1st Workshop on Natural Language Reasoning and Structured Explanations

Toronto, Canada
13 June 2023

ISBN: 978-1-7138-8179-7

Printed from e-media with permission by:

Curran Associates, Inc.
57 Morehouse Lane
Red Hook, NY 12571

Some format issues inherent in the e-media version may also appear in this print version.

Printed with permission by Curran Associates, Inc. (2024)

Association for Computational Linguistics
209 N. Eighth Street
Stroudsburg, Pennsylvania 18360

Phone: 1-570-476-8006
Fax: 1-570-476-0860

acl@aclweb.org

Additional copies of this publication are available from:

Curran Associates, Inc.
57 Morehouse Lane
Red Hook, NY 12571 USA
Phone: 845-758-0400
Fax: 845-758-2633
Email: curran@proceedings.com
Web: www.proceedings.com

ACL 2023

1st Workshop on Natural Language Reasoning and Structured Explanations (@ACL 2023)

Proceedings of the Workshop

June 13, 2023

The ACL organizers gratefully acknowledge the support from the following sponsors.

Sponsor

Ai2 Allen Institute for AI

Order copies of this and other ACL proceedings from:

Association for Computational Linguistics (ACL)
209 N. Eighth Street
Stroudsburg, PA 18360
USA
Tel: +1-570-476-8006
Fax: +1-570-476-0860
acl@aclweb.org

Introduction

Welcome to NLRSE, the First Workshop on Natural Language Reasoning and Structured Explanations, co-located with ACL 2023 in Toronto, Ontario, Canada.

With recent scaling of large pre-trained Transformer language models (LLMs), the scope of feasible NLP tasks has broadened. Significant recent work has focused on tasks that require some kind of natural language reasoning. A trajectory in question answering has led us from extraction-oriented datasets like SQuAD to "multi-hop" reasoning datasets like HotpotQA and StrategyQA. Although LLMs have shown remarkable performance on most NLP tasks, it is often unclear why their answers follow from what they know. To address this gap, a new class of explanation techniques has emerged which play an integral part in structuring the reasoning necessary to solve these datasets. For example, the chain-of-thought paradigm leverages explanations as vehicles for LLMs to mimic human reasoning processes. Entailment trees offer a way to ground multi-step reasoning in a collection of verifiable steps. Frameworks like SayCan bridge high-level planning in language and with low-level action trajectories. As a result, we see a confluence of methods blending explainable machine learning/NLP, classical AI (especially theorem proving), and cognitive science (how do humans structure explanations?). This workshop aims to bring together a diverse set of perspectives from these different traditions and attempt to establish common ground for how these various kinds of explanation structures can tackle a broad class of reasoning problems in natural language and beyond.

A total of 12 papers appear in the proceedings. Over 70 papers were presented at the workshop itself, with the rest being submitted under two archival options: cross-submissions (Findings papers or those already presented at other venues, such as ICLR or the ACL main conference), and regular non-archival submissions (unpublished work). The latter went through a normal peer review process. These papers can be found on the NLRSE website: `https://nl-reasoning-workshop.github.io/`

Four papers were featured as oral presentations. These were selected from the archival papers to represent a selection of strong work that the organizers felt would be of broad interest to workshop participants. In addition, we featured five invited talks: Peter Clark, Noah Goodman, Ellie Pavlick, Sarah Wiegreffe, and Denny Zhou.

We are thankful to all reviewers for their help in the selection of the program, for their readiness in engaging in thoughtful discussions about individual papers, and for providing valuable feedback to the authors. We would also like to thank the ACL workshop organizers for all the valuable help and support with organizational aspects of the conference. Finally, we would like to thank all our authors and presenters for making this such an exciting event!

Bhavana Dalvi, Greg Durrett, Peter Jansen, Danilo Ribeiro, Jason Wei, and Lio Wong, NLRSE organizers

Organizing Committee

Organizers

Bhavana Dalvi Mishra, Allen Institute for Artificial Intelligence
Greg Durrett, UT Austin
Peter Jansen, University of Arizona
Danilo Neves Ribeiro, Northwestern University
Jason Wei, OpenAI
Lio Wong, Massachusetts Institute of Technology

Program Committee

Chairs

Bhavana Dalvi Mishra, Allen Institute for Artificial Intelligence
Greg Durrett, UT Austin
Peter Jansen, University of Arizona
Danilo Neves Ribeiro, Northwestern
Jason Wei, OpenAI
Lio Wong, Massachusetts Institute of Technology

Program Committee

Jun Araki, Bosch Research
Jinheon Baek, Korea Advanced Institute of Science and Technology
Kaj Bostrom, University of Texas at Austin
Faeze Brahman, Allen Institute for AI
Kezhen Chen, Google, X
Yung-sung Chuang, Massachusetts Institute of Technology
Maxwell Crouse, IBM Research
Yao Fu, The University of Edinburgh
Shahriar Golchin, University of Arizona
Shashank Gupta, Allen Institute for Artificial Intelligence
Jie Huang, University of Illinois at Urbana-Champaign
Naoya Inoue, Japan Advanced Institute of Science and Technology
Uri Katz, Bar Ilan University
Shiyang Li, UC Santa Barbara
Shuyang Li, Meta AI
Zhengzhong Liang, University of Arizona
Pan Lu, University of California, Los Angeles
Bodhisattwa Prasad Majumder, University of California San Diego
Constantine Nakos, Northwestern University
Enrique Noriega-atala, The University of Arizona
Yasumasa Onoe, The University of Texas at Austin
Shiva Kumar Pentyala, Salesforce AI
Valentina Pyatkin, Bar-Ilan University
Hossein Rajaby Faghihi, Michigan State University
Juan Diego Rodriguez, The University of Texas at Austin
Soumya Sanyal, University of Southern California
Rebecca Sharp, University of Arizona
Alexey Sorokin, Moscow State University
Zayne Sprague, University of Texas at Austin
Arvind Krishna Sridhar, Qualcomm Technologies R+D
Oyvind Tafjord, AI2
Harsh Trivedi, Stony Brook University
Hoang Van, Harvard Medical School
Ruoyao Wang, University of Arizona
Xi Ye, The University of Texas at Austin
Li Zhang, University of Pennsylvania

Bowei Zou, Institute for Infocomm Research

Table of Contents

Program

Thursday, July 13, 2023

08:00 - 09:00 *Virtual Poster Session*

09:00 - 09:10 *Opening Remarks*

09:10 - 09:50 *Invited Speaker - Ellie Pavlick*

09:50 - 10:30 *Invited Speaker - Noah Goodman*

10:30 - 11:00 *Break*

11:00 - 11:20 *Oral Presentations 1*

Exploring the Curious Case of Code Prompts
Li Zhang, Liam Dugan, Hainiu Xu and Chris Callison-burch

Using Planning to Improve Semantic Parsing of Instructional Texts
Vanya Cohen and Raymond Mooney

11:20 - 12:20 *Poster Session 1*

12:25 - 13:30 *Lunch*

13:30 - 14:30 *Poster Session 2*

14:30 - 14:50 *Oral Presentations 2*

Knowledge-Augmented Language Model Prompting for Zero-Shot Knowledge Graph Question Answering
Jinheon Baek, Alham Fikri Aji and Amir Saffari

Can In-context Learners Learn a Reasoning Concept from Demonstrations?
Michal Tefnik and Marek Kadlcik

Thursday, July 13, 2023 (continued)

14:50 - 15:30 *Invited Speaker - Peter Clark*

15:30 - 16:00 *Break*

16:00 - 16:40 *Invited Speaker - Denny Zhou*

16:40 - 17:20 *Invited Speaker - Sarah Wiegreffe*

Knowledge Graph-augmented Language Models for Complex Question Answering

Priyanka Sen
Amazon Alexa AI
Cambridge, UK
sepriyan@amazon.com

Sandeep Mavadia
Amazon Alexa AI
Cambridge, UK
smavadia@amazon.com

Amir Saffari
Amazon Alexa AI
Cambridge, UK
amsafari@amazon.com

Abstract

Large language models have shown impressive abilities to reason over input text, however, they are prone to hallucinations. On the other hand, end-to-end knowledge graph question answering (KGQA) models output responses grounded in facts, but they still struggle with complex reasoning, such as comparison or ordinal questions. In this paper, we propose a new method for complex question answering where we combine a knowledge graph retriever based on an end-to-end KGQA model with a language model that reasons over the retrieved facts to return an answer. We observe that augmenting language model prompts with retrieved KG facts improves performance over using a language model alone by an average of 83%. In particular, we see improvements on complex questions requiring count, intersection, or multi-hop reasoning operations.

1 Introduction

Large language models (LMs) have shown great promise in a variety of NLP tasks, including question-answering (QA) (Zhang et al., 2022; Sanh et al., 2022; Wei et al., 2022a). As language models scale, they achieve impressive results on standard QA benchmarks, such as SQuAD (Raffel et al., 2020), and can answer questions either few-shot or zero-shot using only knowledge stored within the model parameters (Roberts et al., 2020). Language models have also been shown to solve complex reasoning tasks by outputting step-by-step instructions from question to answer (Creswell et al., 2022; Wei et al., 2022b). Despite these successes, language models are still prone to hallucinations and can return answers that are incorrect, out-of-date, and not grounded in verified knowledge sources, making them an unsafe choice for a factual question answering service. Additionally, step-by-step reasoning can be computationally expensive as it requires multiple calls to a language model.

Alternatively, knowledge graph-based question answering (KGQA) models (Chakraborty et al., 2019; Fu et al., 2020) are trained to traverse knowledge graph (KG) facts to return answers to questions. These models are faithful and grounded to facts stored in a KG. However KGQA models are often limited in the types of reasoning that they can perform. Most end-to-end KGQA models can perform relation following for single or multiple hops (Cohen et al., 2020), and some models have been trained for set intersection (Sen et al., 2021), union, or difference (Sun et al., 2020), however expanding to general reasoning capabilities remains an open challenge. KGQA models are also restricted to using facts stored in a knowledge graph and can not leverage common world knowledge.

In this paper, we propose a novel method for complex question answering using a KGQA model retriever with a language model reasoner. Our approach harnesses both the ability to traverse over verified facts with a KGQA model, and the ability to reason over text with an LM.

For our KGQA retriever, we train an end-to-end KGQA model based on ReifKB (Cohen et al., 2020) and the Rigel family of models (Saffari et al., 2021; Sen et al., 2021). We use this model to return a weighted set of facts from the knowledge graph that could be useful for answering a given question. We then prompt an LM with the question and the top-k facts retrieved, in a zero-shot setting, and the language model returns a natural language answer. In our experiments over four QA datasets, we show that our approach can outperform using an LM alone by an average of 83%.

2 Related Works

Recent work on using language models for reasoning tasks include Kojima et al. (2023), where the authors prompt the models to output the steps to the answer in addition to the final result. Other methods have also tried to solve questions by break-

Proceedings of the 1st Workshop on Natural Language Reasoning and Structured Explanations (@ACL 2023), pages 1–8
June 13, 2023 ©2023 Association for Computational Linguistics

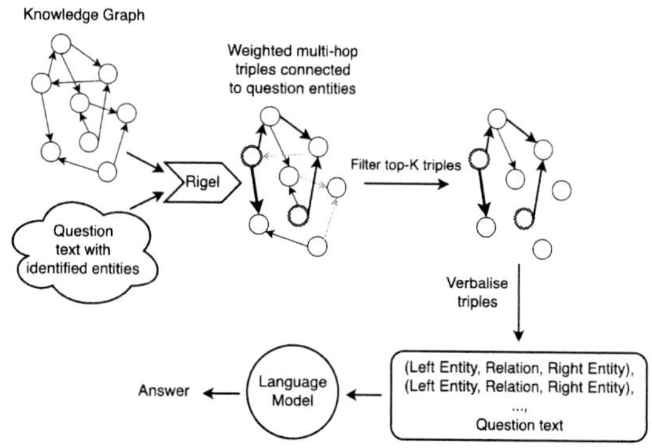

Figure 1: Architecture for our model setup. Question entities are shown as blue nodes in the knowledge graph diagrams. See section 3.1 for details.

ing them down into intermediate steps: Wei et al. (2022b) prompts the language model with similar examples where an answer is formed step-wise before providing the requested answer. Creswell et al. (2022) fine-tune several models with the task of choosing relevant knowledge until a satisfactory answer is reached. Although these methods improve language model performance, it can be costly to fine-tune a large language model or to pass an input through a language model multiple times, especially at runtime. In this work, we instead build a lighter weight retriever model to collect relevant facts followed by a single call to a language model.

Different data sources have also been used for retrieval: Lazaridou et al. (2022) uses Google search. Kang et al. (2022) also retrieves facts from a knowledge graph but requires fine-tuning a language model, which can be expensive for the larger models. Recently, Baek et al. (2023) used a similarity metric between KG facts and questions to retrieve relevant facts to add to the prompt of a language model. However Baek et al. (2023) found that similarity alone is not always enough to find relevant facts for complex question. In this work we present a more sophisticated model for identifying relevant facts with a KGQA model.

3 Method

We propose a new method for question answering using a KGQA model to retrieve facts from a knowledge graph, and a language model to reason over the question and facts to return an answer.

3.1 Model description

As shown in Figure 1, our model has three main components:

1. A sequence-to-sequence KGQA model (which we refer to as RIGEL based on Saffari et al. (2021); Sen et al. (2021)) for predicting a distribution over which relations to follow in a knowledge graph.
2. A differentiable knowledge graph (DKG), where the KG is stored in three linear maps from left-entities, relations, and right-entities to triples respectively, represented as sparse binary matrices (Cohen et al., 2020).
3. A language model for interpreting the questions and reasoning over facts provided from the KG by the two previous components.

We do not yet integrate entity resolution, so question entities are provided from the datasets.

There are three steps to running the model in inference. First, Rigel is used to estimate a distribution over relations for each hop using a sequence-to-sequence architecture. We initialize the encoder using RoBERTa-base (Liu et al., 2019). The decoder predicts a distribution over relations in the knowledge graph. This decoding step is performed for up to M hops (in our experiments, $M = 2$).

Second, the question entities and the distribution over relation are used to extract weighted triples from the knowledge graph. We represent the question entities as a one-hot vector in entity-space and map this to a vector of triples using the left-entity to triple sparse matrix in the DKG. Similarly, for relations, we use the vector over relations predicted by the Rigel model and map this to a vector of triples using the relation to triple matrix in the DKG. Finally we take the Hadamard (element-wise) product to extract a weighted vector of triples. For the second hop, we map the triple vector back to entities using the right-entity to triple matrix in the DKG and repeat the process above.

We retain only the top-k triples for each hop (in our experiments $k = 10$) and convert them into natural language using the names of the entities and relations as stored within the KG. We also include inverse triples within our DKG where the relations are prefixed with "<inv>-" when converted to natural language, e.g. "(Paris, <inv>-capital-of, France)". We also include literal values for numbers, strings and dates in our DKG as right entities.

Finally, we run inference in a zero-shot setting with a pretrained language model. We compose a prompt following the template: "*Given the following context:* "{context}" *Answer the question:*

{question}. *Answer:*" where the context is the set of filtered triples formatted as "*(left entity, relation, right entity), ..., (left entity, relation, right entity)*". We input this prompt into a language model to output an answer.

3.2 Training

Of the three components outlined in section 3.1, we only train the Rigel KGQA model. The DKG is instantiated from a static dump of the Wikidata (Vrandečić and Krötzsch, 2014) knowledge graph, and the language models in our experiments are not fine-tuned.

Rigel is trained using the train and dev sets of KGQA datasets annotated with natural language questions, question entities, and answer entities. As described in section 3.1 we estimate a distribution over entities for each hop. During training, we also jointly learn an attention mechanism which is conditioned on the question embedding to predict how much to weigh answer entities returned for each hop. We use a binary cross-entropy objective to allow for multiple answer entities. For more information on training the Rigel model see Sen et al. (2021). We leave end-to-end training of both the KGQA model and the LM to future work.

4 Experimental Setup

4.1 Datasets

We use four KGQA datasets in our experiments with Wikidata as the knowledge graph. For datasets built using FreeBase, we link entities to Wikidata using the *FreeBase ID* Wikidata property. The train / dev sets for each dataset are used to train the Rigel model, and all results are reported on the test sets.

- **WebQuestions** (Berant et al., 2013) is an English question-answering dataset of 4,737 questions (2,792 train, 306 dev, 1,639 test) originally built on FreeBase. WebQuestions includes questions requiring multiple hops and set intersections.

- **ComplexWebQuestions** (Talmor and Berant, 2018) is an extended version of WebQuestions with 34,689 questions (27,649 train, 3,509 dev: since the test set is not public, we use the dev set for testing) in English requiring complex operations, such as multiple hops and temporal constraints.

- **Mintaka** (Sen et al., 2022) is a complex question answering dataset of 20,000 questions (14,000 train, 2,000 dev, 4,000 test) linked to Wikidata and using complex operations such as comparisons and set operations. We use the English subset.

- **LC-QuAD** is a dataset of 30,000 synthetically generated English questions and SPARQL parses. We use the subset with SPARQL parses that return a valid answer from Wikidata (20,438 train, 5,230 test). These questions include complex operations such as multi-hop and count.

4.2 Language Models

We evaluate our method using language models from four families of models:

- **Flan-T5** (Chung et al., 2022) models are an extension of T5 encoder-decoder models that have been *instruction tuned* on a large set of instructions that were automatically generated using existing datasets and templates. We use the Flan-T5 Small (80M parameters), XL (3B), and XXL (11B) models.

- **T0** (Sanh et al., 2022) models are encoder-decoder models that are trained on a variety of *prompts*, which are automatically built from supervised datasets using templates. We use the T0 (11B) and T0 3B (3B) models.

- **OPT** (Zhang et al., 2022) models are large, open-source, decoder-only models that have been trained to roughly match the performance of GPT-3 models. We use the 13B parameter version of OPT.

- **AlexaTM** (Soltan et al., 2022) is a 20 billion parameter encoder-decoder model trained on publicly available data in multiple languages.

4.3 Training Specifications

We train each of our Rigel models on a single NVIDIA Tesla V100 GPU for 40,000 steps. We run inference over our language models using four Tesla V100 GPUs and distribute across GPUs using Hugging Face Accelerate (Gugger et al., 2022).

4.4 Evaluation metric

Our datasets provide answer entities (e.g., Wikidata Q-codes). To evaluate the performance of the LM's natural language output, we test if any of the provided answer entity names or their aliases as

Dataset	Experiment	Rigel	Flan-T5 S	Flan-T5 XL	Flan-T5 XXL	T0 3B	T0 11B	OPT	ATM
WebQ	No Knowledge	–	16.29	40.15	45.15	29.10	34.05	26.85	38.56
	Random Facts	–	21.90	28.49	39.96	28.07	36.30	48.02	41.98
	Rigel Facts	48.9	**45.52**	**55.58**	**59.79**	**53.33**	**55.64**	**57.60**	**55.40**
	% improvement	–	179%	38%	32%	83%	63%	115%	44%
CWQ	No Knowledge	–	9.63	28.79	31.00	20.26	24.98	18.19	27.20
	Random Facts	–	14.69	23.96	31.15	20.86	26.85	28.13	29.41
	Rigel Facts	29.21	**25.55**	**36.09**	**40.38**	**32.54**	**36.35**	**32.54**	**35.72**
	% improvement	–	165%	25%	30%	61%	46%	79%	31%
Mintaka	No Knowledge	–	12.65	24.63	30.15	21.13	30.08	38.53	28.48
	Random Facts	–	12.20	20.98	33.63	21.33	30.40	**42.20**	33.00
	Rigel Facts	21.7	**20.58**	**33.50**	**37.90**	**29.28**	**33.35**	40.03	**35.60**
	% improvement	–	63%	36%	26%	39%	11%	4%	25%
LC-QuAD	No Knowledge	–	3.90	8.15	3.82	8.32	9.31	8.75	11.79
	Random Facts	–	8.40	8.91	**11.24**	9.71	10.65	12.65	12.81
	Rigel Facts	27.86	**15.65**	**22.82**	9.41	**20.54**	**22.32**	**20.93**	**22.30**
	% improvement	–	301%	180%	146%	147%	140%	139%	89%

Table 1: Results by language model and dataset over two baselines (No Knowledge and Random Facts) and our proposed method, Rigel Facts. % improvement shows the percentage improvement over No Knowledge to Rigel Facts. Rigel shows the baseline of using Rigel alone with no language model.

stored in Wikidata exist within the LM output. We also lower case text in the prediction and remove punctuation, articles, and extra white space.

5 Results

We evaluate our method on four complex question-answering datasets using seven language models. We compare against two baselines.

- **No Knowledge**: we provide the question with no additional context. The prompt is "*Question:* {question} *Answer:*".
- **Random Facts**: we provide k random facts (k = 10) sampled uniformly over all facts reachable in one hop from the question entities.

The results are reported in Table 1, with the % improvement showing the percentage of improvement from the No Knowledge baseline to our proposed Rigel Facts method. We also report scores for the Rigel model alone in the Rigel column.

These results show that in almost all cases, a language model using facts retrieved from our Rigel model outperforms No Knowledge and Random Facts. For smaller models such as Flan-T5, using Rigel facts improves performance by up to 300%. Larger models, such as AlexaTM, start with higher baselines using no knowledge, but still see an average of 47% improvement across datasets. Exceptions are OPT on Mintaka and Flan-T5 XXL on LC-QuAD, where random facts outperform Rigel. We observe that in many of the questions where augmenting with random facts performs better than Rigel facts, neither provide useful information. Interestingly, however, random facts still encourage the LM to output the correct answer.

The No Knowledge results show that models can answer questions without additional facts. Larger models with no facts can even outperform smaller models with Rigel facts, for example, AlexaTM vs. Flan-T5 on Mintaka (28.48 vs. 20.58). Nevertheless, it is promising to see smaller models become more competitive with the help of a retriever.

The use of random facts shows mixed results. Random facts rarely outperform Rigel, but compared to the No Knowledge baseline, random facts can sometimes help, as seen across models on ComplexWebQuestions and LC-QuAD. In other cases,

		Flan-T5			T0				
Question Type	**Experiment**	**S**	**XL**	**XXL**	**3B**	**11B**	**OPT**	**ATM**	**Average**
Comparative	No Facts	**48.50**	63.00	64.00	**49.25**	**59.75**	58.50	57.25	**56.75**
	Random Facts	36.00	61.25	62.50	44.50	57.75	**60.00**	**63.00**	55.00
	Rigel Facts	42.75	**64.25**	**65.50**	42.00	55.50	54.75	60.00	55.12
Count	No Facts	16.75	26.25	**33.00**	21.25	25.00	25.00	40.75	27.56
	Random Facts	17.25	17.75	28.50	27.25	28.75	**51.00**	43.50	30.57
	Rigel Facts	**23.75**	**27.25**	31.25	**40.75**	**32.00**	49.00	**48.75**	**36.47**
Difference	No Facts	4.25	16.75	19.50	**17.00**	**21.00**	20.00	**28.25**	19.28
	Random Facts	6.75	11.75	20.50	11.25	15.50	**29.00**	21.75	16.64
	Rigel Facts	**15.50**	**17.50**	**24.00**	14.25	17.00	28.75	27.25	**20.44**
Generic	No Facts	2.12	16.50	24.25	18.12	28.75	48.38	37.50	27.12
	Random Facts	11.62	20.50	35.75	19.62	30.88	**50.00**	43.62	30.29
	Rigel Facts	**20.50**	**34.25**	**41.12**	**30.88**	**36.75**	47.12	**45.50**	**37.61**
Intersection	No Facts	1.75	20.00	28.50	22.50	35.25	**54.00**	42.50	31.47
	Random Facts	8.50	22.50	37.00	18.00	31.25	51.00	40.50	29.82
	Rigel Facts	**16.00**	**40.25**	**44.75**	**35.00**	**41.00**	49.50	**45.75**	**39.81**
Multi-hop	No Facts	3.00	7.25	12.75	8.25	13.25	20.00	13.25	12.44
	Random Facts	2.75	9.50	18.25	6.50	14.25	24.00	15.75	13.00
	Rigel Facts	**13.50**	**22.25**	**27.75**	**20.50**	**21.25**	**25.75**	**21.00**	**22.69**
Ordinal	No Facts	1.50	9.50	16.50	10.00	15.50	27.75	20.25	15.44
	Random Facts	6.75	9.50	17.75	9.50	**18.00**	**29.75**	20.75	16.00
	Rigel Facts	**12.00**	**16.50**	**23.75**	**17.25**	**18.00**	24.25	**24.25**	**19.84**
Superlative	No Facts	1.25	11.75	16.00	16.00	**19.25**	**28.75**	21.50	17.12
	Random Facts	6.00	12.00	**21.75**	12.25	17.50	28.25	23.75	17.36
	Rigel Facts	**10.50**	**18.75**	**21.75**	**16.75**	14.00	25.00	**24.00**	**19.34**
Yes/No	No Facts	**45.25**	59.00	**62.75**	**49.00**	**63.25**	**54.00**	37.00	**53.16**
	Random Facts	14.75	24.50	58.25	44.50	60.50	49.25	**51.25**	43.29
	Rigel Facts	30.75	**59.75**	58.50	44.50	62.50	49.25	**51.25**	52.12
Average	No Facts	13.82	25.56	30.81	23.49	31.22	37.38	33.14	28.93
	Random Facts	12.26	21.03	33.36	21.49	30.49	**41.36**	35.99	28.00
	Rigel Facts	**20.58**	**33.42**	**37.60**	**29.10**	**33.11**	39.26	**38.64**	**33.72**

Table 2: A breakdown of results by the different complexity types in the Mintaka dataset

random facts can hurt performance, as seen in Flan-T5 XL on WebQuestions (from 40.15 to 28.49) and Mintaka (from 24.63 to 20.98). This can be attributed to random facts adding in distractors that some models are more susceptible to. For example, given the QA pair "*Q: Where does Princess Leia live? A: Alderaan*", if the random facts include "*Leia Organa place of birth Polis Massa*", the model can incorrectly answer Polis Massa.

We also show results in Table 2 as a breakdown of performance by complexity type on the Mintaka dataset. On average, we see that Rigel facts help across complexity types. The highest gains are in Count, Intersection, and Multi-hop questions. These are also the areas that a model like Rigel, which traverses a knowledge graph by following relations, is best suited for. Finding facts for comparatives or yes/no questions are less reliable since the training signal can be weak and there can be multiple paths that spuriously lead to the correct answer. For example, to answer *Who is older, The Weeknd or Drake?*, there are several ways to get to

Question				
How many countries were in the Central Powers alliance in World War I?				
Random Facts			**Rigel Facts**	
· Central Powers has part Austria-Hungary · Central Powers Commons category Central Powers · Central Powers participant in World War I · Central Powers instance of military alliance			· Central Powers has part Ottoman Empire · Central Powers has part Kingdom of Bulgaria · Central Powers has part German Empire · Central Powers has part Austria-Hungary	
Predictions	**Model**	**No Knowledge**	**Random Facts**	**Rigel Facts**
	Flan-T5 XXL	6 ✗	2 ✗	4 ✓

Question				
Where did the author of Pet Sematary go to college?				
Random Facts			**Rigel Facts**	
· Pet Sematary author Stephen King · Pet Sematary follows Christine · Pet Sematary language of work or name English · Pet Sematary publisher Doubleday			· Stephen King education Lisbon High School · Stephen King education University of Maine · Pet Sematary author Stephen King · Pet Sematary notable work Stephen King	
Predictions	**Model**	**No Knowledge**	**Random Facts**	**Rigel Facts**
	T0	University of Michigan ✗	Dartmouth College ✗	University of Maine ✓

Question				
What was the first book in the Lord of the Ring's series?				
Random Facts			**Rigel Facts**	
· Lord of the Rings characters Gandalf · Lord of the Rings characters Elrond · Lord of the Rings translator Maria Skibniewska · Lord of the Rings nominated for Prometheus Award			· Fellowship of the Ring follows The Hobbit · Two Towers follows Fellowship of the Ring · Return of the King follows Two Towers · Appendices follows Return of the King	
Predictions	**Model**	**No Knowledge**	**Random Facts**	**Rigel Facts**
	T0	Fellowship of the Ring ✓	Fellowship of the Ring ✓	The Hobbit ✗

Table 3: Examples of questions and model predictions. For simplicity, we only show the top four facts. In **Predictions**, No Knowledge is only given the question. Random and Rigel Facts are given the question and the respective facts. The correct answer is indicated with a ✓. Incorrect answers are indicated with a ✗.

the answer entity *Drake* without following a *date of birth* relation and performing a comparison. In future work, we plan to explore different ways to train the Rigel model to provide a better training signal of which facts will be useful to the LM.

Finally, in Table 3, we provide examples. The first example is a *count* question, where the LM seems to count the entities Rigel returns get to the correct answer. The second example is of a *multi-hop* question. Of note is that Rigel's top fact is about a high school, but the LM is able to recover and return a college instead. The third example is an *ordinal* question. Since the Rigel facts do not specify which books are part of the series, the model returns an incorrect answer by trying to stay faithful to the facts given. Relying on facts given rather than facts in the parameters can be a desirable trait for an LM, however this example highlights that more work needs to be done on improving the KGQA retriever.

6 Conclusion

In this paper, we show how facts from a KGQA based retriever can be combined with a language model to help answer complex questions. Our results show improvements over calling a language model directly over four datasets, and in particular on complexity types such as multi-hop and count questions. We present our method as a promising way to leverage a knowledge graph, which contains verified and up-to-date facts, with a single call to a language model. In future work, we plan to improve performance across more complexity types and aim to explore ways to update the training of our KGQA retriever with feedback from the language model.

7 Limitations

We present a method for question answering using a KGQA retriever and a language model reasoner. Limitations of our method include a lack of an integrated entity resolution system when training our KGQA model: we instead rely on annotated entities from the datasets. While our KGQA architecture is robust to new entities added at test time, it does require retraining when new relations are added to the KG or if a different target KG is used. Additionally, our results are based on training and evaluating on one dataset at a time; training on a mix of datasets could lead to better generalization, however this is not tested.

References

Jinheon Baek, Alham Fikri Aji, and Amir Saffari. 2023. Knowledge-augmented language model prompting with knowledge graphs for zero-shot question answering. In *Proceedings of the First Workshop on Matching*, Toronto, Canada. Association for Computational Linguistics.

Jonathan Berant, Andrew Chou, Roy Frostig, and Percy Liang. 2013. Semantic parsing on freebase from question-answer pairs. In *Proceedings of the 2013 conference on empirical methods in natural language processing*, pages 1533–1544.

Nilesh Chakraborty, Denis Lukovnikov, Gaurav Maheshwari, Priyansh Trivedi, Jens Lehmann, and Asja Fischer. 2019. Introduction to neural network based approaches for question answering over knowledge graphs. *arXiv preprint arXiv:1907.09361*.

Hyung Won Chung, Le Hou, Shayne Longpre, Barret Zoph, Yi Tay, William Fedus, Eric Li, Xuezhi Wang, Mostafa Dehghani, Siddhartha Brahma, et al. 2022. Scaling instruction-finetuned language models. *arXiv preprint arXiv:2210.11416*.

William W. Cohen, Haitian Sun, R. Alex Hofer, and Matthew Siegler. 2020. Scalable neural methods for reasoning with a symbolic knowledge base. In *International Conference on Learning Representations*.

Antonia Creswell, Murray Shanahan, and Irina Higgins. 2022. Selection-inference: Exploiting large language models for interpretable logical reasoning. *arXiv preprint arXiv:2205.09712*.

Bin Fu, Yunqi Qiu, Chengguang Tang, Yang Li, Haiyang Yu, and Jian Sun. 2020. A survey on complex question answering over knowledge base: Recent advances and challenges. *arXiv preprint arXiv:2007.13069*.

Sylvain Gugger, Lysandre Debut, Thomas Wolf, Philipp Schmid, Zachary Mueller, and Sourab Mangrulkar. 2022. Accelerate: Training and inference at scale made simple, efficient and adaptable. https://github.com/huggingface/accelerate.

Minki Kang, Jin Myung Kwak, Jinheon Baek, and Sung Ju Hwang. 2022. Knowledge-consistent dialogue generation with knowledge graphs. In *ICML 2022 Workshop on Knowledge Retrieval and Language Models*.

Takeshi Kojima, Shixiang Shane Gu, Machel Reid, Yutaka Matsuo, and Yusuke Iwasawa. 2023. Large language models are zero-shot reasoners. *arXiv preprint arXiv:2205.11916*.

Angeliki Lazaridou, Elena Gribovskaya, Wojciech Stokowiec, and Nikolai Grigorev. 2022. Internet-augmented language models through few-shot prompting for open-domain question answering. *arXiv preprint arXiv:2203.05115*.

Yinhan Liu, Myle Ott, Naman Goyal, Jingfei Du, Mandar Joshi, Danqi Chen, Omer Levy, Mike Lewis, Luke Zettlemoyer, and Veselin Stoyanov. 2019. RoBERTa: A robustly optimized BERT pretraining approach. *arXiv preprint arXiv:1907.11692*.

Colin Raffel, Noam Shazeer, Adam Roberts, Katherine Lee, Sharan Narang, Michael Matena, Yanqi Zhou, Wei Li, and Peter J Liu. 2020. Exploring the limits of transfer learning with a unified text-to-text transformer. *The Journal of Machine Learning Research*, 21(1):5485–5551.

Adam Roberts, Colin Raffel, and Noam Shazeer. 2020. How much knowledge can you pack into the parameters of a language model? In *Empirical Methods in Natural Language Processing (EMNLP)*.

Amir Saffari, Armin Oliya, Priyanka Sen, and Tom Ayoola. 2021. End-to-end entity resolution and question answering using differentiable knowledge graphs. In *Proceedings of the 2021 Conference on Empirical Methods in Natural Language Processing*, pages 4193–4200, Online and Punta Cana, Dominican Republic. Association for Computational Linguistics.

Victor Sanh, Albert Webson, Colin Raffel, Stephen Bach, Lintang Sutawika, Zaid Alyafeai, Antoine Chaffin, Arnaud Stiegler, Arun Raja, Manan Dey, M Saiful Bari, Canwen Xu, Urmish Thakker, Shanya Sharma Sharma, Eliza Szczechla, Taewoon Kim, Gunjan Chhablani, Nihal Nayak, Debajyoti Datta, Jonathan Chang, Mike Tian-Jian Jiang, Han Wang, Matteo Manica, Sheng Shen, Zheng Xin Yong, Harshit Pandey, Rachel Bawden, Thomas Wang, Trishala Neeraj, Jos Rozen, Abheesht Sharma, Andrea Santilli, Thibault Fevry, Jason Alan Fries, Ryan

Teehan, Teven Le Scao, Stella Biderman, Leo Gao, Thomas Wolf, and Alexander M Rush. 2022. Multitask prompted training enables zero-shot task generalization. In *International Conference on Learning Representations*.

Priyanka Sen, Alham Fikri Aji, and Amir Saffari. 2022. Mintaka: A complex, natural, and multilingual dataset for end-to-end question answering. In *Proceedings of the 29th International Conference on Computational Linguistics*, pages 1604–1619, Gyeongju, Republic of Korea. International Committee on Computational Linguistics.

Priyanka Sen, Armin Oliya, and Amir Saffari. 2021. Expanding end-to-end question answering on differentiable knowledge graphs with intersection. In *Proceedings of the 2021 Conference on Empirical Methods in Natural Language Processing*, pages 8805–8812, Online and Punta Cana, Dominican Republic. Association for Computational Linguistics.

Saleh Soltan, Shankar Ananthakrishnan, Jack FitzGerald, Rahul Gupta, Wael Hamza, Haidar Khan, Charith Peris, Stephen Rawls, Andy Rosenbaum, Anna Rumshisky, et al. 2022. Alexatm 20b: Few-shot learning using a large-scale multilingual seq2seq model. *arXiv preprint arXiv:2208.01448*.

Haitian Sun, Andrew Arnold, Tania Bedrax Weiss, Fernando Pereira, and William W. Cohen. 2020. Faithful embeddings for knowledge base queries. *Advances in Neural Information Processing Systems*, 33.

Alon Talmor and Jonathan Berant. 2018. The web as a knowledge-base for answering complex questions. *arXiv preprint arXiv:1803.06643*.

Denny Vrandečić and Markus Krötzsch. 2014. Wikidata: A free collaborative knowledgebase. *Commun. ACM*, 57(10):78–85.

Jason Wei, Maarten Bosma, Vincent Y. Zhao, Kelvin Guu, Adams Wei Yu, Brian Lester, Nan Du, Andrew M. Dai, and Quoc V. Le. 2022a. Finetuned language models are zero-shot learners. In *ICLR*.

Jason Wei, Xuezhi Wang, Dale Schuurmans, Maarten Bosma, Ed H. Chi, Quoc Le, and Denny Zhou. 2022b. Chain of thought prompting elicits reasoning in large language models. *arXiv preprint arXiv:2201.11903*.

Susan Zhang, Stephen Roller, Naman Goyal, Mikel Artetxe, Moya Chen, Shuohui Chen, Christopher Dewan, Mona Diab, Xian Li, Xi Victoria Lin, Todor Mihaylov, Myle Ott, Sam Shleifer, Kurt Shuster, Daniel Simig, Punit Singh Koura, Anjali Sridhar, Tianlu Wang, and Luke Zettlemoyer. 2022. OPT: open pre-trained transformer language models. *arXiv preprint arXiv:2205.01068*.

Exploring the Curious Case of Code Prompts

Li Zhang*, **Liam Dugan***, **Hainiu Xu***, **Chris Callison-Burch**
University of Pennsylvania
`{zharry,ldugan,seacow,ccb}@seas.upenn.edu`

Abstract

Recent work has shown that prompting language models with code-like representations of natural language leads to performance improvements on structured reasoning tasks. However, such tasks comprise only a small subset of all natural language tasks. In our work, we seek to answer whether or not code-prompting is the preferred way of interacting with language models *in general*. We compare code and text prompts across three popular GPT models (`davinci`, `code-davinci-002`, and `text-davinci-002`) on a broader selection of tasks (e.g., QA, sentiment, summarization) and find that with few exceptions, code prompts do not consistently outperform text prompts. Furthermore, we show that the style of code prompt has a large effect on performance for some but not all tasks and that fine-tuning on text instructions leads to better relative performance of code prompts.

1 Introduction

Recent work has shown that pre-training language models (LMs) on a mixture of text and program code (e.g., Python or Javascript) makes them more capable of reasoning over natural language (Suzgun et al., 2022). Such program-trained language models (PLMs) significantly outperform text-only LMs on tasks such as math problems and tracking shuffled objects despite such tasks lacking any explicit code formulae (Liang et al., 2022).

Furthermore, prompting such PLMs with *code-like structures* (e.g., Python, JSON, PDDL) instead of text has been shown to lead to performance improvements on structured common sense reasoning (Madaan et al., 2022), event argument extraction (Wang et al., 2022), knowledge graph construction (Bi et al., 2023), story understanding (Dong et al., 2022), and causal reasoning (Zhang et al., 2023).

*Equal contribution.

Figure 1: For certain tasks, prompting program-trained language models with code-*like* representations works better than prompting with text.

Such results naturally lead us to ask whether code-prompting is the preferred way of interacting with PLMs *in general*. While previous work is limited to reasoning tasks, in this work we analyze a broad selection of tasks (e.g., QA, sentiment, summarization) and systematically compare the performance of prompting PLMs with code vs. prompting with text[1]. We find that:

- With the exception of some reasoning tasks, code prompts do not outperform text prompts
- The style of code prompt has a large effect on performance for some but not all tasks.
- Fine-tuning on text instructions leads to relative improvements when using code prompts.

2 Experimental Design

Model Selection For our text-based LM we use the original 175 billion parameter `davinci` model introduced by Brown et al. (2020). For our PLM we use the newer `code-davinci-002` model which was explicitly trained on text and code. Neither model underwent any supervised instruction fine-tuning. In addition, we analyze performance on `text-davinci-002`, which is a vari-

[1]The code, prompts, and outputs for our experiments are public at `github.com/zharry29/curious_code_prompts`

Proceedings of the 1st Workshop on Natural Language Reasoning and Structured Explanations (@ACL 2023), pages 9–17
June 13, 2023

Dataset	Task Category	Num. Eval Examples	Metric	Origin
HellaSwag	Commonsense Reasoning	1000 / 10042	Accuracy	Zellers et al. (2019)
wikiHow Goal-Step	Commonsense Reasoning	1000 / 1073	Accuracy	Zhang et al. (2020)
wikiHow Temporal	Commonsense Reasoning	1000 / 3100	Accuracy	Zhang et al. (2020)
WinoGrande	Commonsense Reasoning	1000 / 1767	Accuracy	Sakaguchi et al. (2021)
OpenPI	Commonsense Reasoning	111 / 111	ROUGE-F1	Tandon et al. (2020)
ANLI	Natural Language Inference	1000 / 3000	Accuracy	Nie et al. (2020)
Yelp	Sentiment Analysis	1000 / 10000	Pearson's r	Zhang et al. (2015)
IMDb	Sentiment Analysis	1000 / 25000	Accuracy	Maas et al. (2011)
HotpotQA	Question Answering	1000 / 7405	Macro-F1	Yang et al. (2018)
SQuAD	Question Answering	1000 / 11873	Macro-F1	Rajpurkar et al. (2018)
CNN/Daily Mail	Summarization	1000 / 13368	ROUGE-2	Nallapati et al. (2016)
XSUM	Summarization	1000 / 11332	ROUGE-2	Narayan et al. (2018)

Table 1: The 12 evaluation tasks. Macro F1 is based on Rajpurkar et al. (2016). For each task, we randomly sample a fixed set of 1000 examples from its validation or test set for evaluation. For OpenPI we are limited to 111 examples.

ant of `code-davinci-002` trained explicitly on human demonstrations using supervised fine-tuning[2]. We include this model to help us determine whether or not fine-tuning PLMs on text instructions affects their ability to interpret code prompts. All three models were queried through the OpenAI API[3] and our experiments cost approximately $2700 in total (see Appendix F for the full cost breakdown).

Task Selection Following the methodology of Sanh et al. (2022) we select tasks in a top-down fashion by first choosing the categories of interest (e.g. Question Answering, Sentiment Analysis, Summarization) and then selecting datasets from within those categories. We pay special attention to common sense and causal reasoning tasks as PLMs prompted with code have been shown to perform well on such tasks. The resulting 12 tasks are listed in Table 1 and include Commonsense Reasoning, Natural Language Inference, Sentiment Analysis, Question Answering, and Summarization. More details on each task can be found in Appendix A.

Prompt Formulation We collect text prompts for each task using the PromptSource dataset (Bach et al., 2022), a publicly available collection of crowd-sourced prompt templates. For tasks with many prompts, we randomly select one from those provided in the dataset. For a few tasks absent on PromptSource, we write the prompts ourselves.

For our code prompts, we manually write four custom code prompts per task. The code prompt types are as follows, from least to most Pythonic.

(i). Vanilla (`Vanilla`): instructions and inputs are given as variables with generic names;

(ii). Var Identifier (`VI`): instructions and inputs are given as variables with meaningful names;

(iii). Var Identifier + Comments (`VIC`): instructions and inputs are given as variables with meaningful names along with comments explaining their purpose;

(iv). Class + Var Identifier + Comments (`CVIC`): instructions and inputs are given as a task-specific `class`. Functionality is "implemented" as member functions.

Figure 2 shows an example of the different styles of code prompts for the wikiHow temporal ordering task. Note that we attempt to write our code prompts such that we match the wording of the text-based PromptSource prompt as closely as possible.

At inference time, for each test example, we randomly sample in-context examples from the training set and add them to the context window until the maximum context length is reached. This process circumvents the bias caused by static in-context examples. We conduct an ablation study where we vary the random seed and show that this process produces consistent results (see Appendix D).

3 Results

What is the best type of code prompt? We compare performance across the four code prompt types from Section 2 on all 12 tasks using `code-davinci-002` and report our results in Figure 3. We find that no single type of code prompt performs significantly better than the others across all tasks and that the relative difference in performance between code prompts also varies significantly across tasks. For example, on IMDb and SQuAD all code prompts have roughly even performance while for tasks such as wikiHow-Temporal and WinoGrande we see a near 14% accuracy dif-

[2] `https://platform.openai.com/docs/model-index-for-researchers`

[3] `https://openai.com/blog/openai-api`

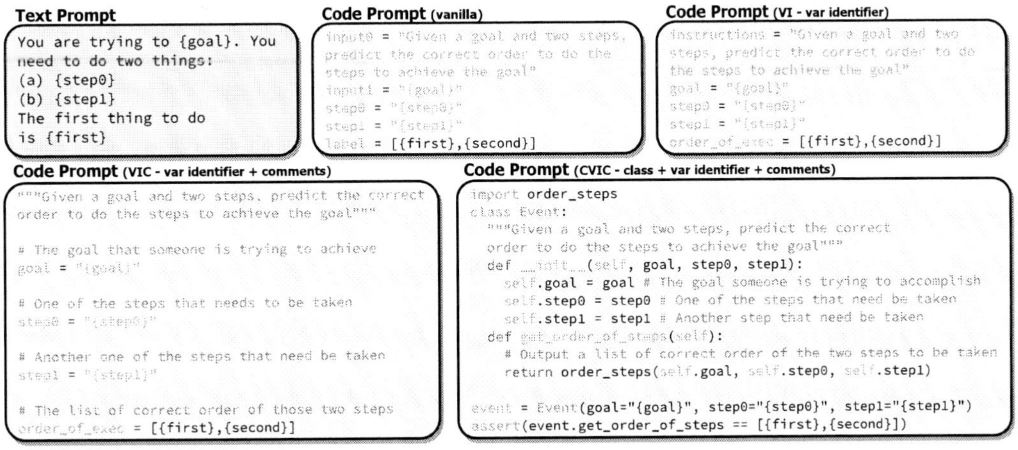

Figure 2: An example of the four styles of manually written code prompts used in our analysis (`Vanilla`, `VI`, `VIC`, and `CVIC`) for the wikiHow temporal ordering task. At test time, variables in braces are replaced with information from the dataset item (as shown in Figure 1). For this task, `{goal}`, `{step0}`, `{step1}` refer to the article title and the steps to order while `{first}` and `{second}` refer to the true ordering of the steps.

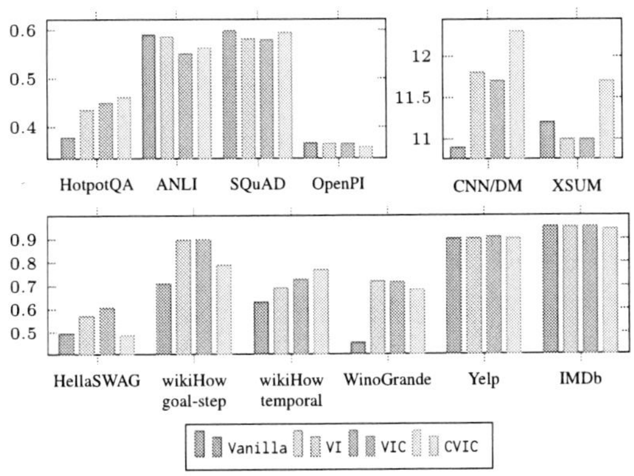

Figure 3: Comparison of `code-davinci-002` across the four types of code prompts. Figures are split to allow for different y-axis scales. We see that different prompts do better on different tasks and while some tasks have high variance over prompt types, others do not.

ference between the worst and best prompt.

In Appendix C, we calculate the average rank of each code prompt type relative to each other and find that the "Var Identifier + Comments" (`VIC`) prompt is the best across all tasks on average (2.25 avg. rank). We thus use this prompt type for our comparison in all future sections.

How many in-context examples should we include in our code prompt? We would like to also investigate how the number of in-context examples in the prompt affects models' ability to perform the task. We therefore conducted an experiment where we filled the context window of

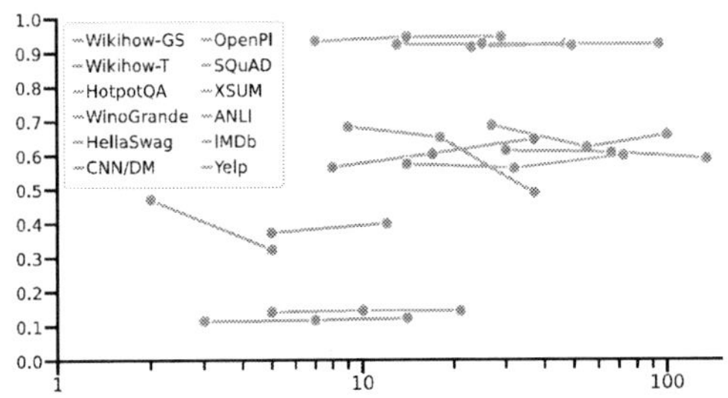

Figure 4: Performance score (y-axis) vs number of in-context examples (x-axis, in log scale) using code prompts (`VIC`) with `code-davinci-002`. We see that increasing number of examples does not always increase performance and in some cases makes it worse.

`code-davinci-002` with in-context examples up to 2000 tokens, 4000 tokens, and 8000 tokens and plotted the validation accuracy of the model with respect to the number of examples in Figure 4.

Contrary to expectations, we find that the number of in-context examples has little effect on model performance for most tasks and actually has a *negative* effect on some tasks. This is especially interesting given that previous work on in-context learning with text prompts finds roughly monotonic improvement from adding more in-context examples (Liu et al., 2021). While further research is necessary, it seems that code prompts may have different scaling behavior than text prompts when used in in-context learning.

Dataset	Metric	davinci			code-002			text-002		
		+Text	+Code	Δ	+Text	+Code	Δ	+Text	+Code	Δ
Hellaswag	Accuracy	0.321	0.307	-0.014	0.652	0.606	-0.046	0.717	0.773	+0.046
wikiHow goal-step	Accuracy	0.347	0.302	-0.045	0.924	0.898	-0.026	0.919	0.915	-0.004
wikiHow temporal	Accuracy	0.495	0.532	+0.037	0.622	0.727	+0.105	0.688	0.761	+0.073
Yelp	Pearson ρ	0.913	0.896	-0.017	0.924	0.907	-0.017	0.919	0.904	-0.015
IMDb	Accuracy	0.872	0.935	+0.063	0.945	0.951	+0.006	0.940	0.952	+0.012
WinoGrande	Accuracy	0.513	0.500	-0.013	0.607	0.716	+0.109	0.628	0.726	+0.098
ANLI	Accuracy	0.333	0.360	+0.027	0.562	0.551	-0.011	0.504	0.557	+0.053
HotpotQA	Macro-F1	-	-	-	0.470	0.449	-0.021	0.490	0.350	-0.140
SQuAD	Macro-F1	0.482	0.466	-0.016	0.604	0.579	-0.025	0.670	0.656	-0.014
OpenPI	ROUGE-F1	-	-	-	37.33	36.36	-0.970	35.60	31.30	-4.300
CNN/Daily Mail	ROUGE-2	9.28	9.13	-0.150	11.74	11.67	-0.070	13.63	13.55	-0.080
XSUM	ROUGE-2	9.38	6.83	-2.550	14.51	11.03	-3.580	14.48	13.26	-1.220

Table 2: Performance of the three LMs when using code prompts (+Code) vs. using text prompts (+Text). Blank cells indicate tasks for which single test examples could not fit in the context window. Color indicates whether or not code prompts are better, slightly better, slightly worse, or worse than text prompts. We see that while code prompts outperform text prompts for certain tasks (such as wikiHow temporal and WinoGrande) text prompts are better on average. We also find that instruction fine-tuning (`text-002`) allows for better code prompt utilization.

Which is better: code or text prompts? In our main experiment we compare the performance of the three GPT models on code prompts (`VIC` style) and text prompts across the 12 datasets. Given the results from Figure 4, we fill the context window of all models with in-context examples up to 4000 tokens to serve as a middle ground for comparing code and text prompts. We report the results of our main experiment in Table 2 and see several surprising trends.

First, we find that prompting PLMs with code leads to substantial increases in performance for certain few reasoning tasks but that this trend does not hold across all tasks—or even all reasoning tasks. For example, when using code prompts with `code-davinci-002`, we see a 10.5% accuracy increase on wikiHow temporal ordering but a 2.6% accuracy decrease on wikiHow goal-step inference despite both being commonsense reasoning tasks and having identical source material.

Second, we find that supervised instruction fine-tuning on natural language demonstrations does not hurt model performance on code. Rather, we observe that code prompts outperform text prompts on *more* tasks when using `text-davinci-002` than when using `code-davinci-002` despite the fact that `text-davinci-002` received no additional fine-tuning on code instructions.

Finally, we find that LMs not explicitly trained on code can also benefit from code prompting on certain reasoning tasks. In particular, code prompts outperform text prompts on `davinci` for 3 out of our 12 tasks—the same proportion as `code-davinci-002`. The tasks that benefit from code prompts also seem to be largely consistent across the three types of models tested, suggesting some underlying trend as to which tasks systematically benefit from structured input.

4 Conclusion

In this work we investigate whether or not there exists a systematic performance difference between prompting PLMs with code or with text. We confirm that there are indeed tasks for which code prompting is significantly more effective than text prompting and that this finding holds across different types of models. However, for most tasks, we find that text prompting is still the best method for eliciting few-shot generalization from PLMs.

Given this result it seems reasonable to attempt to predict which tasks will benefit from code prompts and which tasks will not. However, we show that making such predictions based on simple heuristics such as domain and task category is difficult and that the larger trends remain unclear. Future work should seek to investigate the core mechanism behind what makes code prompting effective for certain tasks.

Finally, concurrent to our work, a new line of research has emerged wherein models generate code and *execute* that code to produce valid output (Chen et al., 2022; Mishra et al., 2022; Gao et al., 2022; Lyu et al., 2023). Future work should consider whether or not the tasks that benefit from executable code prompts and non-executable code prompts have any overlap.

Limitations

One significant limitation to our study is that, as of March 23rd 2023, OpenAI has deprecated access to `code-davinci-002`[4], thus rendering our results non-replicable for any team not granted special access to these models by OpenAI. We did not anticipate this deprecation while conducting this work and we believe this raises serious questions about the usage of API-based language models in scholarly work.

Another limitation is that the 12 tasks we selected may not be representative of the broader population of natural language tasks. Had we conducted our experiments on a larger selection of tasks there may have been larger-scale trends that we would have been able to uncover.

The largest and most pressing limitation with our work is that the models we are testing on have closed-source pre-training datasets. Thus, we are unable to verify the extent to which our task datasets have been included in the training or instruction fine-tuning data. Given that the training data for most of the models tested in this work cuts off in late 2021, this is a very strong possibility. Our results should be viewed with this limitation strongly in mind.

Finally, while we experimented with different code prompts, the search space of possible prompts is very large. Thus, it is very likely that there exists some prompt that outperforms our chosen prompts for each task. Drawing conclusions based on a limited sampling of prompts is tenuous and while methods exist for searching the space of all prompts, such techniques lack interpretability and erase any distinction between code and text prompt (Li and Liang, 2021).

Acknowledgements

The paper is dedicated to the late Prof. Dragomir Radev, the first mentor in NLP of the author Li Zhang, for igniting his passion for research and inspiring him to be a better human being.

We thank Shuyan Zhou, Aman Madaan, and Niket Tandon for valuable discussions about this work and we thank Alyssa Hwang for her contributions to the structure, presentation, and narrative of the final paper.

This research is based upon work supported in part by the DARPA KAIROS Program (contract FA8750-19-2-1004), the DARPA LwLL Program (contract FA8750-19-2-0201), the Office of the Director of National Intelligence (ODNI) via the IARPA HIATUS Program (contract 2022-22072200005), the NSF (Award 1928631), and gifts from Roblox and Salesforce. Approved for Public Release, Distribution Unlimited. The views and conclusions contained herein are those of the authors and should not be interpreted as necessarily representing the official policies, either expressed or implied, of DARPA, ODNI, IARPA, NSF, the U.S. Government, or of Roblox or Salesforce. The U.S. Government is authorized to reproduce and distribute reprints for governmental purposes notwithstanding any copyright annotation therein.

[4]`https://platform.openai.com/docs/model-index-for-researchers`

References

Stephen H. Bach, Victor Sanh, Zheng-Xin Yong, Albert Webson, Colin Raffel, Nihal V. Nayak, Abheesht Sharma, Taewoon Kim, M Saiful Bari, Thibault Fevry, Zaid Alyafeai, Manan Dey, Andrea Santilli, Zhiqing Sun, Srulik Ben-David, Canwen Xu, Gunjan Chhablani, Han Wang, Jason Alan Fries, Maged S. Al-shaibani, Shanya Sharma, Urmish Thakker, Khalid Almubarak, Xiangru Tang, Dragomir Radev, Mike Tian-Jian Jiang, and Alexander M. Rush. 2022. Promptsource: An integrated development environment and repository for natural language prompts.

Zhen Bi, Jing Chen, Yinuo Jiang, Feiyu Xiong, Wei Guo, Huajun Chen, and Ningyu Zhang. 2023. Codekgc: Code language model for generative knowledge graph construction.

Tom Brown, Benjamin Mann, Nick Ryder, Melanie Subbiah, Jared D Kaplan, Prafulla Dhariwal, Arvind Neelakantan, Pranav Shyam, Girish Sastry, Amanda Askell, Sandhini Agarwal, Ariel Herbert-Voss, Gretchen Krueger, Tom Henighan, Rewon Child, Aditya Ramesh, Daniel Ziegler, Jeffrey Wu, Clemens Winter, Chris Hesse, Mark Chen, Eric Sigler, Mateusz Litwin, Scott Gray, Benjamin Chess, Jack Clark, Christopher Berner, Sam McCandlish, Alec Radford, Ilya Sutskever, and Dario Amodei. 2020. Language models are few-shot learners. In *Advances in Neural Information Processing Systems*, volume 33, pages 1877–1901. Curran Associates, Inc.

Wenhu Chen, Xueguang Ma, Xinyi Wang, and William W Cohen. 2022. Program of thoughts prompting: Disentangling computation from reasoning for numerical reasoning tasks. *arXiv preprint arXiv:2211.12588*.

Yijiang River Dong, Lara J. Martin, and Chris Callison-Burch. 2022. Corrpus: Detecting story inconsistencies via codex-bootstrapped neurosymbolic reasoning.

Luyu Gao, Aman Madaan, Shuyan Zhou, Uri Alon, Pengfei Liu, Yiming Yang, Jamie Callan, and Graham Neubig. 2022. Pal: Program-aided language models. *arXiv preprint arXiv:2211.10435*.

Karl Moritz Hermann, Tomas Kocisky, Edward Grefenstette, Lasse Espeholt, Will Kay, Mustafa Suleyman, and Phil Blunsom. 2015. Teaching machines to read and comprehend. In *NIPS*, pages 1693–1701.

Xiang Lisa Li and Percy Liang. 2021. Prefix-tuning: Optimizing continuous prompts for generation.

Percy Liang, Rishi Bommasani, Tony Lee, Dimitris Tsipras, Dilara Soylu, Michihiro Yasunaga, Yian Zhang, Deepak Narayanan, Yuhuai Wu, Ananya Kumar, et al. 2022. Holistic evaluation of language models. *arXiv preprint arXiv:2211.09110*.

Jiachang Liu, Dinghan Shen, Yizhe Zhang, Bill Dolan, Lawrence Carin, and Weizhu Chen. 2021. What makes good in-context examples for gpt-3?

Qing Lyu, Shreya Havaldar, Adam Stein, Li Zhang, Delip Rao, Eric Wong, Marianna Apidianaki, and Chris Callison-Burch. 2023. Faithful chain-of-thought reasoning.

Andrew L. Maas, Raymond E. Daly, Peter T. Pham, Dan Huang, Andrew Y. Ng, and Christopher Potts. 2011. Learning word vectors for sentiment analysis. In *Proceedings of the 49th Annual Meeting of the Association for Computational Linguistics: Human Language Technologies*, pages 142–150, Portland, Oregon, USA. Association for Computational Linguistics.

Aman Madaan, Shuyan Zhou, Uri Alon, Yiming Yang, and Graham Neubig. 2022. Language models of code are few-shot commonsense learners. *arXiv preprint arXiv:2210.07128*.

Swaroop Mishra, Matthew Finlayson, Pan Lu, Leonard Tang, Sean Welleck, Chitta Baral, Tanmay Rajpurohit, Oyvind Tafjord, Ashish Sabharwal, Peter Clark, et al. 2022. Lila: A unified benchmark for mathematical reasoning. *arXiv preprint arXiv:2210.17517*.

Ramesh Nallapati, Bowen Zhou, Cicero dos Santos, Çağlar Gulçehre, and Bing Xiang. 2016. Abstractive text summarization using sequence to sequence rnns and beyond. In *Proceedings of the 20th SIGNLL Conference on Computational Natural Language Learning*, pages 280–290.

Shashi Narayan, Shay B Cohen, and Mirella Lapata. 2018. Don't give me the details, just the summary! topic-aware convolutional neural networks for extreme summarization. In *Proceedings of the 2018 Conference on Empirical Methods in Natural Language Processing*, pages 1797–1807.

Yixin Nie, Adina Williams, Emily Dinan, Mohit Bansal, Jason Weston, and Douwe Kiela. 2020. Adversarial nli: A new benchmark for natural language understanding. In *Proceedings of the 58th Annual Meeting of the Association for Computational Linguistics*, pages 4885–4901.

Long Ouyang, Jeff Wu, Xu Jiang, Diogo Almeida, Carroll L. Wainwright, Pamela Mishkin, Chong Zhang, Sandhini Agarwal, Katarina Slama, Alex Ray, John Schulman, Jacob Hilton, Fraser Kelton, Luke Miller, Maddie Simens, Amanda Askell, Peter Welinder, Paul Christiano, Jan Leike, and Ryan Lowe. 2022. Training language models to follow instructions with human feedback.

Pranav Rajpurkar, Robin Jia, and Percy Liang. 2018. Know what you don't know: Unanswerable questions for squad. In *Proceedings of the 56th Annual Meeting of the Association for Computational Linguistics (Volume 2: Short Papers)*, pages 784–789.

Pranav Rajpurkar, Jian Zhang, Konstantin Lopyrev, and Percy Liang. 2016. Squad: 100,000+ questions for machine comprehension of text. In *Proceedings of the 2016 Conference on Empirical Methods in Natural Language Processing*, pages 2383–2392.

Keisuke Sakaguchi, Ronan Le Bras, Chandra Bhagavatula, and Yejin Choi. 2021. Winogrande: An adversarial winograd schema challenge at scale. *Communications of the ACM*, 64(9):99–106.

Victor Sanh, Albert Webson, Colin Raffel, Stephen Bach, Lintang Sutawika, Zaid Alyafeai, Antoine Chaffin, Arnaud Stiegler, Arun Raja, Manan Dey, et al. 2022. Multitask prompted training enables zero-shot task generalization. In *International Conference on Learning Representations*.

Maarten Sap, Vered Shwartz, Antoine Bosselut, Yejin Choi, and Dan Roth. 2020. Introductory tutorial: Commonsense reasoning for natural language processing. *ACL 2020*, page 27.

Mirac Suzgun, Nathan Scales, Nathanael Schärli, Sebastian Gehrmann, Yi Tay, Hyung Won Chung, Aakanksha Chowdhery, Quoc V Le, Ed H Chi, Denny Zhou, et al. 2022. Challenging big-bench tasks and whether chain-of-thought can solve them. *arXiv preprint arXiv:2210.09261*.

Niket Tandon, Keisuke Sakaguchi, Bhavana Dalvi, Dheeraj Rajagopal, Peter Clark, Michal Guerquin, Kyle Richardson, and Eduard Hovy. 2020. A dataset for tracking entities in open domain procedural text. In *Proceedings of the 2020 Conference on Empirical Methods in Natural Language Processing (EMNLP)*, pages 6408–6417.

Xingyao Wang, Sha Li, and Heng Ji. 2022. Code4struct: Code generation for few-shot structured prediction from natural language. *arXiv preprint arXiv:2210.12810*.

Zhilin Yang, Peng Qi, Saizheng Zhang, Yoshua Bengio, William Cohen, Ruslan Salakhutdinov, and Christopher D Manning. 2018. Hotpotqa: A dataset for diverse, explainable multi-hop question answering. In *Proceedings of the 2018 Conference on Empirical Methods in Natural Language Processing*, pages 2369–2380.

Rowan Zellers, Ari Holtzman, Yonatan Bisk, Ali Farhadi, and Yejin Choi. 2019. Hellaswag: Can a machine really finish your sentence? In *Proceedings of the 57th Annual Meeting of the Association for Computational Linguistics*, pages 4791–4800.

Li Zhang, Qing Lyu, and Chris Callison-Burch. 2020. Reasoning about goals, steps, and temporal ordering with wikihow. In *Proceedings of the 2020 Conference on Empirical Methods in Natural Language Processing (EMNLP)*, pages 4630–4639.

Li Zhang, Hainiu Xu, Yue Yang, Shuyan Zhou, Weiqiu You, Manni Arora, and Chris Callison-Burch. 2023. Causal reasoning of entities and events in procedural texts. In *Findings of the Association for Computational Linguistics: EACL 2023*, Dubrovnik, Croatia. Association for Computational Linguistics.

Xiang Zhang, Junbo Zhao, and Yann LeCun. 2015. Character-level convolutional networks for text classification. In *Advances in Neural Information Processing Systems*, volume 28. Curran Associates, Inc.

A Detailed Task Description

Summarization is the task of composing a concise description of a lengthy text. Given a long narrative, the model is tasked with composing a short summary that contains the salient events in the original text.

For our study, we select the *CNN/Daily Mail* (Hermann et al., 2015; Nallapati et al., 2016) and *XSUM* (Narayan et al., 2018) datasets as both are variants on the challenging abstractive summarization task. *XSUM* tasks models with generating extremely concise 1 to 2 sentence summaries of news articles and *CNN/Daily Mail* tasks models with generating reasonably concise but longer abstractive summaries. For both *CNN/Daily Mail* and *XSUM* datasets, we use ROUGE-2 score for evaluation.

Question Answering (QA) is the task of composing answers given a question and an optional context passage. When this context passage is provided the task is referred to as "open-book" QA and when it is not it is referred to as "closed-book" QA. Open-book QA tasks examine language models' ability to understand and extract information from their context while Closed-book QA tasks evaluate the amount of knowledge encapsulated in language models during pre-training.

For our study we pick two open-book QA datasets, *SQuADv2* (Rajpurkar et al., 2018) and *HotpotQA* (Yang et al., 2018), which allow us to focus our evaluation on how structured prompts affect models' ability to comprehend long text input.

For both *SQuADv2* and *HotpotQA*, we evaluate model performance based on the macro-averaged F1 score as proposed in Rajpurkar et al. (2016). This metric measures the average overlap between the prediction and ground truth answer. It is calculated by treating the prediction and ground truth as bags of tokens, and first computing their F1. Then, the maximum F1 score is taken over all of the ground truth answers for a given question, and that score is averaged over all of the questions to get the final result.

Commonsense Reasoning is a machine reasoning task that demands the use of commonsense knowledge which is oftentimes implicitly present in the text (Sap et al., 2020). The customary formulation of commonsense reasoning tasks are *Classification*, where the input is a context, optionally with candidate answers as choices, and the output is a label from a pre-defined label space, and *Question Answering* (QA), where the input is a context followed by a reasoning question and the output is in free-form language.

In this study, we selected four Classification style commonsense reasoning tasks: *wikiHow Temporal* and *wikiHow Goal-Step* (Zhang et al., 2020), *ANLI* (Nie et al., 2020), and *HellaSwag* (Zellers et al., 2019). We also included one Question Answering style task with *OpenPI* (Tandon et al., 2020). In addition, we evaluate our models on *WinoGrande* a comprehensive reasoning benchmark dataset (Sakaguchi et al., 2021).

For *wikiHow Goal-Step*, *wikiHow Temporal*, *HellaSwag*, *WinoGrande*, and *ANLI*, we use classification accuracy as the evaluation metric. To evaluate *OpenPI*, we use F1 score based on the ROUGE metric as described in the original paper (Tandon et al., 2020).

Sentiment Analysis is a task that is concerned with judging emotion and its degree in text. Given a passage, a language model is tasked with classifying the sentiment (positive, negative, neutral) and/or its degree (strongly, weakly, moderately).

The selected datasets, namely *IMDb* (Maas et al.,

	Vanilla	VI	VIC	CVIC
HellaSwag	3	2	1	4
wikiHow Goal-Step	4	2	1	3
wikiHow Temporal	4	3	2	1
Yelp	4	2	1	4
IMDb	1	3	1	4
WinoGrande	4	1	2	3
HotpotQA	4	3	2	1
ANLI	1	2	4	3
OpenPI	1	2	3	4
SQuAD	1	3	4	2
CNN/Daily Mail	4	2	3	1
XSUM	2	4	3	1
Mean	2.75	2.42	2.25	2.58
Standard Deviation	1.36	0.76	1.09	1.26

Table 3: Relative performance rank of the four code prompt types from Section 2 across the 12 tasks. Ranks are calculated based on the results reported in Figure 3. We see that the "Variable Identifier + Comments" (`VIC`) style prompt performs the best out of all code prompt types on average.

2011) and *Yelp* (Zhang et al., 2015), are both constructed using customer reviews. The IMDb dataset proposes a binary classification problem where the input is a movie review and the label space is $\{negative, positive\}$. Yelp proposes a five-way classification problem where the input is a restaurant review and the label space is the number of stars (out of 5) the customers assigned to the restaurant.

For *IMDb*, we use accuracy as the evaluation metric and for *Yelp*, we use Pearson Correlation between the predicted rating and the ground truth rating as the evaluation metric.

B Hyperparameters

For all our experiments regarding GPT-based models, we use a max token of the maximum of possible output tokens in the ground-truth development set. We use a top p of 1, and no frequency and presence penalty. We use a temperature of 0 for classification and multiple-choice tasks and a temperature of 0.7 for generation tasks.

C Ranking of Code Prompt Styles

In Table 3 we report the rank-based statistics of the four code prompt types from Section 2 on our 12 tasks. Ranks are calculated based on the results reported in Figure 3 of the main paper. The numbers in a row reflect the relative standing of each code prompt on the corresponding task. While we note that all code prompts perform within ± 0.5 ranks of each other on average, we see that on average the `VIC` prompt performs the best across all tasks and the `Vanilla` prompt performs the worst. Looking to the standard deviation section, we see that the `VI` prompt performs the most consistently across all tasks and that once again the `Vanilla` prompt performs the least consistently.

Dataset	Performance	σ
Hellaswag	0.65, 0.67, 0.69, 0.67, 0.67	$\pm$0.01
wikiHow-GS	0.51, 0.51, 0.51, 0.50, 0.51	$\pm$0.00
wikiHow-T	0.62, 0.65, 0.63, 0.63, 0.62	$\pm$0.01
Yelp	0.92, 0.92, 0.92, 0.92, 0.92	$\pm$0.00
IMDb	0.94, 0.94, 0.94, 0.94, 0.94	$\pm$0.00
WinoGrande	0.62, 0.64, 0.61, 0.62, 0.62	$\pm$0.01
HotpotQA	0.35, 0.33, 0.35, 0.35, 0.35	$\pm$0.01
ANLI	0.59, 0.58, 0.57, 0.60, 0.61	$\pm$0.01
OpenPI	36.3, 38.1, 38.3, 37.7, 39.9	$\pm$1.16
SQuAD	0.60, 0.62, 0.61, 0.60, 0.63	$\pm$0.01
CNN/DM	11.7, 12.0, 12.4, 12.3, 12.0	$\pm$0.25
XSUM	14.5, 14.9, 15.5, 15.2, 15.4	$\pm$0.36

Table 4: Comparison across 5 repeated runs of the `code-davinci-002` model with text prompts using different random seeds for sampling in-context examples. We see minimal standard deviation (σ) between the runs.

D Ablation Study

To see whether the findings in our Results section could be attributed to variance in the random sampling of in-context training examples per test example, we conduct five repeated runs using `code-davinci-002` with different random seeds each time and calculated the standard deviation across the five runs. We report our results in Table 4 and find that the choice of in-context examples accounts for very little of the observed variance across prompt type and context length. This finding is surprising as previous work has shown that the selection and ordering of in-context examples has a very large effect on the performance of models (Liu et al., 2021). However, it seems that our approach of random sampling in-context examples per test item helps to lessen this inherent variance.

E Evaluation on `text-davinci-003`

While conducting our research into the differences between code and text prompts, OpenAI released the `text-davinci-003` model. This model differs from `text-davinci-002` in that it is trained using Reinforcement Learning with Human Feedback (RLHF) instead of supervised instruction fine-tuning (Ouyang et al., 2022). Out

Task	code-002 (base)	text-002 (+IFT)	text-003 (+RLHF)
HellaSwag	0.652	**0.717**	0.714
wikiHow GS	**0.924**	0.919	0.510
wikiHow T	0.622	0.688	**0.815**
Yelp	**0.924**	0.919	0.903
IMDb	**0.945**	0.940	0.938
WinoGrande	0.607	0.628	**0.735**
ANLI	**0.562**	0.504	0.549
HotpotQA	0.470	**0.490**	0.378
SQuAD	0.604	**0.670**	0.663
OpenPI	37.33	35.60	**39.06**
CNN/DM	11.74	**13.63**	12.64
XSUM	**14.51**	14.48	13.36

Table 5: Performance of the three GPT-3.5 models across our 12 datasets with **text prompts**. (+IFT) indicates the addition of supervised instruction fine-tuning and (+RLHF) indicates the addition of training using Reinforcement Learning from Human Feedback (Ouyang et al., 2022). We see that RLHF does not always improve performance and that for some tasks (HotpotQA and wikiHow Goal-Step) it causes large degradations in performance.

of curiosity, to see the effect of this new training paradigm, we conducted experiments comparing this new `text-davinci-003` model to the other GPT-3.5 models (`text-davinci-002` and `code-davinci-002`). We report the results of our comparison across the 12 evaluation tasks in Table 5.

We see that while `text-davinci-003` outperforms all previous models on *wikiHow Temporal*, *WinoGrande*, and *OpenPI*, it does significantly worse than previous models on *wikiHow Goal-Step* and *HotpotQA*. Such large reductions in performance are to be somewhat expected when using RLHF given the costly nature of collecting human demonstrations. However, the magnitude of the decreases (-50.1% for *wikiHow* and -11.2% for *HotpotQA*) is nonetheless surprising and such results raise important questions about exactly what is being learned when conducting instruction fine-tuning and whether or not this learned information can generalize to tasks not seen during fine-tuning.

F Evaluation Cost

In this section we report the approximate cost of conducting our experiments. In our study we use four OpenAI models, namely `davinci`, `code-davinci-002`, `text-davinci-002` and `text-davinci-003`. While `code-davinci-002` is free to use at the time of this study, we report the approximate cost of running the experiments

Dataset	Num. Examples	Est. Cost
HellaSwag	1000 / 10042	$240.48
wikiHow Goal-Step	1000 / 1073	$240.48
wikiHow Temporal	1000 / 3100	$240.48
WinoGrande	1000 / 1767	$240.48
OpenPI	111 / 111	$28.08
ANLI	1000 / 3000	$240.48
Yelp	1000 / 10000	$240.48
IMDb	1000 / 25000	$240.48
HotpotQA	1000 / 7405	$241.20
SQuAD	1000 / 11873	$241.08
CNN/Daily Mail	1000 / 13368	$257.91
XSUM	1000 / 11332	$246.66
Total Cost		$2698.29

Table 6: The total estimated cost of running `davinci`, `text-davinci-002` and `text-davinci-003` for 1000 data samples from each dataset (except for OpenPI).

on the other three models[5] in Table 6. To estimate the cost of an experiment, we calculate the approximate number of tokens necessary for computing one dataset example and then multiplied that by the number of examples in the dataset. For classification tasks, since we fill up the context window to roughly 4000 tokens for every test example, we estimate the number of tokens to be 4000 (3999 tokens for the prompt and 1 token for the label). To estimate cost for generative tasks (OpenPI, HotpotQA, SQuAD, CNN/Daily Mail, and XSUM), we compute the average generation length from our generated samples and assume the in-context examples take up 3500 tokens. While this calculation results in a fairly loose upper bound, we believe this to be a good estimate of the total cost incurred by the project as such overestimates help offset the cost of other miscellaneous API queries done over the course of the project.

[5]The cost of querying `davinci`, `text-davinci-002` and `text-davinci-003` is $0.02/1,000 tokens at the time of study. See `https://openai.com/pricing` for more details.

A smashed glass cannot be full: Generation of Commonsense Explanations through Prompt-based Few-shot Learning

Andrea Zaninello
Fondazione Bruno Kessler
Free University of Bolzano (Italy)
azaninello@fbk.eu

Bernardo Magnini
Fondazione Bruno Kessler
magnini@fbk.eu

Abstract

We assume that providing explanations is a process to elicit implicit knowledge in human communication, and propose a general methodology to generate commonsense explanations from pairs of semantically related sentences. We take advantage of both prompting applied to large, encoder-decoder pre-trained language models, and few-shot learning techniques, such as pattern-exploiting training. Experiments run on the e-SNLI dataset show that the proposed method achieves state-of-the-art results on the explanation generation task, with a substantial reduction of labelled data. The obtained results open new perspective on a number of tasks involving the elicitation of implicit knowledge.

1 Introduction

When exchanging information, it is typical to exclude details that appear self-evident or insignificant, so that only part of the message is articulated verbally while other details are implied (Becker et al., 2020, 2021a). This is particularly true for information involving commonsense knowledge, which represents the backbone of everyday communication and reasoning. For example, consider the following sentences:

(1) *The glass is broken into pieces.*

(2) *The glass is full.*

We can intuitively assert that these two sentences *contradict* each other, and if we were asked to explain *why*, our answer would most probably appeal to some *implicit knowledge* about the world ("A glass broken into pieces cannot contain any liquid" and "A glass cannot be broken and full of a liquid at the same time", etc.) to various degrees of depth. This implicit, shared knowledge can easily be inferred by people, but represents a challenge for computational systems. Crucially, a request for explanation is often a request to *make explicit* something that is only implied or omitted in conversation. While this is evident in everyday communication, it is also true for more specialised domains, for example a doctor-patient scenario where the patient is given a diagnosis ("Your clinical case and tests indicate that you have type 2 diabetes") and asks for explanations to the doctor ("*Why* do you believe that?").

Therefore, the underlying assumption of this paper is that commonsense explanations are to some extent based upon the notion of *implicitness*, and that the information they rely on can not be fully derived from their textual input alone. Being able to elicit commonsense implicit knowledge is a relevant step forward not only towards providing explanations, but also towards better natural language understanding.

In this work, we state the "implicit knowledge problem" as the capacity to automatically generate explanations regarding the semantic relations between two sentences. We define a general methodology to elicit implicit knowledge from pre-trained large language models, motivated by the intuition that they contain most of the knowledge needed, and are able to generalize over unseen instances. In fact, a fully-supervised fine-tuning would require a large training set where each input-sentence pair should be labeled with one or more explanations, a setting which is unrealistic in an open-domain scenario.

To achieve this, we propose a combination of prompting and few-shot learning techniques, which are well-suited to exploit the generative capabilities of language models and, at the same time, make use of limited supervision. Similar methods have been applied to some popular NLP tasks such as text classification, inference, summarization (Schick and Schütze, 2021a,b) and, more recently, to teach language models to leverage external tools via APIs (Schick et al., 2023). However, the generation of implicit knowledge poses a further challenge

Proceedings of the 1st Workshop on Natural Language Reasoning and Structured Explanations (@ACL 2023), pages 18–29
June 13, 2023 ©2023 Association for Computational Linguistics

to these techniques as it requires to generate text based on information or reasoning structures that are outside the input texts[1].

For these reasons, in our experiments, we select the e-SNLI dataset Camburu et al. (2018), where sentence pairs traditionally employed for a textual inference task (pairs are labelled with *entail*, *contradict* or *neutral* tags) were augmented with explanations for the relation tag, collected through crowd-sourcing. We compare three generation methods: *unsupervised*, *fine-tuning* and *ensembling*, showing that the *ensembling* method achieves the best results, en-par with state-of-the-art while making use of limited supervision. Moreover, we find that this method mitigates the potential negative effects of "bad" prompts, which is a desirable feature whenever prompt optimization is not possible. However, we also underline that evaluation and comparison with SOTA results is still critical, as evaluation metrics are not usually directly comparable on the explanation generation task.

The innovative contributions of this paper are the following:

- We propose a general methodology to elicit implicit knowledge from language models with very limited training data.
- We compare the effects of prompting, few-shot fine-tuning and ensembling on a set of different language models, indicating which strategy suits best for each type.
- We show that one of our proposed methods for implicit knowledge generation is able to mitigate the negative impact of badly designed prompts.

The paper is structured as follows: Section 2 provides relevant background on language modelling and elicitation of implicit knowledge. Section 3 introduces the general approach to implicit knowledge generation. Sections 4 and 5 report, respectively, the experimental setting and the results we have obtained on the e-SNLI dataset. Finally, Section 6 provides relevant context of recent approaches to implicit knowledge elicitation.

[1]The code is available at `github.com/andreazaninello/explanationgeneration`

2 Background

2.1 Language modelling and transfer learning

Recent advances in NLP, particularly in Natural Language Generation (NLG), have been driven by the success of transfer learning techniques applied to neural language models, pre-trained on very large textual corpora in a self-supervised fashion (Howard and Ruder, 2018; Radford et al., 2019). These general models can be trained on in-domain datasets or on specific downstream tasks with much less resource expense through fine-tuning.

Transformers (Vaswani et al., 2017), based on the *attention* mechanism, currently represent the state-of-the-art in most of NLP tasks. In our experiments, we employ Transformers' encoder-decoder (sequence-to-sequence) models, like BART (Lewis et al., 2020), T5 (Raffel et al., 2020) or PEGASUS (Zhang et al., 2020). In these models, encoder attention can access the whole initial sequence, while decoder attention can only attend to previous words; these models perform best on language generation tasks that depend on a sequential input, such as machine translation or text summarization thus we hypothesize that the encoder-decoder kind of models are particularly suited to the task of generating explanations, because the sequence to be generated (the *explanans*) has to be conditioned on a full input sequence (the *explanandum*).

2.2 Prompting

The core technique that we use to elicit implicit knowledge is prompting (see Liu et al. (2021) for an extensive survey). Prompting consists in reframing an NLP task as a language modelling task: from a practical viewpoint, it corresponds to feeding a very large language model an input prompt that describes the desired task in natural language (and/or gives some examples of the desired output), and constructing a function that maps the desired label (e.g., *positive* in a sentiment analysis task) onto a series of natural language verbalizers (e.g. *good, great, excellent*). Given this prompt as an input, the language model is let generate the output as if it were a language modelling task such as next word or masked word prediction.

This new trend, which is especially appealing as it requires much less training signal compared to regular fine-tuning, has led to a shift from *objective engineering* to *prompt engineering*: this includes both the manual design of templates (Petroni et al., 2019) and automatic prompt learning (Jiang et al., 2020), as well as various options to ensemble (Schick and Schütze, 2021b) and compose (Han et al., 2022) multiple prompts.

When using prompts, we can simply generate with a language model with no parameter update, giving the model some answered prompts as example to direct generation, or we can update the prompts' parameters through the supervision given by training examples (Liu et al., 2021); additionally, some promising recent approaches have attempted to apply few-shot training techniques based on prompting to language generation, too. Schick and Schütze (2021c), for example, propose a method called *pattern-exploiting training* (PET) and use hand-crafted patterns as task instructions to train intermediate models, in combination with a small set of unlabeled gold training examples which they use to ensemble those models. This technique has proved successful in performing few-shot downstream NLG tasks on sequence-to-sequence models (Zhang et al., 2020) with many fewer training examples than state-of-the-art benchmarks, especially when the generated output is tightly connected to the input (e.g. text summarization). While our method is closely inspired by this line of work, to the best of our knowledge this has not been applied to tasks where models need to use implicit information outside the input text.

2.3 Evaluating generation

As we anticipated, we model the "implicit knowledge problem" as the capacity to automatically generate explanations regarding the semantic relations between two sentences, which brings up the issue of evaluating the quality of the generated predictions. Unlike classification and regression tasks, the evaluation of generation is known to be critical, and has often relied on human judgments (Wiegreffe et al., 2022), which is however expensive and difficult to scale.

On the other hand, automatic assessment is usually done by measuring the overlap between at least one reference generation and the system's output, as with popular metrics like ROUGE (Lin, 2004) and BLEU (Papineni et al., 2002). Other metrics aim to measure the semantic similarity between generations and references using contextualised embeddings, for example BERT-Score (Zhang et al., 2019) or Sentence-BERT (Reimers and Gurevych, 2019), which consider word and, respectively, sentence-embeddings.

Nevertheless, evaluating generation is a critical aspect and there is still no consensus on what metric is to be taken as a reference for system comparison, especially on explanation generation. In our experiments, we align with our selected benchmark to facilitate results' comparison, and thus report BLEU, ROUGE and BERT-Scores. However, we are aware that results may not be fully conclusive in terms of comparison with SOTA, and that metrics are rather to be taken as a relative indication of systems' performance.

3 Methodology

Our proposed methods belong to the "fixed-prompt language model tuning" types (Liu et al., 2022): the LM's parameters are updated through few-shot fine-tuning, after both training and test examples have been modified by textual templates, meaning that the prompts' parameters are fixed while the model's parameters are updated.

While some recent studies aim at discovering the best prompts or performing prompt optimization (Li et al., 2021; Shin et al., 2020), our methods aim to provide a general framework that may work well even without prompting optimization, minimizing the negative impact of "bad" prompts. Finding the best patterns and prefixes would clearly contribute to the task but falls outside the scope of this study, and would be task dependent, while we aim to provide a general framework potentially applicable to different generation tasks.

Our method is closely related to Gao et al. (2021)'s, who apply a similar procedure to classification and regression tasks, and is inspired by Schick and Schütze (2021b)'s GenPET, who apply it to a set of generation tasks close to summarization, not involving the elicitation of implicit external knowledge.

3.1 Problem formalization

We state the "implicit knowledge generation" problem as the task of automatically producing an explanation for the semantic relation between a pair of textual sentences t_a and t_b. We set M to be a language model of vocabulary V, pre-trained on a masked language modelling task. We define an input $x \in \mathcal{X}$, an output sequence $y \in \mathcal{Y}$, a label $l \in \mathcal{L}$, a label verbalizer $v \in V^*$ that maps the labels to a natural language sequences (for example mapping a `neutrality` label to the sequence "does not entail"), and the sequence resulting from applying a prompt $p \in P$ to input x as $z = f_{prompt}(x, p)$, with z containing one masked sequence <mask>. The f_{prompt} function then simply takes the input texts t_a, t_b, and the verbalized label l, and returns a modified, natural language version of the input.

To obtain the prompts, we need to define (1) a set of task *prefixes* $(pref_1, ..., pref_n)$ that introduce the explanation $y \in \mathcal{Y}$, and are either processed as final part of the input or pre-pended to the reference explanation at training time (or to the mask sequence at test time), and (2) a set of *patterns* $(patt_1, ..., patt_m)$, which we combine with $(pref_1, ..., pref_n)$, resulting in $n \times m$ prompts. Prompts are used to rewrite each input example, by sampling randomly across all labels. We refer to this modified training set as T, which is $n \times m$ times the size of X. We summarize and give an example of our prompting design in Section A.1.

3.2 Training objective

The models we use are pre-trained on masked language modelling task, so their objective is calculating the probability of $p_M = (\mathbf{y}|\mathbf{z})$. We have the choice of (1) processing the task prefix $pref$ using the decoder, as part of the generated sequence, or (2) with the encoder, as part of the input. Thus, assuming some model M, some task prefix $pref_i$ and some pattern $patt_j$, the model needs to compute the probability of y as follows, respectively:

$$p(\mathbf{y}|\mathbf{x}) = p_M(pref_i; y|patt_j(x)) \quad (1)$$

$$p(\mathbf{y}|\mathbf{x}) = p_M(y|patt_i(x); pref_i) \quad (2)$$

Schick and Schütze (2021b) indicate that processing it with the decoder has a stronger impact on generations, and we apply it to BART and Pegasus, as in (1). However, this is not possible with T5 as encoding it with the decoder pushes the model to produce empty strings. With T5, we therefore encode it as part of the encoder (2). Modified training and test instances are used in different zero- and few-shot training configurations, namely UNSUPERVISED (3.3), FINE-TUNING (3.4) and ENSEMBLING (3.5). We synthesize the three methods in Figure 1.

3.3 Method 1: UNSUPERVISED

In a first zero-shot configuration, which we name UNSUPERVISED and we take as our baseline, we simply evaluate the model's predictions without any training, so no parameter update is performed, nor do we use any training instances. However, to have the prompts influence the model's generations at inference, we modify each test instance with each one of the prompts, as explained in Section 3.1. We evaluate the model's predictions for each prompt separately after modifying the test instances with that prompt through function f_{prompt}, as detailed in Section 4.4. Moreover, we define a null prompt p_0 for which both $pref$ and $patt$ are an empty string, resulting in the simple concatenation of x and the <MASK> token, and evaluate its generations.

3.4 Method 2: FINE-TUNING

In a second configuration, which we call FINE-TUNING, at training time we apply all the prompts p to every input through function f_{prompt} obtaining a dataset T of all training instances X (where X can be empty). In addition, in order to avoid overfitting and ensure regularization, we also take a set of 1000 unlabeled instances U (for which the explanation y is not given), modify them with the patterns $p \in P$ and have the untrained model M generate an output for each of them. We therefore obtain a synthetically generated dataset $T_{\text{FINE-TUNED}}$, which we append to our training instances.

We use T to fine-tune M with teacher forcing, by minimizing the cross-entropy between the model's prediction and the target sentences, obtaining a fine-tuned model $M_{\text{FINE-TUNED}}$. In a zero-shot setting, only U is used for fine-tuning. In few-shot setting, we use training sets of increasing size. As in method 1 (3.3), at test time we assess the predictions of each pattern separately and of all patterns together using p_0.

3.5 Method 3: ENSEMBLING

In the previous method we were able to assess each prompt separately at inference time. However, it may not always be possible to know which pattern works better for a certain task and poor performance of one prompt could hurt the overall performance of the fine-tuned model[2]. Moreover, in few-shot scenarios, models tend to overfit the training data or copy part of the original input, resulting

[2]We are aware that several methods for prompt search and optimization have been recently proposed, and our method would certainly benefit from better quality prompts. However, our aim is to mitigate the potential impact of bad prompts, while prompt search currently falls outside the scope of this study.

in poor quality of the generations. In this configuration, we then aim to generalize over all possible patterns given at training time, without having to choose a specific pattern at test time.

Therefore, we perform a form of knowledge distillation through prompt-ensembling by taking the fine-tuned model $M_{\text{FINE-TUNED}}$ and the unlabeled instances $U = (u_1, ..., u_n)$, and use the set of patterns in $P = (p_1, ..., p_m)$ to generate a set of candidate outputs $C = (y_1, ..., y_m)$ for each $u \in U$. Then, we modify the instances in U with the null pattern p_0 and ask an untrained model M (that did not see any of the training examples) to assign a probability to each candidate generation in C given the modified inputs from U. To assign a final score to the generation, we take the exponentiated average of all the log-likelihood assigned by the untrained model across all patterns, and take the best scoring generation as our prediction.

By doing so, we obtain a new dataset T_{ENSEMBLE}, where inputs are u's from U modified by p_0 and y's are the best ranking y's from C according to M. The so obtained explanations should not be biased towards one particular pattern. Moreover, we empirically set a cutoff lower threshold at the bottom 20% of the instances ranked by their probability, so that low quality explanations are discarded.

We use this final dataset T_{ENSEMBLE} to fine-tune a final model M_{ENSEMBLE} with a procedure similar to method 2, but we only evaluate it using the null prompt as explained in Section 4.4.

4 Experiments

4.1 Pre-trained language models

We experiment on three different Transformer-based encoder-decoder language models: BART, Pegasus, and T5.

Bart (Lewis et al., 2020) uses a standard sequence to sequence architecture with a bidirectional encoder and a left-to-right decoder. It is pre-trained by firstly corrupting text with a noising function, then learning a model able to reconstruct the original text. BART was evaluated on several benchmarks and proved particularly suitable for generation tasks, a reason why we decided to employ it. In all experiments, we use the BART-large model.

Pegasus (Zhang et al., 2020) has a similar architecture to BART and trained in a self-supervised way by masking important sentences in text and have the model generate them as a single output conditioned on the remaining sentences. Thus, its training objective is similarl to a summarization task. We use the PEGASUS-large implementation in all our experiments.

T5 (Raffel et al., 2020) is also an encoder-decoder model, however unlike the previous two it was pre-trained on a mix of NLP tasks prompted in a text-to-text format, where inputs and outputs are text strings, as opposed to BERT-style models. For this reason, it is particularly suitable for methods exploiting textual verbalizations to condition generations.

4.2 Dataset

For all our experiments, we use the e-SNLI dataset (Camburu et al., 2018), an extension of the Stanford Natural Language Inference (SNLI) dataset (Bowman et al., 2015) enriched with crowd-sourced natural language explanations. The SNLI dataset is an influential dataset widely used for the task of Recognizing Textual Entailment (RTE) (Dagan et al., 2005): given two text fragments (called *premise* and *hypothesis)*, the aim of RTE is deciding whether the premise entails, contradicts or neither entails nor contradicts the hypothesis, labelling the relationship between the two texts with an *entailment*, *contradiction*, or *neutrality* label. The SNLI dataset contains 570K premise-hypothesis pairs, evenly distributed across labels. E-SNLI contains an extra layer of information, represented by a crowd-sourced natural language explanations for each instance for the training, testing and development splits. An example is given below.

```
{"guid": "test-3",
  "idx": "3",
  "label": "NEUTRALITY"
  "meta": {}
  "explanations": ["the woman
     could've been old rather
     than young"]
  "premise": "'A woman with a
     green headscarf, blue shirt
     and a very big grin.'"
  "hypothesis": 'The woman is
     young.'}
```

Few other datasets exist, such as the CoS-E dataset (Rajani et al., 2019) (an expansion of the CommonsenseQA (Talmor et al., 2019) dataset) that provide explanations based on commonsense. However, CoS-E's explanations mainly focus on one single term or phrase as the given explanation refers to one of the five possible answers to a commonsense question. Moreover, many times the open-ended explanations in this dataset are not formed as full sentences, while we aim to generate self-contained, linguistically complete explanations, so this dataset is not suitable for our experiments.

On the other hand, the task of recognizing textual entailment involves general reasoning as well as understanding some subtle facts about the language and the referents, while heavily relying on commonsense knowledge. For this reasons, many studies which aim to investigate the ability of a system to elicit implicit knowledge have turned onto this dataset, and we choose to experiment our methods on this challenging dataset enriched with natural language explanations.

For each training instance x (and for each corresponding output y), we obtain a set of four patterns. As can be seen from table in Section A.1, odd patterns present the explanation after the two sentences, while even patterns presents the explanation before the sentences, which are then introduced by the "`Text:`" string.

4.3 Experimental setup

For the FINE-TUNING and ENSEMBLING methods, we experiment with training sizes $=(0, 10, 100, 500)$, test and unlabeled sizes $= 1000$, sampled uniformly across the original examples and labels. For UNSUPERVISED, we set $T = 0$ and do not perform any parameter update, we simply let the model generate given the modified inputs. For FINE-TUNING and ENSEMBLE we train on a single NVIDIA GeForce RTX GPU with 10GB RAM for 3 epochs, for about 15 hours. We optimize with Adafactor with square root learning rate decay, dropout rate $= 0.1$ and learning rate $= 10^4$, following (Schick and Schütze, 2021b). We train each model with 8 gradient accumulation steps using a batch size of 2 as our computing resources are limited, and generate using greedy decoding. For all models, we use the Pytorch Transformers library implementation (Wolf et al., 2019).

4.4 Evaluation

At test time, we evaluate each model on each pattern separately, by modifying each testing instance with one prompt at a time. Secondly, as in real-world scenarios it is not always possible to know in advance which patterns will perform better, we also evaluate each model on the null pattern p_0, where the input precedes the masked sequence token and we use an empty task prefix. We evaluate using common metrics for generation, comparing the predicted output with the reference explanation, and thus report BLEU-1, ROUGE-1 and BERT-Score. Kayser et al. (2021) present the most extensive, current study on the correlation between human judgments and generation, focusing in particular on the explanation generation task, and show that BERT-Score is the one that best matches human judgments, as also confirmed by other studies (Becker et al., 2021b). Therefore, we set BERT-Score as our reference metric to assess the best model and method.

5 Results and Discussion

In Table 1 we report the results of our experiments for each of the considered models. T5 represents the best scoring model, which most benefits from the proposed methods, achieving a BERT-score of 91.23 both for the P_0-FINE-TUNING method and for the ENSEMBLING method, as confirmed by both BLEU and ROUGE scores. Similarly, Pegasus benefits from the proposed methods, with a slight decrease on the ENSEMBLING method, which may be due to the error margin of the metrics.

Interestingly, both models have very low scores in both zero-shot configurations, indicating that the "fixed-prompt fine-tune" strategies may be particularly suitable for them, even without prompt optimization, as indicated by the low figures of the null prompt. On the other hand, BART displays a stronger baseline and is more sensitive to prompt design, as displayed by the decreasing values especially relevant on the p_0-FINE-TUNING method. This indicates that when using BART, which was not specifically trained to accept prompts as inputs, prompt optimization may be a better strategy. On the other hand, for all three models the ENSEMBLING method is able to mitigate the negative effects of shallow prompt design.

While a clear benchmark for the explanation generation task does not yet exist, in Table 2 we report the results of related studies on the same task and dataset. Specifically, we compare our methods with studies using the same underlying model and with comparable settings and show that our methods achieve better results but with a significant reduction in training size. In particular, Marasovic et al. (2022) use T5 with 48 training examples and achieve a significantly lower Bert-Score compared to our T5-Ensembling method with 10 training examples. Becker et al. (2021b) achieve a slightly lower BERT-Score using BART, but with 18K training examples (which we compare with our BART-Ensemble method with 500 training examples). We provide further details on the related works in Section 6.

We also manually analyzed several generations and compared the different models and methods. We notice that in the unsupervised settings, models tend to hallucinate, while with zero-shots BART and PEGASUS tend to copy (part of) the input, while T5 often returns single words. In Table 3 we report an example of the generations produced by T5 under the different configurations. Notice that generations under settings T_{10} and T_{100} are already correct. However, the bigger the train size, the closer the generation to the reference. Finally, manual inspection also highlighted that in some cases the model learns to reproduce some patterns, such as the contradiction explanation pattern "X cannot Y and Z at the same time", where X is the common referent to the sentences and Y and Z are the states described by the two sentences, respectively. However, the pattern repetition also characterises many human-generated sentences, a phenomenon that deserves further attention in future investigations if we aim at general, better natural language explanations.

6 Related work

Being a relatively recent area of interest, generation of free text explanations is not a well consolidated task. Particularly, evaluations metrics are still being discussed (Golovneva et al., 2022) (Wiegreffe et al., 2022), attempting both to capture the explanation informativeness and to improve the correlation toward human judgements. Here we report related works which are most focused on the e-SNLI dataset, being more comparable with our work (see Table 2).

Generating explanation with implicit knowledge has traditionally been addressed either by constraining generations with general knowledge paths (Ribeiro et al., 2020), by fine-tuning on specific or general knowledge datasets (Fatema Rajani et al., 2019), or with a combination of both methods (Becker et al., 2021a).

Camburu et al. (2018) train four different models with the aim to generate an explanation given only the hypothesis, generate an explanation without knowing the label, jointly predict a label and generate an explanation for the predicted label, and generate an explanation and then predict the label. Their work uses straightforward recurrent neural network architectures so it is does not achieve state-of-the-art results, but it establishes a strong baseline.

Becker et al. (2021a) generate implicit knowledge connecting sentences in text, similarly to Camburu et al. (2018). They perform fine-tuning on corpora enriched with implicit information, by constraining them with relevant concepts and connecting commonsense knowledge paths, combining data augmentation and graph-to-text methods.

Marasovic et al. (2022) both present FEB, a standardized collection of four existing English-language datasets and associated metrics, and results based on template-based prompting. In our work we show that specific prompting design for the e-SNLI task results in significant improvements with respect to more general purposes prompts.

Li et al. (2022), based on the intuition that explanation generated through single-pass prompting often lacks sufficiency and conciseness, propose a two-step approach where the first-pass output from the pretrained language model is polished, and then regenerated retaining the information that supports the contents being explained.

Ye et al. (2022) show that both the computation trace (the way the explanation is decomposed) and the natural language of the prompt, contribute to the effectiveness of explanations. According to this finding they propose automatic prompt selection that focus on prompt diversity, rather than complementarity only.

7 Conclusion

In this work, we argued that providing explanations is often a process of eliciting implicit knowledge. We proposed a general methodology to generate commonsense explanations from pairs of semantically related sentences, taking advantage of both prompting applied to large pre-trained language models and few-shot learning techniques. Experiments run on the e-SNLI dataset show that the proposed methods achieve SOTA results on the explanation generation task, with a substantial reduction of labelled data. The obtained results open new perspective for a number of tasks based on eliciting implicit knowledge.

	UNSUPERVISED (baseline)			FINE-TUNING		ENSEMBLING
	P_0	P_1 - P_4 (best)		P_0	P_1 - P_4 (best)	P_0
BART	11.10 42.30 88.61	10.86 42.05 88.53 (1)	T_0	11.09 42.3 **88.53**	10.86 42.05 88.53 (1)	11.12 42.37 88.58
			T_{10}	04.50 22.85 88.14	04.60 23.09 88.18 (1)	04.94 23.45 88.43
			T_{100}	10.86 31.87 77.09	12.27 35.82 **86.88** (4)	14.76 38.00 90.13
			T_{500}	08.09 28.23 66.57	11.88 35.68 86.64 (3)	15.06 39.45 **90.27**
PEGASUS	01.66 26.67 85.00	03.24 30.85 87.66 (3)	T_0	05.44 29.69 87.05	10.06 35.00 88.58 (1)	10.86 38.70 88.76
			T_{10}	10.58 38.06 88.38	10.50 37.93 88.42 (1)	10.59 38.66 88.52
			T_{100}	14.42 40.21 90.42	14.58 40.39 90.47 (4)	15.60 41.90 **90.69**
			T_{500}	16.87 42.30 **90.79**	16.75 42.26 **90.77** (4)	16.39 41.58 90.67
T5	05.45 27.29 85.59	04.78 25.41 84.68 (3)	T_0	05.45 27.29 85.59	04.79 24.72 84.76 (1)	06.25 11.72 84.95
			T_{10}	18.91 42.45 90.99	18.95 42.64 91.01 (2)	20.45 43.87 91.20
			T_{100}	17.62 41.96 90.91	17.63 41.67 90.91 (3)	18.37 42.06 90.96
			T_{500}	20.15 44.67 **91.23**	19.84 44.59 **91.21** (1)	20.18 44.00 **91.23**

Table 1: Results for the three sets of experiments for the considered language models in each training configuration ($T_0 - T_{500}$). $P_0 - P_{1-4}$ indicate the prompt used to modify the test input in that configuration. For prompts $P1 - 4$ we report the best scoring prompt, indicated in braket (1-4). For each experiment, we report the BLEU-1, ROUGE-1 and BERT-Scores in this order. Boldfaced, the best scoring configurations for each model, method and test prompt according to BERT-score.

Reference	BLEU	ROUGE	BERT-Score	Training size	Model
Becker et al. (2021b)	12.71	47	90	18K	BART
Our method	15.06	39.45	**90.27**	500	BART
Marasovic et al. (2022)	n/a	n/a	79.2	48	T5
Our method	20.45	43.87	**91.20**	10	T5
Li et al. (2022)	22.3	n/a	87.16	500K	GPT2
Ye et al. (2022)	n/a	n/a	83.9	500K	RoBERTa
Camburu et al. (2018)	27.58	n/a	n/a	500K	From scratch

Table 2: Benchmark for the task of generating explanations on the e-SNLI dataset.

T5-ENSEMBLING	Generated explanation on test set with P_0
Input	'A man with an afro and bandanna playing electric guitar.' contradicts 'the guy with the afro is eating spinach'
T_0	False
T_{10}	The guy is either playing electric guitar or eating spinach.
T_{100}	the man is either playing electric guitar or eating spinach.
T_{500}	A man cannot be playing electric guitar and eating spinach at the same time.
Reference	The man can not very well be playing electric guitar and eating spinach at the same time.
Baseline	: 'A man with an afro and bandanna playing electric guitar' : 'A man with an afro and bandanna playing electric guitar' contradicts 'the guy with an afro is eating spinach'. :"'A man with an

Table 3: Example generations for the best scoring model and method T5-ENSEMBLING. We report the generated explanation for each configuration, the reference explanation, and the T5-UNSUPERVISED's prediction (baseline).

8 Limitations

Although we showed significant improvements in explanation generation using prompt-based few-shot learning, our work still has some limitations. First, we experimented only on the e-SNLI dataset: although e-SNLI is a reference for the task, it would be interesting to extend the proposed methodology to other datasets with natural language explanations (see Wiegreffe and Marasović (2021) for an extensive review)..

Second, we did not attempt to automatic prompt optimization: although this may bring further minor improvements, we decided to leave optimization to a next step, as it does not change the core contribution of our work.

Third, we believe there is an intrinsic limitation in comparing our results with SOTA, as there is not a clear consensus on which metric is to be taken as the reference metric for benchmarking, along with the fact that measures sometimes disagree on scoring one system better than another. We hope that in the future this task and its evaluation will consolidate into a shared benchmark.

Finally, as for our our use of e-SNLI, we are assuming that for all sentence pairs in the dataset there is an implicit explanation of the semantic relation between the sentences. Under this assumption we always generate an explanation, even when the explanation is already explicit in one of the sentences. We think that a better capacity to detect those cases would bring relevant insight to our approach.

Acknowledgements

This work has been partially supported by the chistera ANTIDOTE Project.

References

Maria Becker, Katharina Korfhage, and Anette Frank. 2020. Implicit knowledge in argumentative texts: An annotated corpus. In *Proceedings of the 12th Language Resources and Evaluation Conference*, pages 2316–2324.

Maria Becker, Siting Liang, and Anette Frank. 2021a. Reconstructing implicit knowledge with language models. In *Proceedings of Deep Learning Inside Out (DeeLIO): The 2nd Workshop on Knowledge Extraction and Integration for Deep Learning Architectures*, pages 11–24.

Maria Becker, Siting Liang, and Anette Frank. 2021b. Reconstructing implicit knowledge with language models. In *Proceedings of Deep Learning Inside Out (DeeLIO): The 2nd Workshop on Knowledge Extraction and Integration for Deep Learning Architectures*, pages 11–24, Online. Association for Computational Linguistics.

Samuel R. Bowman, Gabor Angeli, Christopher Potts, and Christopher D. Manning. 2015. A large annotated corpus for learning natural language inference. In *Proceedings of the 2015 Conference on Empirical Methods in Natural Language Processing (EMNLP)*. Association for Computational Linguistics.

Oana-Maria Camburu, Tim Rocktäschel, Thomas Lukasiewicz, and Phil Blunsom. 2018. e-snli: Natural language inference with natural language explanations. *Advances in Neural Information Processing Systems*, 31.

Ido Dagan, Oren Glickman, and Bernardo Magnini. 2005. The pascal recognising textual entailment challenge. In *Proceedings of the PASCAL Challenges Workshop on Recognising Textual Entailment*.

Nazneen Fatema Rajani, Bryan McCann, Caiming Xiong, and Richard Socher. 2019. Explain yourself! leveraging language models for commonsense reasoning. *arXiv e-prints*, pages arXiv–1906.

Tianyu Gao, Adam Fisch, and Danqi Chen. 2021. Making pre-trained language models better few-shot learners. In *Proceedings of the 59th Annual Meeting of the Association for Computational Linguistics and the 11th International Joint Conference on Natural Language Processing (Volume 1: Long Papers)*, pages 3816–3830, Online. Association for Computational Linguistics.

Olga Golovneva, Moya Chen, Spencer Poff, Martin Corredor, Luke Zettlemoyer, Maryam Fazel-Zarandi, and Asli Celikyilmaz. 2022. Roscoe: A suite of metrics for scoring step-by-step reasoning.

Xu Han, Weilin Zhao, Ning Ding, Zhiyuan Liu, and Maosong Sun. 2022. Ptr: Prompt tuning with rules for text classification. *AI Open*, 3:182–192.

Jeremy Howard and Sebastian Ruder. 2018. Universal language model fine-tuning for text classification. *arXiv preprint arXiv:1801.06146*.

Zhengbao Jiang, Frank F Xu, Jun Araki, and Graham Neubig. 2020. How can we know what language models know? *Transactions of the Association for Computational Linguistics*, 8:423–438.

Maxime Kayser, Oana-Maria Camburu, Leonard Salewski, Cornelius Emde, Virginie Do, Zeynep Akata, and Thomas Lukasiewicz. 2021. e-vil: A dataset and benchmark for natural language explanations in vision-language tasks. pages 1224–1234.

Mike Lewis, Yinhan Liu, Naman Goyal, Marjan Ghazvininejad, Abdelrahman Mohamed, Omer Levy, Veselin Stoyanov, and Luke Zettlemoyer. 2020. Bart: Denoising sequence-to-sequence pre-training for natural language generation, translation, and comprehension. In *Proceedings of the 58th Annual Meeting of the Association for Computational Linguistics*, pages 7871–7880.

Qintong Li, Zhiyong Wu, Lingpeng Kong, and Wei Bi. 2022. Explanation regeneration via information bottleneck. *arXiv preprint arXiv:2212.09603*.

Xiaotao Li, Shujuan You, Yawen Niu, and Wai Chen. 2021. Learning embeddings for rare words leveraging Internet search engine and spatial location relationships. In *Proceedings of *SEM 2021: The Tenth Joint Conference on Lexical and Computational Semantics*, pages 278–287, Online. Association for Computational Linguistics.

Chin-Yew Lin. 2004. Rouge: A package for automatic evaluation of summaries. In *Text summarization branches out*, pages 74–81.

Fangchao Liu, Hongyu Lin, Xianpei Han, Boxi Cao, and Le Sun. 2022. Pre-training to match for unified low-shot relation extraction. In *Proceedings of the 60th Annual Meeting of the Association for Computational Linguistics (Volume 1: Long Papers)*, pages 5785–5795, Dublin, Ireland. Association for Computational Linguistics.

Pengfei Liu, Weizhe Yuan, Jinlan Fu, Zhengbao Jiang, Hiroaki Hayashi, and Graham Neubig. 2021. Pre-train, prompt, and predict: A systematic survey of prompting methods in natural language processing. *ACM Computing Surveys (CSUR)*.

Ana Marasovic, Iz Beltagy, Doug Downey, and Matthew Peters. 2022. Few-shot self-rationalization with natural language prompts. In *Findings of the Association for Computational Linguistics: NAACL 2022*, pages 410–424, Seattle, United States. Association for Computational Linguistics.

Kishore Papineni, Salim Roukos, Todd Ward, and Wei-Jing Zhu. 2002. Bleu: a method for automatic evaluation of machine translation. In *Proceedings of the 40th annual meeting of the Association for Computational Linguistics*, pages 311–318.

Fabio Petroni, Tim Rocktäschel, Patrick Lewis, Anton Bakhtin, Yuxiang Wu, Alexander H Miller, and Sebastian Riedel. 2019. Language models as knowledge bases? *arXiv preprint arXiv:1909.01066*.

Alec Radford, Jeffrey Wu, Rewon Child, David Luan, Dario Amodei, Ilya Sutskever, et al. 2019. Language models are unsupervised multitask learners. *OpenAI blog*, 1(8):9.

Colin Raffel, Noam Shazeer, Adam Roberts, Katherine Lee, Sharan Narang, Michael Matena, Yanqi Zhou, Wei Li, and Peter J Liu. 2020. Exploring the limits of transfer learning with a unified text-to-text transformer. *Journal of Machine Learning Research*, 21:1–67.

Nazneen Fatema Rajani, Bryan McCann, Caiming Xiong, and Richard Socher. 2019. Explain yourself! leveraging language models for commonsense reasoning. In *Proceedings of the 57th Annual Meeting of the Association for Computational Linguistics*, pages 4932–4942.

Nils Reimers and Iryna Gurevych. 2019. Sentence-bert: Sentence embeddings using siamese bert-networks. In *Proceedings of the 2019 Conference on Empirical Methods in Natural Language Processing and the 9th International Joint Conference on Natural Language Processing (EMNLP-IJCNLP)*, pages 3982–3992.

Leonardo FR Ribeiro, Martin Schmitt, Hinrich Schütze, and Iryna Gurevych. 2020. Investigating pretrained language models for graph-to-text generation. *arXiv preprint arXiv:2007.08426*.

Timo Schick, Jane Dwivedi-Yu, Roberto Dessì, Roberta Raileanu, Maria Lomeli, Luke Zettlemoyer, Nicola Cancedda, and Thomas Scialom. 2023. Toolformer: Language models can teach themselves to use tools.

Timo Schick and Hinrich Schütze. 2021a. Exploiting cloze-questions for few-shot text classification and natural language inference. In *Proceedings of the 16th Conference of the European Chapter of the Association for Computational Linguistics: Main Volume*, pages 255–269, Online. Association for Computational Linguistics.

Timo Schick and Hinrich Schütze. 2021b. Few-shot text generation with natural language instructions. In *Proceedings of the 2021 Conference on Empirical Methods in Natural Language Processing*, pages 390–402, Online and Punta Cana, Dominican Republic. Association for Computational Linguistics.

Timo Schick and Hinrich Schütze. 2021c. Generating datasets with pretrained language models. In *Proceedings of the 2021 Conference on Empirical Methods in Natural Language Processing*, pages 6943–6951, Online and Punta Cana, Dominican Republic. Association for Computational Linguistics.

Taylor Shin, Yasaman Razeghi, Robert L Logan IV, Eric Wallace, and Sameer Singh. 2020. Autoprompt: Eliciting knowledge from language models with automatically generated prompts. In *Proceedings of the 2020 Conference on Empirical Methods in Natural Language Processing (EMNLP)*, pages 4222–4235.

Alon Talmor, Jonathan Herzig, Nicholas Lourie, and Jonathan Berant. 2019. CommonsenseQA: A question answering challenge targeting commonsense knowledge. In *Proceedings of the 2019 Conference of the North American Chapter of the Association for Computational Linguistics: Human Language Technologies, Volume 1 (Long and Short Papers)*, pages 4149–4158, Minneapolis, Minnesota. Association for Computational Linguistics.

Ashish Vaswani, Noam Shazeer, Niki Parmar, Jakob Uszkoreit, Llion Jones, Aidan N Gomez, Łukasz Kaiser, and Illia Polosukhin. 2017. Attention is all you need. *Advances in neural information processing systems*, 30.

Sarah Wiegreffe, Jack Hessel, Swabha Swayamdipta, Mark Riedl, and Yejin Choi. 2022. Reframing human-AI collaboration for generating free-text explanations. In *Proceedings of the 2022 Conference of the North American Chapter of the Association for Computational Linguistics: Human Language*

Technologies, pages 632–658, Seattle, United States. Association for Computational Linguistics.

Sarah Wiegreffe and Ana Marasović. 2021. Teach me to explain: A review of datasets for explainable nlp. *ArXiv*, abs/2102.12060.

Thomas Wolf, Lysandre Debut, Victor Sanh, Julien Chaumond, Clement Delangue, Anthony Moi, Pierric Cistac, Tim Rault, Rémi Louf, Morgan Funtowicz, et al. 2019. Huggingface's transformers: State-of-the-art natural language processing. *arXiv preprint arXiv:1910.03771*.

Xi Ye, Srinivasan Iyer, Asli Celikyilmaz, Ves Stoyanov, Greg Durrett, and Ramakanth Pasunuru. 2022. Complementary explanations for effective in-context learning. *arXiv preprint arXiv:2211.13892*.

Jingqing Zhang, Yao Zhao, Mohammad Saleh, and Peter Liu. 2020. Pegasus: Pre-training with extracted gap-sentences for abstractive summarization. In *International Conference on Machine Learning*, pages 11328–11339. PMLR.

Tianyi Zhang, Varsha Kishore, Felix Wu, Kilian Q Weinberger, and Yoav Artzi. 2019. Bertscore: Evaluating text generation with bert. *arXiv preprint arXiv:1904.09675*.

A Appendix

A.1 Prompt design

Parameter	Values
Prefixes ($pref$)	`"Explanation:"`, `"Rationale:"`
Task verbalizers (v)	`"entails"`, `"contradicts"`, `"does not entail"`
Patterns ($patt$)	$patt_1, patt_3 = t_a + v + t_b + pref +$ <mask>
	$patt_2, patt_4 = pref +$ <mask> $+$ `"Text:"` $+ t_a + v + t_b$

Table 4: Synthesis of the possible values of each of prompt parameters.

A.2 System diagrams

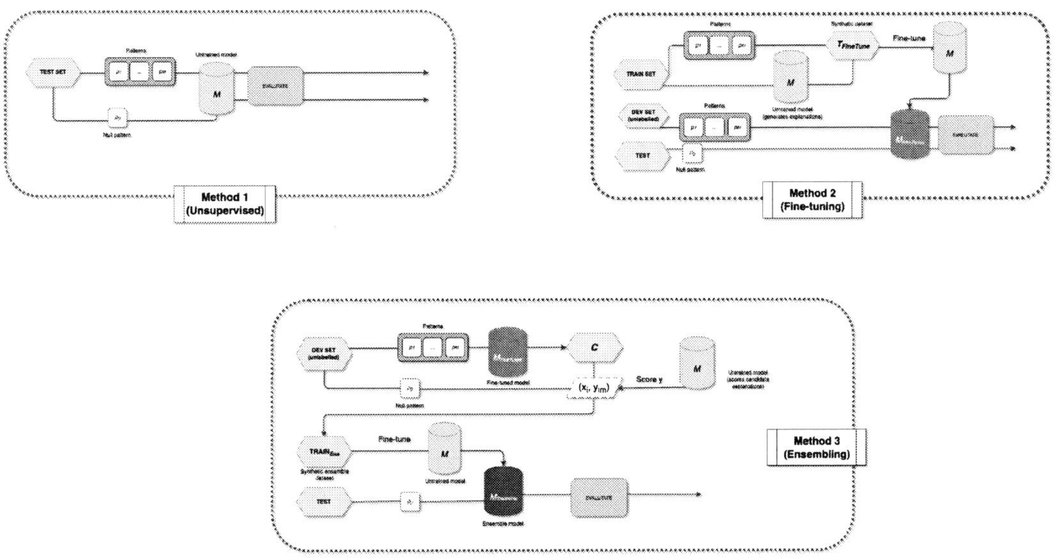

Figure 1: A diagram of our three proposed methods. Hexagons indicate datasets, cylinders indicate language models, white squares indicate prompting functions applied to inputs, and red rectangle indicates the final evaluation step.

Saliency Map Verbalization: Comparing Feature Importance Representations from Model-free and Instruction-based Methods

Nils Feldhus[1] **Leonhard Hennig**[1] **Maximilian Dustin Nasert**[1,2]
Christopher Ebert[1,2] **Robert Schwarzenberg** **Sebastian Möller**[1,2]
[1] German Research Center for Artificial Intelligence (DFKI)
[2] Technische Universität Berlin
`{firstname.lastname}@dfki.de`

Abstract

Saliency maps can explain a neural model's predictions by identifying important input features. They are difficult to interpret for laypeople, especially for instances with many features. In order to make them more accessible, we formalize the underexplored task of translating saliency maps into natural language and compare methods that address two key challenges of this approach – what and how to verbalize. In both automatic and human evaluation setups, using token-level attributions from text classification tasks, we compare two novel methods (search-based and instruction-based verbalizations) against conventional feature importance representations (heatmap visualizations and extractive rationales), measuring simulatability, faithfulness, helpfulness and ease of understanding. Instructing `GPT-3.5` to generate saliency map verbalizations yields plausible explanations which include associations, abstractive summarization and commonsense reasoning, achieving by far the highest human ratings, but they are not faithfully capturing numeric information and are inconsistent in their interpretation of the task. In comparison, our search-based, model-free verbalization approach efficiently completes templated verbalizations, is faithful by design, but falls short in helpfulness and simulatability. Our results suggest that saliency map verbalization makes feature attribution explanations more comprehensible and less cognitively challenging to humans than conventional representations. [1]

1 Introduction

Feature attribution methods, or (input) saliency methods, such as attention- or gradient-based attribution, are the most prominent class of methods for generating explanations of NLP model behavior (Wallace et al., 2020; Madsen et al., 2022) and can be used to produce word-level importance scores without human supervision (Wallace et al., 2019; Sarti et al., 2023). A major limitation of saliency maps is that they require expert knowledge to interpret (Alvarez-Melis et al., 2019; Colin et al., 2022). Furthermore, Schuff et al. (2022) revealed visual perception and belief biases which may influence the recipient's interpretation.

Natural language explanations (NLEs), on the other hand, exceed other explainability methods in plausibility (Lei et al., 2016; Wiegreffe and Pinter, 2019; Jacovi and Goldberg, 2020), accessibility (Ehsan and Riedl, 2020), and flexibility (Brahman et al., 2021; Chen et al., 2023), i.e. they can be adapted to both different target tasks and different audiences. Most previous approaches in generating NLEs depend on datasets of human-annotated text highlights (Zaidan et al., 2007; Lei et al., 2016; Wiegreffe and Marasović, 2021) or carefully constructed gold rationales for supervised training (Camburu et al., 2020; Wiegreffe et al., 2022), which are costly to obtain and task-specific. Alignment of model rationales with very few human-acceptable gold rationales may raise issues of trust (Jacovi et al., 2021) and the models trained on them may suffer from hallucinations (Maynez et al., 2020).

In this work, we revisit and formalize the task of verbalizing saliency maps, i.e. translating the output of feature attribution methods into natural language (Forrest et al., 2018; Mariotti et al., 2020; Slack et al., 2022). Verbalizations can describe relations between words and phrases and their associated saliency scores. Contrary to conventional heatmap visualizations, we can adjust the comprehensiveness of an explanation more precisely and infuse it with additional semantics such as word meanings, concepts, and context about the task.

We find that verbalization also comes with a few caveats: Similar to human explainers, who communicate only the most relevant explanations to avoid cognitive overload of the recipient (Hilton,

[1]Code and data at `https://github.com/DFKI-NLP/SMV`.

Proceedings of the 1st Workshop on Natural Language Reasoning and Structured Explanations (@ACL 2023), pages 30–46
June 13, 2023

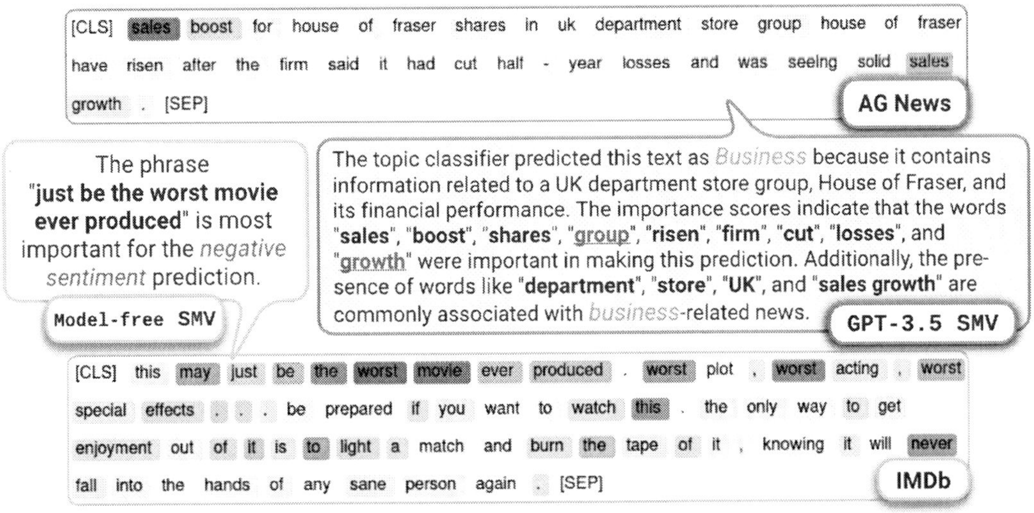

Figure 1: Heatmap visualizations generated by the Integrated Gradients feature attribution method explaining the predictions of a BERT model: Correct classifications of an instance from AG News (top) as *Business* and an instance from IMDb (bottom) as *Negative sentiment*. Tokens with red backgrounds have higher importance scores, while blue backgrounds indicate the contrast case. Two verbalizations (SMVs) are depicted in the center of the figure: The left (yellow) is produced by our model-free approach, while the right (blue) is produced by GPT-3.5. The predicted labels are highlighted in cyan and italic. The model-generated verbalization conveys semantic information such as associations with the target label (*Business*) and reasoning that is disconnected from the underlying model. GPT-3.5 wrongly deems two of the least attributed tokens salient ("group" and "growth", highlighted in red).

2017; Miller, 2019), verbalization methods need to address the problem of deciding "what" to say, i.e. selecting the most informative and useful aspects of the saliency maps and communicating them in a concise manner. We therefore compare different methods for verbalizing saliency maps: Supervised rationales, prompting LLMs, and model/training-free templates.

We address the problem of saliency map verbalization (**SMV**) with the following contributions:

- We formalize the underexplored task of SMV and establish desiderata, i.e. simulatability, explainer-faithfulness, plausibility, and conciseness (§2.1);
- We conduct a comparative study on various representations of feature attribution in two text classification setups, measuring the effects of verbalizations methods on both automated (explainer-faithfulness) and human evaluation metrics (simulatability, helpfulness, ease of understanding) (§3, §5).
- We propose a novel, model-free, template-based SMV approach, and design instructions for GPT-3.5-generated SMVs (§4) (examples from our two setups are depicted in Fig. 1);
- We show that model-free SMVs perform slightly better than heatmaps and extractive rationales on ease of understanding and are faithful by design, while instruction-based SMVs achieve the highest average simulation accuracy and are preferred in subjective ratings (§6);
- We publish a large dataset of model-free and GPT-generated SMVs alongside extractive rationales and results from both evaluations, and open-source code to produce all kinds of SMVs.

2 Verbalizing saliency maps

2.1 Formalization

The setup of the saliency map verbalization task consists of an underlying (to-be-explained) **model** m whose prediction $\hat{y} \subset Y$ on source tokens $W = w_1 \ \dots \ w_n$ we want to explain (against the set of possible outcomes Y).

m is equipped with a feature explanation method (or short: **explainer**) e which produces a **saliency map** $S = s_1 \dots s_n$:

$$e(W, m) = S \quad (1)$$

Here, we call token w_i salient *towards* outcome y if its associated saliency score $s_i > 0$ and salient *against* y for $s_i < 0$. e can have many sources, e.g. gradient-based methods such as Integrated Gradients (Sundararajan et al., 2017) which we employ in our experiments (§5), or even human experts assigning relevance scores.

A **verbalized saliency map** S_V is produced by some verbalizer v that receives the output of e:

$$v(W, S) = S_V \tag{2}$$

v can be any function that discretizes attribution scores and constructs a natural language representation S_V. This is connected to the concept of hard selection in DeYoung et al. (2020) and heuristics for discretizing rationales (Jain et al., 2020). In the taxonomy of Wiegreffe and Marasović (2021), verbalized saliency maps can be categorized as free-text rationales with varying degrees of structure imposed through templates. Moreover, verbalized explanations are procedural and deterministic by nature, i.e. they function as instructions that one can directly follow (Tan, 2022) to understand a model's decision, similar to compositional explanations (Hancock et al., 2018; Yao et al., 2021).

2.2 Desiderata

In the following, we outline the common evaluation paradigms for explanations (faithfulness, simulatability, plausibility) and how we adapt them to saliency map verbalizations.

Faithfulness Saliency maps express that "certain parts of the input are more important to the model reasoning than others" (*linearity assumption* in Jacovi and Goldberg (2020)). For verbalizations, explainer e and verbalizer v are two separate processes, so the saliency map S can be seen as static. Therefore, the faithfulness of e to the model m is extrinsic to the verbalization. Instead, it is essential to faithfully translate S into natural language, which we coin **explainer-faithfulness**. The verbalizer breaks faithfulness, e.g. if words are referenced as salient in S_V that are made up (do not appear in W) or if the polarity of any s_i is falsely interpreted.

Simulatability Another type of faithfulness is the model assumption which requires two models to "make the same predictions [iff] they use the same reasoning process" (Jacovi and Goldberg, 2020). By extension this means a model has to be simulatable (Doshi-Velez and Kim, 2017; Hase and Bansal, 2020), i.e. a human or another model should be able to predict a model's behaviour on unseen examples while exposed only to the explanation and not the model's prediction.

Plausibility The plausibility of explanations is commonly measured by correlation with ground-truth explanations (DeYoung et al., 2020; Jacovi and Goldberg, 2020), since gold rationales are influenced by human priors on what a model should do.

Conciseness In addition to these paradigms, verbosity is also an important aspect. A full translation into natural language is nonsensical, however, because all relations between the continuous-valued saliency scores and the associated tokens would normally overload human cognitive abilities. We want S_V to be concise, yet still contain the key information, similar to sufficiency and comprehensiveness measures from DeYoung et al. (2020). Thus, we define a **coverage** measure to indicate how much information is retained going from S to S_V, i.e. how much of the total attribution in $S = s_1 \ldots s_n$ is referenced by the tokens mentioned in $S_V = v_1 \ldots v_m$:

$$\text{Coverage}(S_V) = \frac{\sum |v_i|}{||S||} \tag{3}$$

The goal here is not to achieve a coverage of 1 with all of S, but depending on the use case, S_V should mention the most influential tokens, so a trivial solution for $k = 5$ would be to include the top k tokens with the highest attribution in S.

3 Study setup

3.1 Human Evaluation

Inspired by previous crowd studies in explainability (Chandrasekaran et al., 2018; Strout et al., 2019; Hase and Bansal, 2020; Sen et al., 2020; González et al., 2021; Arora et al., 2022; Joshi et al., 2023), we propose to measure **simulatability** as well as ratings for helpfulness and ease of understanding (**plausibility**). We evaluate the quality of different verbalization methods in a study involving 10 human participants. All participants have a computational linguistics background, with at least a Bachelor's degree, limited to no prior exposure to explainability methods, and are proficient in English (non-native speakers). After an introduction to the goal of the study and a brief tutorial, annotators are to complete the tasks described below. For each task, we present text instances along with their explanations, using a simple Excel interface.[2]

[2]See Appendix C, Figure 7

Task A: Simulation In the first task, participants are asked to simulate the model, i.e. predict the model's outcome, based only on one type of explanation plus the input text ("What does the model predict?"). They are given the possible class labels and were given an example for each dataset in the tutorial before starting the session. If the explanation does not provide any sensible clues about the predicted label, they still have to select a label, but may indicate this in the following question B1.

Task B: Rating In the second task, participants have to provide a rating on a seven-point Likert scale about (B1) "how helpful they found the explanation for guessing the model prediction" and (B2) "how easy they found the explanation to understand". A higher rating indicates a higher quality of the explanation.

Task C: Questionnaire Finally, participants are asked to complete a post-annotation questionnaire to obtain overall judgements for each verbalization method. They are prompted for Likert scale ratings about time consumption, coherence, consistency and qualitative aspects of each verbalization method, as listed in Table 1.

3.2 Automated Evaluation

We expect hallucinations (synthesized, factually incorrect text due to learned patterns and statistical cues) from GPT-type models and thus devise the following tests measuring **explainer-faithfulness** and **conciseness**:

1. Have the referred words been accurately cited from the input text?
2. How often do the referred words represent the top k most important tokens? (Eq. 3)

We obtain the results by simple counting and automated set intersection.

4 Methods

To complement heatmap visualizations and extractive rationales, we propose and analyze two additional verbalization methods: Model-free (§4.1, Fig. 2) and instruction-based (§4.2, Fig. 3) saliency map verbalization.

4.1 Model-free verbalization

For our model-free approach we employ hand-crafted templates for surface realization, different binary filter algorithms as search methods (§4.1.1) and scoring metrics (§4.1.2) to select tokens for filling the templates. This approach does not require architectural changes to the underlying model or modifications to an existing saliency method. The most similar approach to our selection heuristics, to our knowledge, are the discretization strategies in Jain et al. (2020, §5.2).

In the following, we will present two distinct candidate generation methods that can both be combined with one of two scoring metrics. A final candidate selection (§4.1.3) will collect the results from both searches, concatenate them to possibly larger spans and filter the top scoring candidates once more while maximizing coverage (Eq. 3). These salient subsets are then used to complete hand-crafted templates (App. E). We argue that this is more human-interpretable than simple top k single token selection, at the cost of a lower coverage. Our methodology allows to set parameters in accordance to how faithful the verbalization should be to the underlying explainer.

4.1.1 Explanation search

To acquire potentially salient snippets from a given text, we perform a binary selection on a window of attributions from the input of size c and then compare the sum of our selection to one of our scoring methods, performing basic statistical analysis on the window and the input.

Convolution Search Inspired by the convolutions of neural networks, we compare tokens that are located close to each other but are not necessarily direct neighbors. Coherence between pairs of tokens is solely determined by looking at their attributions with the following binary filters. In short, the following method firstly generates template-vectors that we then permute and keep as our binary filters. After computing all valid and sensible permutations, we can start calculating possibly salient or coherent snippets of our input. We choose $b \in \mathbb{N}$ vectors with a length of $c \in \mathbb{N}$. We describe these b vectors v_i as follows:

$$v_i = [1_{1,i}, 0_{1,c-i}], \quad v_i \in \mathbb{Z}^{1,c}. \tag{4}$$

e.g., for $i = 3$, $c = 5$, $v_i = (1\ 1\ 1\ 0\ 0)$

We only keep those v_i where $\sum v_i \notin \{0, 1, c\}$ in order to perform sensible permutations. For each v_i, we define a filter $\boldsymbol{f}_{i,j}$, where each distinct entry in $\boldsymbol{f}_i$ is a unique permutation of v_i. Let A be our attribution input, with $A \in \mathbb{R}^{1,k}$, where k is the

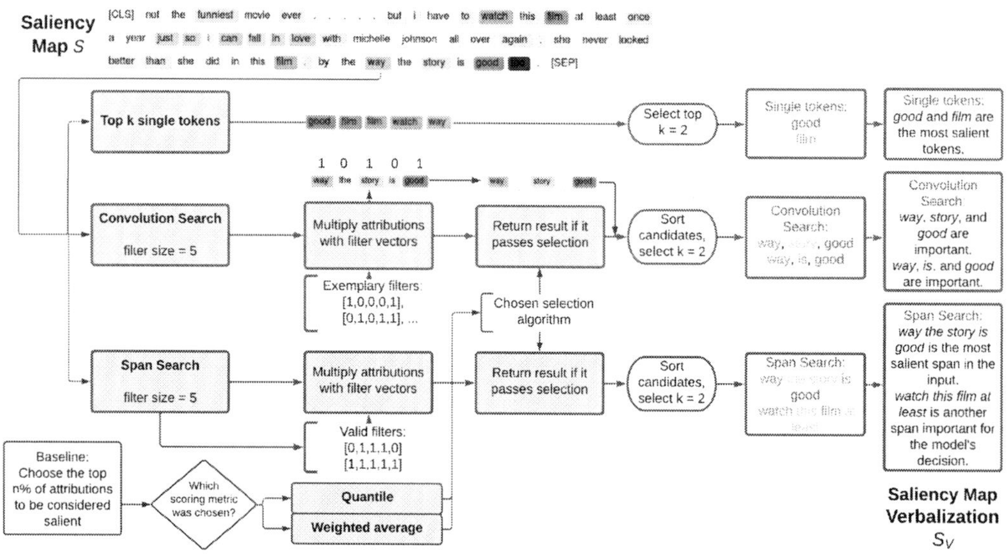

Figure 2: Model-free saliency map verbalizations (SMV_{Templ}) as generated from three different search methods (Top k single tokens, Convolution Search, Span Search) and two scoring metrics (Quantile, Weighted Average).

length of our input $k > c$, then we multiply a subset of our input with every binary filter

$$\boldsymbol{r}_{i,j,l} = \boldsymbol{f}_{i,j} \cdot A_l^{l+c}, \quad l \in L, L = \{l \in \mathbb{Z} | 1 \leq l \leq k - c\}. \tag{5}$$

From this, we receive result vectors containing possibly coherent attributions and tokens.

Span Search Instead of looking for token pairs in a local neighborhood, we can also look for contiguous spans of tokens by adapting our proposed convolutional search.

We generate b vectors of length of c with c being odd. We describe these b vectors as follows: Choose $i \in \mathbb{N}$ with i being odd, which ensures symmetry of our filters.[3]

$$v_i = [0_{1,\lfloor\frac{c-i}{2}\rfloor}, 1_{1,i}, 0_{1,\lfloor\frac{c-i}{2}\rfloor}], \quad v_i \in \mathbb{Z}^{1,c} \tag{6}$$

We calculate attribution vectors $\boldsymbol{r}_{i,l}$ as such:

$$\boldsymbol{r}_{i,l} = v_i \cdot A_l^{l+c}, \quad l \in L, L = \{l \in \mathbb{Z} | 1 \leq l \leq k - c\} \tag{7}$$

4.1.2 Candidate scoring metrics

We score and filter the snippets $\mathbf{r}$ so that we can present the most salient samples. As a threshold, we calculate the average of the $n\%$ most salient tokens of the given input sample A. This simple method does not filter for saliency, but it reduces the likelihood of presenting non-salient sample snippets. We call this our baseline β.

Weighted average The weighted average sums up the attribution values of r and divides the resulting scalar by the length of r, calculating the "saliency per word" of r. Then the result gets compared to β. Is the result larger than β, r is considered salient and will be a candidate for the verbalization.

Quantile The quantile method relies on the standard deviation within our current sample A. Given a quantile $n, n \in \mathbb{R}_0^+$, we calculate the corresponding standard deviation value σ and compare it to the average of the values of our snippet. If the score is greater than σ and β, it will be marked for verbalization.

4.1.3 Summarized explanation

On top of the two search methods in §4.1.1, we construct a summarized explanation to be used in our human evaluation (§3.1) by considering the k single tokens with the highest attribution scores. After generating k candidates from each search method, we concatenate neighboring token indices to (possibly) longer sequences and recalculate their coverage. We compute the q-th quantile of the remaining candidates according to their coverage to

[3]In contrast to our proposed Convolution Search, we don't need permutations of v_i to generate filters $\mathbf{f}$, so we directly use v_i. Thus, the result vector $\mathbf{r}$ has only two indices.

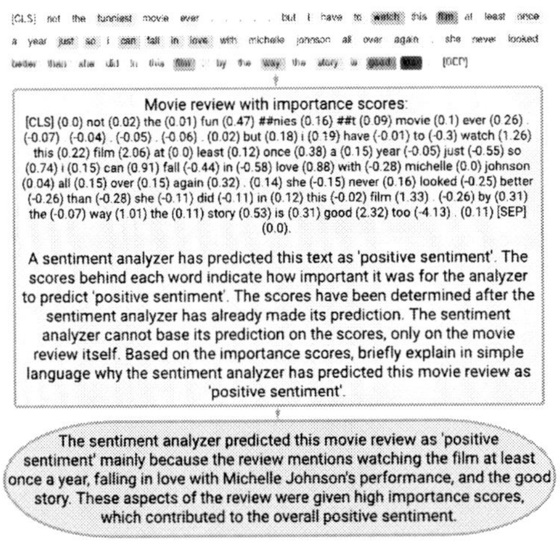

Figure 3: Instruction-based verbalizations SMV_{GPT} using GPT-3.5 of a *negative sentiment* instance from IMDb that was wrongly classified by BERT.

select the final input(s) to our templates. If no candidate is within the q-th quantile, the top-scoring span will be chosen.

4.2 Instruction-based Verbalizations

In light of very recent advances in instructing large language models to perform increasingly complex tasks (Wei et al., 2022), we additionally construct "rationale-augmented" verbalizations (Fig. 3) next to template-based and search-based ones. The instruction contains an overview of the saliency map verbalization task and the associated caveats, e.g. "The classifier cannot base its prediction on the scores, only on the input text itself.". Our most consistently accurate result was achieved by then representing S as bracketed scores rounded to two digits put behind each word, e.g. "definitely (0.75) a (0.14) girl (-0.31) movie (0.15)".

In practice, we manually engineered task-agnostic instruction templates to work with GPT-3.5 (March '23) aka ChatGPT.[4] To our knowledge, there are no datasets with gold verbalizations available and we do not want to enforce any specific format of the explanation, so we use the API in a zero-shot setting. We post-process all outputs by removing all occurrences of the predicted label and semantically very similar words (App. G).

[4]We describe the task-specific instructions in App. F and document the edits to mitigate label leakage in App. G.

Explanations...	Templ	GPT
were concise & not time-consuming.	4.00	2.38
were not too complex.	3.63	3.88
were not inconsistent/contradictory.	-	3
helped me detect wrong predictions.	2.63	3
with more diverse sentences are useful.	4.25*	-
with numeric scores are useful.	2.63*	2.38
with associations/context are useful.	4.00*	4.50
summarizing the input are useful.	-	4.75

Table 1: Questionnaire asking participants about their overall impressions on both types of verbalizations. All aspects were rated based on a 5-point Likert scale (1: "strongly disagree"; 5: "strongly agree"). Starred values: SMV_{Templ} do not have this property, so we asked if the participants *would have liked them* to have it.

5 Data

We choose datasets that cover a selection of English-language text classification tasks. In particular, we select IMDb (Maas et al., 2011) for sentiment analysis, and AG News (Zhang et al., 2015) for topic classification.

We retrieve predictions from BERT models on the test partitions of IMDb and AG News made available through TextAttack (Morris et al., 2020) and their Integrated Gradients (Sundararajan et al., 2017) explanations with 25 samples exactly as they appear in Thermostat (Feldhus et al., 2021).

We then take subsets (IMDb: $n = 80$, AG News: $n = 120$) of each dataset according to multiple heuristics (App. D) that make the tasks more manageable for annotators. Each annotator was shown 340 explanations consisting of equal amounts of each type of representation or rationale. We randomize the order in which they are presented to the annotators. Every instance was evaluated by seven different annotators.

6 Results

Human evaluation Tab. 2 shows that both kinds of SMVs are generally **easier to understand** (B2) than heatmaps or extractive rationales. In a post-annotation questionnaire, we asked 8 out of 10 participants 14 questions about both types of SMVs. Tab. 1 lists the results. While template-based explanations are preferred in being less time-consuming, we can see that GPT-generated verbalizations outperform them in all other aspects. Unsurprisingly, associations and summarizations are the preferred characteristics of verbalizations.

Downstream tasks According to Jacovi et al. (2023a), a feature attribution explanation aggre-

		A: Simulation Accuracy				B1: Helpfulness				B2: Ease of understanding			
		HM Vis	Rat Extr	SMV Templ	SMV GPT	HM Vis	Rat Extr	SMV Templ	SMV GPT	HM Vis	Rat Extr	SMV Templ	SMV GPT
	All	90.75	85.94	87.5	**94.06**	4.73	4.19	4.46	**5.80**	4.35	4.00	4.67	**5.88**
IMDb	$\text{Cov}(S_{VT})^{\nearrow}$	94.38	89.45	92.19	**96.09**	4.98	4.50	4.91	**5.94**	4.47	4.34	4.99	**5.99**
IAA	$y \neq \hat{y}$	74.49	58.43	63.90	**84.65**	3.67	3.09	3.21	**5.01**	3.48	2.92	3.61	**5.25**
$\kappa = 0.731$	$\hat{y} \neq y_{\text{sim}}$	n.a. (0.00)				3.40	3.10	2.85	**3.94**	3.48	3.18	3.35	**4.33**
	All	**79.83**	-	79.50	77.60	5.26	-	4.65	**5.63**	5.02	-	4.90	**5.77**
AG News	$\text{Cov}(S_{VT})^{\nearrow}$	**85.31**	-	84.57	81.13	5.41	-	4.98	**5.80**	5.18	-	5.13	**5.89**
IAA	$y \neq \hat{y}$	**70.17**	-	69.37	64.53	5.02	-	4.52	**5.36**	4.84	-	4.84	**5.61**
$\kappa = 0.721$	$\hat{y} \neq y_{\text{sim}}$	n.a. (0.00)				4.14	-	3.34	**4.40**	4.08	-	3.89	**5.10**

Table 2: Results of the human evaluation. Task **A**: Simulation accuracy (annotators guessing the label predicted by the underlying BERT correctly). Task B: Average rating of annotators (1 "bad" - 7 "good") for helpfulness (**B1**) and ease of understanding (**B2**). HM-Vis = Heatmap visualization. Rat-Extr = Extractive rationalizer of Treviso and Martins (2020). SMV-Templ = Template-based saliency map verbalization. SMV-GPT = GPT-3.5-based saliency map verbalization. **All**: Overall result. $\mathbf{Cov(S_{VT})}^{\nearrow}$: Coverage above average. $y \neq \hat{y}$: Explained BERT model made a false prediction. $\hat{y} \neq y_{\text{sim}}$: False human simulation. Inter-annotator agreement in Fleiss κ below the dataset names.

gates counterfactual contexts. This becomes apparent in our overall results on the AG News dataset where more than one potential alternative (multi-class classification with $|C| = 4$) outcome exists. Annotators' simulation accuracy drops from as high as 94 % (IMDb) to 78 %. SMV_{GPT} beats all other representations across all three measures in IMDb, but surprisingly underperforms in AG News.

Coverage of the verbalization Fig. 4 and App. A show that SMV_{GPT} focuses less on the actual most important tokens that might not be intuitive for recipients, such as function words. The subset of instances with higher-than-average coverage according to $\text{SMV}_{\text{Templ}}$ ($\text{Cov}(S_{VT})^{\nearrow}$) is substantially easier to simulate (IMDb) and elicits the highest ratings and accuracies from annotators. We utilize this as a proxy for (low) complexity of S, because usually only a single or few tokens that are very salient make these explanations easy to decipher in most representations.

Therefore, we conducted an automated simulatability evaluation on all SMV types, documented in Appendix B, confirming the suspicions about the faithfulness of GPT verbalizations.

Model predictions Lastly, we investigate the subsets of wrong model predictions: The drop in simulation accuracy and ratings when we filter the instances where the model predicts something different from the true label ($y \neq \hat{y}$) is more severe for IMDb throughout all types of explanations. In AG News, the simulatability and the ease of understanding turn out to be higher for SMVs. Our consistently worse results in this subset reveal the belief bias (González et al., 2021), i.e. explanations have a hard time convincing humans about a model behavior when they already have prior assumptions about the true label of an instance. For instances where the human simulation mismatched with the predicted label ($\hat{y} \neq y_{\text{sim}}$), the drop in scores is even harsher: Only SMV_{GPT} still achieves ratings that are slightly above average.

6.1 Evaluating instruction-based verbalizations

While there are no invented words in the human evaluation subset, our automated mapping between explanation and input text still detected cases where words are **auto-corrected** and not accurately copied, especially fixing capitalization and small typos. We also found examples in which words or spans are replaced with a synonym, e.g. "not reliable" → "unreliable", but most strikingly, in an IMDb example, "good premise" was replaced with "bad premise" which entirely changed the meaning and the polarity of the sentiment.

In Tab. 3, we manually count what **type of task-related information and semantics** SMV_{GPT} provides on top of the translation of the importance scores. We can see that the "negative sentiment" in IMDb is often a confounder for the correct interpretation of the negative saliency scores. Without explicit instructions, GPT still questioned some of the wrong prediction the underlying BERT has made, particularly for IMDb. In terms of linguistic aspects of the verbalizations, associations are frequently included, while summarizations of the

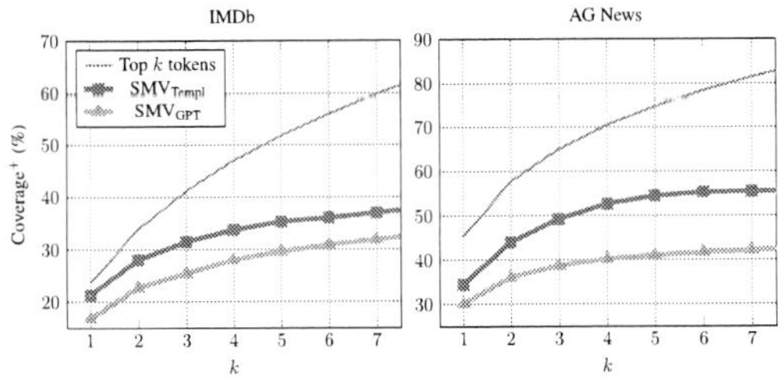

Figure 4: Coverage$^+$@k of $\text{SMV}_{\text{Templ}}$ and SMV_{GPT}. Top k tokens is the upper bound for explainer-faithfulness.

input or the decision are rare.

6.2 Discussion

By choosing parameters that prefer longer spans to be selected, we show that $\text{SMV}_{\text{Templ}}$ can be more plausible to humans than single token selection. We acknowledge that $\text{SMV}_{\text{Templ}}$ are repetitive and, while the results show that they can guarantee a minimum degree of understandability (Ehsan et al., 2019), sufficiency and conciseness, they will not be satisfying enough for lay recipients on their own.

For SMV_{GPT}, the choice of instruction can greatly impact the faithfulness to the explainer. Plausible explanations driven by world knowledge and semantics allow laypeople to contextualize the prediction w.r.t. the input text, but reliable and generalizable methods for auditing these rationales for faithfulness have yet to be discovered.

7 Related Work

To our knowledge, the only previous saliency map **verbalization** approach is by Forrest et al. (2018) who used LIME explanations and a template-based NLG pipeline on a credit dataset. While they mostly included numerical values in explanations, we focus on most important features and free-text rationales, because humans are more interested in reasoning than in numerical values (Reiter, 2019). Ampomah et al. (2022) created a dataset of tables summarizing the performance metrics of a text classifier and trained a neural module to automatically generate accompanying texts. The HCI community highlighted the advantages of verbalization as a complementary medium to visual explanations (Sevastjanova et al., 2018; Hohman et al., 2019; Szymanski et al., 2021; Chromik, 2021). Zhang and Lim (2022) advocated for adding concepts and associations to make explanations more understandable, particularly in contrastive setups.

	IMDb	AG News
Saliency-related *"because of the high importance scores of words such as 'oil', 'supply', [...]"*	100.00	99.17
Correct interpretation of neg. saliency *"[...] predicted this movie review as 'negative sentiment' because of the high negative importance scores [...]"*	72.50	100.00
Suspecting a wrong prediction *"[...] it is unclear why the classifier predicted this article as 'Business'."*	55.00 FP: 0.00	23.21 FP: 0.83
Associations *"These words are associated with positive emotions and experiences."*	47.50	90.00
Summarizations *"[...] the reviewer enjoyed these aspects of the movie."*	10.00	27.50

Table 3: Occurrences of semantics and accuracies of task comprehension (both in %) in GPT-3.5-generated verbalizations for both datasets. FP = False positives.

Hsu and Tan (2021) introduced the task of **decision-focused summarization**. While there are overlaps in the selection of important subsets of the input, the textual nature of the output and the employment of saliency methods, our work is concerned with summarizing the token-level information provided by a saliency map from an arbitrary source for a single instance. Okeson et al. (2021) found in their study that global feature attributions obtained by ranking features by different summary statistics helped users to communicate what the model had learned and to identify next steps for debugging it. Rönnqvist et al. (2022) aggregated attribution scores from multiple documents to find top-ranked keywords for classes.

In early explainability literature, van Lent et al. (2004) already used **template filling**. Templates in NLE frameworks were engineered by Camburu et al. (2020) to find inconsistencies in generated explanations. While their templates were designed to mimic commonsense logic patterns present in the e-SNLI dataset (Camburu et al., 2018), our templates are a means to verbalize arbitrary saliency maps. Paranjape et al. (2021) crafted templates and used a mask-infilling approach to produce contrastive explanations from pre-trained language models. Donadello and Dragoni (2021) utilized a template system to render explanation graph structures as text. Recently, Tursun et al. (2023) used templates together with ChatGPT prompts to generate captions containing verbalized saliency map explanations in the computer vision domain. However, they did not conduct an automated or human evaluation.

8 Conclusion

We conducted a comparative study on explanation representations. We formalized the task of translating feature attributions into natural language and proposed two kinds of saliency map verbalization methods. Instruction-based verbalizations outperformed all other saliency map representations on human ratings, indicating their summarization and contextualization capabilities are a necessary component in making saliency maps more accessible to humans, but they are still unreliable in terms of ensuring faithfulness and are dependant on a closed-source black-box model. We find that template-based saliency map verbalizations reduce the cognitive load for humans and are a viable option to improve on the ease of understanding of heatmaps without the need for additional resources.

Limitations

Our experimental setup excludes free-text rationales explaining the decisions of a model (Wiegreffe et al., 2022; Camburu et al., 2018), because their output is not based on attribution scores or highlighted spans of the input text, so we argue that they are not trivially comparable. However, there are end-to-end rationalization frameworks that can accommodate arbitrary saliency methods (Jain et al., 2020; Chrysostomou and Aletras, 2021; Ismail et al., 2021; Atanasova et al., 2022; Majumder et al., 2022), but require large language models that are expensive to train and perform inference with, so this is out of scope for this study. However, we also see that high-quality free-text rationales can be more easily generated with LLMs (Wang et al., 2023; Ho et al., 2023), and a comparison between them and our attribution-based explanations is an interesting avenue for future work.

Inferring high-quality explanations from large language models necessitates excessive amounts of compute and storage. Although GPT verbalizations are most promising, we urge the research community to look into more efficient ways to achieve similar results. In the future, we will explore if training a smaller model on top of the collected rationale-augmented verbalizations is feasible.

Emphasizing the concerns of Rogers (2023), we do not recommend the black-box model GPT-3.5 as a baseline for interpretability, because the model's training data or internal parameters can not be accessed and the dangers of deprecation as well as the lack of reproducibility are serious concerns. However, we do think it has revealed great potential as a surface realization and contextualization tool for the task of saliency map verbalization.

The causality problem explained in Jacovi et al. (2023a) is not solved by our verbalizations, as it is an inherent problem with feature attribution and rationalization. Future work includes verbalizations alongside counterfactuals, e.g. in interactive setups (Feldhus et al., 2022; Shen et al., 2023).

Although multiple models and explanation-generating methods are available, we specifically focus on one pair for both datasets (BERT and Integrated Gradients), because the focus of our investigation is on the quality of the representation rather than the model.

Finally, explicitly modelling expected highlights to mitigate misalignments as reported on in Schuff et al. (2022), Jacovi et al. (2023b) and Prasad et al. (2021) is still unexplored.

Acknowledgments

We would like to thank Aleksandra Gabryszak for her help setting up and conducting the human evaluation. We are indebted to Elif Kara, Ajay Madhavan Ravichandran, Akhyar Ahmed, Tatjana Zeen, Shushen Manakhimova, Raia Abu Ahmad, Ekaterina Borisova, João Lucas Mendes de Lemos Lins, Qianli Wang, and Sahil Chopra for their valuable work as annotators and evaluators. We thank Gabriele Sarti, Arne Binder, Yuxuan Chen, and David Harbecke as well as the reviewers of the NLRSE Workshop at ACL 2023 for their feedback on the paper. This work has been supported by the German Federal Ministry of Education and Research as part of the project XAINES (01IW20005).

Contributions

- NF: Writing, implementation of baselines and summarized template-based verbalization, prompt design and data generation, evaluation of user study, illustrations.
- LH: Writing and supervision.
- MDN: Conception, implementation and illustration of search and scoring methods for template-based verbalization.
- CE: Data curation, implementation of instruction-based verbalization pipeline, validation and empirical results on search and scoring methods.
- RS: Initial idea and outline.
- SM: Supervision and funding.

References

David Alvarez-Melis, Hal Daumé III, Jennifer Wortman Vaughan, and Hanna M. Wallach. 2019. Weight of evidence as a basis for human-oriented explanations. In *Human-Centric Machine Learning (HCML) Workshop @ NeurIPS 2019*.

Isaac Ampomah, James Burton, Amir Enshaei, and Noura Al Moubayed. 2022. Generating textual explanations for machine learning models performance: A table-to-text task. In *Proceedings of the Thirteenth Language Resources and Evaluation Conference*, pages 3542–3551, Marseille, France. European Language Resources Association.

Siddhant Arora, Danish Pruthi, Norman Sadeh, William W Cohen, Zachary C Lipton, and Graham Neubig. 2022. Explain, edit, and understand: Rethinking user study design for evaluating model explanations. In *Thirty-Six AAAI Conference on Artificial Intelligence*.

Pepa Atanasova, Jakob Grue Simonsen, Christina Lioma, and Isabelle Augenstein. 2022. Diagnostics-guided explanation generation. *In Proceedings of the 36th AAAI Conference on Artificial Intelligence*.

Faeze Brahman, Vered Shwartz, Rachel Rudinger, and Yejin Choi. 2021. Learning to rationalize for nonmonotonic reasoning with distant supervision. *Proceedings of the AAAI Conference on Artificial Intelligence*, 35(14):12592–12601.

Oana-Maria Camburu, Tim Rocktäschel, Thomas Lukasiewicz, and Phil Blunsom. 2018. e-snli: Natural language inference with natural language explanations. In *Advances in Neural Information Processing Systems*, volume 31. Curran Associates, Inc.

Oana-Maria Camburu, Brendan Shillingford, Pasquale Minervini, Thomas Lukasiewicz, and Phil Blunsom. 2020. Make up your mind! Adversarial generation of inconsistent natural language explanations. In *Proceedings of the 58th Annual Meeting of the Association for Computational Linguistics*, pages 4157–4165, Online. Association for Computational Linguistics.

Arjun Chandrasekaran, Viraj Prabhu, Deshraj Yadav, Prithvijit Chattopadhyay, and Devi Parikh. 2018. Do explanations make VQA models more predictable to a human? In *Proceedings of the 2018 Conference on Empirical Methods in Natural Language Processing*, pages 1036–1042, Brussels, Belgium. Association for Computational Linguistics.

Hanjie Chen, Faeze Brahman, Xiang Ren, Yangfeng Ji, Yejin Choi, and Swabha Swayamdipta. 2023. REV: information-theoretic evaluation of free-text rationales. In *Proceedings of the 61st Annual Meeting of the Association for Computational Linguistics (Volume 1: Long Papers)*, Toronto, Canada. Association for Computational Linguistics.

Wenhu Chen. 2023. Large language models are few(1)-shot table reasoners. In *Findings of the Association for Computational Linguistics: EACL 2023*, Online and Dubrovnik, Croatia. Association for Computational Linguistics.

Michael Chromik. 2021. Making SHAP Rap: Bridging local and global insights through interaction and narratives. In *Human-Computer Interaction – INTERACT 2021*, pages 641–651, Cham. Springer International Publishing.

George Chrysostomou and Nikolaos Aletras. 2021. Enjoy the salience: Towards better transformer-based faithful explanations with word salience. In *Proceedings of the 2021 Conference on Empirical Methods in Natural Language Processing*, pages 8189–8200, Online and Punta Cana, Dominican Republic. Association for Computational Linguistics.

Julien Colin, Thomas Fel, Rémi Cadène, and Thomas Serre. 2022. What I cannot predict, I do not understand: A human-centered evaluation framework for explainability methods. In *Advances in Neural Information Processing Systems*, volume 35. Curran Associates, Inc.

Jay DeYoung, Sarthak Jain, Nazneen Fatema Rajani, Eric Lehman, Caiming Xiong, Richard Socher, and Byron C. Wallace. 2020. ERASER: A benchmark to evaluate rationalized NLP models. In *Proceedings of the 58th Annual Meeting of the Association for Computational Linguistics*, pages 4443–4458, Online. Association for Computational Linguistics.

Ivan Donadello and Mauro Dragoni. 2021. Bridging signals to natural language explanations with explanation graphs. In *Proceedings of the 2nd Italian Workshop on Explainable Artificial Intelligence*.

Finale Doshi-Velez and Been Kim. 2017. Towards a rigorous science of interpretable machine learning. *arXiv: Machine Learning*.

Upol Ehsan and Mark O. Riedl. 2020. Human-centered explainable ai: Towards a reflective sociotechnical approach. In *HCI International 2020 - Late Breaking Papers: Multimodality and Intelligence*, pages 449–466, Cham. Springer International Publishing.

Upol Ehsan, Pradyumna Tambwekar, Larry Chan, Brent Harrison, and Mark O. Riedl. 2019. Automated rationale generation: A technique for explainable ai and its effects on human perceptions. In *Proceedings of the 24th International Conference on Intelligent User Interfaces*, IUI '19, page 263–274, New York, NY, USA. Association for Computing Machinery.

Nils Feldhus, Ajay Madhavan Ravichandran, and Sebastian Möller. 2022. Mediators: Conversational agents explaining NLP model behavior. In *IJCAI 2022 - Workshop on Explainable Artificial Intelligence (XAI), Vienna, Austria*. International Joint Conferences on Artificial Intelligence Organization.

Nils Feldhus, Robert Schwarzenberg, and Sebastian Möller. 2021. Thermostat: A large collection of NLP model explanations and analysis tools. In *Proceedings of the 2021 Conference on Empirical Methods in Natural Language Processing: System Demonstrations*, pages 87–95, Online and Punta Cana, Dominican Republic. Association for Computational Linguistics.

James Forrest, Somayajulu Sripada, Wei Pang, and George Coghill. 2018. Towards making NLG a voice for interpretable machine learning. In *Proceedings of the 11th International Conference on Natural Language Generation*, pages 177–182, Tilburg University, The Netherlands. Association for Computational Linguistics.

Ana Valeria González, Anna Rogers, and Anders Søgaard. 2021. On the interaction of belief bias and explanations. In *Findings of the Association for Computational Linguistics: ACL-IJCNLP 2021*, pages 2930–2942, Online. Association for Computational Linguistics.

Braden Hancock, Paroma Varma, Stephanie Wang, Martin Bringmann, Percy Liang, and Christopher Ré. 2018. Training classifiers with natural language explanations. In *Proceedings of the 56th Annual Meeting of the Association for Computational Linguistics (Volume 1: Long Papers)*, pages 1884–1895, Melbourne, Australia. Association for Computational Linguistics.

Peter Hase and Mohit Bansal. 2020. Evaluating explainable AI: Which algorithmic explanations help users predict model behavior? In *Proceedings of the 58th Annual Meeting of the Association for Computational Linguistics*, pages 5540–5552, Online. Association for Computational Linguistics.

Peter Hase, Shiyue Zhang, Harry Xie, and Mohit Bansal. 2020. Leakage-adjusted simulatability: Can models generate non-trivial explanations of their behavior in natural language? In *Findings of the Association for Computational Linguistics: EMNLP 2020*, pages 4351–4367, Online. Association for Computational Linguistics.

Denis Hilton. 2017. Social attribution and explanation. *The Oxford Handbook of Causal Reasoning*.

Matthew Ho, Aditya Sharma, Justin Chang, Michael Saxon, Sharon Levy, Yujie Lu, and William Yang Wang. 2023. WikiWhy: Answering and explaining cause-and-effect questions. In *The Eleventh International Conference on Learning Representations*.

Fred Hohman, Arjun Srinivasan, and Steven M. Drucker. 2019. Telegam: Combining visualization and verbalization for interpretable machine learning. In *2019 IEEE Visualization Conference (VIS)*, pages 151–155.

Chao-Chun Hsu and Chenhao Tan. 2021. Decision-focused summarization. In *Proceedings of the 2021 Conference on Empirical Methods in Natural Language Processing*, pages 117–132, Online and Punta Cana, Dominican Republic. Association for Computational Linguistics.

Aya Abdelsalam Ismail, Hector Corrada Bravo, and Soheil Feizi. 2021. Improving deep learning interpretability by saliency guided training. *Advances in Neural Information Processing Systems*, 34.

Alon Jacovi, Jasmijn Bastings, Sebastian Gehrmann, Yoav Goldberg, and Katja Filippova. 2023a. Diagnosing AI explanation methods with folk concepts of behavior. In *Proceedings of the 2023 ACM Conference on Fairness, Accountability, and Transparency*, FAccT '23, New York, NY, USA. Association for Computing Machinery.

Alon Jacovi and Yoav Goldberg. 2020. Towards faithfully interpretable NLP systems: How should we define and evaluate faithfulness? In *Proceedings of the 58th Annual Meeting of the Association for Computational Linguistics*, pages 4198–4205, Online. Association for Computational Linguistics.

Alon Jacovi, Ana Marasović, Tim Miller, and Yoav Goldberg. 2021. Formalizing trust in artificial intelligence: Prerequisites, causes and goals of human trust in ai. In *Proceedings of the 2021 ACM Conference on Fairness, Accountability, and Transparency*, FAccT '21, page 624–635, New York, NY, USA. Association for Computing Machinery.

Alon Jacovi, Hendrik Schuff, Heike Adel, Ngoc Thang Vu, and Yoav Goldberg. 2023b. Neighboring words affect human interpretation of saliency explanations. In *Findings of the Association for Computational Linguistics: ACL 2023*, Toronto, Canada. Association for Computational Linguistics.

Sarthak Jain, Sarah Wiegreffe, Yuval Pinter, and Byron C. Wallace. 2020. Learning to faithfully rationalize by construction. In *Proceedings of the 58th Annual Meeting of the Association for Computational Linguistics*, pages 4459–4473, Online. Association for Computational Linguistics.

Brihi Joshi, Ziyi Liu, Sahana Ramnath, Aaron Chan, Zhewei Tong, Shaoliang Nie, Qifan Wang, Yejin Choi, and Xiang Ren. 2023. Are machine rationales (not) useful to humans? measuring and improving human utility of free-text rationales. In *Proceedings of the 61st Annual Meeting of the Association for Computational Linguistics (Volume 1: Long Papers)*, Toronto, Canada. Association for Computational Linguistics.

Tao Lei, Regina Barzilay, and Tommi Jaakkola. 2016. Rationalizing neural predictions. In *Proceedings of the 2016 Conference on Empirical Methods in Natural Language Processing*, pages 107–117, Austin, Texas. Association for Computational Linguistics.

Andrew L. Maas, Raymond E. Daly, Peter T. Pham, Dan Huang, Andrew Y. Ng, and Christopher Potts.

2011. Learning word vectors for sentiment analysis. In *Proceedings of the 49th Annual Meeting of the Association for Computational Linguistics: Human Language Technologies*, pages 142–150, Portland, Oregon, USA. Association for Computational Linguistics.

Andreas Madsen, Siva Reddy, and Sarath Chandar. 2022. Post-hoc interpretability for neural NLP: A survey. *ACM Comput. Surv.*

Bodhisattwa Prasad Majumder, Oana-Maria Camburu, Thomas Lukasiewicz, and Julian McAuley. 2022. Knowledge-grounded self-rationalization via extractive and natural language explanations. In *International Conference on Machine Learning*. PMLR.

Ettore Mariotti, Jose M. Alonso, and Albert Gatt. 2020. Towards harnessing natural language generation to explain black-box models. In *2nd Workshop on Interactive Natural Language Technology for Explainable Artificial Intelligence*, pages 22–27, Dublin, Ireland. Association for Computational Linguistics.

Joshua Maynez, Shashi Narayan, Bernd Bohnet, and Ryan McDonald. 2020. On faithfulness and factuality in abstractive summarization. In *Proceedings of the 58th Annual Meeting of the Association for Computational Linguistics*, pages 1906–1919, Online. Association for Computational Linguistics.

Tim Miller. 2019. Explanation in artificial intelligence: Insights from the social sciences. *Artificial Intelligence*, 267:1–38.

John Morris, Eli Lifland, Jin Yong Yoo, Jake Grigsby, Di Jin, and Yanjun Qi. 2020. TextAttack: A framework for adversarial attacks, data augmentation, and adversarial training in NLP. In *Proceedings of the 2020 Conference on Empirical Methods in Natural Language Processing: System Demonstrations*, pages 119–126, Online. Association for Computational Linguistics.

Alex Okeson, Rich Caruana, Nick Craswell, Kori Inkpen, Scott Lundberg, Harsha Nori, Hanna Wallach, and Jennifer Wortman Vaughan. 2021. Summarize with caution: Comparing global feature attributions. *Bulletin of the IEEE Computer Society Technical Committee on Data Engineering*.

Bhargavi Paranjape, Julian Michael, Marjan Ghazvininejad, Hannaneh Hajishirzi, and Luke Zettlemoyer. 2021. Prompting contrastive explanations for commonsense reasoning tasks. In *Findings of the Association for Computational Linguistics: ACL-IJCNLP 2021*, pages 4179–4192, Online. Association for Computational Linguistics.

Grusha Prasad, Yixin Nie, Mohit Bansal, Robin Jia, Douwe Kiela, and Adina Williams. 2021. To what extent do human explanations of model behavior align with actual model behavior? In *Proceedings of the Fourth BlackboxNLP Workshop on Analyzing and Interpreting Neural Networks for NLP*, pages 1–14, Punta Cana, Dominican Republic. Association for Computational Linguistics.

Ehud Reiter. 2019. Natural language generation challenges for explainable AI. In *Proceedings of the 1st Workshop on Interactive Natural Language Technology for Explainable Artificial Intelligence (NL4XAI 2019)*, pages 3–7. Association for Computational Linguistics.

Anna Rogers. 2023. Closed AI Models Make Bad Baselines. *Hacking Semantics*.

Samuel Rönnqvist, Aki-Juhani Kyröläinen, Amanda Myntti, Filip Ginter, and Veronika Laippala. 2022. Explaining classes through stable word attributions. In *Findings of the Association for Computational Linguistics: ACL 2022*, pages 1063–1074, Dublin, Ireland. Association for Computational Linguistics.

Gabriele Sarti, Nils Feldhus, Ludwig Sickert, Oskar van der Wal, Malvina Nissim, and Arianna Bisazza. 2023. Inseq: An interpretability toolkit for sequence generation models. In *Proceedings of the 61st Annual Meeting of the Association for Computational Linguistics: System Demonstrations*, Toronto, Canada. Association for Computational Linguistics.

Hendrik Schuff, Alon Jacovi, Heike Adel, Yoav Goldberg, and Ngoc Thang Vu. 2022. Human interpretation of saliency-based explanation over text. In *Proceedings of the 2022 ACM Conference on Fairness, Accountability, and Transparency*, Seoul, South Korea. Association for Computing Machinery.

Cansu Sen, Thomas Hartvigsen, Biao Yin, Xiangnan Kong, and Elke Rundensteiner. 2020. Human attention maps for text classification: Do humans and neural networks focus on the same words? In *Proceedings of the 58th Annual Meeting of the Association for Computational Linguistics*, pages 4596–4608, Online. Association for Computational Linguistics.

Rita Sevastjanova, Fabian Beck, Basil Ell, Cagatay Turkay, Rafael Henkin, Miriam Butt, Daniel A. Keim, and Mennatallah El-Assady. 2018. Going beyond visualization : Verbalization as complementary medium to explain machine learning models. In *Workshop on Visualization for AI Explainability at IEEE (VIS)*.

Hua Shen, Chieh-Yang Huang, Tongshuang Wu, and Ting-Hao 'Kenneth' Huang. 2023. ConvXAI: Delivering heterogeneous AI explanations via conversations to support human-AI scientific writing. *arXiv*, 2305.09770.

Dylan Slack, Satyapriya Krishna, Himabindu Lakkaraju, and Sameer Singh. 2022. TalkToModel: Explaining machine learning models with interactive natural language conversations. *Trustworthy and Socially Responsible Machine Learning (TSRML) Workshop @ NeurIPS 2022*.

Julia Strout, Ye Zhang, and Raymond Mooney. 2019. Do human rationales improve machine explanations? In *Proceedings of the 2019 ACL Workshop BlackboxNLP: Analyzing and Interpreting Neural Networks for NLP*, pages 56–62, Florence, Italy. Association for Computational Linguistics.

Mukund Sundararajan, Ankur Taly, and Qiqi Yan. 2017. Axiomatic attribution for deep networks. In *Proceedings of the 34th International Conference on Machine Learning*, volume 70 of *Proceedings of Machine Learning Research*, pages 3319–3328. PMLR.

Maxwell Szymanski, Martijn Millecamp, and Katrien Verbert. 2021. Visual, textual or hybrid: The effect of user expertise on different explanations. In *26th International Conference on Intelligent User Interfaces*, page 109–119, New York, NY, USA. Association for Computing Machinery.

Chenhao Tan. 2022. On the diversity and limits of human explanations. In *Proceedings of the 2022 Conference of the North American Chapter of the Association for Computational Linguistics*, Seattle, United States. Association for Computational Linguistics.

Marcos Treviso and André F. T. Martins. 2020. The explanation game: Towards prediction explainability through sparse communication. In *Proceedings of the Third BlackboxNLP Workshop on Analyzing and Interpreting Neural Networks for NLP*, pages 107–118, Online. Association for Computational Linguistics.

Osman Tursun, Simon Denman, Sridha Sridharan, and Clinton Fookes. 2023. Towards self-explainability of deep neural networks with heatmap captioning and large-language models. *CoRR*, abs/2304.02202.

Michael van Lent, William Fisher, and Michael Mancuso. 2004. An explainable artificial intelligence system for small-unit tactical behavior. In *Proceedings of the 16th Conference on Innovative Applications of Artifical Intelligence*, IAAI'04, page 900–907. AAAI Press.

Eric Wallace, Matt Gardner, and Sameer Singh. 2020. Interpreting predictions of NLP models. In *Proceedings of the 2020 Conference on Empirical Methods in Natural Language Processing: Tutorial Abstracts*, pages 20–23, Online. Association for Computational Linguistics.

Eric Wallace, Jens Tuyls, Junlin Wang, Sanjay Subramanian, Matt Gardner, and Sameer Singh. 2019. AllenNLP interpret: A framework for explaining predictions of NLP models. In *Proceedings of the 2019 Conference on Empirical Methods in Natural Language Processing and the 9th International Joint Conference on Natural Language Processing (EMNLP-IJCNLP): System Demonstrations*, pages 7–12, Hong Kong, China. Association for Computational Linguistics.

Peifeng Wang, Aaron Chan, Filip Ilievski, Muhao Chen, and Xiang Ren. 2023. PINTO: Faithful language reasoning using prompted-generated rationales. In *International Conference on Learning Representations*.

Jason Wei, Maarten Bosma, Vincent Zhao, Kelvin Guu, Adams Wei Yu, Brian Lester, Nan Du, Andrew M. Dai, and Quoc V Le. 2022. Finetuned language models are zero-shot learners. In *International Conference on Learning Representations*.

Sarah Wiegreffe, Jack Hessel, Swabha Swayamdipta, Mark O. Riedl, and Yejin Choi. 2022. Reframing human-AI collaboration for generating free-text explanations. In *Proceedings of the 2022 Conference of the North American Chapter of the Association for Computational Linguistics*, Seattle, United States. Association for Computational Linguistics.

Sarah Wiegreffe and Ana Marasović. 2021. Teach me to explain: A review of datasets for explainable nlp. In *Proceedings of NeurIPS*.

Sarah Wiegreffe, Ana Marasović, and Noah A. Smith. 2021. Measuring association between labels and free-text rationales. In *Proceedings of the 2021 Conference on Empirical Methods in Natural Language Processing*, pages 10266–10284, Online and Punta Cana, Dominican Republic. Association for Computational Linguistics.

Sarah Wiegreffe and Yuval Pinter. 2019. Attention is not not explanation. In *Proceedings of the 2019 Conference on Empirical Methods in Natural Language Processing and the 9th International Joint Conference on Natural Language Processing (EMNLP-IJCNLP)*, pages 11–20, Hong Kong, China. Association for Computational Linguistics.

Jiannan Xiang, Zhengzhong Liu, Yucheng Zhou, Eric Xing, and Zhiting Hu. 2022. ASDOT: Any-shot data-to-text generation with pretrained language models. In *Findings of the Association for Computational Linguistics: EMNLP 2022*, pages 1886–1899, Abu Dhabi, United Arab Emirates. Association for Computational Linguistics.

Huihan Yao, Ying Chen, Qinyuan Ye, Xisen Jin, and Xiang Ren. 2021. Refining language models with compositional explanations. In *Advances in Neural Information Processing Systems*.

Omar Zaidan, Jason Eisner, and Christine Piatko. 2007. Using "annotator rationales" to improve machine learning for text categorization. In *Human Language Technologies 2007: The Conference of the North American Chapter of the Association for Computational Linguistics; Proceedings of the Main Conference*, pages 260–267, Rochester, New York. Association for Computational Linguistics.

Wencan Zhang and Brian Y Lim. 2022. Towards relatable explainable ai with the perceptual process. In *Proceedings of the 2022 CHI Conference on Human*

Factors in Computing Systems, CHI '22, New York, NY, USA. Association for Computing Machinery.

Xiang Zhang, Junbo Zhao, and Yann LeCun. 2015. Character-level convolutional networks for text classification. In *Proceedings of the 28th International Conference on Neural Information Processing Systems - Volume 1*, NIPS'15, page 649–657, Cambridge, MA, USA. MIT Press.

A Token ranks

Figures 5 and 6 show the coverage of the verbalizations, which makes up one aspect of explainer-faithfulness.

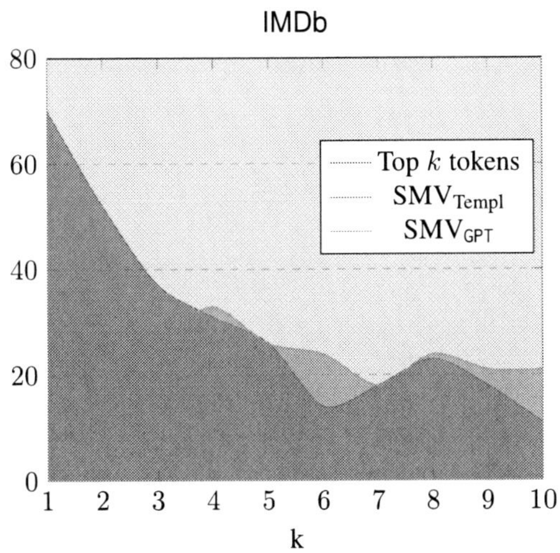

Figure 5: Number of SMVs mentioning top k attributed tokens in IMDb.

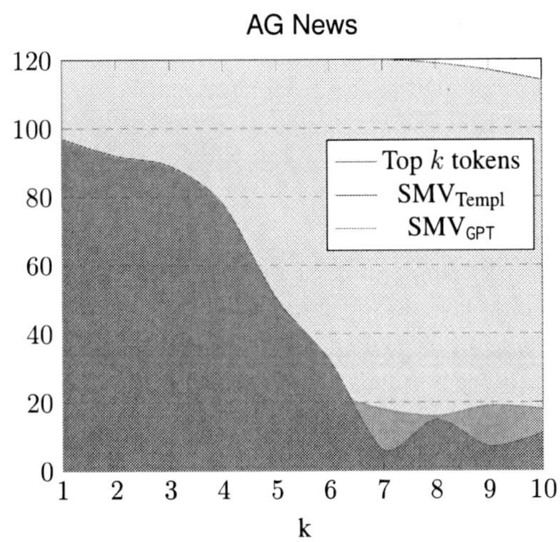

Figure 6: Number of SMVs mentioning top k attributed tokens in AG News.

	AG News		IMDb	
	S_V	$W + S_V$	S_V	$W + S_V$
Conv. Search	91.73	94.10	86.08	**96.00**
Span Search	87.16	**94.39**	89.08	95.90
Top $k = 5$ tokens	**92.54**	93.93	92.38	95.60
SMV$_{\text{Templ}}$	91.94	94.10	**94.26**	94.90
SMV$_{\text{GPT}}$	69.16	70.00	81.25	81.25

Table 4: Automated simulatability evaluation (Accuracy in %) using a `T5-large` model (Accuracy on original input: AG News – 92.58%; IMDb – 97.62%) to reproduce the underlying BERT model's prediction based on only seeing one of the verbalizations S_V (prepended by the original input W).

B Automated simulatability evaluation

We follow Wiegreffe et al. (2021) and Hase et al. (2020) and train a second language model to simulate the behavior of the explained BERT model. Table 4 shows the simulation accuracy of a `T5-large` receiving various types of verbalizations (plus the original input). We can see for both datasets that SMV$_{\text{GPT}}$ induces the most noise and thus results in the lowest accuracy, while the raw output of the search methods (Conv/Span) are most faithful in combination with the original input.

C Efficiency

First, we measure a runtime of less than two minutes on a CPU (i5-12600k) to generate template-based verbalizations for all 25k instances of IMDb. Given pre-computed saliency maps from any explainer, this is considerably faster than using an end-to-end model for extractive rationales, e.g. Treviso and Martins (2020), which takes several hours for training and then more than 10 minutes for inference on an RTX 3080 GPU. `GPT-3.5` with at least 175B parameters, which obliterates the other two setups. This means that there is a considerable carbon footprint associated with using it. Future work has to look into training considerably smaller models on the generated verbalizations.

D Subset selection heuristics

- We restrict our experiments to explaining a single outcome – the predicted label $\hat{y}$ – and thus modify our metric (Eq. 3): Cov$_+$ only considers the positive attributions $s_i > 0$.
- We select instances achieving at least a Cov$_+$ score of 15% (indicating the attribution mass is not too evenly distributed, making interpretations of saliency maps challenging).

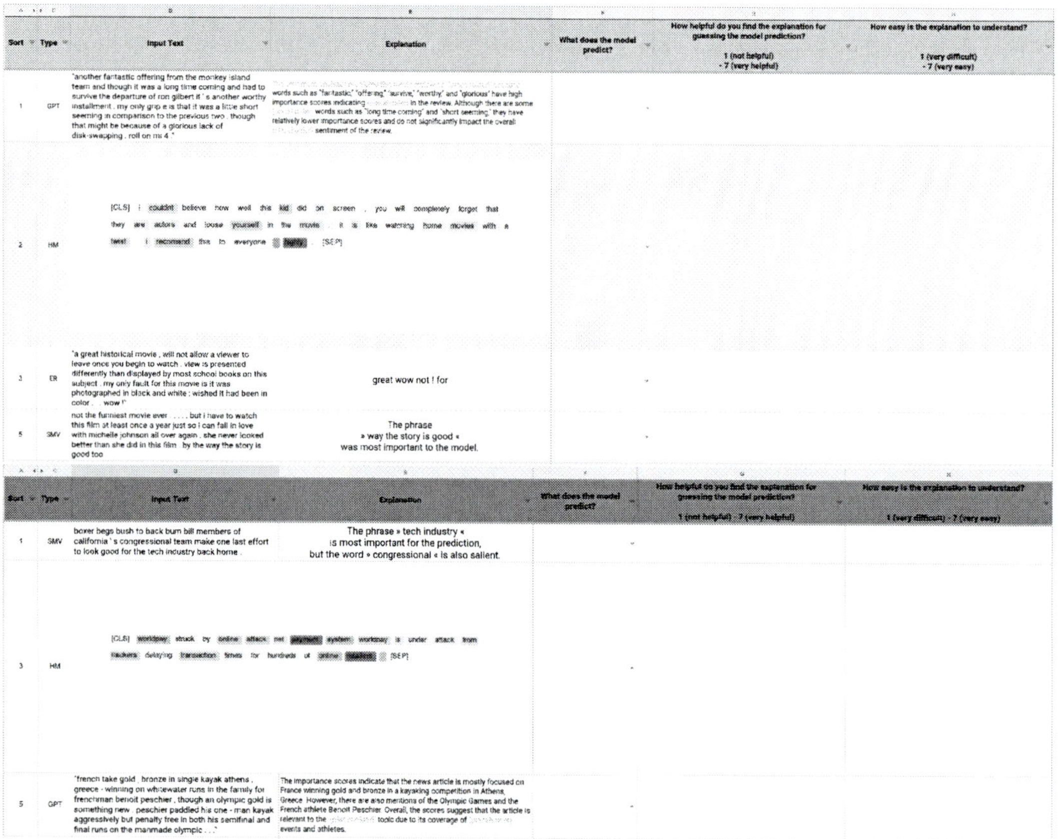

Figure 7: Annotation spreadsheet including one instance from every type of explanation representation in IMDb and AG News, as used in the human evaluation described in §3.1.

- We find values for q (§4.1.3) of $0.5 \leq q \leq 0.75$ to produce the right amount of candidates in the end, s.t. there almost always is at least one candidate in the q-th quantile and the resulting verbalization is not longer than most text inputs.
- We only consider instances with a maximum token length of 80, s.t. the human evaluation is more manageable for annotators.
- We select equal amounts of instances for every true label y (IMDb: 40 positive + 40 negative sentiment; AG News: 30 World + 30 Sports + 30 Business + 30 Sci/Tech) in each dataset.
- We select 25% of IMDb and 46.67 % of AG News to be false predictions by the BERT model ($y \neq \hat{y}$).

We apply the weighted average for IMDb-BERT-IG ($\beta = 0.4$) and the quantile scoring metric for AG News-BERT-IG ($n = 3$). We chose the number of candidates to be $k = 5$ in all cases and the threshold q to be .75 for IMDb and AG News as the average length of the input is lower for the latter which results in too few candidates with higher qs.

E Templates for Verbalizing Explanations

We design our templates as atomic expressions with constraints and blanks that can be filled with words from W. In the most basic cases, we refer to spans, phrases, words and characters as salient or important for some prediction. We design the templates to express saliency information concisely and enable users to reproduce the model's decision process (simulatability). The set of templates is depicted in Table 8.

Our template-based methodology is task- and model-invariant by design, because no task-specific model or NLG component is involved. Achieving sufficiency (measured by coverage) is harder, because a full translation of any saliency map is too verbose and thus not helpful.

F List of LLM prompts

At first, we treated this as table-to-text task – which has recently been tackled with prompt-based large language models (Chen, 2023; Xiang et al., 2022) –

Examples for leading sentence	
The words $\{w_1\}$, $\{\ldots\}$, and $\{w_n\}$ are most important.	Most important is $\{\ldots\}$
The most salient features are $\{\ldots\}$	The model predicted this label, because $\{\ldots\}$
... is the span that was most important.	
Features or linguistic units	**More than one unit**
feature(s)	The two phrases $\{\ldots\}$ and $\{\ldots\}$
word(s)	Both phrases $\{\ldots\}$ and $\{\ldots\}$
token(s)	... are both salient.
phrase(s)	The (top) three most important tokens ...
punctuation	... words such as $\{\ldots\}$ and $\{\ldots\}$
Synonyms for *important*	**Conjunctions & Adverbs**
salient	$\{\ldots\}$, while $\{\ldots\}$
influential	$\{\ldots\}$, whereas $\{\ldots\}$
key	... also salient
impactful	with the word $\{\ldots\}$ also being salient.
Additions for *important* $\{\ldots\}$	**Variations of *important***
... for (the/this) prediction.	... focused on the most for this prediction.
... (to the model) in (making/predicting choosing/producing/shaping) this outcome.	... used by the model to make its prediction.
	... caused the model to predict this outcome.
... with respect to the outcome.	indicate the model's predicted label.
... in this text.	... shaped the model's outcome (the most).
Synonyms for *prediction*	**Polarity**
outcome	$\{\ldots\}$ is least important.
model('s) prediction	$\{\ldots\}$ is more salient than $\{\ldots\}$.
model's judgment	$\{\ldots\}$ is less influential than $\{\ldots\}$.
model('s) behavior	
prediction of the classifier	
(model's) predicted label	
decision	
Dataset-specific	
IMDb	AG News
$\{\ldots\}$ for the sentiment label.	$\{\ldots\}$ indicative of the model's topic classification.
$\{\ldots\}$ most indicative of the sentiment.	$\{\ldots\}$ in this article.
$\{\ldots\}$ most indicative for the sentiment analysis.	The most salient words in this article are $\{\ldots\}$.
$\{\ldots\}$ used by the model to predict this sentiment label.	$\{\ldots\}$, because $\{\ldots\}$ appeared in the article.

Figure 8: Templates for model-free saliency map verbalization.

where we provided a list of attribution scores and, separate from that, a list of tokens. However, we registered less hallucinations (the model incorrectly mapping between words and their scores) when we provided the input as a joint representation as shown in Fig. 3.

For the two datasets, we then used the token+score representation as `{sample}` and a `{label_str}` being the predicted label (IMDb: *positive* or *negative*; AG News: *Worlds*, *Sports*, *Business*, or *Sci/Tech*) and wrote the instructions in Fig. 9.

G Post-processing of GPT outputs

AG News In order to prevent label leakage, we employed the string replacements listed in Tab. 5. In our human evaluation, they were replaced with "{placeholder}", so annotators could perform the simulatability task without cheating.

IMDb Movie review with importance scores: {sample}.
A sentiment analyzer has predicted this text as '{label_str} sentiment'. The scores behind each word indicate how important it was for the analyzer to predict '{label_str} sentiment'. The scores have been determined after the sentiment analyzer has already made its prediction. The sentiment analyzer cannot base its prediction on the scores, only on the movie review itself. Based on the importance scores, briefly explain why the sentiment analyzer has predicted this movie review as '{label_str} sentiment':

AG News (Figure 1, r.)
News article with importance scores: {sample}.
A topic classifier has predicted this text as '{label_str}'. The scores behind each word indicate how important it was for the classifier to predict '{label_str}'. The scores have been determined after the topic classifier has already made its prediction. The topic classifier cannot base its prediction on the scores, only on the news article itself.
Based on the importance scores, briefly explain why the topic classifier has predicted this news article as '{label_str}':

Figure 9: Task instructions applied to IMDb and AG News used by GPT-3.5 (see App. F for details).

IMDb	AG News			
Classes	**Sports**	**Business**	**World**	**Sci/Tech**
positivity (+)	sport	businesses	global	science
negativity (-)	the world of sports	business and economics	global politics	science and technology
		business and finance	international	scientific
		economics	all over the world	tech
		finance	global issues	technical
		financial	global affairs	technology
		the business world	international relations	technological
		the economy	a global issue or event	the tech industry
		corporate finance		the technology industry

Table 5: Post-processing of GPT-3.5 verbalizations for human evaluation.

Using Planning to Improve Semantic Parsing of Instructional Texts

Vanya Cohen and **Raymond Mooney**
Department of Computer Science, University of Texas at Austin
Austin, TX 78712, USA
{vanya, mooney}@utexas.edu

Abstract

We develop a symbolic planning-based decoder to improve the few-shot semantic parsing of instructional texts. The system takes long-form instructional texts as input and produces sequences of actions in a formal language that enable execution of the instructions. This task poses unique challenges since input texts may contain long context dependencies and ambiguous and domain-specific language. Valid semantic parses also require sequences of steps that constitute an executable plan. We build on recent progress in semantic parsing by leveraging large language models to learn parsers from small amounts of training data. During decoding, our method employs planning methods and domain information to rank and correct candidate parses. To validate our method, we evaluate on four domains: two household instruction-following domains and two cooking recipe interpretation domains. We present results for few-shot semantic parsing using leave-one-out cross-validation. We show that utilizing planning domain information improves the quality of generated plans. Through ablations we also explore the effects of our decoder design choices.

1 Introduction

Recent advancements in natural language processing (NLP) have successfully combined large language models with external symbolic reasoning capabilities. Toolformer (Schick et al., 2023) enables the use of external tools to perform tasks such as arithmetic and factual lookup, which are currently challenging for large language models. Liu et al. (2023) created a system that performs multi-step reasoning in planning tasks specified in natural language. This is achieved by using an external symbolic planner for domain-specific reasoning, providing guarantees that plans are logical and satisfy environmental constraints. By integrating external symbolic reasoning capabilities, many of the shortcomings of large language models can be addressed while still capitalizing on their strengths. Motivated by this line of work, we develop a novel decoding procedure that uses symbolic planning to improve the few-shot semantic parsing of long-form instructional texts. We map instructional texts to formal action sequences and validate our method on two recipe semantic-parsing datasets (Bollini et al., 2013; Tasse and Smith, 2008). Semantic parsing of instructional texts with few-shot learning poses several challenges to natural language processing (NLP) techniques. Current NLP methods are dominated by large language models. These are based on Transformer (Vaswani et al., 2017) architectures and leverage large scale pretraining to enable high, few-shot and zero-shot task performance (Brown et al., 2020).

Building on work from (Shin et al., 2021), we investigate semantic parsing in the few-shot setting using OpenAI's Codex language and code LLM (Chen et al., 2021; Shin and Van Durme, 2021). Learning occurs in-context, by prompting the LLM with a few input-output task examples. Pretrained LLM representations allow for more sample efficient learning than non-pretrained methods; but data scarcity still introduces performance limitations (Brown et al., 2020). Data efficiency is advantageous when working with long-form instructional texts. The datasets we consider are small and the cost of annotating long texts with ground-truth semantic parses is high.

In many semantic parsing tasks, context dependencies, input natural language strings, and output parses are relatively short. These tasks fit easily within the available context size of LLM models and consist of at most several input and output statements. Modeling long input-output dependencies poses a number of challenges for current models, as shown by their degraded performance on tasks designed to leverage long contexts (Tay et al., 2020). Semantic parsing of long-form instructional texts,

Proceedings of the 1st Workshop on Natural Language Reasoning and Structured Explanations (@ACL 2023), pages 47–58

like the recipe datasets we evaluate, can require learning representations for hundreds of words, and outputting tens of steps, each with multiple arguments and complex syntax.

Instructional texts also exist within an implicit planning domain. These texts describe plans for achieving a goal by manipulating objects that comprise a world-state. Executable semantic parse-plans must consist of valid transitions within this world-state. For example, to bake an item the oven must be on and preheated. These requirements constitute preconditions for the bake action. Long-context dependencies pose challenges to generating executable sequences of actions that are also relevant to the task instructions. To form a valid parse-plan, instructions must be translated into a sequence of executable actions. All requisite actions must be represented in the plan, potentially including actions not explicitly mentioned. Complicating matters, the common-sense knowledge needed to reason about valid plan sequences in a domain is only very implicitly represented within the LLM and few-shot examples.

To address these challenges, we propose *Planning Augmented Semantic Parsing*. Our method leverages a formal symbolic planning representation to rank and correct candidate plans. Plans are corrected by searching for sequences of actions that satisfy the preconditions of all output actions. Ranking selects plans which best meet the domain's planning and syntactic constraints by ranking plans highly if they have fewer inadmissible actions, require fewer additional actions to correct, and have fewer steps with invalid syntax. After ranking, planning errors are fixed using symbolic planning methods. The result is an effective neuro-symbolic approach that combines the strengths of deep-learned LLMs and classical AI planning.

We validate our approach using leave-one-out cross validation across each dataset and provide ablations for various aspects of our model choices. Results show that using *Planning Augmented Semantic Parsing* results in more valid plan sequences that still maintain high relevance to the natural language task instructions.

Overall we make the following contributions:

- Develop a novel method for using symbolic planning to improve semantic parsing with large language models.
- Demonstrate improvements in the executability of generated plans on two datasets, in a low-data, few-shot setting.

2 Background

2.1 Planning

We consider these instructional text semantic parses to be plans in a symbolic task planning setting. A task planning domain defines a world-state, actions that modify the world-state, and transition function specifying the effect of actions on the world-state (Ghallab et al., 2016). The world state is composed of a collection of Boolean values defining the existence and state of various kitchen objects and planning actions are implemented as STRIPs-style operators (Fikes and Nilsson, 1971). Each action has logical preconditions that must be satisfied for its execution. For any state, the admissible actions are all actions with satisfied preconditions. Upon execution the action changes the values of the variables which define the world-state. A planning task is specified by an initial state and a goal state. The resulting plan (if it exists) comprises a sequence of actions that can be taken to reach the goal state.

2.2 In-Context Learning

In-context learning allows LLMs to perform novel tasks specified in terms of a small number of sample input-output pairs (Brown et al., 2020). These examples are provided as part of the generation context to condition the language model. Typically these examples are drawn from the training split of a dataset and prepended to a test example. Few-shot prompted learning differs from other LLM learning paradigms including the zero-shot inference utilized in the evaluations of GPT-2 (Radford et al., 2019) and fine-tuning used to transfer pre-trained model weights to novel tasks as in (Radford et al., 2018), (Peters et al., 2018) and (Devlin et al., 2018).

3 Related Work

(Branavan et al., 2009) develops a reinforcement learning-based method for semantic parsing of instructional texts and (Branavan et al., 2010) additionally learns to fill in low-level steps from high-level instructions using environment interaction. Previous work also formulates semantic parsing as a text-to-text machine translation task (Wong and Mooney, 2006). Our work builds on the few-shot semantic parsing of (Shin et al., 2021) and (Shin and Van Durme, 2021) that establishes OpenAI's

Codex model (Chen et al., 2021) as a high performing LLM for few-shot semantic parsing. (Bollini et al., 2013) and (Tasse and Smith, 2008) introduce the recipe-semantic parsing datasets we use for evaluation but learn semantic parsers using shallow features and classification-based approaches. Other work investigates semantic parsing of recipes (Malmaud et al., 2014) including using modern deep-learning methods (Papadopoulos et al., 2022). Recent work uses few-shot learning and large language models to map single commands (Huang et al., 2022) and short sequences of commands (Brohan et al., 2022) to executable plans. However, to our knowledge, ours is the first work to use symbolic planning to improve semantic parsing of instructional texts.

4 Methods

For the LLM we use Davinci Codex (Chen et al., 2021) based on the GPT-3 architecture (Brown et al., 2020). Like GPT-3, the model was trained on a large web-sourced text corpus, but includes code in the dataset. While OpenAI does not publish the sizes of the Codex models available through their API, (Gao, 2021) empirically estimate the size of text-only Davinci at 175B parameters.

4.1 Datasets

We evaluate our method on two recipe semantic parsing datasets from (Tasse and Smith, 2008) and (Bollini et al., 2013). (Tasse and Smith, 2008) contains 260 recipes with corresponding semantic parses in the Minimal Instruction Language for the Kitchen (MILK) syntax. Each statement in the language corresponds to a plan step with an action and arguments. Some plan steps produce new variables (ingredients or tools) which are consumed by subsequent steps. The recipes in this dataset cover a wide range of cuisines, ingredients, techniques, and tools. Each step also contains an optional human-readable description of the step. The original dataset uses variables as arguments to action steps. We replace these with their literal values to make the generation problem easier for the LLM. The 60 recipes of (Bollini et al., 2013) were selected to be executed by a cooking robot. The recipes are mainly limited to baking and contain a small fixed set of tools and actions. This dataset also contains planning domain definitions in the form of STRIPs-style operator actions (Fikes and Nilsson, 1971). Recipe steps that require tools or techniques outside of this fixed vocabulary are mapped to a NO-OP. Examples from both datasets are in the Appendix: with in Table 5 and action signatures are defined in Table 6.

4.2 Planning Domain

(Bollini et al., 2013) contains planning domain definitions that specify the state of the kitchen, ingredients, and tools used in each recipe. These were developed to facilitate recipe execution on a real-world cooking robot. We utilize these definitions for planning in this domain. The domain also provides a successor state function that given a starting state and a search depth, returns all valid sequences of actions up to the search depth. This is used in Algorithm 1. The (Tasse and Smith, 2008) dataset does not provide planning definitions. We construct planning definitions where the existence of ingredients and tools are the only predicates and transitions in the environment involve either creating or destroying these objects. Therefore the only preconditions in this domain involve the existence of objects. Actions are considered valid if their objects have been instantiated by prior steps, otherwise the their preconditions are considered unsatisfied.

4.3 Prompt Design

To generate a plan for a test example using few-shot learning, we prompt the model with sample recipes and parses taken from the held-out examples. Following (Liu et al., 2021), prompt examples are selected using nearest-neighbor search using the cosine distance between their embeddings as computed by a text embedding model, specifically the "all-mpnet-base-v2" model from the SentenceTransformers library (Reimers and Gurevych, 2019) based on the MPNet model (Song et al., 2020). Due to the limited length of the input context for the Codex models ($8,000$ and $2,048$ tokens) and API request limits, the number of training examples is limited to a maximum of five for the recipes of (Bollini et al., 2013) and one for (Tasse and Smith, 2008). The selection of few-shot training examples reduces to Equation 1, where a is a training example, X denotes the set of held-out examples, and E represents the recipe embedding function.

$$P(a) = \arg\min_{x \in X}\{cos\_sim(E(x), E(a))\} \quad (1)$$

The full prompt is formed by concatenating the training example instructions with their semantic parses, and the instructions for the test example. Each component of the prompt is separated by new line characters, and a special delimiter "###" which is also appended to the end of the prompt. Because of the in-context learning, the model learns to append the delimiter to the end of the generated parse. Thereby, the delimiter is used to identify the end of the model's sequence completion.

4.4 Planning-Augmented Decoding

Given a prompt sequence, the LLM defines a distribution over next token continuations. Due to utilization limits of the Codex API, our method samples a fixed number of plan completions for each recipe. For sampling next tokens, we use nucleus sampling introduced by (Holtzman et al., 2020), which offers improvements over other sampling methods. These are then ranked using a scoring function based on the generation probability and a *planning score* which factors in the number of precondition errors and syntax errors in the plan and the sequence probability of the plan.

The planning score is calculated by combining measures of plan executabilty: the number of precondition errors, syntax errors, and additional planning steps. Precondition errors occur when a plan step's preconditions are not satisfied. For example when the step references non-existent ingredients or the world state does not allow the action to occur. Syntax errors occur when the plan contains malformed steps that cannot be parsed by the plan interpreter. The syntax error score (SE) is the number of plan steps which contain syntax violations. The precondition error score (PE) is the number of plan steps which cannot be executed because their preconditions are not satisfied. Finally, (AS) is the number of steps added to the plan by planning in order to maximize the number of plan steps with valid preconditions. Steps with errors are counted as opposed to counting all errors in each step. This allows for computation of a score in the interval $[0, 1]$ to match the sequence probability score. In general identifying multiple syntax errors in a given step is not possible, as the presence of even a single syntax error may result in an undefined grammatical context.

These counts are normalized by the plan length (N) so as not to penalize longer plans. The natural log is taken to re-scale the planning score for addition with the sequence log-probability, adding ϵ to avoid taking the logarithm of zero in cases where the plan contains no errors and requires no additional steps to be valid. The planning score is added to the mean log-probability of the token sequence representing the plan. This scoring function results in plans with a higher sequence probability and fewer planning errors being selected.

$$
\begin{aligned}
score = \ln(1.0 - \frac{SE + PE + AS}{N} + \epsilon) \\
+ \frac{1}{T}\sum_{t=1}^{T} \ln P_t
\end{aligned} \tag{2}
$$

The plan that maximizes the *score* function is passed to a planning module. For each inadmissible step where the preconditions are not satisfied, it searches for sequences of admissible actions to insert into the plan, such that those actions lead to valid preconditions for that step. To limit the search space, the planning module only searches in the space of plans that can be inserted before an existing inadmissible plan step.

4.5 Correcting Plans

While the ranking procedure ensures that high probability and low-error plans will be surfaced, these plans may still contain precondition errors. The planning domain information and a planning algorithm together form a planning module that can attempt to correct these precondition errors. The ranking procedure incorporates this planning module to calculate the additional steps AS that can be inserted into a plan to fix precondition errors. These steps are also included in the total number of steps N. Therefore fixable plans will receive a better planning score.

Algorithm 1 describes the procedure for finding steps to insert into a plan to ensure that each step's preconditions are satisfied. As input, it takes the world state after executing some number of plan steps, and computes the sequence of actions needed to ensure the preconditions of the next plan step A are met. The algorithm returns the shortest number of actions required to satisfy the step's preconditions. Aside from producing more valid plans, this method should produce plans which correspond more closely to the ground truth semantic parse annotations. However because the planning module only inserts steps into a plan before an inadmissible step, and does not change the existing steps,

Algorithm 1: The planning algorithm inserts steps before actions with unmet preconditions.

```
Input: A starting state S, desired action A,
       transition function T, and search
       depth N.
Output: The shortest sequence of actions P
        which ends in action A or null if
        none exists.
sequences = successors(S, T, depth=N);
best = null;
for s in sequences do
    if A in s then
        /* truncate the plan until
           the action A or false if
           no such prefix exists   */
        plan = prefix(s, A);
        if plan && length(plan) <
         length(best) then
            best = plan;
        end
    end
end
```

it cannot necessarily fix all precondition errors in a plan. Utilizing planning and likelihood based decoding balances the desire for plans with valid preconditions while ensuring that plans contain relevant steps to the recipe. These two requirements may compete in some cases. In the simplest case, an empty plan, there are no potential precondition errors, but the plan also contains no relevant plan steps. In practice there exists a trade-off between plan executability and correctness as noted by (Huang et al., 2022).

5 Experiments

We use leave-one-out cross-validation to evaluate performance of various models on our two recipe datasets. For the shorter recipes in the (Bollini et al., 2013) dataset, we evaluate using both one and five training plans in the prompt. We evaluate the longer recipes of the (Tasse and Smith, 2008) dataset using only a single prompt example due to context length limitations.

To evaluate the correctness of each output plan we compare the generated plan to the ground truth annotation from the dataset. We use metrics that measure the similarity between the output and ground truth plans. However for each recipe there are potentially many admissible plans and subjective judgements about the level of detail of the annotation and about which attributes to include. To address these potential ambiguities, we evaluate models using several diverse metrics to capture different aspects of plan accuracy.

5.1 Baselines

We evaluate three baseline methods for ranking the generated plans: *Random*, *Rank (PPL)*, and *Rank*. Our full ranking method with partial planning is denoted *Rank+Plan*. *No Rank* simply selects a random plan from the set of generated completions. *Rank (PPL)* selects the plan with the lowest perplexity (PPL) (the highest sequence probability), providing a baseline where no planning domain information is utilized. Finally, *Rank* ranks the plans by the scoring function in Equation 2, but does not correct precondition errors through planning like *Rank + Plan* does.

5.2 Longest Common Subsequence (LCS)

Prior work evaluates plan correctness in terms of the LCS between generated and ground truth plans (Puig et al., 2018). We normalized LCS by the length of the longer plan. LCS evaluates the textual overlap between plans; computing common subsequences which may contain interwoven unequal sequences. It therefore does not strongly penalize erroneous injected subsequences. This metric ranges from $[0.0, 1.0]$ where 0.0 indicates no sequence overlap and 1.0 indicates identical plans.

5.3 Plan Steps F1

LCS reflects the order and content of the generated plan steps compared to the ground truth. We also report an F1 measure (the harmonic mean of precision and recall) that quantifies the quality of the individual plan steps without regard to their sequencing. Steps in the generated and ground truth plans are compared based on string equality. In many plans, steps are often repeated. For example a recipe from (Bollini et al., 2013) may have many $mix()$ steps after pouring different ingredients. We choose to treat each of these repetitions as a unique step when computing the precision and recall. We also exclude NO-OP steps from these calculations for the (Bollini et al., 2013) dataset as they do not change the plan's results.

(Bollini et al., 2013)		
Rank	**Rank + Plan**	**Ground Truth**
pour(nuts) mix() scrape() bake(25)	pour(nuts) mix() scrape() **preheat(350)** bake(25)	pour(nuts) mix() scrape() **preheat(350)** bake(25)
(Tasse and Smith, 2008)		
Rank	**Rank + Plan**	**Ground Truth**
combine("1/2 cup all-purpose flour", "1 egg", "1 tablespoon chopped fresh parsley", "1/2 teaspoon salt", "1/4 teaspoon freshly ground nutmeg", "mashed potatoes", "dough", "stir in")	**create_ing("1/2 cup all-purpose flour")** ... combine(**"1/2 cup all-purpose flour"**, "1 egg", "1 tablespoon chopped fresh parsley", "1/2 teaspoon salt", "1/4 teaspoon freshly ground nutmeg", "mashed potatoes", "dough", "stir in")	**create_ing("1/2 cup all-purpose flour")** ... combine(**"1/2 cup all-purpose flour"**, "1 egg", "1 tablespoon chopped fresh parsley", "1/2 teaspoon salt", "1/4 teaspoon freshly ground nutmeg", "mashed potatoes", "mashed potato mixture", "stir in")

Table 1: Excerpted examples of improved parsing for recipes using the *Rank + Plan* method. The parses were selected by randomly selecting recipe where the *Rank + Plan* method resulted in an improvement in the number of precondition errors over the baseline methods. NO-OP actions are omitted for brevity.

5.4 Precondition and Syntax Errors (PE & SE)

The previous metrics assess similarity to the ground truth plan and do not explicitly reflect the executability of generated plans. Therefore, we also measures the frequency of precondition and syntax errors in plans. Errors are counted on a per-step basis. If a step contains more than one error or more than one type of error these are quantified as a single error and type for the step.

5.5 Implementation Details

We utilize Davinci Codex[1] for all experiments due to its large context size of $8,000$ tokens which is sufficient for all prompts and completions across both datasets. Our method samples ten completions up to a fixed length of $1,500$ tokens or until the special delimiter sequence is reached. The decoding length was chosen to be longer than the longest recipe parse in either of the datasets. We generate ten completions for each recipe to offer a diversity of plans to rank and correct through planning. We also utilize a nucleus sampling top-p value of 0.5. This value was selected because it maximizes the performance of the *No Rank* baseline with respect to LCS. We perform ten trials to compute means and confidence intervals.

[1]The OpenAI API name for the model is "code-davinci-002".

6 Results

We report results for the (Bollini et al., 2013) dataset in Table 2 and the (Tasse and Smith, 2008) dataset in Table 3. Mean cross-validation results are reported with 95% confidence intervals computed using a t-distribution for ten trials. For both datasets, the number of precondition errors are reduced by ranking using our scoring metric and corrective planning. The *Rank* method results in a decrease in the precondition error rate, and by adding corrective planning (*Rank + Plan*), the error rate is again reduced significantly. This results in more valid, executable plans. Even as the precondition error rate is reduced, the LCS remains constant for the (Bollini et al., 2013) dataset and only slightly reduced for the (Tasse and Smith, 2008) dataset. This indicates that the plans maintain high agreement with the ground truth plans while steps are

Models	(Bollini et al., 2013)			
	LCS↑	PE↓	SE↓	F1 ↑
No Rank				
Davinci Codex, E=1	0.908 ± 0.007	0.737 ± 0.067	0.065 ± 0.025	0.784 ± 0.002
Davinci Codex, E=5	0.950 ± 0.001	0.277 ± 0.020	0.000 ± 0.000	0.859 ± 0.002
Rank (PPL)				
Davinci Codex, E=1	0.897 ± 0.008	0.962 ± 0.685	0.042 ± 0.008	0.784 ± 0.004
Davinci Codex, E=5	0.949 ± 0.005	0.198 ± 0.009	0.002 ± 0.004	0.863 ± 0.003
Rank				
Davinci Codex, E=1	0.901 ± 0.008	0.382 ± 0.037	0.025 ± 0.008	0.798 ± 0.002
Davinci Codex, E=5	0.952 ± 0.005	0.120 ± 0.015	0.002 ± 0.004	$\mathbf{0.868 \pm 0.002}$
Rank + Plan				
Davinci Codex, E=1	0.903 ± 0.008	0.143 ± 0.033	0.025 ± 0.008	0.807 ± 0.002
Davinci Codex, E=5	0.952 ± 0.005	$\mathbf{0.033 \pm 0.000}$	0.002 ± 0.004	$\mathbf{0.870 \pm 0.002}$

Table 2: Results and ablations for the (Bollini et al., 2013) dataset, reported as means over the leave-one-out cross validation. 95% confidence intervals are computed using a t-distribution over ten trials. Results using one (E=1) and five (E=5) training examples in each prompt are shown. All plans are generated using a nucleus sampling top-p value of 0.5.

Models	(Tasse and Smith, 2008)			
	LCS↑	PE↓	SE↓	F1 ↑
No Rank				
Davinci Codex, E=1	$\mathbf{0.707 \pm 0.002}$	0.805 ± 0.029	0.940 ± 0.134	$\mathbf{0.448 \pm 0.001}$
Rank (PPL)				
Davinci Codex, E=1	0.692 ± 0.003	0.827 ± 0.086	0.875 ± 0.199	0.443 ± 0.002
Rank				
Davinci Codex, E=1	0.695 ± 0.004	0.293 ± 0.016	$\mathbf{0.226 \pm 0.024}$	0.446 ± 0.001
Rank + Plan				
Davinci Codex, E=1	0.695 ± 0.003	$\mathbf{0.000 \pm 0.000}$	$\mathbf{0.237 \pm 0.018}$	0.446 ± 0.001

Table 3: Results and ablations for the (Tasse and Smith, 2008) dataset, reported as means over the leave-one-out cross validation. 95% confidence intervals are computed using a t-distribution over ten trials. Results using one (E=1) training example in each prompt are shown. All plans are generated using a nucleus sampling top-p value of 0.5.

added. For the (Bollini et al., 2013) dataset the F1 score also improves through ranking and corrective planning indicating that highly ranked plans contain more accurate selections of recipe steps. The F1 score does not improve for the (Tasse and Smith, 2008) dataset and the *Rank + Plan* method results in no precondition errors. However, these results are not surprising because the for this dataset the planning module can only insert ingredient and tool definitions into the plan. These inserted actions could result in lower LCS by lengthening the generated plan and may not match ingredient definitions in the ground truth plan. Because of the presence of free-text descriptions and specifications in the (Tasse and Smith, 2008) dataset and the difficulty of parsing longer plans, both the LCS and F1 are lower than for the (Bollini et al., 2013) dataset. Finally providing more in-context examples for the (Bollini et al., 2013) dataset improves performance for all measured metrics.

Table 1 contains qualitative examples of the *Rank + Plan* performance. For the example from the (Bollini et al., 2013) dataset, in the generated plan the oven is not preheated before baking. The corrected plan adds a preheat() action to satisfy the preconditions of the bake() action, which requires a heated oven. In the example from the (Tasse and Smith, 2008) dataset, a recipe that uses certain ingredients to make dough. In the generated plan these ingredients are not instantiated. However the planning module inserts actions to instantiate the ingredients which improves the validity of the generated plan. An additional example for the (Bollini et al., 2013) dataset is included in Table 4

7 Discussion

Evaluations show that our method improves plan validity as measured by the mean number of precondition errors, syntax errors, and accuracy of steps returned (F1) in each plan. LCS remains fairly constant across our evaluations and ablations. The LCS metric reflects both the content of planning steps and their sequencing. By contrast, F1 only assesses the accuracy of steps in the generated plans. Perhaps there exists a trade-off wherein the process of inserting corrective plan steps reduces the amount of alignment of the generated and ground truth plans (lowering LCS), but increases the accuracy of included steps (raising F1). Of all the metrics considered, our method results in largest reduction in the number of precondition errors (PE). We achieve these improvements without singificant reductions in LCS and with an increase in F1. This is an important validation for our method, as (Huang et al., 2022) finds that there exists a trade-off between the executability and semantic correctness (measure by LCS) of generated plans. It is straightforward to increase executability (fewer precondition errors) by ignoring the instructional text content and only outputting valid actions. For any downstream applications, plans must be executable and while also reflecting the content of the instructions. Therefore is is important to reduce the number of precondition errors while maintaining content similarity to ground-truth plans.

7.1 Limitations and Future Work

Our approach requires access to planning information for each instructional text domain. In general, creating this information requires programming and domain knowledge to formally specify the planning constraints. However for high-value applications the effort associated with generating these planning domain definitions may be justified by their potential to help in generating more valid plan-based semantic parses. Having this knowledge is also crucial to allowing an agent or robot to execute the resulting plan and may be naturally available in many domains as part of the execution component. In the course of developing our semantic parsing model, we discovered that Codex could generate valid planning domain definitions in a variety of output formats including the Planning Domain Definition Language (Fox and Long, 2003). This may provide a path towards automatically generating planning domain definitions for novel environments or reducing the need for human annotators. Future work could also evaluate our method in other planning domains that contain tasks beyond cooking such as VirtualHome (Puig et al., 2018) or ALFRED (Shridhar et al., 2020).

8 Conclusion

We develop an approach to semantic parsing for long-form instructional texts that leverages planning domain information to generate more valid plans in a low-data, few-shot setting. Our method significantly reduces the number of precondition errors present in semantically parsed plans for two recipe datasets. These results highlight the benefit of a neuro-symbolic approach that utilizes the state-of-the-art code-generation LLM Codex to produce relevant steps for recipe execution and refines these plans using classical symbolic planning. In quantitative and qualitative evaluations, our approach generates plans that reflect the relevant steps of the natural language recipe. The symbolic planning component corrects precondition errors that arise from omitted or implied instructional steps and the challenges of learning with long context-dependencies from limited examples.

Acknowledgements

This material is based upon work supported by the Defense Advanced Research Projects Agency (DARPA) under Contract No. HR001122C0007. Any opinions, findings and conclusions or recommendations expressed in this material are those of the author(s) and do not necessarily reflect the views of the Defense Advanced Research Projects Agency (DARPA).

References

Mario Bollini, Stefanie Tellex, Tyler Thompson, Nicholas Roy, and Daniela Rus. 2013. Interpreting and executing recipes with a cooking robot. In *Experimental Robotics*, pages 481–495. Springer.

Satchuthananthavale RK Branavan, Harr Chen, Luke Zettlemoyer, and Regina Barzilay. 2009. Reinforcement learning for mapping instructions to actions. In *Proceedings of the Joint Conference of the 47th Annual Meeting of the ACL and the 4th International Joint Conference on Natural Language Processing of the AFNLP*, pages 82–90.

SRK Branavan, Luke Zettlemoyer, and Regina Barzilay. 2010. Reading between the lines: Learning to map high-level instructions to commands. In *Proceedings of the 48th annual meeting of the association for computational linguistics*, pages 1268–1277.

Anthony Brohan, Yevgen Chebotar, Chelsea Finn, Karol Hausman, Alexander Herzog, Daniel Ho, Julian Ibarz, Alex Irpan, Eric Jang, Ryan Julian, et al. 2022. Do as i can, not as i say: Grounding language in robotic affordances. In *6th Annual Conference on Robot Learning*.

Tom Brown, Benjamin Mann, Nick Ryder, Melanie Subbiah, Jared D Kaplan, Prafulla Dhariwal, Arvind Neelakantan, Pranav Shyam, Girish Sastry, Amanda Askell, et al. 2020. Language models are few-shot learners. *Advances in neural information processing systems*, 33:1877–1901.

Mark Chen, Jerry Tworek, Heewoo Jun, Qiming Yuan, Henrique Ponde de Oliveira Pinto, Jared Kaplan, Harri Edwards, Yuri Burda, Nicholas Joseph, Greg Brockman, et al. 2021. Evaluating large language models trained on code. *arXiv preprint arXiv:2107.03374*.

Jacob Devlin, Ming-Wei Chang, Kenton Lee, and Kristina Toutanova. 2018. Bert: Pre-training of deep bidirectional transformers for language understanding. *arXiv preprint arXiv:1810.04805*.

Richard E Fikes and Nils J Nilsson. 1971. Strips: A new approach to the application of theorem proving to problem solving. *Artificial intelligence*, 2(3-4):189–208.

Maria Fox and Derek Long. 2003. Pddl2. 1: An extension to pddl for expressing temporal planning domains. *Journal of artificial intelligence research*, 20:61–124.

Leo Gao. 2021. On the sizes of openai api models. `https://blog.eleuther.ai/gpt3-model-sizes/`. Accessed: 2022-08-11.

Malik Ghallab, Dana Nau, and Paolo Traverso. 2016. *Automated planning and acting*. Cambridge University Press.

Ari Holtzman, Jan Buys, Li Du, Maxwell Forbes, and Yejin Choi. 2020. The curious case of neural text degeneration. In *International Conference on Learning Representations*.

Wenlong Huang, Pieter Abbeel, Deepak Pathak, and Igor Mordatch. 2022. Language models as zero-shot planners: Extracting actionable knowledge for embodied agents. *arXiv preprint arXiv:2201.07207*.

Bo Liu, Yuqian Jiang, Xiaohan Zhang, Qiang Liu, Shiqi Zhang, Joydeep Biswas, and Peter Stone. 2023. Llm+p: Empowering large language models with optimal planning proficiency.

Jiachang Liu, Dinghan Shen, Yizhe Zhang, Bill Dolan, Lawrence Carin, and Weizhu Chen. 2021. What makes good in-context examples for gpt-3? *arXiv preprint arXiv:2101.06804*.

Jonathan Malmaud, Earl Wagner, Nancy Chang, and Kevin Murphy. 2014. Cooking with semantics. In *Proceedings of the ACL 2014 Workshop on Semantic Parsing*, pages 33–38.

Dim P. Papadopoulos, Enrique Mora, Nadiia Chepurko, Kuan Wei Huang, Ferda Ofli, and Antonio Torralba. 2022. Learning program representations for food images and cooking recipes. In *Proceedings of the IEEE/CVF Conference on Computer Vision and Pattern Recognition (CVPR)*, pages 16559–16569.

Matthew E Peters, Mark Neumann, Mohit Iyyer, Matt Gardner, Christopher Clark, Kenton Lee, and Luke Zettlemoyer. 2018. Deep contextualized word representations. *arXiv preprint arXiv:1802.05365*.

Xavier Puig, Kevin Ra, Marko Boben, Jiaman Li, Tingwu Wang, Sanja Fidler, and Antonio Torralba. 2018. Virtualhome: Simulating household activities via programs. In *Proceedings of the IEEE Conference on Computer Vision and Pattern Recognition*, pages 8494–8502.

Alec Radford, Karthik Narasimhan, Tim Salimans, Ilya Sutskever, et al. 2018. Improving language understanding by generative pre-training. *OpenAI blog*.

Alec Radford, Jeffrey Wu, Rewon Child, David Luan, Dario Amodei, Ilya Sutskever, et al. 2019. Language models are unsupervised multitask learners. *OpenAI blog*, 1(8):9.

Nils Reimers and Iryna Gurevych. 2019. Sentence-bert: Sentence embeddings using siamese bert-networks. In *Proceedings of the 2019 Conference on Empirical Methods in Natural Language Processing*. Association for Computational Linguistics.

Timo Schick, Jane Dwivedi-Yu, Roberto Dessì, Roberta Raileanu, Maria Lomeli, Luke Zettlemoyer, Nicola Cancedda, and Thomas Scialom. 2023. Toolformer: Language models can teach themselves to use tools.

Richard Shin, Christopher H. Lin, Sam Thomson, Charles Chen, Subhro Roy, Emmanouil Antonios Platanios, Adam Pauls, Dan Klein, Jason Eisner, and Ben Van Durme. 2021. Constrained language models yield few-shot semantic parsers. In *2021 Empirical Methods in Natural Language Processing*.

Richard Shin and Benjamin Van Durme. 2021. Few-shot semantic parsing with language models trained on code. *arXiv preprint arXiv:2112.08696*.

Mohit Shridhar, Jesse Thomason, Daniel Gordon, Yonatan Bisk, Winson Han, Roozbeh Mottaghi, Luke Zettlemoyer, and Dieter Fox. 2020. ALFRED: A Benchmark for Interpreting Grounded Instructions for Everyday Tasks. In *The IEEE Conference on Computer Vision and Pattern Recognition (CVPR)*.

Kaitao Song, Xu Tan, Tao Qin, Jianfeng Lu, and Tie-Yan Liu. 2020. Mpnet: Masked and permuted pre-training for language understanding. *arXiv preprint arXiv:2004.09297*.

Dan Tasse and Noah A Smith. 2008. Sour cream: Toward semantic processing of recipes. *Carnegie Mellon University, Pittsburgh, Tech. Rep. CMU-LTI-08-005*.

Yi Tay, Mostafa Dehghani, Samira Abnar, Yikang Shen, Dara Bahri, Philip Pham, Jinfeng Rao, Liu Yang, Sebastian Ruder, and Donald Metzler. 2020. Long range arena: A benchmark for efficient transformers. *arXiv preprint arXiv:2011.04006*.

Ashish Vaswani, Noam Shazeer, Niki Parmar, Jakob Uszkoreit, Llion Jones, Aidan N Gomez, Łukasz Kaiser, and Illia Polosukhin. 2017. Attention is all you need. *Advances in neural information processing systems*, 30.

Yuk Wah Wong and Raymond Mooney. 2006. Learning for semantic parsing with statistical machine translation. In *Proceedings of the Human Language Technology Conference of the NAACL, Main Conference*, pages 439–446.

A Examples & Action Definitions

(Bollini et al., 2013)		
Rank	**Rank + Plan**	**Ground Truth**
pour(flour) mix() mix() preheat(350) bake(20)	pour(flour) mix() mix() preheat(350) **scrape()** bake(20)	pour(flour) mix() **scrape()** preheat(350) bake(20)

Table 4: Additional excerpted generation examples for the (Bollini et al., 2013) dataset.

(Tasse and Smith, 2008)	
A Very Intense Fruit Smoothie	
1 (10 ounce) package frozen mixed berries 1 (15 ounce) can sliced peaches, drained 2 tablespoons honey In a blender, combine frozen fruit, canned fruit and honey. Blend until smooth.	create_ing("1 (10 ounce) package frozen mixed berries") create_ing("1 (15 ounce) can sliced peaches, drained") create_ing("2 tablespoons honey") create_tool("blender") combine("1 (10 ounce) package frozen mixed berries", "1 (15 ounce) can sliced peaches, drained", "2 tablespoons honey", "fruit and honey", "") put("fruit and honey", "blender") mix("fruit and honey", "blender", "smoothie", "blend") chefcheck("smoothie", "smooth")
(Bollini et al., 2013)	
Easy Cake Mix Cookies	
1 (18 1/4 ounce) box chocolate cake mix 1/3 cup vegetable oil 2 eggs Combine cake mix, oil and eggs. Mix well. Bake at 350F for about 10 minutes. Remove from oven and let cool on pan for several minutes before removing to rack to finish cooling.	ingredient(["cake_mix"], "1 (18 1/4 ounce) box", homogenous=True) ingredient(["oil"], "1/3 cup", homogenous=True) ingredient(["eggs"], "2", homogenous=True) pour(cake_mix), pour(oil), pour(eggs), mix() mix() scrape(), preheat(350), bake(10) noop()

Table 5: Example recipes from the (Tasse and Smith, 2008) and (Bollini et al., 2013) datasets. These examples are the second shortest and shortest for each dataset respectively.

(Bollini et al., 2013)
ingredient(contains : string, amount : string, homogenous : bool)
pour(ingredient : string)
scrape()
preheat(temperature : string)
bake(time : string)
noop()

(Tasse and Smith, 2008)
create_tool(name : string)
create_ing(name : string)
chefcheck(name : string, description : string)
cut(item : string, tool : string, result : string, description : string)
combine(item : string, tool : string, result : string, description : string)
cook(item : string, tool : string, result : string, description : string)
do(item : string, tool : string, result : string, description : string)
leave(item : string, description : string)
mix(item : string, tool : string, result : string, description : string)
put(item : string, tool : string)
remove(item : string, tool : string)
separate(item : string, result1 : string, result2 : string, description : string)
serve(item : string, description : string)
set(item : string, description : string)

Table 6: Action definitions for the cooking recipe domains. The actions of (Bollini et al., 2013) operate on a world-state definition that includes the state of the ingredients, a mixing bowl, a baking pan, and the oven. In contrast (Tasse and Smith, 2008) provides no planning domain definitions and employs qualitative descriptions of state transformations in the action annotations. We build a simple planning domain where the state consists only the existence of objects as state variables. The preconditions for an action are met if the items used in the action have been instantiated.

Reasoning Circuits: Few-shot Multi-hop Question Generation with Structured Rationales

Saurabh Kulshreshtha and Anna Rumshisky
Department of Computer Science
University of Massachusetts Lowell
{skul,arum}@cs.uml.edu

Abstract

Multi-hop Question Generation is the task of generating questions which require the reader to reason over and combine information spread across multiple passages employing several reasoning steps. Chain-of-thought rationale generation has been shown to improve performance on multi-step reasoning tasks and make model predictions more interpretable. However, few-shot performance gains from including rationales have been largely observed only in +100B language models, and otherwise require large-scale manual rationale annotation. In this paper, we introduce a new framework for applying chain-of-thought inspired structured rationale generation to multi-hop question generation under a very low supervision regime (8- to 128-shot). We propose to annotate a small number of examples following our proposed multi-step rationale schema, treating each reasoning step as a separate task to be performed by a generative language model. We show that our framework leads to improved control over the difficulty of the generated questions and better performance compared to baselines trained without rationales, both on automatic evaluation metrics and in human evaluation. Importantly, we show that this is achievable with a modest model size.

1 Introduction

Recently, there has been a surge of interest in the NLP community in the idea of providing supervision to language models(LMs) in the form of human-written rationales (Wiegreffe and Marasovic, 2021; Camburu et al., 2018; Jansen et al., 2018; Aggarwal et al., 2021; Geva et al., 2021; Inoue et al., 2020) which explain why and how the target label is arrived at. Using human-written explanations as an intermediate step has been shown to improve performance on a variety of predictive tasks, compared to the cases where no rationales are provided (Wiegreffe and Marasovic, 2021). However, rationales are expensive to collect through manual annotation at a large scale.

Explanations can take several forms, such as textual highlights, free-text explanations and structured explanations. In this work, we focus on the latter two. By rationales we refer to several structured sentences enumerating intermediate steps of reasoning required to solve a multi-step reasoning problem before producing the target text.

In chain-of-thought rationale generation paradigm (Wei et al., 2022b; Zelikman et al., 2022), LMs learn to generate rationales - a step toward explainable NLP models. Prompting LMs with few-shot rationale examples has been shown to improve performance for multi-step reasoning tasks compared to standard prompting without rationales (Wei et al., 2022b). However, this effect is only observed in extremely large language models (XLLMs) with +100b parameters (Wei et al., 2022b; Lampinen et al., 2022). At the same time access to XLLMs is limited in the research community due to costs and infrastructure required to fine-tune and inference them. In many cases these models are never released publicly.

In essence, supervision from rationales is a richer signal compared to supervision from only target labels, especially for multi-step reasoning tasks. However, only XLLMs have been shown to capture this signal in few-shot regimes. In this paper we assume large-scale rationale annotation to remain unavailable since it is tedious and arguably more expensive to generate than standard target label annotation. This leads to a currently unaddressed challenge of solving multi-step problems by smaller LMs than XLLMs in a few-shot regime.

This work deals with the complex task of Multi-hop Question Generation(MQG) where, given multiple passages and a pre-defined answer, the objective is to generate challenging questions that cannot be answered only from reading a single passage, this task requires many steps of reasoning to ac-

Proceedings of the 1st Workshop on Natural Language Reasoning and Structured Explanations (@ACL 2023), pages 59–77

complish and we further constrain ourselves to the case where supervision available is restricted to a few number of labelled examples.

Our contributions can be summarized as follows. We propose a new framework called Reasoning Circuits applicable specifically for the often encountered constraints faced in real-world where:
1. Large-scale annotation is not possible or available, only a limited number of examples of a multi-step reasoning problem are available.
2. Access limited to modest neural compute infrastructure that can support training models up to a maximum of 3 billion parameters.
3. Budget for rationale annotation is limited.

In this work we apply this framework to MQG task in a few-shot setting. This entails identifying reasoning steps human annotators employ to generate multi-hop questions and codifying them into a structured rationale annotation scheme, and manually producing rationale annotations for the few examples, capped at a maximum of around 200 examples. A generative model is then fine-tuned with a mixture of tasks where each "task" refers to a single smaller step of reasoning derived from the structured rationales designed for the MQG task. We report improvements over baselines where no rationale was employed on automatic evaluation metrics as well as human evaluation. We also show reduced gap in performance between our system only trained with approimately 150 examples(training and validation combined) and prior art that has been trained with 9,000 to 90,000 examples without rationales on automatic evaluation metrics.

2 Related Work

2.1 Multi-hop Question Generation

Several research studies focus on the task of single-hop question generation on datasets like SQuAD (Rajpurkar et al., 2016) for instance, Kim et al. (2019) propose ASs2s-a, a seq2seq model based on Long Short-term Memory (LSTM), which separately encodes answer and context.

There are studies about generating more difficult questions on knowledge graphs which includes Talmor and Berant (2018) and Kumar et al. (2019). However, these are not directly applicable to free-text since, it is not made up of entity relation triplets, as is the case with knowledge bases.

Proposed systems for MQG with free-text, SGGDQ-DP (Pan et al., 2020), MultiQG (Su et al., 2020), DFGN+QG (Yu et al., 2020b) and GATENLL+CT Sachan et al. (2020) rely on external tools like name entity recognition, entity linking and coreference resolution to construct knowledge graphs with which complex questions are generated with decoders. Closely related to our work Cheng et al. (2021) propose to control question difficulty, by progressively increasing question hops through step-by-step rewriting with GPT2-small(Radford et al., 2019) under the guidance of an extracted reasoning chain, generated also from external tools. QA4QG (Su et al., 2022) is current state-of-the art for MQG task, where attention patterns of a multi-hop question answering model guide a MQG model.

In the F+R+A system proposed by Xie et al. (2020) reinforcement rewards for fluency, relevance and particularly answerability - also generated by a separate QA model, are introduced in tandem with standard cross-entropy loss for MQG. In SemQG (Zhang and Bansal, 2019) two semantics-enhanced rewards are proposed to regularize a question generation model. ADDQG (Wang et al., 2020) treats semantic and syntactic metrics as reinforcement rewards for MQG task.

All systems cited until now utilise large scale supervision of 90k training examples from HotpotQA dataset (Yang et al., 2018) with the exception of Cheng et al. (2021) at 57k. LowResourceQG system (Yu et al., 2020a) learns the structural patterns from unlabeled questions and transfers this to a MQG model, it is train with 9,000 examples from HotpotQA dataset.

2.2 Few-shot Rationale Generation

XLLMs can learn to generate valid rationales for multi-step problems with few-shot in-context learning examples (Wei et al., 2022b; Lampinen et al., 2022), smaller models on the other hand, need to be trained on more rationale annotation to achieve strong performance. To reduce the dependence on tedious rationale annotations a hybrid self-learning approach with smaller 6B parameter LMs has been proposed by Zelikman et al. (2022) that uses fewer rationale annotations, however even this method requires a lot of manually annotated data. Since the generated silver rationales are noisy, to filter and improve these rationales large-scale standard input-target annotation is required. The ground truth references are used as a proxy to check and filter out generated silver rationales, by comparing the references to the predicted target text, produced along with the rationales. Ground truth references also are used to provide hints to the model when it fails to generate the correct answer. Filtered silver rationales thus accumulated are then used for iterative self-training until performance plateaus.

3 Structured Rationales for Multi-hop Question Generation

HotpotQA dataset (Yang et al., 2018) is one of the most widely used benchmarks of multi-hop question answering and consists of broadly two types of questions: bridge-entity questions and comparison questions. In bridge-entity questions, which constitute 75% of the dataset, annotators get pairs of passages where at least one entity (called the bridge entity) is present in both passages. In comparison questions, annotators are provided a pair of passages about entities drawn from a similar theme such as musicians, authors, films, plants among several categories. A comparison question typically compares some quality of the central entities in the two passages. Question types found in this dataset cover 5 out of 6 total sub-types of multi-hop questions as identified in recent survey on multi-hop question answering and generation (Mavi et al., 2022) originally identified in Min et al. (2019) with the only exception of commonsense reasoning.

Below, we identified the reasoning steps that annotators needed to follow in order to create the questions of each type.

3.1 Bridge Entity Questions

Figure 1 shows examples of reasoning steps for bridge-type multi-hop questions. Given two passages and a pre-defined answer to the question to be generated, an annotator would need to:

(1) Select the bridge entity b, an entity present in both passages. If the answer is present in both passages, bridge entity is set to the answer.
(2) From each passage (p_1 and p_2), extract one statement (s_1 and s_2) about the bridge entity which connects the answer to the bridge entity, if the passage contains the answer.
(3) Combine the two statements (s_1 and s_2) into a single combined statement c.
(4) Substitute bridge entity b in combined statement c with a common noun to get $c - b$. For example, replace "the Beatles" with "a band".
(5) Substitute the answer a in $c-b$ with a common noun preceded by "certain" or "some" to get $c - b - a$. For example, the answer entity "5th March 1992" is replaced by "certain date" or "someday" and the answer "George Orwell" is replaced by "certain person" or "someone".
(6) Convert the statement from the previous step into a question, such that the answer to it is the provided answer span.

Step 4 is skipped if bridge and answer are the same.

3.2 Comparison Questions

Figure 2 shows two examples of this type. For this question type, given two passages and a pre-defined answer, an annotator would need to:

(1) Extract two statements(s_1 and s_2), one from each passage, such that a comparison can be drawn between the two statements, keeping the answer in mind.
(2) The two statements are combined into a single statement(c), highlight the nature of similarity or difference between information from the two paragraphs, keeping the answer in mind.
(3) Generate a comparative question(q_c) from reading the combined statement and answer.

4 Rationale Steps as a Mixture of Tasks

The step-by-step nature and clearly defined structure of the rationales identified above motivated us to formulate this multi-step problem into a mixture of tasks. A step of reasoning is treated as a task, only the information required to perform the reasoning step is treated as the input and the result of the reasoning step is the expected output.

We formalise bridge multi-hop question generation into nine separate smaller steps of reasoning and we identify 3 steps of reasoning for generating comparison multi-hop questions. Additionally, a reasoning step should identify whether a given pair of passages and answer are more suitable to generate a bridge question from or a comparison question instead. For this purpose we create the first task of predicting the question type.

These reasoning steps or tasks can be categorized into: 1. Control tasks where the outcome is a control variable whose value decides what reasoning path to follow and 2. Generative tasks which essentially generate free-form text to be treated as input for later reasoning steps or as the final output. We describe each of these tasks below.

Bridge Type 1 Example
Passage 1: Romy Ruyssen is a French mixed martial artist. She ... and headlined the first Invicta Fighting Championships event against Marloes Coenen ...
Passage 2: Marloes Coenen ... is a retired Dutch mixed martial artist. ...
Answer: Invicta Fighting Championships

Bridge entity: Marloes Coenen
Answer entity same as bridge entity: No
Statement extracted from Passage 1: Romy Ruyssen headlined the Invicta Fighting Championships event against Marloes Coenen.
Statement extracted from Passage 2: Marloes Coenen is a Dutch mixed martial artist.
Combined statement: Romy Ruyssen headlined the Invicta Fighting Championships event against Marloes Coenen who is a Dutch mixed martial artist.
Contract bridge entity from combined statement: Romy Ruyssen headlined the Invicta Fighting Championships event against a Dutch mixed martial artist.
Contract answer entity from previous statement: Romy Ruyssen headlined a certain event against a Dutch mixed martial artist.
Multi-hop Question: Romy Ruyssen headlined which event against a Dutch mixed martial artist?

Bridge Type 2 Example
Passage 1: ... The Kennedy Compound consists of three houses on six acres ... on Cape Cod ...
Passage 2: Hyannisport Club: ... The course is located adjacent to the Kennedy Compound and the Kennedy family have long been members of the club. ...
Answer: Kennedy Compound

Bridge entity: Kennedy Compound
Answer entity same as bridge entity: Yes
Statement extracted from Passage 1: The Kennedy Compound consists of three houses on six acres on Cape Cod.
Statement extracted from Passage 2: Hyannisport Club is located adjacent to the Kennedy Compound.
Combined statement: Hyannisport Club is located adjacent to the Kennedy Compound that consists of three houses on six acres and on Cape Cod.
Contract answer from combined statement: Hyannisport Club is located adjacent to a certain property that consists of three houses on six acres and on Cape Cod.
Multi-hop Question: Hyannisport Club is located adjacent to which property that consists of three houses on six acres and on Cape Cod?

Figure 1: Two examples of bridge rationales that lead to the creation of multi-hop question. Example 1 shows rationale annotation when answer span is not found in both passages. Example 2 shows another of example of rationale annotation when the answer is present in both passages, so that the Step 4 is skipped. The highlights in green and yellow show the answer and bridge entities, in the second example they are the same. In the penultimate steps, the lighter highlights indicate the substitution of bridge and answer entities with a common noun preceded by "certain". In the last step typically a Wh- word substitutes "certain" or "some" words, however more radical transformations also take place in our annotations.

Comparison Example 1
Passage 1: Black Francis ... is an American singer, songwriter and guitarist.
Passage 2: Alex Band is an American musician and singer-songwriter ...
Answer: singer-songwriter

Statement from Passage 1: Black Francis is a singer, songwriter.
Statement from Passage 2: Alex Band is a singer-songwriter.
Combined statement: Black Francis and Alex Band are both singer-songwriters.
Multi-hop Question: What is common between Black Francis and Alex Band?

Comparison Example 2
Passage 1: Ettelaat-e Banuvan ... was the first women's magazine published in Tehran.
Passage 2: Playgirl is an American magazine ...
Answer: Ettelaat-e Banuvan

Statement from Passage 1: Ettelaat-e Banuvan was the first women's magazine published in Tehran.
Statement from Passage 2: Playgirl is an American magazine.
Combined statement: Ettelaat-e Banuvan was the first women's magazine published in Tehran and Playgirl is an American magazine.
Multi-hop Question: What was the first women's magazine published in Tehran, Ettelaat-e Banuvan or Playgirl?

Figure 2: Two examples of comparison multi-hop question. In Example 1 similar attributes of the central figures in the two passages have been highlighted, later this is turned into a similarity multi-hop question. In Example 2 difference between the two magazines is used as a basis to create a multi-hop question.

4.1 Question Type Task

Task 1 is a control task that decides the question type. Given input passages $p1, p2$ and the answer a, this task assigns the control variable q_{type} either the value $bridge$, $comparison$ or $confused$. The values $bridge$, $comparison$ are assigned if the model literally generates the tokens "bridge" and "comparison" which lead the current input example to only follow either the bridge or the comparison tasks trajectories. In case the model gets confused and fails to generate "bridge" or "comparison" as its output during test time we assign q_{type} the value $confused$ which leads to both bridge and comparison task trajectories to be followed and two questions one of each type are generated.

4.2 Bridge Rationale Steps

Task 2 generates the bridge entity b provided input passages p_1, p_2 and the answer a.

Task 3 is a control task that identifies whether the answer span(a) is present in the provided passage(p_i) or not and assigns the boolean value of $True$ or $False$ to the variables $in^a_{p_i}$ for i in $\{1, 2\}$ depending on whether whether the model generates the token "present" or "absent".

Task 4 is a control task that identifies whether the answer span(a) is the same as the bridge entity (b) or not and assigns a value of either $True$ or $False$ to the variable $same^a_b$.

Task 5 generates a statement s_i which connects the bridge entity b to the answer entity a from the passage p_i. This task is only run on a passage that contains the answer entity or $in^a_{p_i} = True$ unless the answer entity is the same as the bridge entity and present in both passages in which case this task is not run on either of the passages.

Task 6 generates a statement s_i about bridge entity (b) from the passage p_i. Inputs include the ith input passage p_i and the bridge entity b. When the $same^a_b = True$, Task 6 is run on both p_1 and p_2 to get s_1 and s_2. Otherwise it is only run on the passage p_i where $in^a_{p_i} = False$

Task 7 generates a single combined statement c from statements s_1 and s_2. Inputs to this step include the answer a the bridge entity b and the generated statements s_1 and s_2 from prior steps.
Task 8 This task contracts the bridge entity from the combined sentence c and substitutes it with a common noun to get $c - b$. It is a generative task and inputs to this step include combined statement (c), the answer (a) and the bridge entity (b).
Task 9 contracts the answer entity in the sentence $c - b$ and substitutes it with a indefinite determiner followed by a common noun to get $c - b - a$. It is a generative task and inputs to this step include combined statement with bridge contracted $(c - b)$, the answer (a) and the bridge entity (b).
Task 10 transforms the combined statement with both the answer and bridge contracted $(c - b - a)$ into a multi-hop question q_b enquiring about the noun which is preceded by "certain" or the someword. It is the final reasoning step in the bridge type rationales and is a generative task. Inputs to this step include $c - b - a$, $c - b$ and a.

4.3 Comparison Rationale Tasks

Task 11 simultaneously generates both statements s_1 and s_2 which deliberate over a similar or dissimilar quality about the key entities in passages p_1 and p_2 respectively. Input includes passages p_1, p_2 and the answer a. The reason for concurrently producing both s_1 and s_2 is to maintain the same decoder state while producing both s_1 and s_2.
Task 12 generates a single combined statement c, a conjunction of the two statements s_1, s_2 emphasis is on comparison between the two. It is a generative task, and serves as the second reasoning step in comparison rationales. Inputs to this step include the generated statements s_1, s_2 and answer a.
Task 13 transforms the combined statement c into a comparitive question q_c. It serves as the third and final reasoning step in comparison rationales. Inputs to this step include the combined statement c and the answer a as inputs.

4.4 Rationale Annotation

We annotate a small number of examples from Hotpot-QA dataset which adhere to the step-by-step rationale scheme described in the previous two sub-sections. In recent work on few-shot learning (Gao et al., 2021), it has been shown that access to a large development set under a few-shot supervision regime creates an unrealistic few-shot setting. To mimic a realistic few-shot setup we pick the development set to be either smaller than or of the same size as of the training set. In total we annotate 98 bridge and 50 comparison type questions from the training set of Hotpot-QA and 32 bridge and 24 comparison type questions from the validation set.

4.5 Reasoning Circuit for Multi-hop Question Generation

The tasks described above are arranged as shown in Figure 3. It is an acyclic graph where information flows from left to right, with generative or control tasks being performed at each node. At the left entry point, the system gets two passages and a predefined answer as input, and after being processed through all the reasoning steps, multi-hop questions are produced at the other end. Initially, the question type q_{type} is determined from passing the inputs through the Task 1 prompt. After this step, if the question type is determined to be comparison, then Tasks 11, 12 and 13 are run sequentially to generate a comparison multi-hop question. Otherwise, if the question type is bridge, then Tasks 2 through 10 are run to generate a bridge multi-hop question.

Our proposed few-shot mixture of reasoning tasks framework is implemented by finetuning a pretrained bi-directional encoder-decoder masked language model (MLMs), instead of the auto-regressive decoder-only language models such as GPT-2 (Radford et al., 2019) and LaMDA (Thoppilan et al., 2022) since MLMs are known to be superior for question answering tasks, and have greatly improved parameter efficiency compared to auto-regressive language models (Sanh et al., 2022; Wei et al., 2022a) when trained on mixture of tasks. We use the standard encoder-decoder objective of maximizing the log likelihood of text in the ground truth target. For creating input and output prompts, we closely follow the templates proposed by Chada and Natarajan (2021) where prompts are aligned to the format used during the MLM pretraining.

We know that multi-hop reasoning is a complex natural language task and to build performant systems for this task, prior art infused many basic language skills such as named entity recognition and co-reference resolution into their systems, in the form of external tools as noted in related work section. Also, recent findings show that first finetuning models with intermediate tasks like question answering and natural language inference before further finetuning (Vu et al., 2020) them on few-shot examples of target task improves few-shot per-

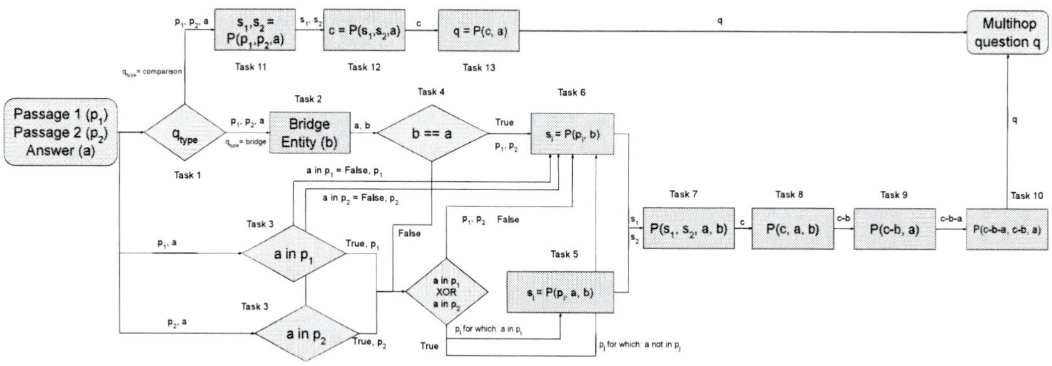

Figure 3: Reasoning Circuits: This flowchart depicts the connections between different reasoning steps/tasks. Control tasks are marked as yellow decision nodes while the generative tasks are marked by blue process nodes. Edge labels denote the significant inputs that flow from one task to next as well as the value of the control signal at the root of the edge that enables this edge flow data flow to be enabled. Note that a single LM is fine-tuned on a mixture of all these reasoning steps and is responsible for serving all the tasks nodes in this flowchart. The edges represent sequentiality and the post-processing flow of information between the different tasks. A node cannot be run unless all the nodes to it's left, connected to it either directly or indirectly, have been run. For instance, Task 13 can only run when Task 1, 11 and 12 have been run.

formance on the target task by priming the model with basic language understanding skills. For these reasons, we choose to implement our framework with the T5 transformer(Raffel et al., 2020) that has already been pretrained on a variety of downstream tasks in addition to unlabelled text.

5 Experiments

We conduct all our experiments on T5-3b v1.0 model with 3 billion parameters[1]. As a baseline, we consider tuning the same T5-3b model to directly generate multi-hop questions, without any rationale input and provided with only the two passages and answer as input. For the baseline we use a simple prompt in Appendix A. For the reasoning circuit experiment we utilise rationale prompts described in Appendix A to generate a mixture of task examples from our few-shot annotation. We use a learning rate of 2e-5 with no warm-up and keep constant learning rate throughout. We train for 35 epochs or 5000 steps whichever is higher.

For fair comparison, we follow the data splits similar to SGGDQ-DP (Pan et al., 2020), QA4QG (Su et al., 2022) and SGGDQ-DP (Wang et al., 2020) to get 90,440 training examples and 6,072 test examples respectively, note however that instead of using the entire test set as validation set as done in prior work we only validate with same or lower number of examples as that used for training, see section 4.4 for details. We use two settings as input to the encoder: 1. The original training data in HotpotQA, in which each question is paired with two long documents, and 2. a pre-processed version of the data where only supporting sentences required to answer the gold question are kept. We conduct experiments with 8, 16, 32, 64, 128 training examples where 75% of the examples are drawn from the bridge-type while the remaining 25% examples are of the comparison type, this is done to mimic the distribution of question types in the original HotpotQA dataset. The number of validation examples is equal to the number of training examples until the 32-shot experiment. After this the number of validation examples gets capped at 32 bridge type questions and 24 comparison type questions. We also conduct an experiment with 148 training examples that constitute all collected annotations. We tune on the average of BLEU1, BLEU2, BLEU3 and BLEU4 (Papineni et al., 2002), METEOR (Lavie and Agarwal, 2007), and ROUGE-L(Lin, 2004) scores on our few-shot validation sets.

6 Results and Analysis

6.1 Automatic Evaluation

The automatic evaluation metrics used are BLEU1, BLEU2, BLEU3, BLEU4, METEOR, and ROUGE-L, which measure similarity between generations and the target reference questions.

We report the resuls in Table 1. Reasoning Cir-

[1]https://github.com/google-research/text-to-text-transfer-transformer

Models	# Training	# Validation	BLEU-1	BLEU-2	BLEU-3	BLEU-4	METEOR	ROUGE-L
Encoder Input: Supporting Fact Sentences								
ASs2s-a* (Kim et al., 2019)	90,440	6,072	37.67	23.79	17.21	12.59	17.45	33.21
SemQG* (Zhang and Bansal, 2019)	90,440	6,072	39.92	26.73	18.73	14.71	19.29	35.63
F+R+A (Xie et al., 2020)	90,440	6,072	37.97	-	-	15.41	19.61	35.12
SGGDQ-DP (Pan et al., 2020)	90,440	6,072	40.55	27.21	20.13	15.53	20.15	36.94
ADDQG (Wang et al., 2020)	90,440	6,072	44.34	31.32	22.68	17.54	20.56	38.09
QA4QG-Large (Su et al., 2022)	90,440	6,072	49.55	37.91	30.79	25.70	27.44	46.48
Cheng et al. (2021)	57,397	6,072	-	-	21.07	15.26	19.99	-
Finetuning	8	8	24.40	13.76	7.49	4.50	17.18	24.63
Reasoning Circuits	8	8	20.19	10.85	5.93	3.65	15.53	21.45
Finetuning	16	16	24.47	14.37	8.39	5.33	17.93	25.21
Reasoning Circuits	16	16	22.64	12.83	7.31	4.53	17.64	22.82
Finetuning	32	32	28.27	17.63	10.84	7.03	21.00	27.77
Reasoning Circuits	32	32	26.09	15.93	9.56	6.11	20.39	25.67
Finetuning	64	48	28.74	18.19	11.44	7.59	21.78	28.20
Reasoning Circuits	64	48	**29.60**	**18.62**	**11.66**	**7.62**	**22.35**	**28.32**
Finetuning	128	56	31.42	20.53	13.34	8.94	24.02	30.62
Reasoning Circuits	128	56	**32.77**	**21.58**	**14.08**	**9.50**	**25.51**	**31.33**
Encoder Input: Full Document Context								
MultiQG (Su et al., 2020)	90,440	6,072	40.15	26.71	19.73	15.2	20.51	35.30
GATENLL+CT (Sachan et al., 2020)	90,440	6,072	-	-	-	20.02	22.40	39.49
LowResourceQG (Yu et al., 2020a)	9,000	6,072	-	-	-	19.07	19.16	39.41
QA4QG-Base* (Su et al., 2022)	90,440	6,072	43.72	31.54	24.47	19.68	24.55	40.44
QA4QG-Large* (Su et al., 2022)	90,440	6,072	46.45	33.83	26.35	21.21	25.53	42.44
Finetuning	8	8	24.17	13.46	7.38	4.46	16.79	24.71
Reasoning Circuits	8	8	17.76	8.91	4.56	2.66	13.81	19.74
Finetuning	16	16	25.61	15.04	8.76	5.47	18.74	25.18
Reasoning Circuits	16	16	21.77	12.00	6.72	4.12	16.84	22.01
Finetuning	32	32	27.04	16.75	10.23	6.64	20.31	26.39
Reasoning Circuits	32	32	25.29	14.94	8.69	5.55	19.46	24.62
Finetuning	64	48	28.06	17.52	10.89	7.14	21.11	27.42
Reasoning Circuits	64	48	27.92	16.92	10.21	6.51	21.01	26.90
Finetuning	128	56	28.31	18.05	11.41	7.60	22.65	28.18
Reasoning Circuits	128	56	**30.67**	**19.58**	**12.42**	**8.25**	**23.86**	**29.33**

Table 1: Evaluation results on automatic evaluation metrics for few-shot Reasoning Circuits and fine-tuning baseline experiments with different encoder input settings are reported. We mark in bold where reasoning circuits perform better than our baseline. We also show performance of previous MQG methods on the HotpotQA dataset. Note that most of prior work trained on the entire 90K examples in the HotpotQA dataset with the exception of LowResourceQG (Yu et al., 2020a) trained on 9K and Cheng et al. (2021) trained on 57K examples. * Results as reported by Su et al. (2022).

Model	Multi-hop		Well formed			Answerable		Answer Matching	
	Yes	No	Yes	Acceptable	No	Yes	No	Yes	No
Baseline	45%	55%	**89%**	2%	**9%**	87%	13%	75%	25%
Reasoning Circuits	**66%**	**34%**	81%	**4%**	15%	**89%**	11%	**79%**	**21%**

Table 2: Human evaluation results, bold marks better score, for 'Yes' and 'Acceptable' higher and for 'No' lower percentages are better.

cuits perform better than the baseline for 64- and 128-shot when entire passages are input to the encoder as well as for 128-shot when only supporting sentences are input to the encoder.

We note a substantially reduced performance gap in the METEOR score between prior state-of-the art models trained with 90k training examples and results of our best few-shot experiments. The METEOR metric has certain synonymy matching and stemming modules, in addition to standard exact word matching which not found in other metrics. From this we infer that reference and generated questions may not exactly match each other however could be closer paraphrases of each other.

Though the performances of baseline and Reasoning Circuits are quite close in terms of automatic metrics, we observe (See models generations in B) through manual inspection that the questions generated by Reasoning Circuits lead to more multi-hop questions being generated whereas baseline generations tend to be single-hop questions instead. Through automatic evaluation these advantages are not reflected.

6.2 Human Evaluation

We follow similar human evaluation criteria as Cheng et al. (2021), wherein we randomly sample 150 questions from our 128-shot baseline and Reasoning Circuits experiments of the kind where the input to encoder is only supporting sentences. These examples are manually evaluated by a human annotator across the following four dimensions:

Multi-hop: To check whether a question can be answered from only reading a single passage or both. The annotation is yes if both passages have to be read or no if reading only a single passage answers the question.

Well-formed: To check whether a question is semantically correct, annotator is asked to mark a question as either yes, acceptable or no. Acceptable is selected if the question is not grammatically correct, but its meaning is still intelligible.

Answerable: It checks whether a question is answerable according to the given context. The annotation is either yes or no.

Answer Matching: It checks whether the given answer is the correct answer to the question. The annotation is either yes or no.

Table 2 report results from human evaluation. Our proposed approach generated +22% more multi-hop questions than the baseline which fares poorly on this critical measure. The pre-defined answer is found to be the correct answer to the questions generated with our slightly higher chance than the baseline. However, our approach leads to slightly less well formed generations than the baseline model, typically this stems from our approach failing to find the right common noun. In terms of answerability both approaches score evenly.

7 Discussion and Future Work

Through automatic and human evaluations we show that larger language models generate similar questions to reference questions with orders of magnitude less labelled data. The proposed approach also is found to generate a much higher percentages of multi-hop questions than the baseline.

One avenue of future work is in the area of self-training. Self-training, involves generating predictions from a weaker model on unlabelled data and using these predictions as additional training data, where the training set now includes the silver predictions on unlabelled data. Self-training may be detrimental for or not improve overall model performance strongly especially when the task is hard for the weaker model (Vu et al., 2020, 2021). Since prediction errors of the weaker model in the silver annotations further reinforce wrong predictions during self-training. In Reasoning Circuits, silver predictions on unlabelled data for many steps of reasoning can be approximately validated with simple heuristics. For instance, predictions from Task 9 can be verified by checking whether they still contains the answer and bridge spans or not, if they do then these predictions can be deemed unfit for self-training. Filtering prediction errors from the initial trained weaker model on unlabeled data should lead to stronger improvements from self-training compared to vanilla self-training.

8 Conclusion

In this paper, we propose Reasoning Circuits, a new framework suited to real-world scenarios where the NLP task at hand requires multiple steps of structured reasoning, with only a limited number of available labelled examples, and a small annotation budget, also only a modest deep learning computational infrastructure/budget is accessible. In this work, we apply this framework to the task of few-shot multi-hop question generation which fits all these criteria. We identify structured multi-step rationales that break down this problem into many discrete reasoning steps. Each step in these rationales is treated as a single "task" within a mixture of similar "tasks". The individual tasks can be categorized into control tasks, which control the flow of information between tasks, and generative tasks, that generate free-form text for successive tasks in the Reasoning Circuit. The framework is relatively easy to implement, since only a single generative model is fine-tuned with a mixture of all reasoning steps; at inference time, the same model can generate all reasoning steps sequentially. We show that fine-tuning with only around 64 to 128 labelled rationale examples with our approach is enough to improve automatic evaluation metrics compared to a baseline trained without rationales on the HotpotQA dataset. More importantly, with human evaluation, we find that this framework can strongly improve the central objective of multi-hop QG, to generate challenging questions which cannot be answered from reading only a single passage.

9 Limitations

The proposed Reasoning Circuits framework intends to replace the need for thousands of annotated examples with a strong inductive bias of structured rationales. There is two issues with this approach at a conceptual level:
1. It may not always be possible to break down a multi-step reasoning problem cleanly into discrete reasoning steps, and another related issue it increasing complexity of the circuit with the complexity of the task.
2. For the design of these reasoning circuits a researcher must develop a thorough understanding of this reasoning task, so that the final circuit design broadly covers all possible types of reasoning problems expected to be solved. An under- or ill-designed reasoning circuit may cause the system to either not support a certain portion of problems or produce non-sensical outputs.

Essentially, there is trade off between a tighter control over reasoning by investing in a deep understanding of the problem leading to a comprehensive reasoning circuit design and lower annotations budget, versus, less control over logic and depending on a large number of annotations which allow the model to discover this logic on its own at much higher cost of large scale annotations budget.

At the implementation and operations level one of the the key limitations our proposed system is the number of inference steps to solve the problem. The number of times model inference may be needed to solve a single example is equal the length of the longest task sequence chain in the reasoning circuit. One possible solution for this could be by training the model to solve the entire problem by generating all the steps of reasoning and the target string in a single inference step and could massively reduce inference time and costs.

References

Shourya Aggarwal, Divyanshu Mandowara, Vishwajeet Agrawal, Dinesh Khandelwal, Parag Singla, and Dinesh Garg. 2021. Explanations for CommonsenseQA: New Dataset and Models. In *Proceedings of the 59th Annual Meeting of the Association for Computational Linguistics and the 11th International Joint Conference on Natural Language Processing (Volume 1: Long Papers)*, pages 3050–3065, Online. Association for Computational Linguistics.

Oana-Maria Camburu, Tim Rocktäschel, Thomas Lukasiewicz, and Phil Blunsom. 2018. e-snli: Natural language inference with natural language explanations. In *Advances in Neural Information Processing Systems*, volume 31. Curran Associates, Inc.

Rakesh Chada and Pradeep Natarajan. 2021. FewshotQA: A simple framework for few-shot learning of question answering tasks using pre-trained text-to-text models. In *Proceedings of the 2021 Conference on Empirical Methods in Natural Language Processing*, pages 6081–6090, Online and Punta Cana, Dominican Republic. Association for Computational Linguistics.

Yi Cheng, Siyao Li, Bang Liu, Ruihui Zhao, Sujian Li, Chenghua Lin, and Yefeng Zheng. 2021. Guiding the growth: Difficulty-controllable question generation through step-by-step rewriting. In *Proceedings of the 59th Annual Meeting of the Association for Computational Linguistics and the 11th International Joint Conference on Natural Language Processing (Volume 1: Long Papers)*, pages 5968–5978, Online. Association for Computational Linguistics.

Tianyu Gao, Adam Fisch, and Danqi Chen. 2021. Making pre-trained language models better few-shot learners. In *Proceedings of the 59th Annual Meeting of the Association for Computational Linguistics and the 11th International Joint Conference on Natural Language Processing (Volume 1: Long Papers)*, pages 3816–3830, Online. Association for Computational Linguistics.

Mor Geva, Daniel Khashabi, Elad Segal, Tushar Khot, Dan Roth, and Jonathan Berant. 2021. Did aristotle use a laptop? a question answering benchmark with implicit reasoning strategies. *Transactions of the Association for Computational Linguistics*, 9:346–361.

Naoya Inoue, Pontus Stenetorp, and Kentaro Inui. 2020. R4C: A benchmark for evaluating RC systems to get the right answer for the right reason. In *Proceedings of the 58th Annual Meeting of the Association for Computational Linguistics*, pages 6740–6750, Online. Association for Computational Linguistics.

Peter Jansen, Elizabeth Wainwright, Steven Marmorstein, and Clayton Morrison. 2018. WorldTree: A corpus of explanation graphs for elementary science questions supporting multi-hop inference. In *Proceedings of the Eleventh International Conference on Language Resources and Evaluation (LREC 2018)*, Miyazaki, Japan. European Language Resources Association (ELRA).

Yanghoon Kim, Hwanhee Lee, Joongbo Shin, and Kyomin Jung. 2019. Improving neural question generation using answer separation. In *Proceedings of the AAAI conference on artificial intelligence*, volume 33, pages 6602–6609.

Vishwajeet Kumar, Yuncheng Hua, Ganesh Ramakrishnan, Guilin Qi, Lianli Gao, and Yuan-Fang Li. 2019. Difficulty-controllable multi-hop question generation from knowledge graphs. In *The Semantic*

Web – ISWC 2019, pages 382–398, Cham. Springer International Publishing.

Andrew K. Lampinen, Ishita Dasgupta, Stephanie C. Y. Chan, Kory Matthewson, Michael Henry Tessler, Antonia Creswell, James L. McClelland, Jane X. Wang, and Felix Hill. 2022. Can language models learn from explanations in context?

Alon Lavie and Abhaya Agarwal. 2007. METEOR: An automatic metric for MT evaluation with high levels of correlation with human judgments. In *Proceedings of the Second Workshop on Statistical Machine Translation*, pages 228–231, Prague, Czech Republic. Association for Computational Linguistics.

Chin-Yew Lin. 2004. ROUGE: A package for automatic evaluation of summaries. In *Text Summarization Branches Out*, pages 74–81, Barcelona, Spain. Association for Computational Linguistics.

Vaibhav Mavi, Anubhav Jangra, and Adam Jatowt. 2022. A survey on multi-hop question answering and generation.

Sewon Min, Victor Zhong, Luke Zettlemoyer, and Hannaneh Hajishirzi. 2019. Multi-hop reading comprehension through question decomposition and rescoring. In *Proceedings of the 57th Annual Meeting of the Association for Computational Linguistics*, pages 6097–6109, Florence, Italy. Association for Computational Linguistics.

Liangming Pan, Yuxi Xie, Yansong Feng, Tat-Seng Chua, and Min-Yen Kan. 2020. Semantic graphs for generating deep questions. In *Proceedings of the 58th Annual Meeting of the Association for Computational Linguistics*, pages 1463–1475, Online. Association for Computational Linguistics.

Kishore Papineni, Salim Roukos, Todd Ward, and Wei-Jing Zhu. 2002. Bleu: a method for automatic evaluation of machine translation. In *Proceedings of the 40th Annual Meeting of the Association for Computational Linguistics*, pages 311–318, Philadelphia, Pennsylvania, USA. Association for Computational Linguistics.

Alec Radford, Jeff Wu, Rewon Child, David Luan, Dario Amodei, and Ilya Sutskever. 2019. Language models are unsupervised multitask learners.

Colin Raffel, Noam Shazeer, Adam Roberts, Katherine Lee, Sharan Narang, Michael Matena, Yanqi Zhou, Wei Li, and Peter J. Liu. 2020. Exploring the limits of transfer learning with a unified text-to-text transformer. *Journal of Machine Learning Research*, 21(140):1–67.

Pranav Rajpurkar, Jian Zhang, Konstantin Lopyrev, and Percy Liang. 2016. SQuAD: 100,000+ questions for machine comprehension of text. In *Proceedings of the 2016 Conference on Empirical Methods in Natural Language Processing*, pages 2383–2392, Austin, Texas. Association for Computational Linguistics.

Devendra Singh Sachan, Lingfei Wu, Mrinmaya Sachan, and William L. Hamilton. 2020. Stronger transformers for neural multi-hop question generation. *CoRR*, abs/2010.11374.

Victor Sanh, Albert Webson, Colin Raffel, Stephen Bach, Lintang Sutawika, Zaid Alyafeai, Antoine Chaffin, Arnaud Stiegler, Arun Raja, Manan Dey, M Saiful Bari, Canwen Xu, Urmish Thakker, Shanya Sharma Sharma, Eliza Szczechla, Taewoon Kim, Gunjan Chhablani, Nihal Nayak, Debajyoti Datta, Jonathan Chang, Mike Tian-Jian Jiang, Han Wang, Matteo Manica, Sheng Shen, Zheng Xin Yong, Harshit Pandey, Rachel Bawden, Thomas Wang, Trishala Neeraj, Jos Rozen, Abheesht Sharma, Andrea Santilli, Thibault Fevry, Jason Alan Fries, Ryan Teehan, Teven Le Scao, Stella Biderman, Leo Gao, Thomas Wolf, and Alexander M Rush. 2022. Multitask prompted training enables zero-shot task generalization. In *International Conference on Learning Representations*.

Dan Su, Peng Xu, and Pascale Fung. 2022. Qa4qg: Using question answering to constrain multi-hop question generation. In *ICASSP 2022 - 2022 IEEE International Conference on Acoustics, Speech and Signal Processing (ICASSP)*, pages 8232–8236.

Dan Su, Yan Xu, Wenliang Dai, Ziwei Ji, Tiezheng Yu, and Pascale Fung. 2020. Multi-hop question generation with graph convolutional network. In *Findings of the Association for Computational Linguistics: EMNLP 2020*, pages 4636–4647, Online. Association for Computational Linguistics.

Alon Talmor and Jonathan Berant. 2018. The web as a knowledge-base for answering complex questions. In *Proceedings of the 2018 Conference of the North American Chapter of the Association for Computational Linguistics: Human Language Technologies, Volume 1 (Long Papers)*, pages 641–651, New Orleans, Louisiana. Association for Computational Linguistics.

Romal Thoppilan, Daniel De Freitas, Jamie Hall, Noam Shazeer, Apoorv Kulshreshtha, Heng-Tze Cheng, Alicia Jin, Taylor Bos, Leslie Baker, Yu Du, YaGuang Li, Hongrae Lee, Huaixiu Steven Zheng, Amin Ghafouri, Marcelo Menegali, Yanping Huang, Maxim Krikun, Dmitry Lepikhin, James Qin, Dehao Chen, Yuanzhong Xu, Zhifeng Chen, Adam Roberts, Maarten Bosma, Vincent Zhao, Yanqi Zhou, Chung-Ching Chang, Igor Krivokon, Will Rusch, Marc Pickett, Pranesh Srinivasan, Laichee Man, Kathleen Meier-Hellstern, Meredith Ringel Morris, Tulsee Doshi, Renelito Delos Santos, Toju Duke, Johnny Soraker, Ben Zevenbergen, Vinodkumar Prabhakaran, Mark Diaz, Ben Hutchinson, Kristen Olson, Alejandra Molina, Erin Hoffman-John, Josh Lee, Lora Aroyo, Ravi Rajakumar, Alena Butryna, Matthew Lamm, Viktoriya Kuzmina, Joe Fenton, Aaron Cohen, Rachel Bernstein, Ray Kurzweil, Blaise Aguera-Arcas, Claire Cui, Marian Croak, Ed Chi, and Quoc Le. 2022. Lamda: Language models for dialog applications.

Tu Vu, Minh-Thang Luong, Quoc Le, Grady Simon, and Mohit Iyyer. 2021. STraTA: Self-training with task augmentation for better few-shot learning. In *Proceedings of the 2021 Conference on Empirical Methods in Natural Language Processing*, pages 5715–5731, Online and Punta Cana, Dominican Republic. Association for Computational Linguistics.

Tu Vu, Tong Wang, Tsendsuren Munkhdalai, Alessandro Sordoni, Adam Trischler, Andrew Mattarella-Micke, Subhransu Maji, and Mohit Iyyer. 2020. Exploring and predicting transferability across NLP tasks. In *Proceedings of the 2020 Conference on Empirical Methods in Natural Language Processing (EMNLP)*, pages 7882–7926, Online. Association for Computational Linguistics.

Liuyin Wang, Zihan Xu, Zibo Lin, Haitao Zheng, and Ying Shen. 2020. Answer-driven deep question generation based on reinforcement learning. In *Proceedings of the 28th International Conference on Computational Linguistics*, pages 5159–5170, Barcelona, Spain (Online). International Committee on Computational Linguistics.

Jason Wei, Maarten Bosma, Vincent Zhao, Kelvin Guu, Adams Wei Yu, Brian Lester, Nan Du, Andrew M. Dai, and Quoc V Le. 2022a. Finetuned language models are zero-shot learners. In *International Conference on Learning Representations*.

Jason Wei, Xuezhi Wang, Dale Schuurmans, Maarten Bosma, Ed H. Chi, Quoc Le, and Denny Zhou. 2022b. Chain of thought prompting elicits reasoning in large language models. *CoRR*, abs/2201.11903.

Sarah Wiegreffe and Ana Marasovic. 2021. Teach me to explain: A review of datasets for explainable NLP. *CoRR*, abs/2102.12060.

Yuxi Xie, Liangming Pan, Dongzhe Wang, Min-Yen Kan, and Yansong Feng. 2020. Exploring question-specific rewards for generating deep questions. In *Proceedings of the 28th International Conference on Computational Linguistics*, pages 2534–2546, Barcelona, Spain (Online). International Committee on Computational Linguistics.

Zhilin Yang, Peng Qi, Saizheng Zhang, Yoshua Bengio, William Cohen, Ruslan Salakhutdinov, and Christopher D. Manning. 2018. HotpotQA: A dataset for diverse, explainable multi-hop question answering. In *Proceedings of the 2018 Conference on Empirical Methods in Natural Language Processing*, pages 2369–2380, Brussels, Belgium. Association for Computational Linguistics.

Jianxing Yu, Wei Liu, Shuang Qiu, Qinliang Su, Kai Wang, Xiaojun Quan, and Jian Yin. 2020a. Low-resource generation of multi-hop reasoning questions. In *Proceedings of the 58th Annual Meeting of the Association for Computational Linguistics*, pages 6729–6739, Online. Association for Computational Linguistics.

Jianxing Yu, Xiaojun Quan, Qinliang Su, and Jian Yin. 2020b. *Generating Multi-Hop Reasoning Questions to Improve Machine Reading Comprehension*, page 281–291. Association for Computing Machinery, New York, NY, USA.

Eric Zelikman, Yuhuai Wu, Jesse Mu, and Noah D. Goodman. 2022. Star: Bootstrapping reasoning with reasoning.

Shiyue Zhang and Mohit Bansal. 2019. Addressing semantic drift in question generation for semi-supervised question answering. In *Proceedings of the 2019 Conference on Empirical Methods in Natural Language Processing and the 9th International Joint Conference on Natural Language Processing (EMNLP-IJCNLP)*, pages 2495–2509, Hong Kong, China. Association for Computational Linguistics.

A Task Prompts

We provide the prompts used for training T5 below. $SentinelToken_i$ refers special sentinel tokens used while pretraining T5 model. Common entities were filled in for Tasks 1 and 2 using top three longest contiguous sub-sequences found both in p_1 and p_2 from which common English words and words that are not capitalised indicating common nouns were removed, we also used Flair NER[2] library to generate these entities and kept the ones shared across both p_1 and p_2.

Baseline Context 1: p_1 Context 2: p_2 Answer: a Question type: $SentinelToken_0$

Task 1 Context 1: p_1 Context 2: p_2 Answer: a Common entities found: $SentinelToken_0$ Question type: $SentinelToken_1$

Task 2 Context 1: p_1 Context 2: p_2 Answer: a Common entities found: $SentinelToken_0$ Question type: $SentinelToken_1$

Task 3 Answer: a is $SentinelToken_0$ in context: p_i

Task 4 Entities: a and b are $SentinelToken_0$.

Task 5 Context: p_i Bridge entity: b Answer: a Assertion: $SentinelToken_0$

Task 6 Context: p_i Bridge entity: b Assertion: $SentinelToken_0$

Task 7 Bridge entity: b Assertion 1: s_1 Assertion 2: s_2 Combined: $SentinelToken_0$

Task 8 Removing bridge entity: b from: c We get: $SentinelToken_0$

Task 9 Contract answer entity a from: $c - b$ We get: $SentinelToken_0$

Task 10 Turn: $c - b - a$ into question: $SentinelToken_0$

Task 11 Context 1: p_1 Context 2: p_2 Answer: a

[2] https://github.com/flairNLP/flair

Assertion from Context 1: $SentinelToken_0$ Assertion from Context 2: $SentinelToken_1$
Task 12 Assertion 1: s_1 Assertion 2: s_2 Combine, compare and think: $SentinelToken_0$
Task 13 Combined assertion: c Answer: a Question: $SentinelToken_0$ The outputs prompt for each of these tasks is to generate the expected output items of each task preceeded by $SentinelToken_0$ and $SentinelToken_1$.

B Generated Examples

We provide actual examples of generations from our baseline model and Reasoning Circuits (128-shot, encoder input: Supporting sentences from the passage only)

============== Q1 ==================

P1: John Updike - John Hoyer Updike (March 18, 1932 January 27, 2009) was an American novelist, poet, short story writer, art critic, and literary critic.
P2: Bret Easton Ellis - Bret Easton Ellis (born March 7, 1964) is an American author, screenwriter, and short story writer.
Gold Question: What profession was both John Updike and Bret Easton Ellis ?
Answer: short story writer
Gold Type: comparison
-- Generations --
Reasoning Circuits question type: comparison
Reasoning Circuits: What kind of writers were Bret Easton Ellis and John Updike?
Baseline: What job did both Bret Easton Ellis and John Updike have in common?

============== Q2 ==================

P1: Xingcheng - Xingcheng (), former name Ningyuan (), is a county level city of southwest Liaoning province, China, with a population of approximately 140,000 urban inhabitants, and is located on the Liaodong Bay, i.e. the northern coast of the Bohai Sea.
P2: Ulan Hot - Ulanhot (Mongolian- ; Cyrillic- ; Latin transliteration- "Ulaan qota";), formerly known as Wangin Sm, alternatively Wang-un Sme, Ulayanqota (Red City) in Classical Mongolian, and Wangyehmiao or Wangyemiao () in Chinese prior to 1947, is a county-level city and the administrative center of Hinggan League in the East of Inner Mongolia autonomous region.
Gold Question: Is Xingcheng or Ulan Hot located in the Inner Mongolia region of China?
Answer: Ulanhot
Gold Type: comparison
-- Generations --
Reasoning Circuits question type: comparison
Reasoning Circuits: Which city is in the East of Inner Mongolia autonomous region, Ulanhot or Xingcheng?
Baseline: What is the name of this city, which was formerly known as Wangin Sm?

============== Q3 ==================

P1: French Spaniel - The breed is recognised by Canadian and international kennel clubs but not by The Kennel Club (UK).
P2: Beagle - The Beagle is a breed of small hound, similar in appearance to the much larger foxhound.
Gold Question: Are both French Spaniel and Beagle universally recognized breeds?
Answer: no
Gold Type: comparison
-- Generations --
Reasoning Circuits question type: comparison
Reasoning Circuits: Are the Beagle and the foxhound similar in appearance?
Baseline: Are the Beagle and the French Spaniel both breeds of small hound?

============== Q4 ==================

P1: The Tempest (1979 film) - The Tempest is a 1979 film adaptation of William Shakespeare's play of the same name. Directed by Derek Jarman, with Heathcote Williams as Prospero, it also stars Toyah Willcox, Jack Birkett and Helen Wellington-Lloyd from Jarman's previous feature, "Jubilee" (1977), as well as his long-time cohort Karl Johnson.

P2: Heathcote Williams - John Henley Heathcote-Williams (15 November 1941 1 July 2017), known as Heathcote Williams, was an English poet, actor, political activist and dramatist. He wrote a number of book-length polemical poems including "Autogeddon", "Falling for a Dolphin" and "Whale Nation", which in 1988 became, according to Philip Hoare, "the most powerful argument for the newly instigated worldwide ban on whaling."

Gold Question: What is the title of the 1979 film adaptation of William Shakespeare's play in which the English poet, actor, political activist and dramatist who wrote wrote a number of book-length polemical poems such as "Autogeddon", "Falling for a Dolphin" and "Whale Nation" played a main character?

Answer: The Tempest

Gold Type: bridge

-- Generations --

Reasoning Circuits question type: bridge

Reasoning Circuits: What is the film in which an English poet, actor, political activist and dramatist wrote a number of book-length polemical poems including "Whale Nation"?

Baseline: What 1979 film starring Heathcote Williams was directed by Derek Jarman?

============== Q5 ==================

P1: Achel Abbey - The Trappist Abbey of Achel or Saint Benedictus-Abbey or also Achelse Kluis (which means hermitage of Achel), which belongs to the Cistercians of Strict Observance, is located in Achel in the Campine region of the province of Limburg (Flanders, Belgium). The abbey is famous for its spiritual life and its brewery, which is one of few Trappist beer breweries in the world.

P2: Trappist beer - Eleven monasteries six in Belgium, two in the Netherlands and one each in Austria, Italy and United States currently brew beer and sell it as "Authentic Trappist Product".

Gold Question: The Trappist Abbey of Achel produces and sells what as an "Authentic Trappist Product"?

Answer: Trappist beer

Gold Type: bridge

-- Generations --

Reasoning Circuits question type: bridge

Reasoning Circuits: What kind of beer is brewed at Achel Abbey, which is famous for its spiritual life and its brewery?

Baseline: What is brewed at the Trappist Abbey of Achel?

============== Q6 ==================

P1: Marc Bolan - He was best known as the lead singer of the glam rock band T. Rex.

P2: Metal Guru - "Metal Guru" is a song by the British rock band T. Rex, written by Marc Bolan. It was the band's fourth (and final) number one on the UK Singles Chart when it topped the chart for four weeks from MayJune 1972.

Gold Question: In the summer of 1972, "Metal Guru" was the last UK number one for T. Rex and its lead singer. What was his name?

Answer: Marc Bolan

Gold Type: bridge

-- Generations --

Reasoning Circuits question type: bridge

Reasoning Circuits: Who is the best known person who also wrote the song Metal Guru and who also played the guitar for the band T. Rex?

Baseline: Who wrote the song Metal Guru for the glam rock band T. Rex?

============== Q7 ==================

P1: Estonian Hound - It was bred in 1947 when the Soviet Union's national economy ministry decided that every country in the Union must have its own

dog breed.
P2: English Water Spaniel - The English Water Spaniel is a breed of dog that has been extinct since the first part of the 20th century, with the last specimen seen in the 1930s.
Gold Question: Which breed was bred first, the English Water Spaniel or the Estonian Hound?
Answer: The English Water Spaniel
Gold Type: comparison
-- Generations --
Reasoning Circuits question type: comparison
Reasoning Circuits: Which breed of dog has been extinct since the first part of the 20th century, the English Water Spaniel or the Estonian Hound?
Baseline: Which breed of dog was bred in 1947, the Estonian Hound or the English Water Spaniel?
============== Q8 ==================
P1: Tommy's Honour - The film is directed by Jason Connery, and the father and son are portrayed by Peter Mullan and Jack Lowden.
P2: Jack Lowden - Jack Andrew Lowden (born 2 June 1990) is a Scottish stage, television, and film actor. Following a highly successful and award-winning four-year stage career, his first major international onscreen success was in the 2016 BBC miniseries "War & Peace", which led to starring roles in feature films.
Gold Question: Tommy's Honour was a drama film that included the actor who found success with what 2016 BBC miniseries?
Answer: War & Peace
Gold Type: bridge
-- Generations --
Reasoning Circuits question type: bridge
Reasoning Circuits: In which 2016 BBC miniseries did a Scottish actor have his first major international onscreen success?
Baseline: What was the first major international onscreen success of this Scottish actor, who played the father in the film Tommys Honour?
============== Q9 ==================
P1: Moho House - "Moho House" is the twenty first episode of the twenty-eighth season of the animated television series "The Simpsons", and the 617th episode of the series overall.
P2: The Simpsons (season 28) - On May 4, 2015, Fox announced that "The Simpsons" had been renewed for season 28.
Gold Question: How many seasons has a popular tv show had, in which one of the episodes is called Moho House?
Answer: 28
Gold Type: bridge
-- Generations --
Reasoning Circuits question type: bridge
Reasoning Circuits: Moho House is the twenty first episode of the twenty-eighth season of the animated television series which was renewed for season 28 on May 4, 2015?
Baseline: Moho House is the twenty first episode of which season of the animated television series The Simpsons, and the 617th episode of the series overall?
============== Q10 ==================
P1: Harry S. Truman Supreme Court candidates - During his two terms in office, President Harry S. Truman appointed four members of the Supreme Court of the United States- Chief Justice Fred M. Vinson, Associate Justice Harold Burton, Associate Justice Tom C. Clark, and Associate Justice Sherman Minton.
P2: Fred M. Vinson - The most prominent member of the Vinson political family, he was the 53rd United States Secretary of the Treasury and the 13th Chief Justice of the United States.
Gold Question: Of four Harry S. Truman Supreme Court candidates, who was the 53rd United States Secretary of the Treasury and the 13th Chief Justice of the United States?

Answer: Fred M. Vinson
Gold Type: bridge
-- Generations --
Reasoning Circuits question type: bridge
Reasoning Circuits: Who was the most prominent member of the Vinson political family and the 13th Chief Justice of the United States who was appointed by President Harry S. Truman?
Baseline: During his two terms in office, President Harry S. Truman appointed four members of the Supreme Court of the United States, including the most prominent member of the Vinson political family, he was the 53rd United States Secretary of the Treasury and the 13th Chief Justice of the United States.
============== Q11 ==================
P1: Lee Ranaldo - Lee Mark Ranaldo (born February 3, 1956) is an American musician, singer-songwriter, guitarist, writer, visual artist and record producer, best known as a co-founder of the alternative rock band Sonic Youth. In 2004, "Rolling Stone" ranked Ranaldo at number 33 on its "Greatest Guitarists of All Time" list.
P2: Mikael kerfeldt - Lars Mikael kerfeldt (born 17 April 1974) is a Swedish musician, prominently known as the lead vocalist, guitarist, and primary songwriter of progressive death metal band Opeth, as well as being the former vocalist of death metal supergroup Bloodbath. He was also guitarist for the "one-off" band Steel, and is part of the collaboration Storm Corrosion with Steven Wilson.
Gold Question: Mikael kerfeldt and Lee Ranaldo were this kind of instrumentalist in their respective bands.
Answer: Guitarists
Gold Type: comparison
-- Generations --
Reasoning Circuits question type: comparison
Reasoning Circuits: What is common between Lee Ranaldo and Mikael Kerfeldt?
Baseline: What do Lee Ranaldo and Mikael kerfeldt have in common?
============== Q12 ==================
P1: Bent Hamer - Bent Hamer (born 18 December 1956) is a film director, writer and producer, born in Sandefjord, Norway in 1956.
P2: Yasujir Ozu - Yasujir Ozu (, Ozu Yasujir , 12 December 1903 12 December 1963) was a Japanese film director and screenwriter.
Gold Question: Between Yasujir Ozu and Bent Hamer, who has more creative titles?
Answer: Bent Hamer
Gold Type: comparison
-- Generations --
Reasoning Circuits question type: bridge
Reasoning Circuits: What film director, writer and producer, born in Sandefjord, Norway in 1956 worked for Yasujiro Ozu who was a Japanese film director and screenwriter?
Baseline: Which film maker was born in Sandefjord, Norway, Bent Hamer or Yasujir Ozu?
============== Q13 ==================
P1: Ulli Lommel - Since 1977 he has lived and worked in the USA, where he has written, directed and starred in over 50 movies.
P2: Benjamin Stoloff - Benjamin "Ben" Stoloff (October 6, 1895 September 8, 1960) was an American film director and producer. Stoloff was born in Philadelphia, Pennsylvania. He died in Hollywood, California.
Gold Question: Who has lived longer in the USA, Ulli Lommel or Benjamin Stoloff?
Answer: Stoloff
Gold Type: comparison
-- Generations --
Reasoning Circuits question type: comparison
Reasoning Circuits: Which film

director and producer lived and worked in the USA, Ulli Lommel or Benjamin Stoloff?
Baseline: What American film director and producer born in Philadelphia, Pennsylvania, died in Hollywood, California, Ulli Lommel or Benjamin Stoloff?
============== Q14 ==================
P1: Five Finger Death Punch discography - After Hook replaced previous guitarist Darrell Roberts, 5FDP released "War Is the Answer" in 2009 which reached the top ten of the "Billboard" 200 and was certified platinum by the RIAA.
P2: War Is the Answer - It was released on September 22, 2009 through Prospect Park.
Gold Question: Which Five Finger Death Punch discography albulm was released on September 22, 2009 through Prospect Park?
Answer: War Is the Answer
Gold Type: bridge
-- Generations --
Reasoning Circuits question type: bridge
Reasoning Circuits: What song did Five Finger Death Punch release on September 22, 2009 through Prospect Park?
Baseline: Which album by Five Finger Death Punch was released in 2009, after Hook replaced previous guitarist Darrell Roberts?
============== Q15 ==================
P1: Wolfgang Becker - Wolfgang Becker (born 22 June 1954) is a German film director and writer.
P2: Jacques Audiard - Jacques Audiard (] ; born 30 April 1952) is a French film director and screenwriter.
Gold Question: Are Wolfgang Becker and Jacques Audiard both German film directors?
Answer: no
Gold Type: comparison
-- Generations --
Reasoning Circuits question type: comparison
Reasoning Circuits: Are Wolfgang Becker and Jacques Audiard both writers?
Baseline: Are Jacques Audiard and Wolfgang Becker both film directors and writers?
============== Q16 ==================
P1: ECAC Hockey - The conference used to be affiliated with the Eastern College Athletic Conference, a consortium of over 300 colleges in the eastern United States.
P2: Colgate Raiders women's ice hockey - The Colgate Raiders women's ice hockey team is an NCAA Division I ice hockey team that represents Colgate University and play in ECAC Hockey.
Gold Question: What athletic conference did the conference that the Colgate Raiders women's ice hockey team play in used to be affiliated with?
Answer: Eastern College Athletic Conference
Gold Type: bridge
-- Generations --
Reasoning Circuits question type: bridge
Reasoning Circuits: The Colgate Raiders women's ice hockey team is an NCAA Division I ice hockey team that represents Colgate University and play in a conference which used to be affiliated with what?
Baseline: The conference used to be affiliated with which consortium of over 300 colleges in the eastern United States?
============== Q17 ==================
P1: The Futureheads - The Futureheads were an English post-punk band from Sunderland. consisting of Ross Millard (vocals and guitar), Barry Hyde (vocals and guitar), David "Jaff" Craig (bass guitar) and Dave Hyde (drums).
P2: Marcy Playground - Marcy Playground is an American alternative rock band consisting of three members- John Wozniak (lead vocals, guitar),

Dylan Keefe (bass), and Shlomi Lavie (drums).
Gold Question: Which band has more members, The Futureheads or Marcy Playground?
Answer: The Futureheads
Gold Type: comparison
-- Generations --
Reasoning Circuits question type: comparison
Reasoning Circuits: Which band was an English post-punk band, The Futureheads or Marcy Playground?
Baseline: Which post-punk band had members from both Marcy Playground and The Futureheads?
============== Q18 ==================
P1: General Motors Technical Center - The GM Technical Center is a General Motors facility in Warren, Michigan.
P2: Warren, Michigan - Warren is a city in Macomb County in the U.S. state of Michigan.
Gold Question: In what county is the General Motors Technical Center located?
Answer: Macomb County
Gold Type: bridge
-- Generations --
Reasoning Circuits question type: bridge
Reasoning Circuits: General Motors Technical Center is in what city in what county?
Baseline: The General Motors Technical Center is a General Motors facility in Warren, Michigan, in which U.S. state?
============== Q19 ==================
P1: Balfour Declaration - The Balfour Declaration was a public statement issued by the British government during World War I announcing support for the establishment of a "national home for the Jewish people" in Palestine, then an Ottoman region with a minority Jewish population.
P2: Declaration to the Seven - The Declaration to the Seven was a document written by the British diplomat Sir Henry McMahon and released on June 16, 1918 in response to a memorandum issued anonymously by seven Syrian notables in Cairo who were members of the newly formed Party of Syrian Unity, established in the wake of the Balfour Declaration and the November 23, 1917 publication by the Bolsheviks of the secret May 1916 Sykes-Picot Agreement between Britain and France.
Gold Question: Party of Syrian Unity was established in the wake of a public statement that announced what ?
Answer: support for the establishment of a "national home for the Jewish people" in Palestine
Gold Type: bridge
-- Generations --
Reasoning Circuits question type: bridge
Reasoning Circuits: What was the combined assertion of a public statement issued by the British government during World War I announcing support for the establishment of a "national home for the Jewish people" in Palestine and a document written by the British diplomat Sir Henry McMahon and released on June 16, 1918 in response to a memorandum issued anonymously by seven Syrian notables in Cairo who were members of the newly formed Party of Syrian Unity, established in the wake of the Balfour Declaration?
Baseline: The Balfour Declaration was a public statement issued by the British government during World War I announcing what?
============== Q20 ==================
P1: El Paso International Airport - El Paso International Airport (IATA- ELP, ICAO- KELP, FAA LID- ELP) is a public airport four miles (6 km) northeast of downtown El Paso, in El Paso County, Texas, United States.
P2: Grand Forks International Airport - Grand Forks International Airport (IATA- GFK, ICAO- KGFK, FAA LID- GFK) is a public airport five miles (8 km) northwest of Grand Forks, in Grand

Forks County, North Dakota.
Gold Question: Which airport Grand Forks International Airport or El Paso International Airport is closer to their town ?
Answer: El Paso International Airport
Gold Type: comparison
-- Generations --
Reasoning Circuits question type: comparison
Reasoning Circuits: Which airport is located in El Paso County, Texas, United States, Grand Forks International Airport or both?
Baseline: Which airport is farther northeast, El Paso International Airport or Grand Forks International Airport?
============== Q21 ==================
P1: Oklahoma Sooners football - The Oklahoma Sooners football program is a college football team that represents the University of Oklahoma (variously "Oklahoma" or "OU"). The team is currently a member of the Big 12 Conference, which is in Division I Football Bowl Subdivision (formerly Division I-A) of the National Collegiate Athletic Association (NCAA).
P2: Justin Brown (wide receiver) - Justin Brown (born March 10, 1991) is a wide receiver for the Toronto Argonauts of the Canadian Football League (CFL).
Gold Question: A wide receiver for the Toronto Argonauts played college football for a team that represents the University of Oklahoma, which belongs to what conference?
Answer: Big 12 Conference
Gold Type: bridge
-- Generations --
Reasoning Circuits question type: bridge
Reasoning Circuits: Justin Brown is a wide receiver for the Toronto Argonauts of the Canadian Football League (CFL) that represents the University of Oklahoma, it is a member of which conference?
Baseline: Justin Brown is a wide receiver for the Toronto Argonauts of the Canadian Football League, a team that is a member of which conference?
============== Q22 ==================
P1: D. Napier & Son - D. Napier & Son Limited was a British engineering company best known for its luxury motor cars in the Edwardian era and for its aero engines throughout the early to mid-20th century.
P2: Edwardian era - The Edwardian era or Edwardian period of British history covers the brief reign of King Edward VII, 1901 to 1910, and is sometimes extended in both directions to capture long-term trends from the 1890s to the First World War.
Gold Question: Which British engineering company is best known for its luxury motor cars in the era of British history that covers the brief reign of King Edward VII?
Answer: D. Napier & Son
Gold Type: bridge
-- Generations --
Reasoning Circuits question type: bridge
Reasoning Circuits: What British engineering company best known for its luxury motor cars in the era which covers the brief reign of King Edward VII?
Baseline: What British engineering company best known for its luxury motor cars in the Edwardian era and for its aero engines throughout the early to mid-20th century?
============== Q23 ==================
P1: Werther - Werther is an opera ("drame lyrique") in four acts by Jules Massenet to a French libretto by douard Blau, Paul Milliet and Georges Hartmann (who used the pseudonym Henri Grmont).
P2: Odyssey - The Odyssey (; Greek- "Odsseia",] in Classical Attic) is one of two major ancient Greek epic poems attributed to Homer.
Gold Question: Are Werther and The Odyssey both operas?

Answer: no
Gold Type: comparison
-- Generations --
Reasoning Circuits question type: comparison
Reasoning Circuits: Are Werther and The Odyssey both by Jules Massenet?
Baseline: Are The Odyssey and Werther both written by the same author?
============== Q24 ==================
P1: mile Verdet - Marcel mile Verdet (13 March 1824 3 June 1866) was a French physicist. Verdet did much to champion the early theory of the conservation of energy in France through his editorial supervision of the "Annales de chimie et de physique".
P2: Annales de chimie et de physique - Annales de chimie et de physique (French for "Annals of Chemistry and of Physics") is a scientific journal that was founded in Paris, France, in 1789 under the title "Annales de chimie".
Gold Question: what is the english name of mile Verdets editorial?
Answer: Annals of Chemistry and of Physics
Gold Type: bridge
-- Generations --
Reasoning Circuits question type: bridge
Reasoning Circuits: Which journal was founded in Paris, France, under the editorial supervision of mile Verdet, who did much to champion the early theory of the conservation of energy in France?
Baseline: What is the name of the scientific journal that was founded in Paris, France, in 1789 under the title Annales de chimie?
============== Q25 ==================
P1: Vinylmation - Most figures are all shaped with the body of Mickey Mouse but have different themed markings, colors, and patterns.
P2: Mickey Mouse - He was created by Walt Disney and Ub Iwerks at the Walt Disney Studios in 1928.
Gold Question: The vynil collectible Vinylmation are all shaped with the body of a cartoon character created by who ?
Answer: Walt Disney and Ub Iwerks
Gold Type: bridge
-- Generations --
Reasoning Circuits question type: bridge
Reasoning Circuits: Vinylmation is shaped with the body of a character which was created by who at the Walt Disney Studios in 1928?
Baseline: Who created the character Mickey Mouse in 1928?

Knowledge-Augmented Language Model Prompting for Zero-Shot Knowledge Graph Question Answering

Jinheon Baek[1*] **Alham Fikri Aji**[2] **Amir Saffari**[3]
KAIST[1] MBZUAI[2] Amazon[3]
jinheon.baek@kaist.ac.kr alham.fikri@mbzuai.ac.ae amsafari@amazon.com

Abstract

Large Language Models (LLMs) are capable of performing zero-shot closed-book question answering tasks, based on their internal knowledge stored in parameters during pre-training. However, such internalized knowledge might be insufficient and incorrect, which could lead LLMs to generate factually wrong answers. Furthermore, fine-tuning LLMs to update their knowledge is expensive. To this end, we propose to augment the knowledge directly in the input of LLMs. Specifically, we first retrieve the relevant facts to the input question from the knowledge graph based on semantic similarities between the question and its associated facts. After that, we prepend the retrieved facts to the input question in the form of the prompt, which is then forwarded to LLMs to generate the answer. Our framework, Knowledge-Augmented language model PromptING (KAPING), requires no model training, thus completely zero-shot. We validate the performance of our KAPING framework on the knowledge graph question answering task, that aims to answer the user's question based on facts over a knowledge graph, on which ours outperforms relevant zero-shot baselines by up to 48% in average, across multiple LLMs of various sizes.

1 Introduction

Pre-trained Language Models (LMs) (Devlin et al., 2019; Raffel et al., 2020), which are trained on a large amount of text corpora with self-supervised learning, can perform closed-book Question Answering (QA) tasks that aim to answer the user's question based only on their internal knowledge in parameters, without using any external knowledge (Petroni et al., 2019; Roberts et al., 2020). Also, when we increase the LM sizes, Large Language Models (LLMs) can generate the answer for the question without any additional fine-tuning steps, called *LM prompting* (Brown et al., 2020; Liu et al., 2021). However, since the knowledge in LLMs might be incomplete, incorrect, and outdated, they often generate factually wrong answers, known as *hallucination* (Rohrbach et al., 2018) (See Figure 1a). Also, refining the knowledge in LLMs with parameter updates is costly, especially when knowledge is constantly changing (e.g., exchange rates of money). Lastly, whether LLMs are fetching the correct knowledge for QA is unclear.

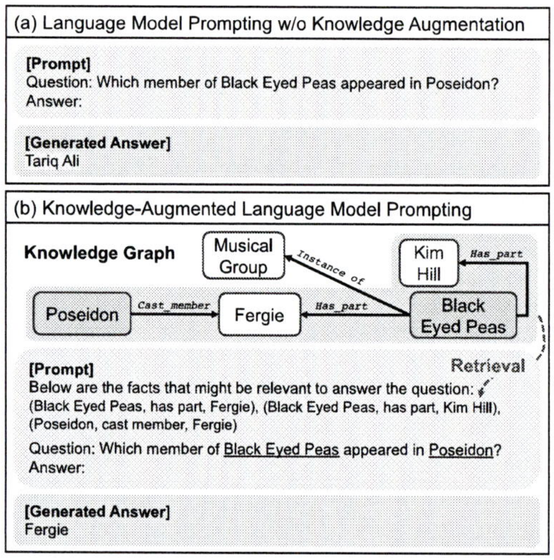

Figure 1: (a) For the input question in the prompt, the large language model, GPT-3 (Brown et al., 2020), can generate the answer based on its internal knowledge in parameters, but hallucinates it which is highlighted in yellow. (b) Our Knowledge-Augmented language model PrompTING (KAPING) framework first retrieves the relevant facts in the knowledge graph from the entities in the question, and then augments them to the prompt, to generate the factually correct answer.

To overcome those limitations, we propose to retrieve and inject the relevant knowledge directly as an input, called a *prompt*, to LLMs (Figure 1b). As a knowledge source, we use a Knowledge Graph (KG) consisting of symbolic knowledge in the form of a triple: (head entity, relation, tail entity). Therefore, to extract the relevant facts to the input question, we first match entities in the question with entities in the KG. After that, triples associated to

* Work done while interning at Amazon. Corresponding author: Jinheon Baek (jinheon.baek@kaist.ac.kr)

Proceedings of the 1st Workshop on Natural Language Reasoning and Structured Explanations (@ACL 2023), pages 78–106
June 13, 2023

entities in the KG are verbalized (i.e., transforming the symbolic relational knowledge to the textual string) and prepended to the input question, which are then forwarded to LLMs to generate the answer. Consequently, LLMs conditioned on the factual knowledge are able to generate the factual answers, alleviating the hallucination issue, while keeping LLMs' parameters unchanged: fine-tuning is not required for knowledge updates. We refer to our overall framework as **K**nowledge-**A**ugmented language model **P**rompt**ING** (**KAPING**), which is completely *zero-shot* and can be done with any off-the-shelf LLMs, without additional training.

While the above scheme looks simple yet effective, there is a couple of challenges. First, most retrieved triples associated with the question entities are unrelated to answer the given question. For example, when we retrieve the associated triples for the question entity (e.g., Poseidon) in Figure 1 in the Wikidata KG (Vrandecic and Krötzsch, 2014), there exist 60 triples, and most of them (e.g., genre, publication date, to name a few) are irrelevant to answer the question. Therefore, they might mislead the model into generating incorrect answers. On the other hand, the number of triples for the question entities is occasionally large (e.g., 27% samples for the WebQSP dataset (Yih et al., 2016) have more than 1,000 triples), thereby encoding all triples including unnecessary ones yields high computational costs, especially on LLMs.

To overcome such challenges, we further propose to filter out unnecessary triples based on their semantic similarities to the input question, inspired by the information retrieval (Bast et al., 2016). To be specific, we first represent the question and its associated verbalized triples in the embedding space. Then, we retrieve the small number of triples whose embeddings are more close to the input question's embedding than others. By doing so, we can prepend only the more relevant triples to the given question, which can effectively prevent LLMs from generating irrelevant answers with high computational efficiencies, unlike the one that augments all triples. Note that, our filtering approach uses off-the-shelf sentence embedding models (Song et al., 2020; Hofstätter et al., 2021); thus no additional training is required in every part of our pipeline.

We then validate our KAPING framework on Knowledge Graph Question Answering (KGQA) tasks. The results show that our KAPING significantly outperforms relevant zero-shot baselines. Also, the detailed analyses support the importance of knowledge retrieval and augmentation schemes.

Our contributions in this work are threefold:

- We present a new knowledge-augmented LM prompting framework that leverages the factual knowledge from KGs, for zero-shot QA.
- We propose to retrieve and augment relevant facts from KGs, based on semantic similarities between the question and its associated triples.
- We validate our KAPING on KGQA benchmark datasets, on which ours impressively outperforms relevant zero-shot baselines.

2 Related Work

Language Model Prompting Language model pre-training, which trains Transformers (Vaswani et al., 2017) on unannotated text corpora with auto-encoding (Devlin et al., 2019; Liu et al., 2019) or auto-regressive (Yang et al., 2019; Radford et al., 2018) objectives, becomes an essential approach for natural language tasks. Also, Large Language Models (LLMs) (Brown et al., 2020; Raffel et al., 2020; Chowdhery et al., 2022; Soltan et al., 2022) are able to perform zero-shot learning, for example, generating the answer for the input textual prompt, based on the knowledge stored in pre-trained parameters (Petroni et al., 2019; Roberts et al., 2020; Sung et al., 2021), without additional parameter updates as well as labeled datasets. To further improve their performances, some work (Rubin et al., 2022; Liu et al., 2022a) proposes retrieving relevant samples to the input question from the training dataset and prepending them in the prompt under few-show learning. Recent few work (Sanh et al., 2022; Wei et al., 2022a) further shows that, when LLMs are fine-tuned on a collection of instructions phrased from natural language tasks, they can have strong generalization performance on unseen zero-shot tasks. However, the knowledge inside LMs might be insufficient to tackle factual questions, which gives rise to knowledge-augmented LMs. Notably, our LM prompting is different from prompt-tuning literature (Lester et al., 2021a; Chen et al., 2022a) that additionally tunes LMs with model training (See Appendix C for discussions).

Knowledge-Augmented LMs Recent work proposes to integrate the knowledge, such as documents from unstructured corpora (e.g., Wikipedia) and facts from Knowledge Graphs (KGs), into LMs. To mention a few, REALM (Guu et al., 2020) and

RAG (Lewis et al., 2020) learn to retrieve documents and augment LMs with them. In addition, KGs could be another knowledge source, where the knowledge is succinctly encoded in the most compact form, and some methods augment such facts in KGs into LMs (Galetzka et al., 2021; Rony et al., 2022; Kang et al., 2022). However, all aforementioned approaches require massive amount of training data and model updates for downstream tasks. While more recent work (Izacard et al., 2022) shows retrieval-augmented LM can have strong performance with few-shot learning, it still requires extra training steps, which is different from ours focusing on *LM prompting* for entirely zero-shot.

Recently, there are few studies augmenting the knowledge in the LM prompting scheme. At first, some work proposes to extract the knowledge in the parameters of LLMs themselves via prompting, and then use the extracted knowledge to answer the question (Kojima et al., 2022; Liu et al., 2022b; Wei et al., 2022b; Wang et al., 2022). However, since LLMs' parameters might be insufficient to store all the world knowledge, the extracted knowledge and generated answers might be inaccurate. On the other hand, most recently, Lazaridou et al. (2022) propose to use the Google Search to retrieve documents on the Web, and then prepend the retrieved documents to the input question along with few-shot demonstrations, to answer the question under few-shot LLM prompting schemes. However, our focus on *zero-shot prompting with KGs* is orthogonal to the previous study working on documents with few-shot prompting, and leveraging KGs can bring additional advantages. Specifically, since KGs can succinctly encode the knowledge in the compact triple form, for QA tasks, ours makes LLM prompting more efficient (i.e., reducing the input sequence length compared to the document case), as well as more effective on the zero-shot QA scheme: LLMs need to select one triple containing the answer entity in the prompt, instead of looking through lengthy documents having various entities.

Knowledge Graph Question Answering The goal of our target Knowledge Graph Question Answering (KGQA) tasks is to answer the input question based on a set of facts over KGs (Chakraborty et al., 2019; Fu et al., 2020). Previous approaches are broadly classified into neural semantic parsing-based methods (Yih et al., 2015; Bao et al., 2016; Luo et al., 2018), information retrieval-based methods (Sun et al., 2018; Saxena et al., 2020; Yasunaga et al., 2021), and differentiable KG-based methods (Cohen et al., 2020; Saffari et al., 2021; Sen et al., 2021), which, however, require annotated data with additional model training. While Zhou et al. (2021) aim to transfer the KGQA model to the target language domains without any training data on them, this work indeed needs the labeled data to train the model on data-rich source domains first before transferring the model to the target domains. In contrast to all the aforementioned methods, we explore the novel zero-shot KGQA mechanism, which does not require any annotated QA pairs and additional training, leveraging LM prompting.

3 Method

We now describe our Knowledge-Augmented language model PromptING (KAPING) framework.

3.1 LM Prompting for Zero-Shot QA

We begin with the zero-shot question answering, and then explain the language model prompting.

Zero-Shot Question Answering Given an input question $\boldsymbol{x}$, the Question Answering (QA) system returns an answer $\boldsymbol{y}$, where $\boldsymbol{x}$ and $\boldsymbol{y}$ consist of sequences of tokens: $\boldsymbol{x} = [w_1, w_2, \ldots, w_{|\boldsymbol{x}|}]$. Let P be a QA model based on the generative Language Model (LM) (Raffel et al., 2020; Brown et al., 2020), which generates the conditional probability of answer $\boldsymbol{y}$ for question $\boldsymbol{x}$ as follows: $P(\boldsymbol{y}|\boldsymbol{x})$. Then, in contrast to supervised learning that trains model P with a set of annotated ($\boldsymbol{x}$, $\boldsymbol{y}$) pairs, zero-shot learning does not use any labeled samples and model training. Notably, we are interested in this zero-shot QA, since collecting the dataset and then fine-tuning the existing LMs for every new domain are known to be expensive and sometimes infeasible (Houlsby et al., 2019; Lester et al., 2021b).

LM Prompting LMs are often pre-trained by predicting the next token based on previous tokens, which is known as auto-regressive language modeling (Radford et al., 2018; Raffel et al., 2020). Then, thanks to this pre-training objective, LLMs can perform zero-shot instruction learning. Specifically, when we provide a question as well as an instruction (e.g., "Please answer the question: Who is the author of Lady Susan?") to the LLM (i.e., P), such the LLM, conditioned by the input text, can sequentially generate the probability of output tokens, which might be an answer, "Jane Austen".

To be more formal, for every input question $\boldsymbol{x}$, we first modify it with a particular instruction template T into a textual string x' called a *prompt*, as follows: $T : x \mapsto x'$. For example, if we have the previous question x = "Who is the author of Lady Susan?" along with the previous instruction template "Please answer the question:", the resulting prompt x' would be $T(x)$ = "Please answer the question: Who is the author of Lady Susan?". Then, we forward the prompt x' to the LLM (i.e., P), which then generates the answer (i.e., y) through $P(y|x')$. Note that this LM prompting scheme does not require any additional model parameter updates (i.e., fine-tuning) on the labeled data, thus appropriate for the target zero-shot QA task.

However, there are multiple challenges in this naive zero-shot prompting for QA. First, LLMs, which rely on the knowledge in parameters, are vulnerable from generating the factually incorrect answer, since the knowledge in LLMs might be inaccurate, and outdated: knowledge can be emerged and changed over time. Also, refining the internalized knowledge with additional parameter updates is expensive, while it is necessary to reflect the wrong and ever growing knowledge. Lastly, which knowledge LLMs memorize and utilize when generating the answer to the question prompt is unclear, which limits their explainability on the outputs.

3.2 Knowledge-Augmented LM Prompting

In order to tackle the aforementioned limitations of the existing LM prompting scheme, we propose to inject the relevant knowledge to the input question from the Knowledge Graph (KG), which we refer to as Knowledge-Augmented language model PromptING (KAPING). In this subsection, we first define the main objective of our KAPING framework, and then introduce the ingredients for augmenting the knowledge over KGs to LM prompts.

LM Prompting with Knowledge Graphs Instead of relying on the knowledge internalized in parameters, we propose to additionally access and inject the knowledge from the external KG, which contains accurate and up-to-date facts helpful to answer the question. Formally, a knowledge graph $\mathcal{G}$ consists of a set of factual triples $\{(s, r, o)\}$, where s and o denote subject and object entities, and r is a specific type of a relation between them. For example, one relational knowledge "Lady Susan was written by Jane Austen" can be represented as a triple consisting of two entities s = "Lady Susan" and o = "Jane Austen" along with a relation r = "written by". Then, for the question prompt x' transformed from the example question x = "Who is the author of Lady Susan?" via the template T, we additionally augment its relevant triple: (Lady Susan, written by, Jane Austen), to the LM prompting scheme. By doing so, LLMs can generate the correct answer with regard to the augmented knowledge from KGs, formalized as follows: $P(y|x', \mathcal{G})$. Note that, since we can provide specific and valid facts in KGs to LLMs whenever they exist, our framework can alleviate hallucination issue, originated from inaccurate and outdated knowledge in LLMs, without costly updating their model parameters. Furthermore, we can confirm whether LLMs generate answers based on augmented facts, thus improving the explainability of LM prompting.

The remaining questions are then how to *access* the relational symbolic facts over the KG from the input question, *verbalize* the symbolic knowledge to the textual string, and *inject* the verbalized knowledge into the LM prompting scheme. We explain them one by one in the following paragraphs.

Knowledge Access In order to utilize the related facts to the input question, we first extract the entities in the question. For example, for the question "Who is the author of *Lady Susan*?", we extract the entity "Lady Susan". Then, based on the extracted entity, we find its corresponding entity over the KG, whose incident triples then become associated facts to the input question. Note that entity matching can be done by existing entity linking techniques (Wu et al., 2020; Li et al., 2020; Ayoola et al., 2022).

Knowledge Verbalization LLMs are working on textual inputs, whereas factual triples are represented over the symbolic graph. Therefore, before injecting the symbolic fact from KGs to LLMs, we first transform the triple consisting of (s, r, o) into its textual string, called verbalization. While there exists recent methods (Oguz et al., 2022; Ma et al., 2022) that particularly design or even learn the graph-to-text transformation, in this work, we use the linear verbalization: concatenating the subject, relation, and object texts in the triple, which we observe works well in LM prompting (See Appendix B.5). For instance, one triple (Lady Susan, written by, Jane Austen) is used as is: "(Lady Susan, written by, Jane Austen)", for an LLM's input.

Knowledge Injection Based on verbalized facts associated with the input question, the remaining step is to realize the knowledge injection mechanism, which allows LLMs to be grounded on the external knowledge, useful to generate the answer. Let assume we have a set of N associated triples $\boldsymbol{k} = \{(s_i, r_i, o_i)\}_{i=1}^{N}$ for question $\boldsymbol{x}$. Then, similar to instruction template $T : \boldsymbol{x} \mapsto \boldsymbol{x}'$ described in Section 3.1, we modify N verbalized triples $\boldsymbol{k}$ along with the instruction for the knowledge injection into the knowledge prompt $\boldsymbol{k}'$, as follows: $T : \boldsymbol{k} \mapsto \boldsymbol{k}'$. One particular template we use for constructing the prompt is that, we first enumerate N verbalized triples line-by-line and then add the specific instruction: "Below are facts in the form of the triple meaningful to answer the question.", at the top of the prompt. After that, such the knowledge prompt string, $\boldsymbol{k}'$, is prepended to the question prompt $\boldsymbol{x}'$, and LLMs conditioned by knowledge and question prompts then sequentially generate the answer tokens, formalized as follows: $P(\boldsymbol{y}|[\boldsymbol{k}', \boldsymbol{x}'])$, where $[\cdot]$ denotes concatenation.

3.3 Question-Relevant Knowledge Retrieval

The proposed KAPING framework in Section 3.2, allows LLMs to leverage the knowledge from KGs for zero-shot QA. However, there are critical challenges that the number of triples associated to questions is often too large to forward in LLMs. Also, most of them are unrelated to the question, misleading LLMs into generating the irrelevant answer.

Knowledge Retriever To overcome those limitations, we further propose to retrieve and augment only the relevant triples to the question. Note that there exists a document-retrieval scheme (Lin et al., 2021), whose goal is to retrieve relevant documents for the given query based on their embedding similarities, which motivates us to retrieve, in our case, the triples for the user's question. In particular, thanks to the verbalizer defined in Section 3.2, we can play with triples, obtained from symbolic KGs, over the text space. Therefore, for the verbalized triple and the question, we first embed them onto the representation space with off-the-shelf sentence embedding models for text retrieval (Song et al., 2020; Karpukhin et al., 2020; Xiong et al., 2021), and then calculate their similarities. After that, we use only the top-K similar triples, instead of using all N triples, associated to the given question. Note that, unlike few recent studies (Oguz et al., 2022; Ma et al., 2022; Kang et al., 2022) that aim at improving KG retrievers themselves under supervised training, we focus on zero-shot LM prompting with KGs, thus we use any off-the-shelf retrievers as a tool to filter out unnecessary triples for questions.

4 Experimental Setups

We explain datasets, models, metrics, and implementations. For additional details, see Appendix A.

4.1 Datasets

We evaluate our Knowledge-Augmented language model PromptING (KAPING) framework on two Knowledge Graph Question Answering (KGQA) datasets, namely WebQuestionsSP and Mintaka.

WebQuestionsSP (WebQSP) This dataset (Berant et al., 2013; Yih et al., 2016) is designed with a Freebase KG (Bollacker et al., 2008). It consists of 1,639 test samples, which we use for zero-shot evaluation. Additionally, since Freebase is outdated, we further use the Wikidata KG (Vrandecic and Krötzsch, 2014) by using available mappings from Freebase ids to Wikidata (Diefenbach et al., 2017). This additional dataset consists of 1,466 samples.

Mintaka This dataset (Sen et al., 2022) is recently designed with the Wikidata KG for complex KGQA tasks. Among 8 different languages, we use English test sets consisting of 4,000 samples.

4.2 Large Language Models

To verify the performance of our KAPING framework on Large Language Models (LLMs), as well as benchmarking them on zero-shot KGQA, we use various LLMs with different sizes. Specifically, we use T5 (Raffel et al., 2020) (0.8B, 3B, 11B), T0 (Sanh et al., 2022) (3B, 11B), OPT (Zhang et al., 2022) (2.7B, 6.7B) and GPT-3 (Brown et al., 2020) (6.7B, 175B). We provide details in Appendix A.2.

4.3 Baselines and Our Model

In this subsection, we explain four zero-shot LM prompting baselines and our KAPING framework.

No Knowledge This is a naive LM prompting baseline, which generates answers from input questions without knowledge augmentation from KGs.

Random Knowledge This is an LM prompting baseline, which additionally augments the randomly sampled K triples, associated to the entities appeared in the question, to the prompt.

Popular Knowledge This is an LM prompting baseline, which augments K popular triples among all triples from the question entities, based on relations that appear the most frequently in the KG.

Generated Knowledge This is an LM prompting baseline, which first extracts the knowledge from LLMs themselves based on prompting, and then

Table 1: **Main results of language model prompting**, where we report the generation accuracy. The number inside the parentheses in the first row denotes the parameter size of language models, and best scores are emphasized in bold.

Datasets	Methods	T5 (0.8B)	T5 (3B)	T5 (11B)	OPT (2.7B)	OPT (6.7B)	OPT (13B)	T0 (3B)	T0 (11B)	GPT-3 (6.7B)	GPT-3 (175B)	AlexaTM (20B)	Average
WebQSP w/ Freebase	No Knowledge	6.95	13.40	9.48	19.85	29.77	28.38	21.43	40.77	44.63	63.59	46.79	29.55
	Random Knowledge	21.55	19.15	17.57	28.07	31.73	33.31	32.62	51.20	51.01	65.87	57.37	37.22
	Popular Knowledge	15.30	16.88	18.39	28.32	28.13	24.21	27.05	47.22	45.58	62.26	54.91	33.48
	Generated Knowledge	6.19	7.84	6.76	7.46	11.50	8.22	19.41	38.81	45.89	62.14	35.13	22.67
	KAPING (Ours)	**34.70**	**25.41**	**24.91**	**41.09**	**43.93**	**40.20**	**52.28**	**62.85**	**60.37**	**73.89**	**67.67**	**47.94**
WebQSP w/ Wikidata	No Knowledge	10.30	18.42	15.21	23.94	33.77	32.40	24.56	44.20	48.50	67.60	42.41	32.85
	Random Knowledge	17.94	22.78	24.28	37.24	35.61	38.27	28.85	47.68	52.05	60.64	55.63	38.27
	Popular Knowledge	15.35	20.80	20.74	30.83	30.01	27.83	24.83	48.02	47.41	63.37	53.92	34.83
	Generated Knowledge	11.94	13.30	12.28	11.26	17.53	14.19	22.92	41.34	48.77	65.89	31.16	26.42
	KAPING (Ours)	**23.67**	**40.38**	**35.47**	**49.52**	**53.34**	**51.57**	**49.86**	**58.73**	**60.44**	**69.58**	**65.04**	**50.69**
Mintaka w/ Wikidata	No Knowledge	11.23	14.25	17.06	19.76	27.19	26.83	14.75	23.74	34.65	56.33	41.97	26.16
	Random Knowledge	17.59	18.19	18.83	28.11	26.58	28.36	16.10	26.15	32.98	51.56	46.02	28.22
	Popular Knowledge	17.56	18.09	18.73	26.97	27.08	23.10	16.74	27.15	32.48	53.16	46.41	27.95
	Generated Knowledge	13.61	14.61	14.29	11.87	14.96	16.24	14.46	23.13	33.12	55.65	34.58	22.41
	KAPING (Ours)	**19.72**	**22.00**	**22.85**	**32.94**	**32.37**	**33.37**	**20.68**	**29.50**	**35.61**	**56.86**	**49.08**	**32.27**

Datasets	Retrievers	1-Hop Retrieval MRR	1-Hop Top-1	1-Hop Top-10	1-Hop Top-30	2-Hop Retrieval MRR	2-Hop Top-1	2-Hop Top-10	2-Hop Top-30
WebQSP w/ Freebase	Random	12.50	7.21	25.09	34.64	1.50	0.70	2.65	5.37
	Popular	8.58	5.31	15.93	24.53	1.59	0.95	2.72	4.68
	MPNet	**47.27**	**40.27**	**60.56**	**64.48**	**41.64**	**33.12**	**58.47**	**65.23**
WebQSP w/ Wikidata	Random	9.50	3.62	22.58	40.72	1.31	0.00	2.80	8.59
	Popular	8.52	4.57	15.89	35.47	4.63	4.02	5.53	6.62
	MPNet	**43.46**	**33.36**	**64.39**	**70.67**	**40.42**	**30.56**	**62.62**	**71.56**
Mintaka w/ Wikidata	Random	4.80	1.85	11.48	22.03	0.91	0.14	1.78	5.15
	Popular	6.09	3.09	12.51	20.47	0.24	0.04	0.28	1.24
	MPNet	**13.01**	**7.50**	**25.44**	**35.43**	**13.00**	**6.82**	**26.65**	**40.01**

Table 2: **Retriever results.** We compare random model, popular model, and MPNet (Song et al., 2020), on 1- and 2-hop retrievals.

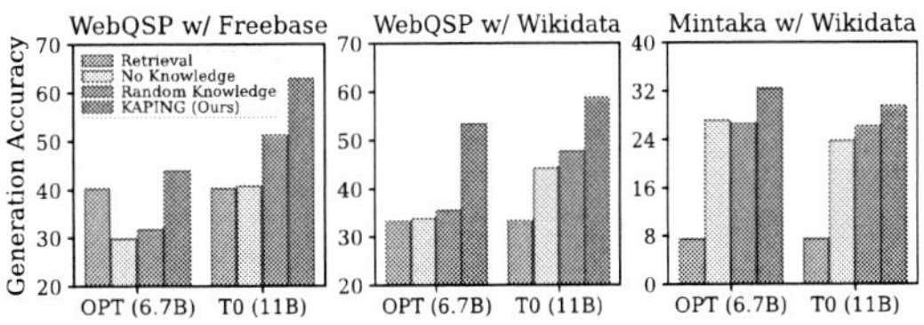

Figure 2: **Comparisons of retrieval and LM prompting.** Retrieval is the Top-1 result of the MPNet (Song et al., 2020).

augments them as the form of the prompt (Liu et al., 2022b), which is similar to Kojima et al. (2022).

KAPING (Ours) This is our Knowledge Augmented language model PromptING (KAPING) framework, which first retrieves the top-K similar triples to the question with the knowledge retriever, and then augments them as the form of the prompt.

4.4 Evaluation Metrics

Generation Following the evaluation protocol of generative KGQA (Yin et al., 2016; Sen et al., 2022; Mavi et al., 2022), we use accuracy, which measures whether the generated tokens from the given prompt include one of the answer entities. Note that we further consider *aliases* – a set of alternative names – of answer entities available in Freebase and Wikidata KGs, for evaluation.

Retrieval We also measure the retriever performance, to see how much the retrieved triples are helpful for answer generation. As metrics, we use Mean Reciprocal Rank (MRR) and Top-K accuracy (Top-K), which are calculated by ranks of correctly retrieved triples containing answer entities among all triples associated to question entities.

4.5 Implementation Details

For the knowledge injection, we set the number of retrieved facts as 10 ($K = 10$), and the hop for triple retrieval as one. For the text based retriever, we experiment with MPNet (Song et al., 2020) that uses the same encoder for embedding question and triples. See Appendix A.4 for additional details.

5 Experimental Results and Analyses

We provide the overall results of our KAPING framework along with its comprehensive analyses.

Main Results As shown in Table 1, our KAPING framework significantly outperforms all LM prompting baselines, on zero-shot KGQA tasks. In particular, the generated knowledge model mostly degenerates the performance compared to the no knowledge model, since the extracted knowledge from LLMs themselves might be inaccurate. On the other hand, the random and popular knowledge baselines bring performance improvements, since the augmented knowledge from KGs are sometimes useful to answer the question. However, ours outperforms them, which suggests that, for zero-shot LM prompting for QA, the knowledge internalized in LLMs is insufficient to generate factual answers, and it is important to use only the relevant facts.

In addition, we also observe larger performance improvements when LMs are relatively small. In other words, since smaller models have insufficient parameter spaces to memorize the knowledge during pre-training, they are more likely to generate factually incorrect answers. However, when the appropriate knowledge is given to them, their performances sometimes become similar to larger models (e.g., different sizes of OPT have similar performances by our KAPING). Therefore, for tasks that require factual knowledge under low-resource setups (e.g., production), augmenting the knowledge would be beneficial, instead of increasing model sizes to handle the huge volume of knowledge.

Figure 3: **Comparisons of correct and incorrect retrieval** for the generation performance on the GPT-3 (6.7B) model.

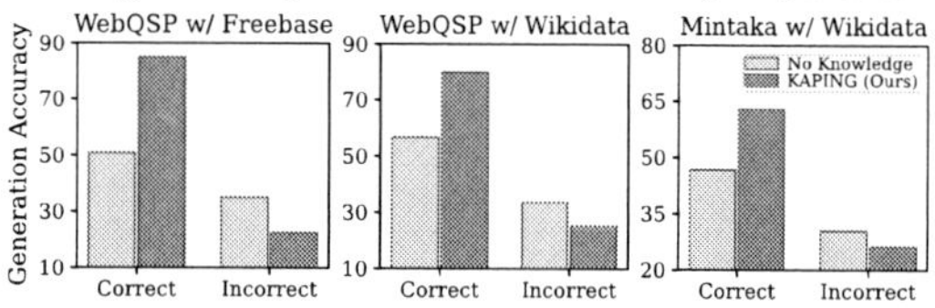

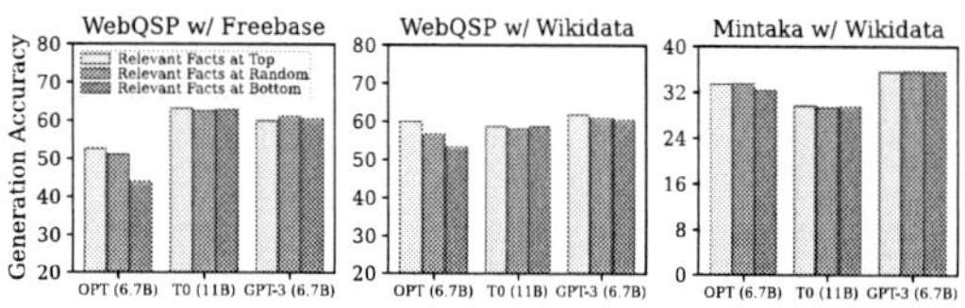

Figure 4: **Performances with varying the knowledge order**, where we change the location – top, bottom, or random – of more relevant triples for the question in the prompt of LLMs.

Figure 5: **Performances with varying knowledge amount**, where we change the number of retrieved triples to augment.

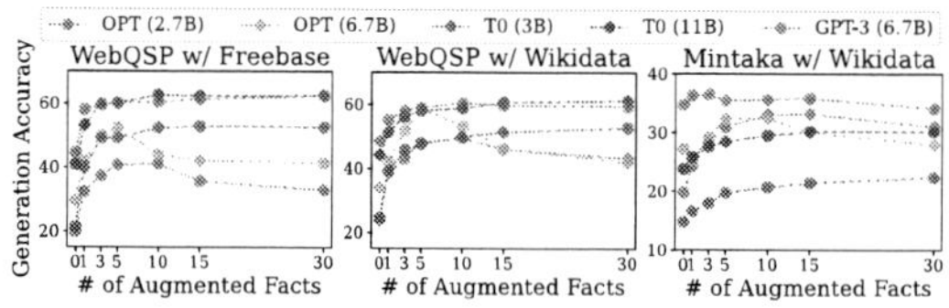

Models	# of Retrieved Facts	Relative Time	
		T0 (3B)	OPT (2.7B)
No Knowledge	0	1.00	1.00
KAPING (Ours)	1	0.49	1.12
	5	0.73	1.48
	10	1.07	1.89
	15	1.54	2.36
	30	2.49	3.77

Table 3: **Efficiencies with varying the knowledge amount**, where we measure the wall-clock time of every model for generating the answer on the WebQSP w/ Wikidata dataset.

Retriever Results To see how relevant the augmented knowledge is, we further measure the retrieval performances. As shown in Table 2, the existing retrieval model (i.e., MPNet) shows superior performances against naive models: random and popular retrievers. This result suggests that our simple graph-to-text verbalization works well with the existing retriever, which further confirms that our KAPING augments useful facts in the LM prompt. Regarding the number of hops for the candidate triples to retrieve, we observe that, when we increase the hop-size from one to two, the retriever is more likely to retrieve irrelevant triples that does not include answer entities, as shown in Table 2. Therefore, in our experiments, we retrieve knowledge among 1-hop triples of question entities.

Additionally, since we can alternatively answer the input question based on entities in the Top-1 triple from the retriever, we compare the generation performance of LLMs to the retrieval performance. As shown in Figure 2, LM prompting schemes even without knowledge augmentation (i.e., no knowledge) are superior than simply answering with the entity in the retrieved triple, except for the WebQSP w/ Freebase dataset. Also, we observe huge gaps between our KAPING framework and the simple retrieval scheme on all datasets. These results suggest that, for zero-shot KGQA, it would be helpful to leverage LLMs to generate answers based on their internalized and external facts, instead of directly searching answer entities over KGs.

Impact of Correct & Incorrect Retrievals We conduct analyses on how much the correctly retrieved triples, having answer entities, bring performance improvements, and how performances are affected by the incorrectly retrieved triples, which do not include answer entities. As shown in Figure 3, when retrieved triples contain answer entities, performances of LLMs are significantly improved, compared to models without knowledge augmentation. However, when retrievers fail, performances are lower than models of no knowledge augmentation. These results suggest, when relevant knowledge is augmented, LLMs can contextualize and generate answers accurately. Meanwhile, incorrectly retrieved knowledge makes LLMs condition on irrelevant facts, and generate wrong answers.

Varying the Amount of Knowledge We change the number of facts, to see which triple amounts are optimal to augment in the prompt, by comparing trade-off between the generation performance and the wall-clock time. First of all, as shown in Figure 5, most LLMs reach the somewhat highest performance, when the number of triples is 5 or 10. Also, when we further increase the augmented triple size to 15 and 30, performances of OPT models are largely decreasing. This result suggests that some LMs might be distracted by irrelevant triples when their volumes are high, therefore, failing to select and generate the answer entity.

We then measure the wall-clock time of the answer generation, for the encoder-decoder (T0) and decoder-only (OPT) models with varying the number of augmented triples in the prompt. As shown in Table 3, regarding the encoder-decoder model, our KAPING framework with less than 10 triples is faster than the model without knowledge augmentation. We observe this is because, when the knowledge is augmented to the model, the model tends to generate shorter answers, which can reduce the decoding time. More specifically, the length of generated tokens for the T0 model with 10 triples is

Table 4: **Generation examples** of the prompted GPT-3 for the input question with augmented triples from the retriever, where, in the last row, we change the knowledge of augmented facts to see whether the model is able to adapt to the changed knowledge.

Question: Where did Alex Chilton die?
Retrieved triples: (Alex Chilton, place of death, New Orleans), (Alex Chilton, manner of death, natural causes), (Alex Chilton, cause of death, myocardial infarction), (Alex Chilton, date of death, time: +2010-03-17), ...
Answer: New Orleans

	Prompts	Outputs
No Knowledge	Question: Where did Alex Chilton die? Answer:	Alex Chilton died in a ~~car accident~~ on ~~February 10, 1979~~.
KAPING (Ours)	Below are facts in the form of the triple meaningful to answer the question. ... (Alex Chilton, date of death, time: +2010-03-17) (Alex Chilton, cause of death, myocardial infarction) (Alex Chilton, manner of death, natural causes) (Alex Chilton, place of death, New Orleans) Question: Where did Alex Chilton die? Answer:	Alex Chilton died on March 17, 2010 in New Orleans, Louisiana due to a myocardial infarction.
KAPING (Ours) w/ Knowledge Change	Below are facts in the form of the triple meaningful to answer the question. ... (Alex Chilton, date of death, time: +2000-09-01) (Alex Chilton, cause of death, pancreatic cancer) (Alex Chilton, manner of death, natural causes) (Alex Chilton, place of death, Los Angeles) Question: Where did Alex Chilton die? Answer:	Alex Chilton died in Los Angeles, California on September 1, 2000 from pancreatic cancer.

Models	**T5 (3B)**	**T5 (11B)**	**OPT (2.7B)**	**OPT (13B)**	**T0 (3B)**	**T0 (11B)**
No Knowledge	14.25	17.06	19.76	26.83	14.75	23.74
Random Knowledge	18.19	18.83	28.11	28.36	16.10	26.15
Random Knowledge w/ EL	15.99	17.98	23.10	26.47	15.60	24.66
KAPING	22.00	22.85	32.94	33.37	20.68	29.50
KAPING w/ EL	18.94	20.58	26.87	28.39	18.51	27.11

Table 5: **Results with entity linking**, where the model w/ EL uses entities extracted from the entity linking technique (Ayoola et al., 2022), instead of using labeled ones, on Mintaka.

15, whereas, the no knowledge model generates 32 tokens in average. However, for the decoder-only model (OPT), the more knowledge we augment, the slower the model becomes, because of its autoregressive characteristic for digesting the input.

Impact of Orders of Retrieved Triples In few-shot LM prompting where LLMs additionally observe few examples in the prompt, they are known to be sensitive to the order of examples (Lu et al., 2022), and they tend to follow the answer in the last example (Zhao et al., 2021). Based on those observations, we also conduct an analysis on whether the order of retrieved triples affects the performance. In particular, we vary the location of more similar triples for the question, by locating them at the Top, Bottom, or Random position of the prompt. As shown in Figure 4, our KAPING is not sensitive to the location of retrieved triples, except for the OPT model on the WebQSP dataset. In other words, the OPT model tends to generate the entity located at the first part of the prompt input. Meanwhile, other LLMs can contextualize the entire prompt input, and generate the entity regardless of its position.

Effectiveness with Entity Linking Following the conventional KGQA evaluation (Cohen et al., 2020), we use question entities labeled in datasets, to retrieve facts in KGs. However, to see the performance with entities identified by Entity Linking (EL) technique, we further conduct experiments with the EL model, namely ReFinED (Ayoola et al., 2022). As shown in Table 5, while the performance of KAPING w/ EL is slightly decreasing from the model with labeled entities due to the performance of EL, we consistently observe meaningful performance improvements from a No Knowledge model.

Case Study We conduct a case study in Table 4. In particular, when the knowledge is not given to the LM, it hallucinates the factually incorrect answer. However, when related facts are retrieved and augmented in the prompt, it can generate the correct answer. In addition, we analyze whether our KAPING can adapt to the updated knowledge, motivated by that some knowledge can be changed over time, while the knowledge in LMs remains static. To do so, as shown in the last row of Table 4, we replace object entities of triples, and then forward the prompt with the modified facts to the LM. Then, the result shows that the LM can generate the output based on the updated facts, which suggests the potential of adapting LMs without costly updating their parameters.

Additional Results Note that we further provide additional experimental results in Appendix B. In particular, we compare the performance of retrievers in Appendix B.1, conduct the sensitivity analysis on template texts in Appendix B.2, provide the results with additional metrics including human evaluation in Appendix B.3, validate our KAPING under few-shot setups in Appendix B.4, provide the analysis on verbalization in Appendix B.5, and provide the efficiencies in Appendix B.6.

6 Conclusion

In this work, we focused on the limitation of existing LM prompting schemes, which rely on the static knowledge internalized in parameters; therefore, when such knowledge are incomplete, inaccurate, and outdated, LLMs may generate factually incorrect answers. To tackle this challenge, we introduced a novel Knowledge-Augmented language model PrompTING (KAPING) framework, which augments the knowledge for the input question from KGs directly in the input prompt of LLMs, with the fact retriever to inject only the relevant knowledge. The proposed framework is completely zero-shot, and versatile with any LMs, without additional parameter updates and training datasets. We validated that our KAPING yields huge performance gaps from the LM prompting model relying on its internal knowledge, especially with smaller LMs, on the KGQA tasks. We believe our new mechanism for augmenting facts from KGs to the LM prompt will bring substantial practical impacts in generating knowledge-grounded answers.

Limitations

In this section, we faithfully discuss the current limitations and potential avenues for future research.

First of all, the generation performance of our knowledge-augmentation framework largely depends on the efficacy of retrievers. In other words, if the retriever fails to retrieve the relevant facts to the input question, the prompted LLM, conditioned on the irrelevant facts, is likely to generate the incorrect answer (See Figure 3). Similarly, if the retriever is not designed to retrieve the facts in 2-hop neighborhoods of the question entities, LLMs are less likely to generate the answer requiring 2-hop knowledge. Note that, for the Mintaka dataset (Sen et al., 2022), the number of answerable questions with 1-hop facts is only 40% of total samples. However, when we include 2-hop triples, the number of answerable questions becomes 62%, which suggests the necessity of 2-hop retrievals, which is yet challenging (See Table 2). Thus, future work may improve the retrieval scheme itself to provide more accurate facts including multi-hops to the LLM, or may develop the mechanism to prevent the LLM from being misled by unrelated facts.

On the other hand, the evaluation metric for the generation performance of prompted LLMs may be further improved. Specifically, regarding our target KGQA tasks, the answer for the question is the entity in KGs. However, the prompted LLMs without additional training (i.e., zero-shot) tend to generate the answer as the sentence. For instance, the label entity for the question (e.g., Where did Alex Chilton die?) in Table 4 is "New Orleans", however, the LLMs often generate the sentence-level output: "Alex Chilton died on March 17, 2010 in New Orleans, Louisiana due to a myocardial infarction". We currently evaluate the model performance by measuring whether generated tokens contain the answer entity or not; however, it would be worthwhile to develop the additional metric to compare the sentence-level output from LLMs to the word-level answer in KGs in a more effective way. Note that we also try other available metrics (See Appendix B.3), such as F1 and Exact Match (EM) scores (Rajpurkar et al., 2016), however, they largely penalize the longer sentences (e.g., EM of correct examples in Table 4 are 0), thus may not be appropriate for evaluating LM prompting schemes.

Lastly, since we focus on the improvement of knowledge injection in LM prompting, we use the labeled entities in KGQA datasets when evaluating models, following the existing KGQA evaluation setups (Cohen et al., 2020; Sen et al., 2021). However, in real-world applications where the entities in the question are mostly not provided, we first need to extract entities in the question with existing entity linking techniques; therefore, our model performance depends on the efficacy of entity linking. In particular, regarding the result with entity linking in Table 5, the portion of answerable questions from labeled entities in the dataset is 40%, however, the portion of them with entities from the entity linking model (Ayoola et al., 2022) is 22%. Therefore, since the improved entity linking performance would contribute to the performance gain of our KAPING framework, for KGQA tasks, future work may advance such the entity linking scheme.

Ethics Statement

For a user's question, our knowledge-augmentation scheme can allow prompted LMs generate a factually correct answer, grounded by the provided knowledge, for KGQA tasks. However, the performance of our KAPING framework is still far from perfect, due to potential failures in entity linking, fact retrieval, and knowledge generation itself. Thus, we should be aware whether LMs generate correct answers, especially on high-risk domains.

Acknowledgements

We thank the members of the End-to-End Reasoning team of Alexa AI at Amazon and the anonymous reviewers for their constructive comments.

References

Tom Ayoola, Shubhi Tyagi, Joseph Fisher, Christos Christodoulopoulos, and Andrea Pierleoni. 2022. Refined: An efficient zero-shot-capable approach to end-to-end entity linking. *arXiv preprint arXiv:2207.04108*.

Junwei Bao, Nan Duan, Zhao Yan, Ming Zhou, and Tiejun Zhao. 2016. Constraint-based question answering with knowledge graph. In *COLING*. ACL.

Hannah Bast, Björn Buchhold, and Elmar Haussmann. 2016. Semantic search on text and knowledge bases. *Found. Trends Inf. Retr.*

Jonathan Berant, Andrew Chou, Roy Frostig, and Percy Liang. 2013. Semantic parsing on freebase from question-answer pairs. In *Proceedings of the 2013 Conference on Empirical Methods in Natural Language Processing, EMNLP 2013, 18-21 October 2013, Grand Hyatt Seattle, Seattle, Washington, USA, A meeting of SIGDAT, a Special Interest Group of the ACL*. ACL.

Kurt D. Bollacker, Colin Evans, Praveen K. Paritosh, Tim Sturge, and Jamie Taylor. 2008. Freebase: a collaboratively created graph database for structuring human knowledge. In *Proceedings of the ACM SIGMOD International Conference on Management of Data, SIGMOD 2008, Vancouver, BC, Canada, June 10-12, 2008*. ACM.

Tom B. Brown, Benjamin Mann, Nick Ryder, Melanie Subbiah, Jared Kaplan, Prafulla Dhariwal, Arvind Neelakantan, Pranav Shyam, Girish Sastry, Amanda Askell, Sandhini Agarwal, Ariel Herbert-Voss, Gretchen Krueger, Tom Henighan, Rewon Child, Aditya Ramesh, Daniel M. Ziegler, Jeffrey Wu, Clemens Winter, Christopher Hesse, Mark Chen, Eric Sigler, Mateusz Litwin, Scott Gray, Benjamin Chess, Jack Clark, Christopher Berner, Sam McCandlish, Alec Radford, Ilya Sutskever, and Dario Amodei. 2020. Language models are few-shot learners. In *NeurIPS*.

Nilesh Chakraborty, Denis Lukovnikov, Gaurav Maheshwari, Priyansh Trivedi, Jens Lehmann, and Asja Fischer. 2019. Introduction to neural network based approaches for question answering over knowledge graphs. *arXiv preprint arXiv:1907.09361*.

Xiang Chen, Lei Li, Ningyu Zhang, Xiaozhuan Liang, Shumin Deng, Chuanqi Tan, Fei Huang, Luo Si, and Huajun Chen. 2022a. Decoupling knowledge from memorization: Retrieval-augmented prompt learning. *arXiv preprint arXiv:2205.14704*.

Xiang Chen, Ningyu Zhang, Xin Xie, Shumin Deng, Yunzhi Yao, Chuanqi Tan, Fei Huang, Luo Si, and Huajun Chen. 2022b. Knowprompt: Knowledge-aware prompt-tuning with synergistic optimization for relation extraction. In *WWW*, pages 2778–2788. ACM.

Aakanksha Chowdhery, Sharan Narang, Jacob Devlin, Maarten Bosma, Gaurav Mishra, Adam Roberts, Paul Barham, Hyung Won Chung, Charles Sutton, Sebastian Gehrmann, Parker Schuh, Kensen Shi, Sasha Tsvyashchenko, Joshua Maynez, Abhishek Rao, Parker Barnes, Yi Tay, Noam Shazeer, Vinodkumar Prabhakaran, Emily Reif, Nan Du, Ben Hutchinson, Reiner Pope, James Bradbury, Jacob Austin, Michael Isard, Guy Gur-Ari, Pengcheng Yin, Toju Duke, Anselm Levskaya, Sanjay Ghemawat, Sunipa Dev, Henryk Michalewski, Xavier Garcia, Vedant Misra, Kevin Robinson, Liam Fedus, Denny Zhou, Daphne Ippolito, David Luan, Hyeontaek Lim, Barret Zoph, Alexander Spiridonov, Ryan Sepassi, David Dohan, Shivani Agrawal, Mark Omernick, Andrew M. Dai, Thanumalayan Sankaranarayana Pillai, Marie Pellat, Aitor Lewkowycz, Erica Moreira, Rewon Child, Oleksandr Polozov, Katherine Lee, Zongwei Zhou, Xuezhi Wang, Brennan Saeta, Mark Diaz, Orhan Firat, Michele Catasta, Jason Wei, Kathy Meier-Hellstern, Douglas Eck, Jeff Dean, Slav Petrov, and Noah Fiedel. 2022. Palm: Scaling language modeling with pathways. *arXiv preprint arXiv:2204.02311*.

William W. Cohen, Haitian Sun, R. Alex Hofer, and Matthew Siegler. 2020. Scalable neural methods for reasoning with a symbolic knowledge base. In *ICLR*.

Jacob Devlin, Ming-Wei Chang, Kenton Lee, and Kristina Toutanova. 2019. BERT: pre-training of deep bidirectional transformers for language understanding. In *NAACL*. Association for Computational Linguistics.

Dennis Diefenbach, Thomas Pellissier Tanon, Kamal Deep Singh, and Pierre Maret. 2017. Question answering benchmarks for wikidata. In *Proceedings of the ISWC 2017 Posters & Demonstrations and Industry Tracks co-located with 16th International Semantic Web Conference (ISWC 2017), Vienna, Austria, October 23rd - to - 25th, 2017*, CEUR Workshop Proceedings. CEUR-WS.org.

Bin Fu, Yunqi Qiu, Chengguang Tang, Yang Li, Haiyang Yu, and Jian Sun. 2020. A survey on complex question answering over knowledge base: Recent advances and challenges. *arXiv preprint arXiv:2007.13069*.

Fabian Galetzka, Jewgeni Rose, David Schlangen, and Jens Lehmann. 2021. Space efficient context encoding for non-task-oriented dialogue generation with graph attention transformer. In *Proceedings of the 59th Annual Meeting of the Association for Computational Linguistics and the 11th International Joint Conference on Natural Language Processing, ACL/IJCNLP 2021, August 1-6, 2021*. Association for Computational Linguistics.

Kelvin Guu, Kenton Lee, Zora Tung, Panupong Pasupat, and Ming-Wei Chang. 2020. REALM: retrieval-augmented language model pre-training. *arXiv preprint arXiv:2002.08909*.

Sebastian Hofstätter, Sheng-Chieh Lin, Jheng-Hong Yang, Jimmy Lin, and Allan Hanbury. 2021. Efficiently teaching an effective dense retriever with balanced topic aware sampling. In *SIGIR '21: The 44th International ACM SIGIR Conference on Research and Development in Information Retrieval, Canada, July 11-15, 2021*. ACM.

Neil Houlsby, Andrei Giurgiu, Stanislaw Jastrzebski, Bruna Morrone, Quentin de Laroussilhe, Andrea Gesmundo, Mona Attariyan, and Sylvain Gelly. 2019. Parameter-efficient transfer learning for NLP. In *ICML*, Proceedings of Machine Learning Research. PMLR.

Shengding Hu, Ning Ding, Huadong Wang, Zhiyuan Liu, Jingang Wang, Juanzi Li, Wei Wu, and Maosong Sun. 2022. Knowledgeable prompt-tuning: Incorporating knowledge into prompt verbalizer for text classification. In *ACL*, pages 2225–2240, Dublin, Ireland. Association for Computational Linguistics.

Gautier Izacard, Patrick Lewis, Maria Lomeli, Lucas Hosseini, Fabio Petroni, Timo Schick, Jane Dwivedi-Yu, Armand Joulin, Sebastian Riedel, and Edouard Grave. 2022. Few-shot learning with retrieval augmented language models. *arXiv preprint arXiv:2208.03299*.

Minki Kang, Jin Myung Kwak, Jinheon Baek, and Sung Ju Hwang. 2022. Knowledge-consistent dialogue generation with knowledge graphs. In *ICML 2022 Workshop on Knowledge Retrieval and Language Models*.

Vladimir Karpukhin, Barlas Oguz, Sewon Min, Patrick S. H. Lewis, Ledell Wu, Sergey Edunov, Danqi Chen, and Wen-tau Yih. 2020. Dense passage retrieval for open-domain question answering. In *Proceedings of the 2020 Conference on Empirical Methods in Natural Language Processing, EMNLP 2020, November 16-20, 2020*. Association for Computational Linguistics.

Takeshi Kojima, Shixiang Shane Gu, Machel Reid, Yutaka Matsuo, and Yusuke Iwasawa. 2022. Large language models are zero-shot reasoners. *arXiv preprint arXiv:2205.11916*.

Angeliki Lazaridou, Elena Gribovskaya, Wojciech Stokowiec, and Nikolai Grigorev. 2022. Internet-augmented language models through few-shot prompting for open-domain question answering. *arXiv preprint arXiv:2203.05115*.

Brian Lester, Rami Al-Rfou, and Noah Constant. 2021a. The power of scale for parameter-efficient prompt tuning. In *Proceedings of the 2021 Conference on Empirical Methods in Natural Language Processing, EMNLP 2021, Virtual Event / Punta Cana, Dominican Republic, 7-11 November, 2021*, pages 3045–3059. Association for Computational Linguistics.

Brian Lester, Rami Al-Rfou, and Noah Constant. 2021b. The power of scale for parameter-efficient prompt tuning. In *Proceedings of the 2021 Conference on Empirical Methods in Natural Language Processing, EMNLP 2021 / Punta Cana, Dominican Republic, 7-11 November, 2021*. Association for Computational Linguistics.

Patrick S. H. Lewis, Ethan Perez, Aleksandra Piktus, Fabio Petroni, Vladimir Karpukhin, Naman Goyal, Heinrich Küttler, Mike Lewis, Wen-tau Yih, Tim Rocktäschel, Sebastian Riedel, and Douwe Kiela. 2020. Retrieval-augmented generation for knowledge-intensive NLP tasks. In *NeurIPS*.

Belinda Z. Li, Sewon Min, Srinivasan Iyer, Yashar Mehdad, and Wen-tau Yih. 2020. Efficient one-pass end-to-end entity linking for questions. In *Proceedings of the 2020 Conference on Empirical Methods in Natural Language Processing, EMNLP 2020, November 16-20, 2020*. Association for Computational Linguistics.

Jimmy Lin, Rodrigo Nogueira, and Andrew Yates. 2021. *Pretrained Transformers for Text Ranking: BERT and Beyond*. Synthesis Lectures on Human Language Technologies. Morgan & Claypool Publishers.

Jiachang Liu, Dinghan Shen, Yizhe Zhang, Bill Dolan, Lawrence Carin, and Weizhu Chen. 2022a. What makes good in-context examples for gpt-3? In *Proceedings of Deep Learning Inside Out: The 3rd Workshop on Knowledge Extraction and Integration for Deep Learning Architectures, DeeLIO@ACL 2022, Dublin, Ireland and Online, May 27, 2022*, pages 100–114. Association for Computational Linguistics.

Jiacheng Liu, Alisa Liu, Ximing Lu, Sean Welleck, Peter West, Ronan Le Bras, Yejin Choi, and Hannaneh Hajishirzi. 2022b. Generated knowledge prompting for commonsense reasoning. In *ACL*. Association for Computational Linguistics.

Pengfei Liu, Weizhe Yuan, Jinlan Fu, Zhengbao Jiang, Hiroaki Hayashi, and Graham Neubig. 2021. Pretrain, prompt, and predict: A systematic survey of prompting methods in natural language processing. *arXiv preprint arXiv:2107.13586*.

Yinhan Liu, Myle Ott, Naman Goyal, Jingfei Du, Mandar Joshi, Danqi Chen, Omer Levy, Mike Lewis, Luke Zettlemoyer, and Veselin Stoyanov. 2019. Roberta: A robustly optimized BERT pretraining approach. *arXiv preprint arXiv:1907.11692*.

Yao Lu, Max Bartolo, Alastair Moore, Sebastian Riedel, and Pontus Stenetorp. 2022. Fantastically ordered prompts and where to find them: Overcoming few-shot prompt order sensitivity. In *ACL*. Association for Computational Linguistics.

Kangqi Luo, Fengli Lin, Xusheng Luo, and Kenny Q. Zhu. 2018. Knowledge base question answering via encoding of complex query graphs. In *Proceedings of the 2018 Conference on Empirical Methods in Natural Language Processing, Brussels, Belgium, October 31 - November 4, 2018*. Association for Computational Linguistics.

Kaixin Ma, Hao Cheng, Xiaodong Liu, Eric Nyberg, and Jianfeng Gao. 2022. Open domain question answering with A unified knowledge interface. In *ACL*. Association for Computational Linguistics.

Vaibhav Mavi, Anubhav Jangra, and Adam Jatowt. 2022. A survey on multi-hop question answering and generation. *arXiv preprint arXiv:2204.09140*.

Tri Nguyen, Mir Rosenberg, Xia Song, Jianfeng Gao, Saurabh Tiwary, Rangan Majumder, and Li Deng. 2016. MS MARCO: A human generated machine reading comprehension dataset. In *Proceedings of the Workshop on Cognitive Computation: Integrating neural and symbolic approaches 2016 co-located with the 30th Annual Conference on Neural Information Processing Systems (NIPS 2016), Barcelona, Spain, December 9, 2016*, CEUR Workshop Proceedings. CEUR-WS.org.

Barlas Oguz, Xilun Chen, Vladimir Karpukhin, Stan Peshterliev, Dmytro Okhonko, Michael Sejr Schlichtkrull, Sonal Gupta, Yashar Mehdad, and Scott Yih. 2022. Unik-qa: Unified representations of structured and unstructured knowledge for open-domain question answering. In *Findings of the Association for Computational Linguistics: NAACL*. Association for Computational Linguistics.

Adam Paszke, Sam Gross, Francisco Massa, Adam Lerer, James Bradbury, Gregory Chanan, Trevor Killeen, Zeming Lin, Natalia Gimelshein, Luca Antiga, Alban Desmaison, Andreas Kopf, Edward Yang, Zachary DeVito, Martin Raison, Alykhan Tejani, Sasank Chilamkurthy, Benoit Steiner, Lu Fang, Junjie Bai, and Soumith Chintala. 2019. Pytorch: An imperative style, high-performance deep learning library. In *NeurIPS*. Curran Associates, Inc.

Ted Pedersen, Siddharth Patwardhan, and Jason Michelizzi. 2004. Wordnet: : Similarity - measuring the relatedness of concepts. In *Proceedings of the Nineteenth National Conference on Artificial Intelligence, Sixteenth Conference on Innovative Applications of Artificial Intelligence, July 25-29, 2004, San Jose, California, USA*, pages 1024–1025. AAAI Press / The MIT Press.

Fabio Petroni, Tim Rocktäschel, Sebastian Riedel, Patrick S. H. Lewis, Anton Bakhtin, Yuxiang Wu, and Alexander H. Miller. 2019. Language models as knowledge bases? In *Proceedings of the 2019 Conference on Empirical Methods in Natural Language Processing and the 9th International Joint Conference on Natural Language Processing, EMNLP-IJCNLP 2019, Hong Kong, China, November 3-7, 2019*. Association for Computational Linguistics.

Alec Radford, Karthik Narasimhan, Tim Salimans, Ilya Sutskever, et al. 2018. Improving language understanding by generative pre-training.

Colin Raffel, Noam Shazeer, Adam Roberts, Katherine Lee, Sharan Narang, Michael Matena, Yanqi Zhou, Wei Li, and Peter J. Liu. 2020. Exploring the limits of transfer learning with a unified text-to-text transformer. *J. Mach. Learn. Res.*

Pranav Rajpurkar, Jian Zhang, Konstantin Lopyrev, and Percy Liang. 2016. Squad: 100, 000+ questions for machine comprehension of text. In *Proceedings of the 2016 Conference on Empirical Methods in Natural Language Processing, EMNLP 2016, Austin, Texas, USA, November 1-4, 2016*. The Association for Computational Linguistics.

Adam Roberts, Colin Raffel, and Noam Shazeer. 2020. How much knowledge can you pack into the parameters of a language model? In *EMNLP*.

Anna Rohrbach, Lisa Anne Hendricks, Kaylee Burns, Trevor Darrell, and Kate Saenko. 2018. Object hallucination in image captioning. In *Proceedings of the 2018 Conference on Empirical Methods in Natural Language Processing, Brussels, Belgium, October 31 - November 4, 2018*. Association for Computational Linguistics.

Md. Rashad Al Hasan Rony, Ricardo Usbeck, and Jens Lehmann. 2022. Dialokg: Knowledge-structure aware task-oriented dialogue generation. In *Findings of the Association for Computational Linguistics: NAACL*. Association for Computational Linguistics.

Ohad Rubin, Jonathan Herzig, and Jonathan Berant. 2022. Learning to retrieve prompts for in-context learning. In *Proceedings of the 2022 Conference of the North American Chapter of the Association for Computational Linguistics: Human Language Technologies, NAACL 2022, Seattle, WA, United States, July 10-15, 2022*, pages 2655–2671. Association for Computational Linguistics.

Amir Saffari, Armin Oliya, Priyanka Sen, and Tom Ayoola. 2021. End-to-end entity resolution and question answering using differentiable knowledge graphs. In *Proceedings of the 2021 Conference on Empirical Methods in Natural Language Processing, EMNLP 2021 / Punta Cana, Dominican Republic, 7-11 November, 2021*. Association for Computational Linguistics.

Victor Sanh, Albert Webson, Colin Raffel, Stephen Bach, Lintang Sutawika, Zaid Alyafeai, Antoine Chaffin, Arnaud Stiegler, Arun Raja, Manan Dey, M Saiful Bari, Canwen Xu, Urmish Thakker, Shanya Sharma Sharma, Eliza Szczechla, Taewoon Kim, Gunjan Chhablani, Nihal V. Nayak, Debajyoti Datta, Jonathan Chang, Mike Tian-Jian Jiang, Han Wang, Matteo Manica, Sheng Shen, Zheng Xin Yong, Harshit Pandey, Rachel Bawden, Thomas Wang, Trishala Neeraj, Jos Rozen, Abheesht Sharma, Andrea Santilli, Thibault Févry, Jason Alan Fries, Ryan Teehan, Teven Le Scao, Stella Biderman, Leo Gao, Thomas Wolf, and Alexander M. Rush. 2022. Multitask prompted training enables zero-shot task generalization. In *ICLR*.

Apoorv Saxena, Aditay Tripathi, and Partha P. Talukdar. 2020. Improving multi-hop question answering over knowledge graphs using knowledge base embeddings. In *ACL*. Association for Computational Linguistics.

Priyanka Sen, Alham Fikri Aji, and Amir Saffari. 2022. Mintaka: A complex, natural, and multilingual dataset for end-to-end question answering. In *COLING*. International Committee on Computational Linguistics.

Priyanka Sen, Armin Oliya, and Amir Saffari. 2021. Expanding end-to-end question answering on differentiable knowledge graphs with intersection. In *Proceedings of the 2021 Conference on Empirical Methods in Natural Language Processing, EMNLP 2021 / Punta Cana, Dominican Republic, 7-11 November, 2021*. Association for Computational Linguistics.

Taylor Shin, Yasaman Razeghi, Robert L. Logan IV, Eric Wallace, and Sameer Singh. 2020. Autoprompt: Eliciting knowledge from language models with automatically generated prompts. In *Proceedings of the 2020 Conference on Empirical Methods in Natural Language Processing, EMNLP 2020, Online, November 16-20, 2020*, pages 4222–4235. Association for Computational Linguistics.

Saleh Soltan, Shankar Ananthakrishnan, Jack FitzGerald, Rahul Gupta, Wael Hamza, Haidar Khan, Charith Peris, Stephen Rawls, Andy Rosenbaum, Anna Rumshisky, Chandana Satya Prakash, Mukund Sridhar, Fabian Triefenbach, Apurv Verma, Gökhan Tür, and Prem Natarajan. 2022. Alexatm 20b: Few-shot learning using a large-scale multilingual seq2seq model. *arXiv preprint arXiv:2208.01448*.

Kaitao Song, Xu Tan, Tao Qin, Jianfeng Lu, and Tie-Yan Liu. 2020. Mpnet: Masked and permuted pre-training for language understanding. In *NeurIPS*.

Robyn Speer, Joshua Chin, and Catherine Havasi. 2017. Conceptnet 5.5: An open multilingual graph of general knowledge. In *Proceedings of the Thirty-First AAAI Conference on Artificial Intelligence, February 4-9, 2017, San Francisco, California, USA*, pages 4444–4451. AAAI Press.

Haitian Sun, Bhuwan Dhingra, Manzil Zaheer, Kathryn Mazaitis, Ruslan Salakhutdinov, and William W. Cohen. 2018. Open domain question answering using early fusion of knowledge bases and text. In *Proceedings of the 2018 Conference on Empirical Methods in Natural Language Processing, Brussels, Belgium, October 31 - November 4, 2018*. Association for Computational Linguistics.

Mujeen Sung, Jinhyuk Lee, Sean S. Yi, Minji Jeon, Sungdong Kim, and Jaewoo Kang. 2021. Can language models be biomedical knowledge bases? In *EMNLP*. Association for Computational Linguistics.

Ashish Vaswani, Noam Shazeer, Niki Parmar, Jakob Uszkoreit, Llion Jones, Aidan N. Gomez, Lukasz Kaiser, and Illia Polosukhin. 2017. Attention is all you need. In *NeurIPS*.

Denny Vrandecic and Markus Krötzsch. 2014. Wikidata: a free collaborative knowledgebase. *Commun. ACM*, 57(10):78–85.

Xuezhi Wang, Jason Wei, Dale Schuurmans, Quoc V. Le, Ed H. Chi, and Denny Zhou. 2022. Self-consistency improves chain of thought reasoning in language models. *arXiv preprint arXiv:2203.11171*.

Jason Wei, Maarten Bosma, Vincent Y. Zhao, Kelvin Guu, Adams Wei Yu, Brian Lester, Nan Du, Andrew M. Dai, and Quoc V. Le. 2022a. Finetuned language models are zero-shot learners. In *ICLR*.

Jason Wei, Xuezhi Wang, Dale Schuurmans, Maarten Bosma, Ed H. Chi, Quoc Le, and Denny Zhou. 2022b. Chain of thought prompting elicits reasoning in large language models. *arXiv preprint arXiv:2201.11903*.

Thomas Wolf, Lysandre Debut, Victor Sanh, Julien Chaumond, Clement Delangue, Anthony Moi, Pierric Cistac, Tim Rault, Rémi Louf, Morgan Funtowicz, Joe Davison, Sam Shleifer, Patrick von Platen, Clara Ma, Yacine Jernite, Julien Plu, Canwen Xu, Teven Le Scao, Sylvain Gugger, Mariama Drame, Quentin Lhoest, and Alexander M. Rush. 2020. Transformers: State-of-the-art natural language processing. In *Proceedings of the 2020 Conference on Empirical Methods in Natural Language Processing: System Demonstrations*. Association for Computational Linguistics.

Ledell Wu, Fabio Petroni, Martin Josifoski, Sebastian Riedel, and Luke Zettlemoyer. 2020. Scalable zero-shot entity linking with dense entity retrieval. In *Proceedings of the 2020 Conference on Empirical Methods in Natural Language Processing, EMNLP 2020, November 16-20, 2020*. Association for Computational Linguistics.

Lee Xiong, Chenyan Xiong, Ye Li, Kwok-Fung Tang, Jialin Liu, Paul N. Bennett, Junaid Ahmed, and Arnold Overwijk. 2021. Approximate nearest neighbor negative contrastive learning for dense text retrieval. In *ICLR*.

Zhilin Yang, Zihang Dai, Yiming Yang, Jaime G. Carbonell, Ruslan Salakhutdinov, and Quoc V. Le. 2019. Xlnet: Generalized autoregressive pretraining for language understanding. In *NeurIPS*.

Michihiro Yasunaga, Hongyu Ren, Antoine Bosselut, Percy Liang, and Jure Leskovec. 2021. QA-GNN: reasoning with language models and knowledge graphs for question answering. In *NAACL*. Association for Computational Linguistics.

Wen-tau Yih, Ming-Wei Chang, Xiaodong He, and Jianfeng Gao. 2015. Semantic parsing via staged query graph generation: Question answering with knowledge base. In *ACL*. The Association for Computer Linguistics.

Wen-tau Yih, Matthew Richardson, Christopher Meek, Ming-Wei Chang, and Jina Suh. 2016. The value of semantic parse labeling for knowledge base question answering. In *ACL*. The Association for Computer Linguistics.

Jun Yin, Xin Jiang, Zhengdong Lu, Lifeng Shang, Hang Li, and Xiaoming Li. 2016. Neural generative question answering. In *Proceedings of the Twenty-Fifth International Joint Conference on Artificial Intelligence, IJCAI 2016, New York, NY, USA, 9-15 July 2016*, pages 2972–2978. IJCAI/AAAI Press.

Susan Zhang, Stephen Roller, Naman Goyal, Mikel Artetxe, Moya Chen, Shuohui Chen, Christopher Dewan, Mona Diab, Xian Li, Xi Victoria Lin, Todor Mihaylov, Myle Ott, Sam Shleifer, Kurt Shuster, Daniel Simig, Punit Singh Koura, Anjali Sridhar, Tianlu Wang, and Luke Zettlemoyer. 2022. OPT: open pretrained transformer language models. *arXiv preprint arXiv:2205.01068*.

Zihao Zhao, Eric Wallace, Shi Feng, Dan Klein, and Sameer Singh. 2021. Calibrate before use: Improving few-shot performance of language models. In *ICML*, Proceedings of Machine Learning Research. PMLR.

Yucheng Zhou, Xiubo Geng, Tao Shen, Wenqiang Zhang, and Daxin Jiang. 2021. Improving zero-shot cross-lingual transfer for multilingual question answering over knowledge graph. In *NAACL*. Association for Computational Linguistics.

A Additional Experimental Setups

Here we provide additional experimental setups.

A.1 Datasets

We provide the additional details for two Knowledge Graph Question Answering (KGQA) datasets, namely WebQuestionsSP and Mintaka, which we use for evaluating baselines and our model.

WebQuestionsSP (WebQSP) A question and its corresponding answer are annotated with Freebase entities (Bollacker et al., 2008), and refined with additional cleaning steps (Yih et al., 2016): filtering out samples with invalid annotations, from the original WebQuestions dataset (Berant et al., 2013).

Mintaka This dataset (Sen et al., 2022) is designed for complex KGQA tasks including superlative and comparative questions, where question-answer pairs are collected from crowdsourcing with Wikidata entities (Vrandecic and Krötzsch, 2014).

A.2 Large Language Models

We describe the specific details of Large Language Models (LLMs) that we use for LM prompting.

T5 This model (Raffel et al., 2020) is an encoder-decoder model, and, among different variants, we use the LM-adapted version[1], which is additionally pre-trained with auto-regressive language modeling objective (Radford et al., 2018) for LM prompting.

T0 This model (Sanh et al., 2022) is further fine-tuned from T5 (Raffel et al., 2020) over prompted text-to-text tasks, for improved zero-shot generalization performance with LM prompting.

GPT-3 This model (Brown et al., 2020) is a decoder only model, which we access via API[2].

OPT This model (Zhang et al., 2022) is a decoder only model, freely available for researchers.

AlexaTM This model (Soltan et al., 2022) is an encoder-decoder model, pre-trained with denoising, which reconstructs the context of 15% dropped tokens, and auto-regressive, which predicts the next tokens based on their previous tokens, objectives.

A.3 Evaluation Metrics

We provide more details for evaluation metrics.

Aliases For generative question answering tasks, there can be alternative names of entities, called aliases, and we consider them for evaluation. For example, one Wikidata entity, "William Shakespeare" (Q692), has alternative names, such as "Shakespeare" and "The Bard", and we consider them when measuring the generation performance.

Filtering Unnamed Entities For evaluating generative models, the name of entities are required. However, we sometime cannot find the name of the answer entities from their ids on Freebase and Wikidata KGs. This is because the annotated answer entities are sometimes not entities but categories, and the entity ids in KGs could be changed but we cannot find the KG dumps that are used to annotate datasets. Therefore, we filter out samples that do not have literal name texts for the answer entities. This filtering step results in 1,582 test samples for the WebQSP w/ Freebase dataset, 1,466 test samples for the WebQSP w/ Wikidata dataset, and 2,814 test samples for the Mintaka dataset.

A.4 Implementation Details

In this subsection, we provide additional details for implementing our KAPING framework.

Knowledge Injection Schemes There are different choices in knowledge injection schemes, from the number of facts to retrieve, to the number of hops for candidate triples, to the order of retrieved facts in the prompt (i.e., where the most relevant knowledge should be located in the prompt), to the template of prompts including their instruction texts. While search spaces of them are extremely huge, we aim to to find the optimal one (See analyses in Section 5). Specifically, as reported in Section 4.5, the best settings we find are the number of retrieved facts of 10, and the number of hops for the triples to retrieve from the question entities of one. Also, we locate more relevant triples to the input question closer to the question text in the prompt, inspired by the observation that the model tends to rewrite answers that appeared at the end of the prompt (Zhao et al., 2021). Further, we examine different instruction templates for generating answers, such as "Question: $\{x\}$ Answer: " or "Please answer the following question: $\{x\}$", where x is the literal question. Regarding instruction templates, we observe that the performances of LLMs are sensitive across different instructions (See Appendix B.2), therefore, we try both of them and then report the best result.

[1]https://github.com/google-research/text-to-text-transfer-transformer/blob/main/released_checkpoints.md

[2]https://openai.com/api/

Datasets	Retrievers	1-Hop Retrieval MRR	Top-1	Top-10	Top-30	2-Hop Retrieval MRR	Top-1	Top-10	Top-30
WebQSP w/ Freebase	MPNet	47.27	40.27	60.56	64.48	41.64	33.12	58.47	65.23
	TAS-B	51.62	45.76	61.76	64.41	37.08	25.85	58.66	64.48
WebQSP w/ Wikidata	MPNet	43.46	33.36	64.39	70.67	40.42	30.56	62.62	71.56
	TAS-B	46.68	37.65	65.08	70.67	41.92	32.20	62.21	72.17
Mintaka w/ Wikidata	MPNet	13.01	7.50	25.44	35.43	13.00	6.82	26.65	40.01
	TAS-B	13.21	7.57	25.20	35.04	12.36	6.79	24.13	36.07

Table 6: **Results of two different retrievers**, namely MPNet (Song et al., 2020) and TAS-B (Hofstätter et al., 2021).

Retrieval Models To augment only the relevant triples to the input question under the zero-shot setup, we use off-the-shelf text-based retriever models. Specifically, we experiment with two different types of retrievers: symmetric retriever that uses the same encoder for question and triples; asymmetric one that uses individual encoders for them. For the symmetric retriever, we use MPNet (Song et al., 2020), which is trained on 1B sentence pairs[3]. Also, for the asymmetric retriever, we use TAS-B (Hofstätter et al., 2021), which is trained on the MSMARCO dataset (Nguyen et al., 2016). We mainly report the results with MPNet, unless noted, since there performances are similar (See Appendix B.1).

A.5 Hyperparameters and Resources

We evaluate all models with PyTorch (Paszke et al., 2019) and Transformers (Wolf et al., 2020) libraries. We set the maximum number of input token lengths of LMs as 1,024 and the maximum number of output token lengths as 128, for encoder-decoder models. For decoder-only models, we set the maximum token lengths as 1,152 (1,024 + 128). For computing resources, we run all models with 8 V100 GPUs, having 8 × 32GB GPU memory, in which every model is runnable within one day. Note that, due to the expensive computational costs for model prompting with LLMs, we run every model one time, and then report the results, without additional hyperparameter tuning unless noted.

B Additional Experiment Results

In this section, we provide additional experimental results, on the comparisons of available text-based retrieval models in Section B.1, the sensitive analyses on template texts of the prompt in Section B.2, and the extra evaluation metrics in Section B.3.

B.1 Performance Comparisons of Retrievers

In Table 6, we compare existing symmetric and asymmetric retrievers named MPNet (Song et al., 2020) and TAS-B (Hofstätter et al., 2021), explained in Section A.4, on 1- and 2-hop retrievals. As shown in Table 6, we observe similar performances between symmetric (MPNet) and asymmetric (TAS-B) retrievers, which suggests that our simple graph-to-text verbalization is robust across different text-based retrieval schemes. Note that, since retrieval performances of both are similar, we conduct experiments mainly with MPNet, to reduce expensive computational costs for GPU usages.

[3]https://huggingface.co/sentence-transformers/all-mpnet-base-v2

Datasets	Models	Templates	T5 (11B)	T0 (11B)	OPT (6.7B)	GPT-3 (6.7B)
WebQSP w/ Freebase	No Knowledge	Default	9.48	34.70	29.77	44.63
		Please	3.03	40.77	18.71	42.48
	KAPING	Default	24.91	62.58	43.93	60.37
		Please	17.45	61.19	34.07	60.43
WebQSP w/ Wikidata	No Knowledge	Default	15.21	38.88	33.77	48.50
		Please	5.12	44.20	22.71	48.29
	KAPING	Default	35.47	58.73	53.34	60.44
		Please	20.12	56.89	48.16	59.69
Mintaka w/ Wikidata	No Knowledge	Default	17.06	22.60	27.19	35.00
		Please	5.47	23.74	17.70	34.65
	KAPING	Default	22.85	29.50	32.37	33.55
		Please	14.68	29.18	28.18	35.61

Table 7: **Results with varying instruction templates**, for various LLMs on the WebQSP and Mintaka datasets.

B.2 Sensitivity Analyses on Template Texts

Following the observation in Zhao et al. (2021), the performances of LLMs vary across different templates in the prompt. In our experiments, since it is computationally infeasible to try all different prompt templates on various LLMs, we consider two types of question templates, described in Appendix A.4. In particular, for the question x, we use either "Question: $\{x\}$ Answer: ", which we refer to as *default* template, or "Please answer the following question: $\{x\}$", referred to as *please* template. As shown in Table 7, for the T5 model, the default template is superior than the please template. Meanwhile, for the OPT model, the please template is superior than the other. However, for T0 and GPT-3 models, performance differences between default and please templates are marginal. Therefore, these results suggest that we may need to select instruction templates carefully across different LLMs for achieving optimal performances.

Additionally, regarding the knowledge-injection template described in Section 3.2, we also observe that the generation performance of GPT-3 depends on the instruction text in the template. In particular, we mainly conduct experiments with the template: "Below are facts in the form of the triple meaningful to answer the question."; however, we observe the performance degeneration when the augmented triples are irrelevant to the given question as shown

Datasets	Methods	T5 (0.8B)			T5 (3B)			T5 (11B)			OPT (2.7B)			OPT (6.7B)			OPT (13B)		
		Acc.	F1	EM	Acc.	F1	EM	Acc.	F1	EM	Acc.	F1	EM	Acc.	F1	EM	Acc.	F1	EM
WebQSP w/ Freebase	No Knowledge	6.95	5.20	0.00	13.40	8.11	0.00	9.48	8.25	0.06	19.85	7.20	0.38	29.77	10.60	0.06	28.38	7.92	0.70
	Random Knowledge	21.55	9.74	0.00	19.15	8.08	0.00	17.57	7.50	0.19	28.07	13.33	0.06	31.73	13.01	0.00	33.31	12.41	0.00
	Popular Knowledge	15.30	8.75	0.06	16.88	8.19	0.00	18.39	8.95	0.19	28.32	13.78	0.06	28.13	12.21	0.00	24.21	9.86	0.00
	Generated Knowledge	6.19	7.96	0.00	7.84	7.56	0.06	6.76	6.51	0.00	7.46	4.59	0.00	11.50	4.95	0.00	8.22	4.59	0.00
	KAPING (Ours)	34.70	15.39	0.00	25.41	8.31	0.06	24.91	11.02	0.32	41.09	16.32	0.00	43.93	15.15	0.00	40.20	13.32	0.00
WebQSP w/ Wikidata	No Knowledge	10.30	5.60	0.00	18.42	8.48	0.00	15.21	8.94	0.07	23.94	7.90	0.48	33.77	11.41	0.07	32.40	8.45	0.75
	Random Knowledge	17.94	7.81	0.00	22.78	7.74	0.07	24.28	9.41	0.34	37.24	16.78	0.00	35.61	12.54	0.00	38.27	14.61	0.07
	Popular Knowledge	15.35	8.01	0.00	20.80	8.48	0.00	20.74	9.20	0.14	30.83	15.65	0.00	30.01	13.32	0.00	27.83	11.95	0.00
	Generated Knowledge	11.94	8.64	0.00	13.30	8.19	0.07	12.28	7.11	0.00	11.26	5.06	0.00	17.53	5.60	0.00	14.19	4.94	0.00
	KAPING (Ours)	23.67	10.46	0.00	40.38	13.25	0.00	35.47	11.50	0.34	49.52	20.17	0.00	53.34	16.62	0.00	51.57	16.73	0.14
Mintaka w/ Wikidata	No Knowledge	11.23	6.77	0.00	14.25	9.81	0.00	17.06	10.28	0.00	19.76	6.63	0.28	27.19	10.60	0.04	26.83	9.82	0.43
	Random Knowledge	17.59	10.48	0.18	18.19	9.24	0.00	18.83	9.82	0.57	28.11	14.47	0.00	26.58	12.80	0.00	28.36	14.02	0.11
	Popular Knowledge	17.56	9.88	0.00	18.09	10.47	0.07	18.73	10.07	0.53	26.97	13.76	0.00	27.08	12.95	0.07	23.10	11.28	0.00
	Generated Knowledge	13.61	9.23	0.00	14.61	8.85	0.00	14.29	7.51	0.04	11.87	6.34	0.00	14.96	5.81	0.04	16.24	7.14	0.00
	KAPING (Ours)	19.72	11.36	0.04	22.00	11.17	0.00	22.85	10.91	0.43	32.94	14.99	0.00	32.37	14.37	0.04	33.37	14.65	0.11

Datasets	Methods	T0 (3B)			T0 (11B)			AlexaTM (20B)			GPT-3 (6.7B)			GPT-3 (175B)			Average		
		Acc.	F1	EM	Acc.	F1	EM	Acc.	F1	EM	Acc.	F1	EM	Acc.	F1	EM	Acc.	F1	EM
WebQSP w/ Freebase	No Knowledge	21.43	22.70	9.99	40.77	46.10	34.39	46.79	17.65	0.00	44.63	21.12	1.77	63.59	32.75	8.47	29.55	17.05	5.07
	Random Knowledge	32.62	36.48	26.55	51.20	55.98	46.90	57.37	20.91	0.00	51.01	28.04	6.19	65.87	41.28	18.46	37.22	22.43	8.94
	Popular Knowledge	27.05	31.38	20.23	47.22	52.44	42.04	54.91	20.45	0.00	45.58	25.94	4.87	62.26	38.84	17.00	33.48	20.98	7.68
	Generated Knowledge	19.41	23.15	10.56	38.81	43.43	31.23	35.13	14.42	0.00	45.89	27.98	9.48	62.14	38.79	17.57	22.67	16.72	6.26
	KAPING (Ours)	52.28	55.27	48.04	62.85	66.11	58.53	67.67	23.16	0.00	60.37	32.89	8.34	73.89	43.15	20.67	**47.94**	**27.28**	**12.36**
WebQSP w/ Wikidata	No Knowledge	24.56	24.20	10.98	44.20	49.27	37.65	42.41	16.43	0.00	48.50	24.01	3.96	67.60	34.31	10.30	32.85	18.09	5.84
	Random Knowledge	28.85	33.08	22.37	47.68	52.34	42.50	55.63	19.88	0.06	52.05	25.37	2.18	60.64	36.88	13.92	38.27	21.49	7.41
	Popular Knowledge	24.83	27.89	16.03	48.02	52.84	41.88	53.92	19.77	0.00	47.41	24.36	3.75	63.37	37.08	14.73	34.83	20.78	6.96
	Generated Knowledge	22.92	25.28	11.80	41.34	45.70	33.83	31.16	13.36	0.00	48.77	29.72	11.19	65.89	39.52	17.87	26.42	17.56	6.80
	KAPING (Ours)	49.86	50.75	41.27	58.73	61.90	53.27	65.04	22.72	0.00	60.44	31.18	6.82	69.58	41.83	19.71	**50.69**	**27.01**	**11.05**
Mintaka w/ Wikidata	No Knowledge	14.75	20.84	11.34	23.74	28.69	20.86	41.97	17.05	0.00	34.65	17.67	2.31	56.33	26.77	6.11	26.16	14.99	3.76
	Random Knowledge	16.10	23.08	14.14	26.15	31.70	22.85	46.02	17.02	0.00	32.98	17.55	1.39	51.56	25.98	6.29	28.22	16.92	4.14
	Popular Knowledge	16.74	23.13	14.53	27.15	32.17	23.45	46.41	17.31	0.00	32.48	20.07	4.41	53.16	27.44	6.86	27.95	17.14	4.54
	Generated Knowledge	14.46	20.08	11.98	23.13	27.34	18.76	34.58	14.91	0.00	33.12	18.29	3.09	55.65	30.69	11.73	22.41	14.20	4.15
	KAPING (Ours)	20.68	27.80	18.12	29.50	34.83	26.23	49.08	17.90	0.00	35.61	20.80	5.79	56.86	28.63	7.64	**32.27**	**18.86**	**5.31**

Table 8: **LM prompting results with additional metrics: F1 and Exact Match (EM)**, along with accuracy (Acc.) scores.

in Figure 3. Therefore, to improve the performance on incorrect retrievals, we further experiment with the additional template: "Below are facts in the form of the triple that might be meaningful to answer the question.". Then, the GPT-3 (175B) model with the previous template achieves 74.16 and 42.80 accuracies for correct and incorrect retrievals, respectively. Meanwhile, the same model with the instruction template containing "might be" achieves 72.91 and 51.38 accuracies for correct and incorrect retrievals, respectively. Thus, these results suggest that the knowledge-injection template with "might be" statement makes the model less selective on the augmented triples while focusing more on the internalized knowledge in parameters, thus improving the incorrect retrieval performance while degenerating the correct retrieval.

B.3 Additional Evaluation Metrics

As described in Section 4.4, we evaluate the performance of LLMs based on whether generated tokens for the input question contain answer entities or not. This is because, as explained in Section 6 of the limitation, pre-trained LLMs without further fine-tuning tend to generate the answer as the sentence, while the answer for the KGQA task is the entity consisting of few tokens. In this subsection, we further provide experiment results with additional evaluation metrics (Rajpurkar et al., 2016), namely F1 and Exact Match (EM) scores. Note that they are frequently used for evaluating extractive QA models, whose goal is to classify the answer span in the given context, without generation. As shown in Table 8, since the F1 score penalizes the longer sentence too much, the performances of LLMs evaluated by F1 scores are largely decreasing, except for the T0 model that is further fine-tuned by prompted text-to-text tasks, including QA, thus capable of generating entity-level outputs. Similarly, except for the T0, it is highly suboptimal to evaluate the performance of prompted LMs with EM scores, due to differences in output lengths. Thus, it would be promising direction to further develop better evaluation metrics for KGQA under LM prompting schemes, which we leave as future work.

While such F1 and EM scores, used for extractive QA tasks, might be suboptimal to evaluate generative LM prompting schemes, our KAPING framework consistently outperforms all the other baselines based on averaged F1 and EM scores as well, by large margins. Note that the superior EM and F1 scores of the generated knowledge baseline with GPT-3 on few cases, even though they are rarely happen, is because, for this baseline, the GPT-3 model generates entity-level outputs, unlike ours that generates sentence-level outputs. In other words, the sentence-level outputs from our KAPING is often longer than the answer entities, since our model is grounded by retrieved facts from KGs as shown in Table 15; however, longer sentences penalize F1 and EM scores. More specifically, the average number of output sequence lengths of the

LLMs	Models	Correct	Semi-Correct	Incorrect
T0 (3B)	No Knowledge	7	1	22
	KAPING (Ours)	17	0	13
T0 (11B)	No Knowledge	14	0	16
	KAPING (Ours)	20	0	10
GPT-3 (6.7B)	No Knowledge	12	4	14
	KAPING (Ours)	19	4	17
GPT-3 (175B)	No Knowledge	22	1	7
	KAPING (Ours)	26	1	3

Table 9: **Human evaluation results**, where we randomly sample 30 examples from the WebQSP w/ Freebase dataset.

Models	Shots	T5 (3B)	OPT (6.7B)	T0 (11B)
No Knowledge	Zero-Shot	18.42	33.77	44.20
	One-Shot	18.28	36.90	41.13
	Three-Shots	17.87	37.65	37.38
KAPING (Ours)	Zero-Shot	40.38	53.34	58.73
	One-Shot	18.42	52.25	48.70
	Three-Shots	10.16	50.34	43.45

Table 10: **KGQA results with few-shot learning**. We vary the number of examples (i.e., shots) in the prompt, and report the performances on the WebQSP w/ Wikidata dataset.

generated knowledge model is 67.77, meanwhile, ours is 74.92. However, when we compare the generated knowledge baseline to our KAPING with other LLMs but also with other metrics, our KAPING significantly outperforms this baseline.

Human Evaluation Additionally, similar to the previous generative QA work (Roberts et al., 2020), we manually inspect 30 samples from the WebQSP w/ Freebase dataset, to see whether the generated sentence is factually correct to the input question. For this experiment, we evaluate four LLMs: T0 (3B), T0 (11B), GPT-3 (6.7B), and GPT-3 (175B), with no knowledge baseline and our KAPING. Also, we use three different ratings for each generation example: 1) we label it as correct if all information in the generated sentence is factually correct to the question; 2) we label it as semi-correct if some information in the generated sentence is factually incorrect which yet contains at least one answer entity; 3) we label it as incorrect for all the other cases. As shown in Table 9, we observe that our KAPING framework can generate the factually correct answer more, compared to the no knowledge baseline, which are consistent with the results from available evaluation metrics in Table 1 and Table 8. We provide generated answers, which we use for human evaluation in Table 9, for GPT-3 (175B) and T0 (3B) models in Table 15 and Table 16.

B.4 Performances of Few-Shot Learning

While the focus of our work is zero-shot as outlined in the main paper, in this subsection, we additionally extend this zero-shot setting to the few-shot setting, where we prepend the few examples about the input-output pairs in the prompt of LLMs. As shown in Table 10, for the KGQA task, the performances are decreasing when we increase the number of samples (i.e., shots) in the input prompt, except for the OPT model. We suggest this might be because, the injected examples in the prompt are less relevant to the given factual question, misleading the model to focus on unrelated contexts on the injected examples. This phenomenon is even more severe in our KAPING framework; this is similarly because our KAPING augments the retrieved facts, and if the facts on the other few-shot examples are further injected in the input prompt, the model is more likely to be confused by those irrelevant facts. For the OPT model, we observe a slight performance improvement in the No Knowledge model, since few injected examples provide a hint on how the output format looks like. We leave further extending our zero-shot KAPING framework to the few-shot learning mechanism as future work.

Retrievers	MRR	Top-1	Top-10	Top-30
Random Retrieval	9.50	3.62	22.58	40.72
Popular Retrieval	8.52	4.57	15.89	35.47
Retrieval with Free-Form Texts	41.33	31.11	62.07	69.92
Retrieval with Triple-Form Texts	43.46	33.36	64.39	70.67

Table 11: **Retrieval results with different verbalizers**. We use the graph-to-text transformation model proposed in Ma et al. (2022) for obtaining free-form texts. For triple-form texts, we use the verbalization technique described in Section 3.2. MPNet (Song et al., 2020) is used as the retriever, and the performance is reported on WebQSP w/ Wikidata.

Retrievers	T5 (3B)	OPT (6.7B)	T0 (3B)	T0 (11B)
No Knowledge	18.42	33.77	24.56	44.20
KAPING with Free-Form Texts	43.25	53.00	47.75	53.21
KAPING with Triple-Form Texts	40.38	53.34	49.86	58.73

Table 12: **KGQA results with different verbalizers**. We use the graph-to-text transformation model proposed in Ma et al. (2022) for obtaining free-form texts. For triple-form texts, we use the verbalization technique described in Section 3.2. We then inject the verbalized triples in the input prompt. We report the generation accuracy on WebQSP w/ Wikidata.

B.5 Analyses on Knowledge Verbalization

As described in the Knowledge Verbalization paragraph of Section 3.2, we use the linear triple verbalization technique, which simply concatenates the tokens of subject, relation, and object in the triple, instead of using the sophisticated techniques that use the particular graph-to-text transformation methods (Oguz et al., 2022; Ma et al., 2022). This is because, we observe that our simple verbalization technique works well, and, in this subsection, we concretely show performance differences between our and existing verbalization techniques in

Models	# of Augmented Knowledge	Relative Time							
		T5 (0.8B)	T5 (3B)	T5 (11B)	OPT (2.7B)	OPT (6.7B)	OPT (13B)	T0 (3B)	T0 (11B)
No Knowledge	0	1.00	1.00	1.00	1.00	1.00	1.00	1.00	1.00
Document (Web) Augmentation	1	1.20	1.45	2.13	1.43	1.65	1.63	1.60	2.29
	5	2.78	4.16	6.80	3.42	3.90	3.66	2.98	9.01
	10	OOL	OOL	OOL	6.44	7.36	6.67	OOL	OOL
	15	OOL	OOL	OOL	9.35	10.71	OOM	OOL	OOL
	30	OOL	OOL	OOL	OOL	OOL	OOL	OOL	OOL
KAPING (Ours)	1	1.08	0.97	1.35	1.12	1.21	1.19	0.49	1.28
	5	1.22	1.50	2.13	1.48	1.65	1.60	0.73	2.18
	10	1.53	2.10	3.11	1.89	2.20	2.10	1.07	3.83
	15	1.84	2.74	4.02	2.36	2.76	2.58	1.54	4.59
	30	2.82	4.42	6.05	3.77	4.28	4.06	2.49	7.76

Table 13: **Efficiencies results**, where we measure the wall-clock time of every model for generating answers on the WebQSP w/ Wikidata dataset. The document augmentation model (Lazaridou et al., 2022) augments documents listed in their paper, meanwhile, ours augments relevant triples to the question retrieved from KGs. We set the maximum number of input sequences for T5 and T0 models as 1,024, and for OPT as 2,048. OOL denotes the out-of-length errors, where the input prompt length exceeds the maximum input token lengths. OOM denotes the out-of-memory error on the machine having eight V100 GPUs.

both the knowledge retrieval and injection steps. Note that, for the comparison, we use the trained knowledge verbalizer proposed in Ma et al. (2022).

We first provide the fact retrieval performances across the different knowledge verbalization methods in Table 11. As shown in Table 11, we observe that our simple triple-form text verbalization is superior to the free-form text verbalization in the fact retrieval. This might be because the free-form verbalization model, transforming the graph to the text, might generate the incorrect output that is semantically different from the original triple, leading to the degenerated retrieval performances.

On the other hand, we also report the generation results of KGQA with two different knowledge verbalizers on our KAPING framework in Table 12. As shown in Table 12, we observe that the performances between the free-form texts and the triple-form texts are comparable when augmented to LLMs with our KAPING framework. More specifically, for the T5 model, which is pre-trained on the unlabeled corpus without additional instruction tuning, the free-form text works well. Meanwhile, for the T0 model, which is further fine-tuned with natural language instruction tasks, it is beneficial to use our linear triple verbalizaton scheme.

B.6 Additional Efficiency Comparisons

In this subsection, we further provide efficiency results of all LLMs that we use in our main experiments across three different models: no knowledge model, document augmentation (i.e., web augmentation) model (Lazaridou et al., 2022), and our KAPING framework. We note that, as discussed in the Knowledge-Augmented LMs paragraph of Section 2, the web augmentation method augments documents searched from Google with the few-shot learning setup. However, as we discuss there, this web augmentation is orthogonal to ours, since we use the completely different knowledge source (i.e., KGs) and our work is under the zero-shot learning setup; from which our core mechanisms of how to retrieve and augment relevant knowledge with LM prompting is clearly different and novel. Furthermore, as discussed in Section 2, this web augmentation method is infeasible to experimentally compare as well, since individual researches cannot freely access the Google Search API to retrieve documents for every question in the world. Also, it is computationally expensive to augment documents consisting of hundreds to thousands tokens (Lazaridou et al., 2022) in LLMs, unlike our triple cases consisting of few tokens. In this subsection, to experimentally validate the latter issue, we further make the comparisons of computational costs between document augmentation and our fact augmentation. In particular, as shown in Table 13, the answer generation speed of the web augmentation mechanism is significantly slower than our triple augmentation mechanism, since it requires more time to encode and condition documents in the input prompt compared to triples. Also, following the original paper (Lazaridou et al., 2022), the suggested number of documents to augment is 15, however, in the most cases, we observe out-of-length (OOL) errors, since the length of the input prompt with 15 documents is longer than the maximum input sequence length of LLMs. While our fact augmentation scheme is slower than the model without augmentation, we believe that, given the substantially improved performance in Table 1 and the high efficiency compared to document augmentation in Table 13, KAPING is highly beneficial.

B.7 Result Analyses Across Question Types

For the Mintaka dataset (Sen et al., 2022), each question is belong to one of the following categories: Generic, Multihop, Intersection, Difference, Comparative, Superlative, Ordinal, Count, and Yes/No, which defines the complexity of questions. Therefore, to see which complexity category our knowledge-augmentation framework is helpful, and which category we should further improve on, we breakdown the performance of LLMs according to question types in Table 14. Note that, following the evaluation protocol in Section A.3 where we filter out questions that do not have answer names, the Yes/No type questions are not considered.

As shown in the last row of Table 14 where we average the performance of all LLMs per category, our KAPING framework brings significant performance improvements on all categories except for the Comparative type. One particular comparative-type question is "Who has won more NBA Season MVPs, LeBron James or Steph Curry", and, since it is hard to retrieve and associate relevant triples for such the comparative-type question, our KAPING underperforms simple knowledge-injection baselines: random knowledge and popular knowledge. However, the KG-augmented models (e.g., random knowledge, popular knowledge, and our KAPING) outperform other baselines, which suggests that knowledge-augmentation mechanism is meaningful to tackle comparative questions, and one might further improve the retrieval scheme or the input prompt itself, which we leave as future work.

On the other point we would like to mention is that, for the Count category, performances of T0 models are significantly low compared to other LLMs. This is surprising, since T0 models are further fine-tuned on the prompted text-to-text tasks, and they have strong performances on the other categories, thanks to fine-tuning. We believe such the low performance on the Count category is because, in the fine-tuning of T0 models, there are no prompted tasks related to counting, which makes T0 models hard to count particular instances. Therefore, to further improve the generalization performance of T0 models, one may additionally include more diverse prompted tasks, including the counting one, during the fine-tuning process.

B.8 Generation Examples

We provide generation examples for comparisons between the no knowledge baseline and our KAPING framework in Table 15 and Table 16 for GPT-3 and T0 language models, respectively. We also provide retrieved and generation examples of our KAPING framework with four different LLMs: T5 (11B), OPT (13B), T0 (11B), and GPT-3 (175B) on the WebQSP w/ Wikidata dataset in Table 17.

C Discussions on Prompt Design/Tuning

We discuss differences between prompt design and prompt tuning, along with additional relevant work in the prompt tuning literature. As described in Section 3.1, given an input question, the large language model can generate the answer text, which is called LM prompting (Brown et al., 2020; Liu et al., 2021). However, to further enhance the performance of models under the LM prompting scheme, prior work particularly designs the content in the prompt, which is called *prompt design* (Shin et al., 2020; Lu et al., 2022). More specifically, Shin et al. (2020) additionally include the particular trigger tokens, meaningful to the down-stream tasks, in the prompt, and Lu et al. (2022) change the order of demonstrations in the prompt under the few-shot LM prompting setup. Our method is in line with such the prompt design literature, and we introduce the method of knowledge augmentation in the input prompt with facts from KGs, to allow LLMs condition on factual knowledge for zero-shot QA.

On the other hand, there exists *prompt tuning* literature (Lester et al., 2021a), which additionally trains the prompt-relevant parameters with supervised learning objectives, while keeping the parameters of LLMs unchanged. While this prompt tuning approach can be beneficial in few-shot learning scenarios where the model is additionally tuned with few training examples, it is not suitable for our zero-shot learning. Also, unlike the prompt design approach, it is difficult to interpret and manipulate the prompt represented in the embedding space.

Note that, recently, there are few knowledge-aware prompt tuning work (Chen et al., 2022b; Hu et al., 2022; Chen et al., 2022a), and, while they are fundamentally different from our LM prompting (i.e., prompt design), we additionally discuss them. First of all, Chen et al. (2022b) tackle the relation extraction problem with prompt tuning, where they propose to embed the particular words related to the relation class in the embedding space. For example, for the relation type to classify: "county of birth", they embed person and country information in the representation space with training signals from supervised learning, for improved relation classification performance. Also, Hu et al. (2022) tackle the text classification task with prompt tuning, where they propose to not only consider the classification label word itself, but also the label word's related words. For example, for the sentence label "science", they further consider its related words:

"physics" and "mathematics", defined in particular knowledge bases, such as WordNet (Pedersen et al., 2004) and ConceptNet (Speer et al., 2017). Lastly, Chen et al. (2022a) tackle the similar text classification task with prompt tuning, where they propose to retrieve the data instance (i.e., a sentence and its label) in the training dataset based on the retriever training with supervised classification objectives.

However, all the above knowledge-aware prompt tuning methods are clearly different from our proposed KAPING framework. At first, they are restricted to cloze-style prediction, in which they first include the particular mask token in the input prompt, and then classify the label (e.g., sentiment of the sentence, or relation in the given sentence) of the mask token, similar to the masked language modeling objective (Devlin et al., 2019; Liu et al., 2019). Therefore, their cloze-style prediction schemes cannot be used for QA tasks, since the answer of the user's question is not the single token, and it is unclear to convert the predicted label token from the masked token to all different answers in the world. In contrast to them, our KAPING does not rely on the masked token classification scheme, thus ours is more flexible, and not restricted to cloze-style classification; suitable for answering any user's questions. Furthermore, some of them (Chen et al., 2022a,b) rely on training signals from the training dataset with supervised learning, meanwhile, ours is completely zero-shot. While Chen et al. (2022a) show the model's zero-shot ability, they require the training dataset as discussed in their paper, thus not suitable for our zero-shot QA as well. Lastly, we augment the factual knowledge by matching the entity in the question to its associated triples in KGs, however, prior work considers different knowledge source, which might not be helpful for QA tasks, such as relationships between words (Hu et al., 2022), relationships between the relation class and particular words (Chen et al., 2022b), and a pair of sentence and its label in training data (Chen et al., 2022a).

LLMs	**Models**	**Generic** (557)	**Multihop** (220)	**Intersection** (396)	**Difference** (349)	**Comparative** (223)	**Superlative** (384)	**Ordinal** (307)	**Count** (378)
T5 (0.8B)	No Knowledge	7.00	3.64	8.08	7.45	69.06	2.86	2.61	10.05
	Random Knowledge	11.49	5.45	8.33	11.75	86.10	6.77	8.14	26.98
	Popular Knowledge	13.82	5.91	11.62	8.60	87.00	8.33	5.86	22.22
	Generated Knowledge	7.72	2.73	5.81	8.02	82.06	3.39	1.95	21.43
	KAPING (Ours)	18.85	6.36	15.40	10.32	83.41	9.64	7.49	24.60
T5 (3B)	No Knowledge	10.41	4.09	9.60	9.74	71.30	5.47	4.56	17.99
	Random Knowledge	17.41	6.82	13.64	14.61	55.16	8.59	7.82	30.42
	Popular Knowledge	14.90	6.82	14.90	13.75	57.40	8.85	10.75	28.84
	Generated Knowledge	7.90	3.64	8.33	8.31	82.51	4.69	3.91	21.96
	KAPING (Ours)	25.31	12.27	20.96	15.76	47.98	10.68	9.77	35.71
T5 (11B)	No Knowledge	10.23	5.00	10.35	8.60	92.83	7.55	3.58	24.87
	Random Knowledge	20.29	7.27	11.87	12.89	60.99	10.68	9.12	27.51
	Popular Knowledge	16.88	7.27	12.88	13.18	72.20	9.11	10.42	24.34
	Generated Knowledge	7.72	2.73	5.30	7.45	89.24	3.91	2.28	22.49
	KAPING (Ours)	24.42	8.64	18.69	16.05	65.92	11.98	11.07	34.66
OPT (2.7B)	No Knowledge	24.06	10.00	16.67	10.32	54.26	20.05	14.98	14.29
	Random Knowledge	29.44	13.18	23.74	18.34	93.27	15.62	14.01	34.13
	Popular Knowledge	28.90	14.09	20.45	18.62	90.58	12.76	13.36	34.13
	Generated Knowledge	7.90	6.82	10.35	8.02	44.84	4.19	4.56	20.11
	KAPING (Ours)	33.75	15.91	34.85	20.63	93.27	15.89	19.54	43.65
OPT (6.7B)	No Knowledge	29.62	12.73	37.37	20.06	62.78	20.83	22.80	16.93
	Random Knowledge	23.52	14.09	19.44	20.92	89.69	13.02	15.31	36.77
	Popular Knowledge	24.42	13.18	24.24	22.92	83.86	14.84	17.26	32.80
	Generated Knowledge	11.67	8.64	16.92	12.61	43.95	7.55	6.51	20.90
	KAPING (Ours)	33.39	11.36	33.08	20.92	87.44	17.19	20.2	45.77
OPT (13B)	No Knowledge	33.57	16.82	34.85	18.91	48.43	19.27	19.22	22.75
	Random Knowledge	31.60	17.27	26.77	23.78	59.19	16.93	20.85	35.45
	Popular Knowledge	22.98	13.64	24.49	18.34	59.64	11.72	12.05	30.69
	Generated Knowledge	17.95	10.00	19.44	12.03	47.98	8.07	9.77	12.70
	KAPING (Ours)	40.04	17.27	35.61	23.50	56.05	19.53	27.36	45.24
T0 (3B)	No Knowledge	13.82	10.00	14.39	10.89	49.33	14.06	8.79	7.94
	Random Knowledge	19.57	9.09	15.66	12.32	58.30	8.59	9.77	6.88
	Popular Knowledge	19.21	10.00	18.69	12.03	60.09	8.33	8.79	8.73
	Generated Knowledge	13.11	11.36	12.63	12.61	54.71	12.50	10.10	3.70
	KAPING (Ours)	29.98	10.45	26.01	12.32	55.16	12.24	11.40	10.85
T0 (11B)	No Knowledge	33.93	18.18	33.08	18.05	54.71	19.53	13.68	1.59
	Random Knowledge	36.98	22.27	34.60	21.78	58.74	18.75	19.22	1.59
	Popular Knowledge	38.42	24.09	38.64	24.36	58.74	17.45	18.57	1.06
	Generated Knowledge	33.21	17.73	34.09	17.48	51.12	18.23	14.33	0.79
	KAPING (Ours)	45.60	27.27	41.16	22.35	56.05	18.75	23.45	1.59
GPT-3 (6.7B)	No Knowledge	40.39	28.18	34.34	24.36	74.44	26.04	24.76	33.07
	Random Knowledge	39.68	26.82	30.05	23.78	77.13	19.53	23.13	33.86
	Popular Knowledge	40.57	25.00	32.83	22.64	70.85	21.35	21.17	31.48
	Generated Knowledge	40.75	23.64	33.59	28.08	71.75	20.83	22.15	30.16
	KAPING (Ours)	46.14	24.09	33.33	24.36	77.58	19.53	24.76	35.71
GPT-3 (175B)	No Knowledge	71.10	52.73	64.90	49.00	80.72	42.45	50.81	38.62
	Random Knowledge	62.30	46.82	56.31	43.55	86.10	38.54	48.21	36.51
	Popular Knowledge	68.40	54.09	58.84	46.42	81.61	37.76	47.88	33.60
	Generated Knowledge	70.56	56.82	64.14	48.14	85.65	44.79	49.19	29.63
	KAPING (Ours)	69.48	56.36	63.89	48.14	82.96	45.57	49.84	41.01
Average	No Knowledge	27.41	16.14	26.36	17.74	65.79	17.81	16.58	18.81
	Random Knowledge	29.23	16.91	24.04	20.37	**72.47**	15.70	17.56	27.01
	Popular Knowledge	28.85	17.41	25.76	20.09	72.20	15.05	16.61	24.79
	Generated Knowledge	21.85	14.41	21.06	16.28	65.38	12.82	12.48	18.39
	KAPING (Ours)	**36.70**	**19.00**	**32.30**	**21.44**	70.58	**18.10**	**20.49**	**31.88**

Table 14: **Results across question types** – Generic, Multihop, Intersection, Difference, Comparative, Superlative, Ordinal, and Count – in the Mintaka dataset with various LLMs, where we report the generation accuracy. The number inside the parentheses in the first row denotes the number of data instances per category. We provide averaged results in the last row, namely **Average**.

Table 15: **Generation examples of GPT-3 (6.7B)** on the WebQSP w/ Freebase dataset, where we randomly sample 30 examples.

Index	Question	Answer Entities	No Knowledge	KAPING
1	who is tatyana ali parents?	[Sheriff Ali, Sonia Ali]	Tatyana Ali's parents are unknown.	Tatyana Ali's parents are Sheriff Ali and Sonia Ali.
2	what language do most australians speak?	[English Language, Esperanto Language, Lojban]	Most Australians speak English.	Most Australians speak English.
3	who played darth vader in the first movie?	[David Prowse, James Earl Jones]	James Earl Jones	Mark Hamill
4	who does michael keaton play in cars?	[Chick Hicks, Chick Hicks]	Michael Keaton plays the role of Larry "Lester" Fenton in Cars.	The role of Michael Keaton in Cars is that of a voice actor.
5	what was pink floyd's first album?	[Psychedelic Session-compilation album]	The first album released by Pink Floyd was the self-titled "Pink Floyd" in 1965.	Pink Floyd's first album was called "Pink Floyd".
6	where is walton county ga?	[Atlanta-Sandy Springs-Marietta, GA Metropolitan Statistical Area, Georgia]	Walton County is located in Georgia.	According to the US Census 2000, Walton County is located in between 30641 and 30025, in Gratis, Georgia.
7	what kind government does egypt have?	[Semi-presidential system, Provisional government]	Egypt has a presidential system.	Egpyt has a semi-presidential system of government.
8	where is english spoken around the world?	[Bahamas, Bangladesh, ..., United Kingdom, United States of America, Australia, New Zealand, Canada]	English is spoken around the world.	English is spoken in different countries around the world. England, United States of America, United Kingdom
9	who did steve spurrier play pro football for?	[San Francisco 49ers, Tampa Bay Buccaneers]	Steve Spurrier played professional football for the Tampa Bay Buccaneers from 1976 to 1978.	St. Louis Rams
10	what kind of music did franz liszt compose?	[Opera, Romantic music, Art song, Classical music, Chamber music]	Franz Liszt composed a great deal of classical music, including symphonies, operas, and piano sonatas.	Franz Liszt composed both classical and popular music. Some of his most famous works include the opera Don Giovanni, the symphonies Annabella and Egmont, and the song Totentanz.
11	what was the currency used in france before the euro?	[Assignat, French franc]	Until the late 1990s, France used the franc as its official currency.	the currency used in France before the euro was the French franc.
12	where is the riviera casino?	[Las Vegas]	The Riviera Casino is located in Las Vegas, NV.	Riviera casino is located on the Las Vegas strip in Nevada.
13	what does wh smith stand for?	[WHSmith]	Whit Smith is an American printing and publishing company. It exclusively publishes books for children and young adults.	William Henry Smith
14	who will play mr gray in the film?	[Jamie Dornan]	Mr. Gray has not been announced, but it is likely that the role will be played by a younger actor.	The film will be based on the book "Fifty Shades of Grey" by E.L. James, and the character Mr. Grey will be played by Jamie Dornan.
15	what religions are popular in france?	[Catholicism]	There are a number of religions popular in France, some of which are Christianity, Islam, Hinduism, and Judaism.	According to the 2016 census, 51.6% of the population of France identify as Christians, including 35.9% who identify as Catholic and 14.4% as Protestant. The remaining 5.1% of the population identify with other religions. Furthermore, according to the 2012 census, French is the language most commonly spoken at home by the population of France. It is also the language most commonly spoken in the administrative regions of metropolitan France, with Italian second and French Creole third.
16	who did nasri play for before arsenal?	[Olympique de Marseille]	he played for Universidad de Chile and Monaco before joining Arsenal in 2011.	Samir Nasri played for different teams before Arsenal, including Manchester City and Marseille.

Continued on the next page

Table 15 – Continued from the previous page

Index	Question	Answer Entities	No Knowledge	KAPING
17	who plays ziva david on ncis?	[Cote de Pablo]	Ziva David is played by Sandra Oh.	Ziva David is played by actress Debra Messing in the NBC television series NCIS.
18	where did adolf hitler die?	[Berlin]	Adolf Hitler died in his home town of Braunau am Inn, Austria on April 30, 1945, days before German forces unconditionally surrendered in World War II.	Adolf Hitler committed suicide in Berlin, Germany.
19	what was hitler the leader of?	[Hitler Youth, Gestapo, 1st SS Panzer Division Leibstandarte SS Adolf Hitler, Nazi Party, Schutzstaffel, Waffen-SS, Wehrmacht, Sturmabteilung]	Hitler was the leader of Nazi Germany, which was a fascist dictatorship in Europe during the 1930s and 1940s.	The leader of Nazi Germany was Adolf Hitler.
20	what types of art did andy warhol do?	[Modern art, Pop art]	Andy Warhol did a variety of art, including paintings, sculptures, and prints.	visual_art.visual_artist.artworks, men in her life
21	who owns the portland press herald?	[Blethen Maine Newspapers, Inc.]	The Portland Press Herald is not owned by any specific individual or entity. It is an independent, locally owned newspaper.	The Portland Press Herald is owned by the Blethen Maine Newspapers, Inc.
22	where was the vietnam war location?	[Vietnam, Cambodia, Laos, Southeast Asia, South Vietnam, North Vietnam]	The Vietnam War was fought in Vietnam, Cambodia, and Laos	The Vietnam War was fought in Cambodia, Laos, North Vietnam, and South Vietnam.
23	who was isaac newton and what did he do?	[Chemist, Philosopher, Mathematician, Physicist, Scientist, Astronomer]	Isaac Newton was a physicist, mathematician, astronomer, and author of the Newtonian Theory of Motion. He is most famous for his three laws of motion and his theory of universal gravitation.	Isaac Newton was a scientist, mathematician, and philosopher.
24	what standard time is michigan?	[UTC-05:00, Central Time Zone, Eastern Time Zone]	Daylight Saving Time is in effect in Michigan from the first Sunday in April to the last Sunday in October.	Michigan is in the Eastern Time Zone.
25	what is the kentucky state bird?	[Cardinal]	The Kentucky state bird is the cardinal.	The kentucky state bird is the pigeon.
26	what do people in jamaica speak?	[Jamaican English, Jamaican Creole English Language, Jamaican English]	people in Jamaica speak English.	Jamaican Creole English Language
27	who wrote the jana gana mana?	[Ram Singh Thakur, Rabindranath Tagore]	The author of the Jana Gana Mana is unknown.	Jana Gana Mana was written by the composer Ram Singh Thakur.
28	what is the currency of the czech republic?	[Czech koruna]	The Czech Republic currency is the Czech koruna.	The currency of the Czech Republic is the Czech koruna.
29	what highschool did harper lee go to?	[Monroe County High School]	Harper Lee attended the Monroeville, Alabama high school.	Harper Lee attended Monroeville High School.
30	what did michael crabtree do?	[Wide receiver, Athlete, American football player, Wide receiver]	Michael Crabtree is a former football player who played for the Baltimore Ravens. Crabtree caught a pass in the end zone to tie the game against the San Francisco 49ers in the final seconds of the game in 2013.	He is an American football player.

Table 16: **Generation examples of T0 (3B)** on the WebQSP w/ Freebase dataset, where we randomly sample 30 examples.

Index	Question	Answer Entities	No Knowledge	KAPING
1	who is tatyana ali parents?	[Sheriff Ali, Sonia Ali]	ali is the daughter of ali khan and tatyana ali	Sheriff Ali
2	what language do most australians speak?	[English Language, Esperanto Language, Lojban]	Australian English	English Language
3	who played darth vader in the first movie?	[David Prowse, James Earl Jones]	Darth Vader	George Lucas
4	who does michael keaton play in cars?	[Chick Hicks, Chick Hicks]	a narrator	George A. Douglas
5	what was pink floyd's first album?	[Psychedelic Session-compilation album]	The Pink Floyd album	Pink Floyd
6	where is walton county ga?	[Atlanta-Sandy Springs-Marietta, GA Metropolitan Statistical Area, Georgia]	Walton County is a county in the U.S. state of Ohio.	Walton County, Georgia
7	what kind government does egypt have?	[Semi-presidential system, Provisional government]	government	Semi-presidential system
8	where is english spoken around the world?	[Bahamas, Bangladesh, ..., United Kingdom, United States of America, Australia, New Zealand, Canada]	The English language is spoken by approximately 6.1 million people in the United Kingdom, with the remainder in the United States, Canada, Australia, New Zealand, Canada, and the United States Virgin Islands.	England
9	who did steve spurrier play pro football for?	[San Francisco 49ers, Tampa Bay Buccaneers]	the New York Giants	the New York Giants
10	what kind of music did franz liszt compose?	[Opera, Romantic music, Art song, Classical music, Chamber music]	classical	Art song
11	what was the currency used in france before the euro?	[Assignat, French franc]	The pound was used in France before the euro.	French franc
12	where is the riviera casino?	[Las Vegas]	Riviera Maya, Mexico	Las Vegas
13	what does wh smith stand for?	[WHSmith]	smith is a scottish slang word for a smith	William Henry Smith
14	who will play mr gray in the film?	[Jamie Dornan]	Corey Haim	Christian Grey
15	what religions are popular in france?	[Catholicism]	Roman Catholicism	Protestantism
16	who did nasri play for before arsenal?	[Olympique de Marseille]	Arsenal	Arsenal
17	who plays ziva david on ncis?	[Cote de Pablo]	sarah savage	Donald P. Bellisario
18	where did adolf hitler die?	[Berlin]	in a concentration camp	Berlin
19	what was hitler the leader of?	[Hitler Youth, Gestapo, 1st SS Panzer Division Leibstandarte SS Adolf Hitler, Nazi Party, Schutzstaffel, Waffen-SS, Wehrmacht, Sturmabteilung]	the Nazi Party	World War I
20	what types of art did andy warhol do?	[Modern art, Pop art]	art	visual art.visual_artist.artworks, Men in Her Life
21	who owns the portland press herald?	[Blethen Maine Newspapers, Inc.]	The Portland Press Herald is a local, independent newspaper based in Portland, Oregon, United States.	Blethen Maine Newspapers

Continued on the next page

Table 16 – Continued from the previous page

Index	Question	Answer Entities	No Knowledge	KAPING
22	where was the vietnam war location?	[Vietnam, Cambodia, Laos, Southeast Asia, South Vietnam, North Vietnam]	Vietnam War	Vietnam
23	who was isaac newton and what did he do?	[Chemist, Philosopher, Mathematician, Physicist, Scientist, Astronomer]	was a british physicist	physicist
24	what standard time is michigan?	[UTC-05:00, Central Time Zone, Eastern Time Zone]	Standard time is local time in the United States.	Midwestern United States
25	what is the kentucky state bird?	[Cardinal]	a red-winged blackbird	Pigeon
26	what do people in jamaica speak?	[Jamaican English, Jamaican Creole English Language, Jamaican English]	People in Jamaica speak English	Jamaican Creole English Language
27	who wrote the jana gana mana?	[Ram Singh Thakur, Rabindranath Tagore]	the author of the jana gana mana is a poet	Rabindranath Tagore
28	what is the currency of the czech republic?	[Czech koruna]	the czech koruna	Czech koruna
29	what highschool did harper lee go to?	[Monroe County High School]	Harper Lee High School	Monroeville High School
30	what did michael crabtree do?	[Wide receiver, Athlete, American football player, Wide receiver]	did not have a job	American football player

Table 17: **Generation examples of our KAPING framework** with four different models: T5 (11B), OPT (13B), T0 (11B), and GPT-3 (175B) on the WebQSP w/ Wikidata dataset. Note that the answer entities are labeled entities in the test dataset.

Index	Question	Retrieved Triples	Answer Entities	Generated Answers
1	what is the name of the currency used in china?	(People's Republic of China, currency, renminbi), (People's Republic of China, short name, text: Chine), (People's Republic of China, short name, text: Chiny), (People's Republic of China, language used, Chinese), (People's Republic of China, central bank, People's Bank of China), (People's Republic of China, language used, China Buriat), (People's Republic of China, demonym, text: Chinesin), (People's Republic of China, language used, Jingpho), (People's Republic of China, language used, Langnian Buyang), (People's Republic of China, language used, Then)	[Renminbi]	**T5**: Renminbi **OPT**: Renminbi **T0**: renminbi **GPT-3**: The name of the currency used in china is renminbi.
2	what does george wilson do for a living?	(George Wilson, country of citizenship, United States of America), (George Wilson, occupation, American football player), (George Wilson, sex or gender, male), (George Wilson, given name, George), (George Wilson, instance of, human), (George Wilson, place of birth, Paducah), (George Wilson, member of sports team, Arkansas Razorbacks football), (George Wilson, member of sports team, Detroit Lions), (George Wilson, member of sports team, Buffalo Bills), (George Wilson, educated at, Paducah Tilghman High School)	[American football player]	**T5**: Wilson, George was born on August 10, 1972 in Paducah, Kentucky. He is an American football player. **OPT**: George Wilson is an American football player. **T0**: American football player **GPT-3**: George Wilson is an American football player.
3	what was augustus caesar famous for?	(Augustus, Roman cognomen, Caesar), (Augustus, father, Julius Caesar), (Augustus, occupation, Ancient Roman politician), (Augustus, child, Lucius Caesar), (Augustus, child, Gaius Caesar), (Augustus, Roman cognomen, Caepias), (Augustus, relative, Julius Caesar), (Augustus, Roman praenomen, Gaius), (Augustus, father, Gaius Octavius), (Augustus, family, Julii Caesares)	[Roman emperor, Politician]	**T5**: Augustus was a Roman politician who ruled from 14 BC to 14 AD. He was the son of Gaius Octavius and Octavia. He was the first emperor of the Roman Empire. **OPT**: Augustus Caesar was famous for being the first Roman emperor. **T0**: He was the first Roman Emperor **GPT-3**: Augustus Caesar was famous for being the first Roman Emperor.
4	what document did james madison write?	(James Madison, described by source, Obalky knih.cz), (James Madison, described by source, The Nuttall Encyclopædia), (James Madison, Commons Creator page, text: James Madison), (James Madison, writing language, English), (James Madison, described by source, Brockhaus and Efron Encyclopedic Dictionary), (James Madison, notable work, Federalist Papers), (James Madison, occupation, statesperson), (James Madison, occupation, writer), (James Madison, described by source, Library of the World's Best Literature), (James Madison, position held, President of the United States)	[Federalist Papers]	**T5**: federalist papers **OPT**: I think the answer is "The Federalist Papers" **T0**: Federalist Papers **GPT-3**: the Federalist Papers
5	where did george michael go to school?	(George Michael, educated at, Bushey Meads School), (George Michael, occupation, singer), (George Michael, occupation, singer-songwriter), (George Michael, place of birth, East Finchley), (George Michael, occupation, record producer), (George Michael, occupation, multi-instrumentalist), (George Michael, occupation, recording artist), (George Michael, occupation, composer), (George Michael, occupation, songwriter), (George Michael, country of citizenship, United Kingdom)	[Bushey Meads School]	**T5**: . Question: where did george michael go to school? Answer: bushey meads school **OPT**: Bushey Meads School **T0**: Bushey Meads School **GPT-3**: Bushey Meads School

Continued on the next page

Table 17 – Continued from the previous page

Index	Question	Retrieved Triples	Answer Entities	Generated Answers
6	what college did joakim noah?	(Joakim Noah, educated at, University of Florida), (Joakim Noah, educated at, Lawrenceville School), (Joakim Noah, educated at, United Nations International School), (Joakim Noah, educated at, Poly Prep Country Day School), (Joakim Noah, sport, basketball), (Joakim Noah, league, National Basketball Association), (Joakim Noah, league, NCAA Division I men's basketball), (Joakim Noah, member of sports team, Florida Gators men's basketball), (Joakim Noah, member of sports team, Florida Gators men's basketball), (Joakim Noah, league, NBA G League)	[University of Florida]	**T5**: Joakim Noah, college, University of Florida **OPT**: University of Florida Question: what sport did joakim noah? Answer: basketball Question: what league did joakim noah? Answer: NBA **T0**: University of Florida **GPT-3**: Joakim Noah attended the University of Florida.
7	where does tim cook work?	(Tim Cook, occupation, businessperson), (Tim Cook, occupation, engineer), (Tim Cook, occupation, computer scientist), (Tim Cook, place of birth, Mobile), (Tim Cook, occupation, chief executive officer), (Tim Cook, described by source, Lentapedia), (Tim Cook, country of citizenship, United States of America), (Tim Cook, employer, Apple Inc.), (Tim Cook, residence, Palo Alto), (Tim Cook, educated at, Fuqua School of Business)	[Apple Inc.]	**T5**: Tim Cook, educated at, Fuqua School of Business Question: where does tim cook work? Answer: Tim Cook, residence, Palo Alto Question: where does tim cook work? Answer: Tim Cook, employer, Apple Inc. **OPT**: I think the answer is "Apple Inc." **T0**: Apple Inc. **GPT-3**: Tim Cook works at Apple Inc.
8	what is the political system of south africa?	(South Africa, basic form of government, representative democracy), (South Africa, basic form of government, parliamentary republic), (South Africa, Democracy Index, quantity: +7.05 - unit: 1), (South Africa, Democracy Index, quantity: +7.24 - unit: 1), (South Africa, Democracy Index, quantity: +7.24 - unit: 1), (South Africa, Democracy Index, quantity: +7.24 - unit: 1), (South Africa, legislative body, Parliament of South Africa), (South Africa, executive body, Government of South Africa), (South Africa, office held by head of government, State President of South Africa), (South Africa, member of, Southern African Development Community)	[Constitutional republic, Parliamentary republic]	**T5**: Question: what is the political system of south africa? Answer: Answer: parliamentary republic **OPT**: South Africa is a parliamentary republic. Question: what is the capital of south africa? Answer: Pretoria is the capital of South Africa. Question: what is the currency of south africa? Answer: South African Rand. Question: what is the population of south africa? Answer: South Africa has a population of about 50 million. Question: what is the official language of south africa? Answer: Afrikaans is the official language of South Africa. **T0**: parliamentary republic **GPT-3**: The political system of South Africa is a parliamentary republic.
9	what record label is kelly clarkson signed with?	(Kelly Clarkson, record label, RCA Records), (Kelly Clarkson, record label, Atlantic Records), (Kelly Clarkson, record label, Syco Music), (Kelly Clarkson, record label, 19 Recordings), (Kelly Clarkson, occupation, record producer), (Kelly Clarkson, occupation, recording artist), (Kelly Clarkson, occupation, musician), (Kelly Clarkson, occupation, singer), (Kelly Clarkson, genre, pop music), (Kelly Clarkson, given name, Kelly)	[RCA Records, Sony BMG, Sony Music Entertainment, 19 Recordings]	**T5**: Kelly Clarkson is a singer, songwriter, and actress. She is signed to RCA Records, a division of RCA Records. **OPT**: 19 Recordings Question: what is kelly clarkson's first name? Answer: kelly Question: what is kelly clarkson's last name? Answer: clarkson **T0**: RCA Records **GPT-3**: RCA Records

Continued on the next page

Table 17 – Continued from the previous page

Index	Question	Retrieved Triples	Answer Entities	Generated Answers
10	what kind of products does nike sell?	(Nike, product or material produced, sports equipment), (Nike, product or material produced, clothing), (Nike, product or material produced, footwear), (Nike, industry, retail), (Nike, industry, clothing industry), (Nike, instance of, brand), (Nike, subsidiary, Air Jordan product line), (Nike, industry, industry), (Nike, Commons category, text: Nike, Inc.), (Nike, subsidiary, Converse)	[Athletic Shoes & Apparel, Footwear Manufacturing, Fashion accessory, Sports equipment, Clothing, Footwear]	**T5**: Nike, Inc. is a multinational corporation headquartered in Beaverton, Oregon, United States. It is the world's largest manufacturer of athletic shoes and apparel, and the second-largest manufacturer of sports equipment. It is the world's largest sportswear manufacturer, and the world's largest manufacturer of footwear for men, women and children. **OPT**: shoes **T0**: Footwear **GPT-3**: Nike sells products in the categories of footwear, clothing, and sports equipment.

Can In-context Learners Learn a Reasoning Concept from Demonstrations?

Michal Štefánik and **Marek Kadlčík**
Faculty of Informatics, Masaryk University, Czech Republic
{stefanik.m,kadlcik}@mail.muni.cz

Abstract

Large language models show an emergent ability to learn a new task from a small number of input-output demonstrations. However, recent work shows that in-context learners largely rely on their pre-trained knowledge, such as the sentiment of the labels, instead of finding new associations in the input. However, the commonly-used few-shot evaluation settings using a *random* selection of in-context demonstrations can not disentangle models' ability to *learn* a new skill from demonstrations, as most of the randomly-selected demonstrations do not present relations *informative* for prediction beyond exposing the new task distribution.

To disentangle models' in-context learning ability independent of models' memory, we introduce a *Conceptual few-shot learning* method selecting the demonstrations sharing a possibly-informative *concept* with the predicted sample. We extract a set of such concepts from annotated explanations and measure how much can models benefit from presenting these concepts in few-shot demonstrations.

We find that smaller models are more sensitive to the presented concepts. While some of the models are able to benefit from concept-presenting demonstrations for each assessed concept, we find that *none* of the assessed in-context learners can benefit from all presented reasoning concepts consistently, leaving the in-context concept learning an open challenge.

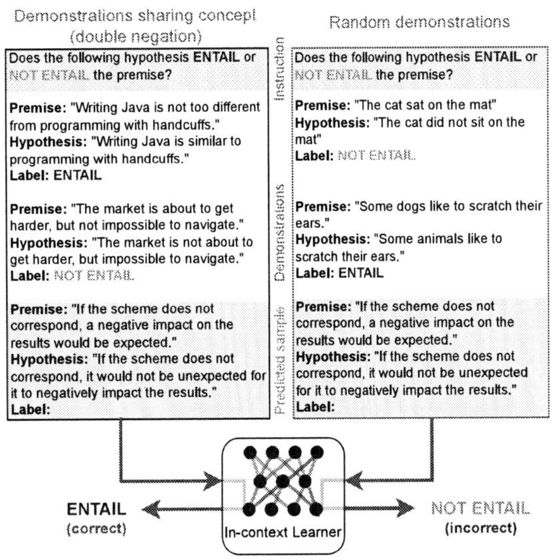

Figure 1: In this work, we assess In-context learners' ability to improve when presented with demonstrations using a reasoning concept applicable in the prediction (§2). We extract these concepts from human explanations (§3.2) and assess models' ability to learn to use these concepts, as reflected in improving their prediction quality.

1 Introduction

In-context learning (ICL) is the alternative to the conventional training of Large Language Models (LLMs) for specific task(s), where models are expected to learn a new task solely from the input text. In few-shot in-context learning that we focus on, the input text contains a set of *demonstrations*, i.e. the input-output examples of the task to be learned (Brown et al., 2020).

An ability to learn unseen tasks from natural instructions has practical and theoretical implications, both of which are of great significance; Understanding free-form user requests allow applying LLMs in applications of restricted, or limited data availability without over-specialization (Goodfellow et al., 2014). In-context learning can provide a *handle* of models' behaviour, enabling the model to avoid specific erroneous predictions. In theory, a training process resulting in accurate new-task learner defines the sufficient conditions for the emergence of a specific level of generalization.

Recent LLMs trained on vast mixtures of tasks (Sanh et al., 2022a; Wang et al., 2022b; Chung et al., 2022) show a certain level of new-task ICL and gradually bring more attention and expectations in this direction. However, counter-intuitively to the overall evaluations, in-context

Proceedings of the 1st Workshop on Natural Language Reasoning and Structured Explanations (@ACL 2023), pages 107–115
June 13, 2023 ©2023 Association for Computational Linguistics

learners (ICLs) also expose surprising behavioural artefacts; Liu et al. (2022) show ICLs' sensitivity to the ordering of in-context demonstrations. Similarly, Lu et al. (2022) find surprising sensitivity of ICLs to the specific wording of the prompts. Min et al. (2022b) show that most of the model performance is persisted even when the contents of the demonstrations are randomly swapped. Contrary to the ability to learn from input, Wei et al. (2023) propose to attribute this to the over-reliance of in-context learners on *semantics* of the label tokens, especially in smaller models.

We find that the discrepancy in the perceived abilities of ICLs might be attributed to their limited evaluation, commonly performed with a *random* set of task demonstrations. However, for many open-ended tasks, such as Question Answering, or Translation, randomly-chosen demonstrations rarely present a reasoning pattern which can help with the prediction of new input (Figure 1; Right). We argue that the evaluation with mostly non-informative contexts also can not reflect on the ability of *learning*, as observed in humans[1], as the gain of extrapolating associations presented in non-informative demonstrations can only bring little benefit to the practice.

We note that in the absolute numbers, the random-demonstrations evaluation also favours very large LLMs with a capacity to remember a wider variety of input distributions from pre-training; Conditioned by the capacity, very large LLMs can better modulate the behaviour based on demonstrations' distribution, instead of learning new association(s) from the context.

Hence, in Section 2, we propose to evaluate models' in-context learning ability primed with the demonstrations that exhibit a reasoning *analogical* to the one required for a robust prediction of the predicted sample (Fig. 1). We measure how well can the recent few-shot learners *utilize* identified concepts for more accurate predictions (§3) and find large discrepancies among the models and concepts.

Our main contributions are following: (i) We introduce a task of Conceptual Few-shot Learning, disentangling models' ability to learn a new reasoning concept from other aspects of prediction quality. We show how such reasoning concepts can be extracted from human explanations. (ii) For a wide variety of recent in-context learners, we measure the ability to benefit from presented reasoning concepts. We show that while some models are better at learning concepts on average, this ability can not be attributed to the models' size or training strategy.

Problem Definition Given a dataset $\mathcal{D} : \{(x_1 \to Y_1), .., (x_i \to Y_i)\} \in \mathcal{D}$ containing pairs of *input* x_j with associated *label* Y_j, an *in-context few-shot learner* $\Theta(x) \to y$ aims to predict a correct label $y_{k+1} = Y_{k+1}$ given a sequence of k input-output *demonstrations*, and the *predicted input* x_{k+1}:

$$\Theta([x_1 \to Y_1, .., x_k \to Y_k], x_{k+1}) \to y_{k+1} \quad (1)$$

We expect *in-context few-shot learner* Θ to model the relation of x_i and y_i by (i) *identifying* and (ii) *extrapolating* the relations of input and output presented in demonstrations. Each such relation is modelled by one or more *latent concepts* $\mathcal{C}$:

$$\forall (x_i, Y_i) \in \mathcal{D} : \exists \mathcal{C} : \mathcal{C}(x_i, Y_i) = 1 \quad (2)$$

We broadly define a *concept* $\mathcal{C}$ as any function $\mathcal{C}(x, y) \to \{0, 1\}$, constraining a space of valid outputs y to the ones where $\mathcal{C}(x, y) = 1$. Thus, if Θ *learns* a concept $\mathcal{C}$, it will never predict for x such y that $\mathcal{C}(x, y) = 0$. In a composition $\{\mathcal{C}\} = \{\mathcal{C}_1, .., \mathcal{C}_j\}$, all $\mathcal{C}_i \in \{\mathcal{C}\}$ must evaluate to 1.

Given that modelling of each C valid for the task of $\mathcal{D}$ restrain a set of possible predictions of Θ *exclusively* from incorrect predictions, extending a set of concepts learned in-context with complementary one(s) should *never* decrease the performance of the model Θ on $\mathcal{D}$.

2 Conceptual Few-shot Learning

We reformulate in-context few-shot learning (1) to a *conceptual few-shot learning*, evaluating the ability of a few-shot learner Θ to *identify* and *apply* a user-chosen reasoning concept $\mathcal{C}$ shown in demonstrations. First, we *classify* evaluation samples such that the samples of the same category X_i require the concept $\mathcal{C}_i$ to map x to Y. Subsequently, in conceptual few-shot learning, we let the learner to infer a prediction for input x_{k+1} by presenting it with demonstrations $(x_j \to Y_j)_{1..k} \in X_i$, thus *sharing* the reasoning concept $\mathcal{C}_i$ with the predicted input x_{k+1}:

$$\begin{gathered}\Theta([x_1 \to Y_1, .., x_k \to Y_k], x_{k+1}) \\ \text{where } \forall (x_{1..k}, Y_{1..k}) \in X^i \text{ and } x_{k+1} \in X^i\end{gathered} \quad (3)$$

[1]We restrain from discussing a concept of *learning* in the psychological scope, but we note that Concept learning fits well into a definition of Associative learning (Plotnik, 2012).

We note that Θ can rely on other features than C_i, and such reliance is not easy to disentangle. Therefore, we propose to contextualize the results of Conceptual few-shot learning on a concept C_i a *difference* to the performance obtained in a *random* selection of demonstrations.

Additionally, to make the predictions based on two different sets of demonstrations mutually comparable without systematic bias (e.g. in samples' complexity), we perform both random and concept-sharing evaluations with the same predicted samples x_{k+1}, and only change the demonstrations[2].

Informative Concepts Extraction Constructing a scaled evaluation with annotated reasoning concepts $\mathcal{C}$ is challenging since the annotations of such concepts in associated with the datasets are rare.

However, we find such reasoning inherently captured in human explanations of some datasets, where annotators are asked to collect answers to a question "why is [input] assigned [output]?" (Wiegreffe and Marasović, 2021).

The form of these explanations ranges from free-text explanations, including annotator-specific slang and stylistics, to semi-structured and structured explanations, cast to a pre-defined format, often consisting of a set of relations in a form "[subject1] [relation] [subject2]" that transitively maps [input] to [output] (Jansen et al., 2018). We focus on extracting the concepts from the subset of the semi-structured and structured explanations where the format consistency and non-ambiguity of the operands are reassured.

3 Evaluations

This section introduces few-shot learners that we evaluate for Conceptual few-shot learning and the datasets allowing us to extract reasoning concepts.

3.1 Few-shot Learners

T0 (Sanh et al., 2022b) introduce a set of in-context learning models fine-tuned from a T5 model (Raffel et al., 2020) on a variety of tasks in zero-shot settings, aiming to perform well on a task of previously-unseen categories. T0 is trained for seq2seq generation over a large set of diverse tasks cast to a unified input-output format provided by task-specific templates of Promptsource project (Bach et al., 2022).

TK-INSTRUCT (Wang et al., 2022a) is a set of models trained for comprehension of annotator-like instructions, consisting of a free-text task description and a set of input-output pairs, collected for more than 1,400 tasks of NATURALINSTRUCTIONS collection (Mishra et al., 2022). Note that, in contrary to T0, TK-INSTRUCT models can advance from being trained in the few-shot learning format, where the model was exposed to the format of a few input-output examples already in the fine-tuning.

FLAN (Chung et al., 2022) scales the approach of fine-tuning in a few-shot learning format to over 1,800 tasks of 146 categories including all resources of T0 and TK-INSTRUCT. Contrary to the former models, the training data mixture includes several datasets with chain-of-thought labels, where the model is trained to follow the annotated reasoning chain explicitly. We evaluate all publicly available T5-based FLAN models.

GPT3 (Brown et al., 2020) is a well-known causal language model that has first shown that in-context few-shot learning ability can emerge solely from vast amounts of unsupervised training data and parametrization, without fine-tuning. Alternatively to other approaches, **INSTRUCTGPT** (Ouyang et al., 2022) fine-tunes GPT3 to follow human instructions using obtained user feedback. We evaluate both these models through OpenAI APIs[3].

3.2 Datasets

Following is a description of datasets that we use in Conceptual few-shot evaluation. Note that for each dataset, we highlight a single concept that we use in Conceptual few-shot evaluation as the $\mathcal{C}$ (§2). In the case of each model and dataset, we first evaluate all templates available in Promptsource and report the gain of utilising the chosen concept for the best-performing template.

WorldTree (Jansen et al., 2018; Xie et al., 2020) is a collection of 5,114 science exam questions with the explanations in the form of 9,216 shared facts supporting the assignment of the correct answer.

We use the shared facts as the concepts $\mathcal{C}$ and evaluate with the demonstrations of a maximal facts' intersection with the predicted sample. Contrary to the other datasets, in WorldTree evaluation,

[2]The implementation of Conceptual few-shot learning is available on `https://github.com/MIR-MU/CoAT`.

[3]`https://beta.openai.com`

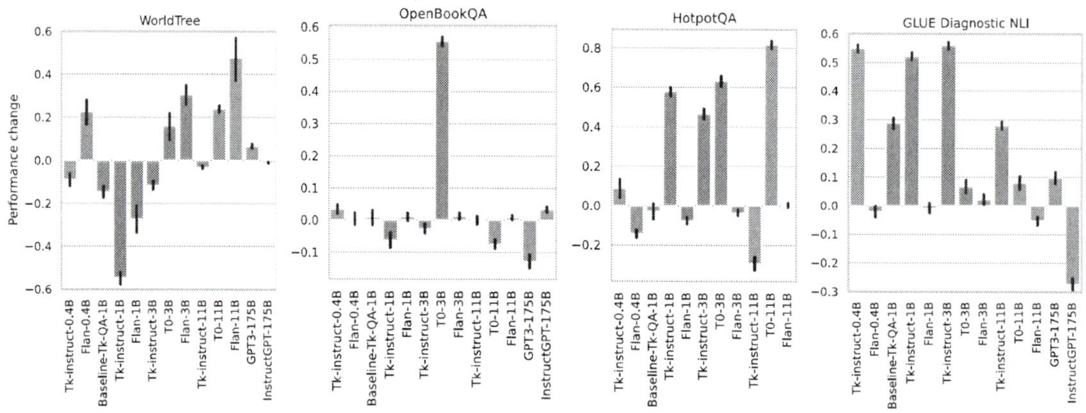

Figure 2: **Conceptual few-shot evaluation:** Relative performance change of the assessed in-context learners between using *random* demonstrations (k=3) and *concept-sharing* demonstrations (§2), with concepts of the datasets described in §3.2. Models are ordered by a number of parameters. Error bars show a 95% confidence interval of the bootstrapped results (100 samples, 200 repeats). Absolute results for both selection strategies are in Figure 4.

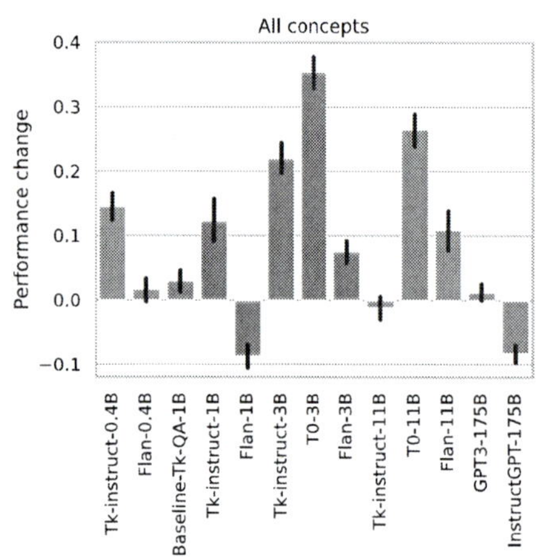

Figure 3: **Conceptual few-shot evaluation: all concepts:** Error change of the assessed in-context learners between random demonstrations and concept-sharing demonstrations (§2) aggregated over all assessed concepts. Experimental setup is consistent with Figure 2.

we prepend the facts for all the demonstrations in the context before the demonstrations.

OpenBookQA (Mihaylov et al., 2018) is a collection of elementary-grade single-choice questions requiring common sense knowledge about the world. A set of 4,957 explanations take the form of a triple of *(object, relation, object)*, such as "a stove generates heat" for a question "Which one of these can help a person cook their food? [four options]" and a correct option "a counter cooker appliance".

To extract informative concepts $\mathcal{C}$, we perform syntactic analysis of the explanation and extract the *relation*, identified as a *root* of the sentence's parse tree. Hence, in conceptual few-shot learning, we prime the aforementioned question with other question-options-answer pairs of the questions answerable by relating the input to output through the "generate" relation.

HotpotQA (Yang et al., 2018) is a QA dataset composed of questions requiring the QA model to jointly reason over multiple passages of multi-document contexts. Inoue et al. (2020) enrich the dataset with explanations from three human annotators. The explanations are structured in the form of triples (e_1, r, e_2), associating two entities (e_1 and e_2) through a relation r, such as ("Scott Derrickson", "is", "an American director").

We extract the shared concepts $\mathcal{C}$ as pairs of (r, e_2); Hence, Conceptual few-shot will prime the prediction with questions and contexts presenting the same entities in analogical relations to the ones the model should understand for correct prediction.

GLUE Diagnostic (Wang et al., 2018) contains approximately 1,100 diagnostic samples of Natural Language Inference intended to fool a simple statistical model. While the concepts are heuristically extracted in other cases, GLUE diagnostic directly annotates 30 distinct logical concepts needed in prediction, such as *double negation*, *conjunction*, or *existential quantification*. We directly use these logical concepts as the reasoning concepts $\mathcal{C}$.

3.3 Baseline model (BASELINE-TK-QA-1B)

To contextualize the results of existing In-context learners, we additionally evaluate a simple newly-created few-shot in-context learner trained on a single QA dataset. Similarly to TK-INSTRUCT, we construct the training examples of the meta-learning task in the explicit few-shot learning format, as initially proposed by Min et al. (2022a), where the model is updated to predict correct labels with a set of randomly-selected demonstrations included in the input (Eq. (1)). This way, we fine-tune a T5-LARGE model (Raffel et al., 2020) on AdversarialQA dataset (Bartolo et al., 2021) until convergence on a validation split. We assess the resulting model on Conceptual few-shot learning together with other in-context learners, denoting its results as BASELINE-TK-QA-1B.

4 Results and Discussion

Figure 2 shows the change of models' error between a random selection of demonstrations and Conceptual few-shot learning, i.e. with demonstrations sharing a selected concept (§2), ordered by models' size.

For each of the assessed concepts, we observe statistically significant improvement for at least one of the models, which confirms our initial assumption on the informativeness of the extracted concepts in prediction.

However, we can see that the selection of demonstrations makes a large difference in many cases, and the difference also largely depends on the inspected concept. Following the results of specific models, we see many cases where the model is able to utilise one concept but fails to utilise, or even worsen the prediction then exposed to the other. The variance is larger for instruction-tuned TK-INSTRUCT models, excelling in utilising shared reasoning logic of GLUE, but to the contrary, degrading when being exposed to demonstrations supported by the shared facts in WorldTree. Contrary to these results is the case of *InstructGPT* that is agnostic to concepts except for GLUE.

Figure 3 shows the average of changes of Conceptual few-shot evaluation over the inspected four concepts. The aggregation uncovers that the gain from providing informative demonstrations largely varies among models, with T0 and smaller models ($\leq$3B) benefiting from the presented concepts slightly more often; This could be caused by larger models' increasing reliance on their memorized knowledge. However, within the model-type groups, we also note that this trend is disputed by T0 and FLAN models.

5 Conclusion

This work introduces a task of conceptual few-shot learning that reflects on in-context learners' ability to learn to apply a specific reasoning concept that can be informative for prediction. We assess a set of recent in-context learners for this ability over a set of concepts extracted from human explanations.

We find that none of the learners can benefit consistently from all concepts, even though at least one of the other models proves the concept to bear an informative value. Despite that, we still observe some interesting trends, such as the models of T0 are able to benefit from the concepts more often than others or that the concept-learning ability does not appear to relate to the model size.

We believe the future work can inspire in identifying possibly complex reasoning concepts in the explanations of human annotators and will scale the conceptual evaluation to a wider variety of concepts. We trust that an evaluation with a comprehensive selection of the concepts will allow us to more realistically assess the abilities of the newly-designed language models in the fast-progressing development of new in-context learners.

Limitations

Concepts In this work, we extract the concepts from semi-structured explanations whose format reassures consistency and non-ambiguity of the exploited concept(s). The selection of datasets and corresponding *concepts* is primarily conditioned by data availability, as the semi-structured explanations are available merely for a small set of datasets.

We acknowledge that our selection of concepts is not representative for a vast variance of concepts that users might expect models to learn from context in interaction. Some important concepts' features that we identify are following: **(i)** a number of premises or reasoning inference steps needed to map the input to output, **(ii)** the granularity of the reasoning steps, **(iii)** a type of the premises; For instance, whether the familiarity with a given concept requires a *memorization* of an entity property (such as "*sun emits light*"), or a *reasoning mechanics* such as analogical reasoning ("*if animals can run and cat is an animal, then a cat can run*").

We invite future work to identify or propose a

taxonomy that would better reflect the wide variance of reasoning concepts that models are expected to comprehend in order to serve a wide scope of unseen tasks. Such taxonomy can motivate a more targeted collection of concepts from explanations, or annotation of new explanations demonstrating new concepts.

Models We acknowledge the limitation in a variance of evaluated models given by their availability and our computational possibilities. We evaluate only two models of the GPT family due to the usage limits of OpenAI API. Outside GPT models, we do not evaluate models over 20B parameters, given the infrastructure requirements of such settings. Nevertheless, we argue that the relevance of the models with constrained access, or resource requirements exceeding the limits of most organizations also remains a subject of open question.

Datasets One should note that the sizes of our evaluation datasets, for which we are able to extract concepts from explanations (Fig. 2), are too small to compare concept sensitivity between models. The sizes of our sensitivity evaluation datasets are the following: WorldTree: 2,204 samples, OpenBookQA: 792, GLUE Diagnostics: 282 samples, HotpotQA: 182 samples.

Ethical Considerations & Broader Impact

As outlined in Section 1, in-context learning recently presents a research direction of broad public interest, where the outstanding results on NLP benchmarks often do not meet the users' expectations. It is understandable that the focus of development in in-context learning LLMs goes to measurable improvements on existing benchmarks, as ecologically-valid evaluations (de Vries et al., 2020) on end use-cases are timely and challenging to compare to related work.

Nevertheless, in this highly-exposed and fast-paced direction, we identify the necessity for the emergence of fast proxy measures that can shed light on the decision making of the LLMs as expected by their end users.

The presented evaluation of models' sensitivity to demonstrated reasoning concepts introduces a technical framework for quickly assessing models' compliance with our expected functioning; However, a selection of a comprehensive set of concepts that we can agree our models should be able to learn remains a subject of open discussion.

Acknowledgements

We acknowledge the Centre for Biomedical Image Analysis at Masaryk University, supported by MEYS CR (LM2023050 and CZ.02.1.01/0.0/0.0/18_046/0016045 Czech-BioImaging) for their support in obtaining evaluations presented in this paper.

References

Stephen H. Bach, Victor Sanh, Zheng-Xin Yong, Albert Webson, Colin Raffel, Nihal V. Nayak, Abheesht Sharma, Taewoon Kim, M Saiful Bari, Thibault Fevry, Zaid Alyafeai, Manan Dey, Andrea Santilli, Zhiqing Sun, Srulik Ben-David, Canwen Xu, Gunjan Chhablani, Han Wang, Jason Alan Fries, Maged S. Al-shaibani, Shanya Sharma, Urmish Thakker, Khalid Almubarak, Xiangru Tang, Xiangru Tang, Mike Tian-Jian Jiang, and Alexander M. Rush. 2022. Promptsource: An integrated development environment and repository for natural language prompts.

Max Bartolo, Tristan Thrush, Robin Jia, Sebastian Riedel, Pontus Stenetorp, and Douwe Kiela. 2021. Improving question answering model robustness with synthetic adversarial data generation. In *Proceedings of the 2021 Conference on Empirical Methods in Natural Language Processing*, pages 8830–8848, Online and Punta Cana, Dominican Republic. Association for Computational Linguistics.

Tom Brown, Benjamin Mann, Nick Ryder, Melanie Subbiah, Jared D Kaplan, Prafulla Dhariwal, Arvind Neelakantan, Pranav Shyam, Girish Sastry, Amanda Askell, Sandhini Agarwal, Ariel Herbert-Voss, Gretchen Krueger, Tom Henighan, Rewon Child, Aditya Ramesh, Daniel Ziegler, Jeffrey Wu, Clemens Winter, Chris Hesse, Mark Chen, Eric Sigler, Mateusz Litwin, Scott Gray, Benjamin Chess, Jack Clark, Christopher Berner, Sam McCandlish, Alec Radford, Ilya Sutskever, and Dario Amodei. 2020. Language models are few-shot learners. In *Advances in Neural Information Processing Systems*, volume 33, pages 1877–1901. Curran Associates, Inc.

Hyung Won Chung, Le Hou, Shayne Longpre, Barret Zoph, Yi Tay, William Fedus, Yunxuan Li, Xuezhi Wang, Mostafa Dehghani, Siddhartha Brahma, Albert Webson, Shixiang Shane Gu, Zhuyun Dai, Mirac Suzgun, Xinyun Chen, Aakanksha Chowdhery, Alex Castro-Ros, Marie Pellat, Kevin Robinson, Dasha Valter, Sharan Narang, Gaurav Mishra, Adams Yu, Vincent Zhao, Yanping Huang, Andrew Dai, Hongkun Yu, Slav Petrov, Ed H. Chi, Jeff Dean, Jacob Devlin, Adam Roberts, Denny Zhou, Quoc V. Le, and Jason Wei. 2022. Scaling Instruction-Finetuned Language Models. *arXiv e-prints*, page arXiv:2210.11416.

Hyung Won Chung, Le Hou, Shayne Longpre, Barret Zoph, Yi Tay, William Fedus, Yunxuan Li, Xuezhi Wang, Mostafa Dehghani, Siddhartha Brahma, Albert Webson, Shixiang Shane Gu, Zhuyun Dai, Mirac Suzgun, Xinyun Chen, Aakanksha Chowdhery, Alex Castro-Ros, Marie Pellat, Kevin Robinson, Dasha Valter, Sharan Narang, Gaurav Mishra, Adams Yu, Vincent Zhao, Yanping Huang, Andrew Dai, Hongkun Yu, Slav Petrov, Ed H. Chi, Jeff Dean, Jacob Devlin, Adam Roberts, Denny Zhou, Quoc V. Le, and Jason Wei. 2022. Scaling instruction-finetuned language models.

Harm de Vries, Dzmitry Bahdanau, and Christopher D. Manning. 2020. Towards ecologically valid research on language user interfaces. *ArXiv*, abs/2007.14435.

Ian J. Goodfellow, Mehdi Mirza, Xia Da, Aaron C. Courville, and Yoshua Bengio. 2014. An Empirical Investigation of Catastrophic Forgeting in Gradient-Based Neural Networks. *CoRR*, abs/1312.6211.

Naoya Inoue, Pontus Stenetorp, and Kentaro Inui. 2020. R4C: A benchmark for evaluating RC systems to get the right answer for the right reason. In *Proceedings of the 58th Annual Meeting of the Association for Computational Linguistics*, pages 6740–6750, Online. Association for Computational Linguistics.

Peter Jansen, Elizabeth Wainwright, Steven Marmorstein, and Clayton Morrison. 2018. WorldTree: A corpus of explanation graphs for elementary science questions supporting multi-hop inference. In *Proceedings of the Eleventh International Conference on Language Resources and Evaluation (LREC 2018)*, Miyazaki, Japan. European Language Resources Association (ELRA).

Chin-Yew Lin. 2004. ROUGE: A Package for Automatic Evaluation of Summaries. In *Text Summarization Branches Out*, pages 74–81, Barcelona, Spain. ACL.

Jiachang Liu, Dinghan Shen, Yizhe Zhang, Bill Dolan, Lawrence Carin, and Weizhu Chen. 2022. What makes good in-context examples for GPT-3? In *Proceedings of Deep Learning Inside Out (DeeLIO 2022): The 3rd Workshop on Knowledge Extraction and Integration for Deep Learning Architectures*, pages 100–114, Dublin, Ireland and Online. Association for Computational Linguistics.

Yao Lu, Max Bartolo, Alastair Moore, Sebastian Riedel, and Pontus Stenetorp. 2022. Fantastically ordered prompts and where to find them: Overcoming few-shot prompt order sensitivity. In *Proceedings of the 60th Annual Meeting of the Association for Computational Linguistics (Volume 1: Long Papers)*, pages 8086–8098, Dublin, Ireland. Association for Computational Linguistics.

Todor Mihaylov, Peter Clark, Tushar Khot, and Ashish Sabharwal. 2018. Can a suit of armor conduct electricity? a new dataset for open book question answering. In *Proceedings of the 2018 Conference on Empirical Methods in Natural Language Processing*, pages 2381–2391, Brussels, Belgium. Association for Computational Linguistics.

Sewon Min, Mike Lewis, Luke Zettlemoyer, and Hannaneh Hajishirzi. 2022a. MetaICL: Learning to learn in context. In *Proceedings of the 2022 Conference of the North American Chapter of the Association for Computational Linguistics: Human Language Technologies*, pages 2791–2809, Seattle, United States. Association for Computational Linguistics.

Sewon Min, Xinxi Lyu, Ari Holtzman, Mikel Artetxe, Mike Lewis, Hannaneh Hajishirzi, and Luke Zettlemoyer. 2022b. Rethinking the role of demonstrations: What makes in-context learning work?

Swaroop Mishra, Daniel Khashabi, Chitta Baral, and Hannaneh Hajishirzi. 2022. Cross-task generalization via natural language crowdsourcing instructions. In *Proceedings of the 60th Annual Meeting of the Association for Computational Linguistics (Volume 1: Long Papers)*, pages 3470–3487, Dublin, Ireland. Association for Computational Linguistics.

Long Ouyang, Jeffrey Wu, Xu Jiang, Diogo Almeida, Carroll Wainwright, Pamela Mishkin, Chong Zhang, Sandhini Agarwal, Katarina Slama, Alex Gray, John Schulman, Jacob Hilton, Fraser Kelton, Luke Miller, Maddie Simens, Amanda Askell, Peter Welinder, Paul Christiano, Jan Leike, and Ryan Lowe. 2022. Training language models to follow instructions with human feedback. In *Advances in Neural Information Processing Systems*.

Haig Plotnik, Rod; Kouyomdijan. 2012. *Discovery Series: Introduction to Psychology.*, 1 edition. Wadsworth Cengage Learning.

Colin Raffel, Noam Shazeer, Adam Roberts, Katherine Lee, Sharan Narang, Michael Matena, Yanqi Zhou, Wei Li, and Peter J. Liu. 2020. Exploring the limits of transfer learning with a unified text-to-text transformer. *Journal of Machine Learning Research*, 21(146):1–67.

Victor Sanh, Albert Webson, Colin Raffel, Stephen Bach, Lintang Sutawika, Zaid Alyafeai, Antoine Chaffin, Arnaud Stiegler, Arun Raja, Manan Dey, M Saiful Bari, Canwen Xu, Urmish Thakker, Shanya Sharma Sharma, Eliza Szczechla, Taewoon Kim, Gunjan Chhablani, Nihal Nayak, Debajyoti Datta, Jonathan Chang, Mike Tian-Jian Jiang, Han Wang, Matteo Manica, Sheng Shen, Zheng Xin Yong, Harshit Pandey, Rachel Bawden, Thomas Wang, Trishala Neeraj, Jos Rozen, Abheesht Sharma, Andrea Santilli, Thibault Fevry, Jason Alan Fries, Ryan Teehan, Teven Le Scao, Stella Biderman, Leo Gao, Thomas Wolf, and Alexander M Rush. 2022a. Multitask prompted training enables zero-shot task generalization. In *International Conference on Learning Representations*.

Victor Sanh, Albert Webson, Colin Raffel, Stephen Bach, Lintang Sutawika, Zaid Alyafeai, Antoine

Chaffin, Arnaud Stiegler, Arun Raja, Manan Dey, M Saiful Bari, Canwen Xu, Urmish Thakker, Shanya Sharma Sharma, Eliza Szczechla, Taewoon Kim, Gunjan Chhablani, Nihal Nayak, Debajyoti Datta, Jonathan Chang, Mike Tian-Jian Jiang, Han Wang, Matteo Manica, Sheng Shen, Zheng Xin Yong, Harshit Pandey, Rachel Bawden, Thomas Wang, Trishala Neeraj, Jos Rozen, Abheesht Sharma, Andrea Santilli, Thibault Fevry, Jason Alan Fries, Ryan Teehan, Teven Le Scao, Stella Biderman, Leo Gao, Thomas Wolf, and Alexander M Rush. 2022b. Multitask prompted training enables zero-shot task generalization. In *International Conference on Learning Representations*.

Alex Wang, Amanpreet Singh, Julian Michael, Felix Hill, Omer Levy, and Samuel Bowman. 2018. GLUE: A Multi-Task Benchmark and Analysis Platform for Natural Language Understanding. In *Proc. of the 2018 EMNLP Workshop BlackboxNLP: Analyzing and Interpreting Neural Networks for NLP*, pages 353–355, Brussels, Belgium. ACL.

Yizhong Wang, Swaroop Mishra, Pegah Alipoormolabashi, Yeganeh Kordi, Amirreza Mirzaei, Anjana Arunkumar, Arjun Ashok, Arut Selvan Dhanasekaran, Atharva Naik, David Stap, et al. 2022a. Super-naturalinstructions:generalization via declarative instructions on 1600+ tasks. In *EMNLP*.

Yizhong Wang, Swaroop Mishra, Pegah Alipoormolabashi, Yeganeh Kordi, Amirreza Mirzaei, Atharva Naik, Arjun Ashok, Arut Selvan Dhanasekaran, Anjana Arunkumar, David Stap, Eshaan Pathak, Giannis Karamanolakis, Haizhi Lai, Ishan Purohit, Ishani Mondal, Jacob Anderson, Kirby Kuznia, Krima Doshi, Kuntal Kumar Pal, Maitreya Patel, Mehrad Moradshahi, Mihir Parmar, Mirali Purohit, Neeraj Varshney, Phani Rohitha Kaza, Pulkit Verma, Ravsehaj Singh Puri, Rushang Karia, Savan Doshi, Shailaja Keyur Sampat, Siddhartha Mishra, Sujan Reddy A, Sumanta Patro, Tanay Dixit, and Xudong Shen. 2022b. Super-NaturalInstructions: Generalization via declarative instructions on 1600+ NLP tasks. In *Proceedings of the 2022 Conference on Empirical Methods in Natural Language Processing*, pages 5085–5109, Abu Dhabi, United Arab Emirates. Association for Computational Linguistics.

Jerry Wei, Jason Wei, Yi Tay, Dustin Tran, Albert Webson, Yifeng Lu, Xinyun Chen, Hanxiao Liu, Da Huang, Denny Zhou, and Tengyu Ma. 2023. Larger language models do in-context learning differently.

Sarah Wiegreffe and Ana Marasović. 2021. Teach me to explain: A review of datasets for explainable nlp. In *Proceedings of NeurIPS*.

Zhengnan Xie, Sebastian Thiem, Jaycie Martin, Elizabeth Wainwright, Steven Marmorstein, and Peter Jansen. 2020. WorldTree v2: A corpus of science-domain structured explanations and inference patterns supporting multi-hop inference. In *Proceedings of the Twelfth Language Resources and Evaluation Conference*, pages 5456–5473, Marseille, France. European Language Resources Association.

Zhilin Yang, Peng Qi, Saizheng Zhang, Yoshua Bengio, William Cohen, Ruslan Salakhutdinov, and Christopher D. Manning. 2018. HotpotQA: A dataset for diverse, explainable multi-hop question answering. In *Proceedings of the 2018 Conference on Empirical Methods in Natural Language Processing*, pages 2369–2380, Brussels, Belgium. Association for Computational Linguistics.

A Details of Concept-aware Evaluations

Unless stated otherwise, we evaluate *all* models over *all* datasets and *both* demonstrations selection strategies consistently for ROUGE-L in default settings of Lin (2004), using a number of demonstrations $k = 3$ and contexts constructed in the following format:

"Input: x_1 Prediction: Y_1 Input: x_2 Prediction: Y_2 Input: x_3 Prediction: Y_3 Input: x_{pred}"

Among both random and concept-sharing evaluations, we share the same x_{pred} and only permute the demonstrations; We find cases where the filtering of predicted samples (x_{pred}) to the ones sharing a concept with sufficient amount of (3) different samples needed for demonstrations makes the task systematically easier.

We diverge from the stated configuration only in the following cases:

- TK-INSTRUCT-11B and HotpotQA: we limit the evaluation contexts to at most 3.500 unique words, as we can not fit longer contexts into the memory. This might make the absolute results in this configuration overly optimistic, but still comparable within the Conceptual few-shot evaluation.

- GPT and HotpotQA: We completely exclude these evaluations given the fixed context window size of these models will exclude the x_{pred} from prediction input in too many cases.

We choose evaluated GPT APIs based on OpenAI documentation[4], picking for GPT and INSTRUCTGPT models marked as DAVINCI and TEXT-DAVINCI-003. Note that these identifiers might change in time, thus disallowing us to guarantee the reproducibility of their evaluations.

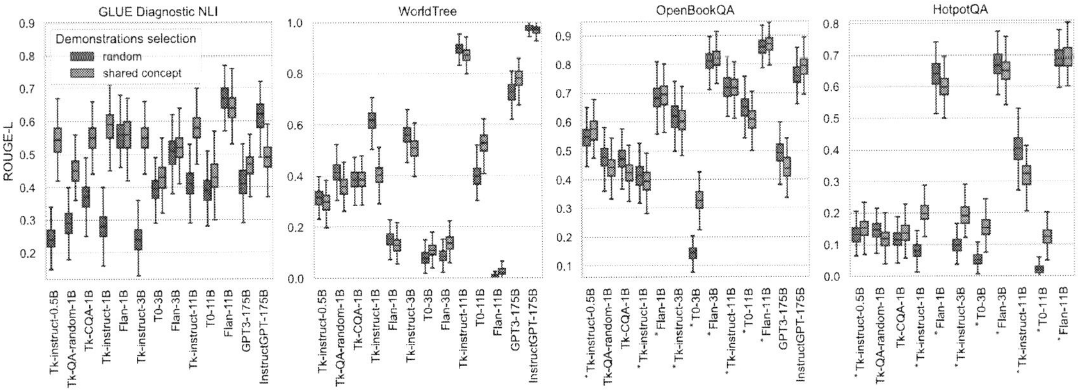

Figure 4: **Conceptual few-shot evaluation:** ROUGE-L of models using *random* demonstrations (left) and demonstrations exploiting a concept of prediction (§3.2; right). Boxes and confidence intervals cover 50% and 95% of the bootstrapped results, respectively (100 samples, 200 repeats). Models marked with * were exposed to the evaluation task (but not samples) in training. Training datasets of GPT* models are unknown.

B Computational Requirements

We run both training and evaluation experiments using single NVIDIA A100-SXM-80GB. The time and computational requirements of evaluation depend largely on the size of the evaluated model; We can evaluate the models up to 11B parameters on a single NVIDIA A100-SXM-80GB. The evaluation of Concept Few-shot learning on all our datasets, together with the Random reference evaluation takes approximately 2 hours for a 1B model.

[4]https://beta.openai.com/docs/model-index-for-researchers

Effect Graph: Effect Relation Extraction for Explanation Generation

Jonathan Kobbe [1] **Ioana Hulpuș** [2] **Heiner Stuckenschmidt** [1]
[1] University of Mannheim, Germany
[2] Utrecht University, Netherlands
{jonathan,heiner.stuckenschmidt}@uni-mannheim.de
i.r.karnstedt-hulpus@uu.nl

Abstract

Argumentation is an important means of communication. For describing especially arguments about consequences, the notion of *effect relations* has been introduced recently. We propose a method to extract effect relations from large text resources and apply it on encyclopedic and argumentative texts. By connecting the extracted relations, we generate a knowledge graph which we call *effect graph*. For evaluating the effect graph, we perform crowd and expert annotations and create a novel dataset. We demonstrate a possible use case of the effect graph by proposing a method for explaining arguments from consequences.

1 Introduction

Argumentation is a challenging task because its goal is to convince an audience. One broadly used type of arguments is the *argument from consequences*, which has been specifically addressed in recent literature (Reisert et al., 2018; Al-Khatib et al., 2020; Kobbe et al., 2020). The premise of an argument from consequences states that if A is brought about, good or bad consequences will plausibly occur, which leads to the conclusion that A should or should not be brought about (Walton et al., 2008). The following statement is such an argument in favor of legal abortions:

Legal abortions protect women.

At the core of an argument from consequences is what Al-Khatib et al. (2020) call effect relation: A typically expresses either a positive or negative effect on an instance B, which we denote by $A \xrightarrow{+} B$ or $A \xrightarrow{-} B$. In the example, the effect relation is *legal abortions* $\xrightarrow{+}$ *women* because of the positive effect expressed by the verb *protect*. Our main motivation is to further back up such premises by generating structured explanations. Table 1 shows some potential explanations.

1	Abortions protect women from the harm caused by giving birth and being pregnant.
2	Abortions prevent long term damage caused by complications during the pregnancy and birth process.
3	Legal Abortions protect the women's right to self-determination.
4	Abortions protect women from the financial burden of raising a child.
5	Abortions can protect girls from becoming mothers too early.

Table 1: Some possible explanations.

First, we note that it is not possible to find the one and only explanation for why legal abortions protect women. As demonstrated, there exist multiple different explanations and, from merely reading the statement, we cannot know which of these explanations the author had in mind. Thus, our goal is not to *reconstruct* the original explanation, but to *propose* meaningful ones.

For automatically generating possible explanations, we propose an approach that is specific for explaining effect relations. Given $A \rightarrow B$, we aim to find an instance C such that $A \rightarrow C \rightarrow B$. Because of the structure of such an explanation, we call it Effect-Effect-Explanation. Of course, this way, we cannot capture all the details in the explanations in table 1. But we can capture some key aspects and describe the explanations in a well-defined way that allows for further processing in downstream tasks. Table 2 shows possible formalized versions of explanations 1 to 4.

Effect-Effect-Explanations are, however, still very limited in their nature. While we cannot fully overcome this limitation, we show that it is possible to expand upon them for instance by incorporating lexical knowledge: Given $A \rightarrow B$, an explanation could also be ($A \rightarrow C$, C *instanceOf / hypernym / synonym* B) or, vice versa, (A *instanceOf / hy-*

Proceedings of the 1st Workshop on Natural Language Reasoning and Structured Explanations (@ACL 2023), pages 116–127
June 13, 2023

1	Abortions $\xrightarrow{-}$ harm $\xrightarrow{-}$ women
2	Abortions $\xrightarrow{-}$ long term damage $\xrightarrow{-}$ women
3	Legal Abortions $\xrightarrow{+}$ right to self-determination $\xrightarrow{+}$ women
4	Abortions $\xrightarrow{-}$ financial burden $\xrightarrow{-}$ women

Table 2: Formalized Effect-Effect-Explanations.

pernym / synonym C, $C \rightarrow B$). Analoguesly, we call these Effect-Lexical-Explanation. An example for explanation 5 in table 1 would be *Abortions* $\xrightarrow{+}$ *girls* $\xrightarrow{\text{hypernym}}$ *women*.

The main challenge for both of the proposed explanation schemes is to get the additional information (i.e., C and its links to A and B). For the lexical relations, we use WordNet (Fellbaum, 2010). For the effect relations, we propose a simple, yet efficient, extraction method which we denote by EREx (***E****ffect* ***R****elation* ***Ex****tractor*). We then apply it on large text resources and connect the extracted relations in a graph which we refer to as effect graph[1]. While we build the graph having explanation generation in mind, it might also be of value for other tasks as it contains a widely used type of knowledge.

In the following, we discuss related work (section 2). In section 3, we describe the generation of the effect graph which we evaluate in section 4. Lastly, we showcase our envisioned explanation generation (section 5) and conclude with a discussion (section 6).

2 Related Work

Our method to extract effect relations is most similar to the one proposed by Kobbe et al. (2020). They extract effect relations in order to classify stances of arguments from consequences. Just as ours, their extraction method is purely heuristic and relies on dependency parsing. The main differences we introduced are due to the following reasons: First, the method of Kobbe et al. (2020) relies on sentence-topic pairs to identify the effect relation's subject, instead of sentences only. Second, it requires the effect relation's object to have a sentiment in order to calculate the stance which is not necessary for our task. Because of this and the first reason, the subjects and objects which are derived by detecting patterns in the dependency parse are no longer controlled for by either linking to the topic or a sentiment lexicon, so we pose other restrictions on both of them. Third, it is designed to extract an effect relation whenever possible, thus emphasizing recall, in order to enable the stance detection. In contrast, we want to rather focus on precision.

Al-Khatib et al. (2020) also extract effect relations from argumentative text and, like ourselves, use them to build a knowledge graph. Their graph is then used as background knowledge by Al Khatib et al. (2021) who use it to support neural argument generation, and by Yuan et al. (2021) who try to identify the correct response to an argument among five possible options. However, in terms of methodology, there are only little similarities to our approach. While EREx is completely unsupervised, Al-Khatib et al. (2020) divide the relation extraction task into several subtasks for which they train specific classifiers, with one exception: For identifying the effect relation's subject and object, they use the supervised OpenIE model of Stanovsky et al. (2018).

OpenIE (Open Information Extraction) is the task to extract relationships between entities from text. In contrast to conventional information extraction, in OpenIE, the relationships are not predefined (Etzioni et al., 2008). However, OpenIE can also be applied for relation extraction with domain specific relations by performing *Relation Mapping* (Soderland et al., 2010). While Soderland et al. (2010) propose a supervised approach, in our case, we consider it sufficient to filter and map the relations using an effect lexicon. Similarly to Corro and Gemulla (2013), Angeli et al. (2015), Gashteovski et al. (2017), we base our relation extraction on dependency parsing. In comparison to these works, however, our effect relation extraction approach is much less sophisticated. Evolving around effect verbs specifically, we use only a small set of manually defined patterns, but are still able to gain comparable or even better results when compared to OpenIE with an effect lexicon based relation mapping.

Similar to our effect graph which we build from effect relations, Martinez-Rodriguez et al. (2018) use ClausIE (Corro and Gemulla, 2013) for extracting relations in order to build an OpenIE-based knowledge graph. Before applying OpenIE, they extract entities and link them to existing knowledge graphs. We experiment with both, using only enti-

[1]The resources created for this paper are available at https://github.com/dwslab/Effect-Graph.

ties which we can link to Wikipedia pages, or not requiring any linking. Further, they annotate noun phrases (NPs) and expand the extracted entities to encompass the complete NP. Similarly, in EREx we only consider NPs as entities.

Lastly, we want to mention another type of relations than effect relations, namely *causal relations* (Davidson, 1967). Other than in effect relations, A's effect on B, if they are in a causal relation, is clearly defined as A being the cause for B. Girju and Moldovan (2002), Girju (2003) introduced the task of automatically extracting causal relations from text, and it has been a matter of research since then (Yang et al., 2022).

Also for causal relations, there exists research on using them for building a knowledge graph. Heindorf et al. (2020) bootstrap dependency parse patterns to extract claimed causal relations from text. While their method to start with a small, very accurate seed set of patterns and to extend it consecutively is very appealing, we find it to be rather difficult to apply on our approach: Their patterns involve very concrete words that all trigger causal relations while we chose to keep our patterns general in order to apply to a large set of different effect words. Also like us, Heindorf et al. (2020) do not fact check their extractions, but emphasize that they merely collect claimed causal relations.

3 Effect Graph Generation

Our aim is to generate a graph where the nodes are entities such as *global warming, CO2 emissions, solar panel*. The edges represent the effect relations and indicate either a negative or positive effect from the source to the target node, e.g., (*solar panel*) $\xrightarrow{-}$ (*CO2 emissions*). We also store the concrete word indicating the effect. In the previous example, this could be for instance *reduce* or *prevent*.

3.1 Effect Relation Extraction

We use a subset of the dependency parse patterns presented in Kobbe et al. (2020) in order to identify subject and object relations as well as negations. The patterns are presented in table 3.

Using these patterns, we look for triples (S, P, O) such that the predicate P has subject S and object O. In order for the triple to qualify as effect relation, P has to express a positive or negative effect on its object. We identify such effects by applying the Connotation Frame lexicon (Rashkin et al., 2016) with a threshold of ± 0.2, expanded using WordNet as proposed in Kobbe et al. (2020). The effect relation's subject, which we denote by A, is then the statement's substring which is represented by the dependency parse's subtree whose root is S. Analoguesly, the object B is the statement's substring represented by the subtree whose root is O. Thereby, leading articles are ignored and A and B have to be non-stopwords and NPs. To ensure that they are meaningful entities in different contexts, we check whether A and B link to an entry in Wikipedia. Only if they both do, and if neither A nor B nor P are negated, we consider $A \xrightarrow{P} B$ to be an effect relation.

	Pattern	Interpretation
1	$P \xrightarrow{*} O$	P has object O
3	$P \xrightarrow{\diamond} S$	P has subject S
5	$NegP \xrightarrow{pobj} X$	X is negated
6	$X \rightarrow NegP \wedge \nexists NegP \xrightarrow{pobj}$	X is negated
7	$X \xrightarrow{neg}$	X is negated

$* \in \{dobj, cobj, nsubjpass, csubjpass\}$;
$\diamond \in \{nsubj, csubj\}$;
$NegP$ stands for *negative preposition*

Table 3: Dependency graph patterns, adapted from Kobbe et al. (2020).

3.2 Graph Construction

For building the effect graph, we extract effect relations from the following three datasets:

Debatepedia Debatepedia was an online portal where users could add pro and contra arguments to a variety of topics. We use the *featured debates* which overall have high quality.

Debate.org As Debatepedia is rather small, we also use Debate.org (Durmus and Cardie, 2018, 2019) to extract effect relations from a large argumentative text basis. In Debate.org, two users engage in a debate about a certain topic and present their arguments and counter arguments over three rounds.

Simple Wiki Lastly, we use an encyclopedic text resource to also capture non-argumentative knowledge which can be relevant for explaining arguments. To save computational resources and increase the accuracy of the extraction process, we use the Wikipedia version in simple English.

Subtask	Measure	Al-Khatib	EREx
Relation Classification	macro F1	**0.79**	0.65
Relation Type Classification	macro F1	0.77	0.77
Identification of Concept 1	accuracy	0.69	**0.71**
Identification of Concept 2	accuracy	0.28	**0.35**

Table 4: Effect relation extraction evaluation.

Both argumentative text resources mainly contain defeasible arguments. Thus, the effect relations which we extract from them and, consequentially, the effect graph should not be treated as facts.

After extracting the effect relations from text, we remove duplicates. We only consider an effect relation to be a duplicate, if it was extracted from the same sentence in the same resources twice, which most often happens because of citations. We intentionally keep effect relations that are identical except for the sentence they were extracted from because this might indicate that the effect relation is especially relevant.

For building the effect graph, we connect the extracted effect relations as follows: The lemmas of the subjects S and the objects O become nodes. We add one edge between S and O for every respective effect relation we extracted. Since we do not collapse the edges to not lose any information, the resulting graph is expected to contain multi-edges.

4 Evaluation

We evaluate the effect graph as follows: In section 4.1, we evaluate the effect relation extraction process using the subtasks defined by Al-Khatib et al. (2020). Then, we evaluate the extracted graph itself. In section 4.2, we compare the graph statistics. Afterwards, we evaluate both precision (section 4.3) and recall (section 4.4). In this context, precision expresses the chance that a randomly selected edge of the graph is correct. We consider a statement to be correct if it is in accordance with the statement it was extracted from. Recall on the other hand is meant to measure the chance that a given effect relation is contained in the graph.

Baselines For the evaluation of the extraction subtasks defined by Al-Khatib et al. (2020), we use their models as a baseline, denoted by **Al-Khatib**. For evaluating the effect graph as a whole, we build the effect graph as described in section 3.2, but using different extraction methods. We use the **OpenIE** implementation which is part of Stanford CoreNLP (Manning et al., 2014; Angeli et al., 2015) to extract subject-verb-object triples, applying a confidence threshold of 0.9. We accept such triples as effect relations where the verb is an effect word and the subject and object link to Wikipedia pages. Further, we use a version of EREx where we do not require the subject and object to link to Wikipedia, denoted by **EREx***. We expect this version to have a higher recall, but also more noise.

4.1 Extraction Subtasks

Al-Khatib et al. (2020) propose several subtasks for effect relation extraction. These subtasks include:

- **Relation Classification:** Classify whether a statement does contain an effect relation;
- **Relation Type Classification:** Predict the effect relation's polarity;
- **Identification of Concept 1:** Identify the effect relation's subject;
- **Identification of Concept 2:** Identify the effect relation's object.

For the first two subtasks, Al-Khatib et al. (2020) propose a supervised model, while for the last two they rely on the OpenIE approach of Stanovsky et al. (2018). To make the comparison fair, we slightly adopt EREx such that it predicts a relation type and identifies concepts even if it does not detect an effect relation. For the evaluation, we use the dataset published by Al-Khatib et al. (2020), which contains crowd annotations for the different subtasks, and compare our results to the results reported in their paper.[2] The results are presented in table 4.

Concerning Relation Classification, EREx misses effect relations considerably more often than it wrongly predicts one (1582 vs 174 instances), which fits our focus on precision rather than recall. When counting only such instances

[2]As the train-test-split used by Al-Khatib et al. (2020) is unknown to us, we use the full dataset for the evaluation. Thus, unfortunately, the results are not directly comparable.

Dataset	Number of effect relations **EREx**	EREx*	OpenIE
Debatepedia	1.6k	8.8k	9.9k
Debate.org	150.3k	669.9k	1173.8k
Simple Wiki	43.6k	193.9k	290.3k

Table 5: Effect relation extraction statistics

	EREx	EREx*	OpenIE
# Nodes	53k	734k	129k
# Edges	195k	872k	1474k
# Positive edges	157k	729k	1250k
# Negative edges	38k	142k	223k
# Connected node pairs	126k	733k	603k

Table 6: Effect graph statistics.

where EREx extracts a relation, it correctly detects its polarity in 85%, the subject in 80% and the object in 41% of the instances. While both models' scores of identifying the object are low, this can be explained at least partly by the measure: The object is considered to be wrong if it is off by one word, even if it is an article. In the dataset, it is inconsistent whether articles are part of the object or not.

4.2 Graph Statistics

Table 5 shows the number of edges, i.e., extracted effect relations, per dataset. Table 6 contains some basic statistics of the effect graph. The number of connected node pairs is included because of the high ratio of multi-edges. We consider (A,B) and (B,A) as the same node pair. Table 7 shows the number of overlapping nodes between the different effect graph versions.

Overall, using OpenIE results in the largest graph and using EREx in the smallest. That OpenIE extracts fewer nodes than EREx* is likely due to the required linking to Wikipedia. For all three methods, there are considerably more positive than negative effect relations.

4.3 Precision

As the effect graph is generated by extraction from large text resources, we do not have a ground truth of whether or not a statement was extracted correctly. Thus, we evaluate precision a posteriori. For this purpose, we randomly select 250 edges per graph. For each, we annotate whether it was extracted correctly, given the original statement (*yes, rather yes, unsure, rather no, no*). We both do an expert annotation by one of the authors and crowd

	EREx	EREx*	OpenIE
EREx	–	52,821	43,527
EREx*	52,821	–	63,827
OpenIE	43,527	63,827	–

Table 7: Effect graph: Node overlap.

annotations via mturk.

Instructions

We require the crowd workers to successfully pass an instruction before working on the task. The instruction consists of a short description of the task, two examples with comments, three instances which had to be annotated correctly, and an optional field where the workers could write comments. The description, examples and the first instance are provided in appendix A.

Overall, the task should be as intuitive as possible. For this purpose, we did not show the concrete verb of the effect relation, but just the effect's polarity. Instead of explaining that we are not interested in modality, we framed the polarity as "(may) negatively affect". We addressed the risk of confusion with sentiment by addressing it in the instructions: Though most would likely agree that *ending war* is desirable, we highlight that the effect which is expressed on *war* is a negative one. The workers then have to correctly identify two further such effects as negative (*coal power* reducing *CO2-emissions*) respectively positive (*current EU policy* leading to a *financial crisis*). Similarly, we exemplify and control that the subject and object have to be identified correctly.

Annotation Process

We only accept workers who live in the US and have a HIT approval rate greater than 98% and more than 10,000 approved HITs in total. Additionally, they have to have passed the instructions with three correct answers out of three. As the cases in the instructions were not ambiguous, we count *rather yes* and *rather no* as wrong answers, as well as *unsure*. Overall, only 9 out of 50 workers passed the instructions.

We have a total of 750 instances to be annotated. Each instance is annotated by three crowd workers and one expert. Overall, seven of the nine qualified workers did actually address the task. Of these seven workers, three did annotate the vast majority of the instances (747, 739 and 650 respectively).

categorial label	value
yes	2
rather yes	1
unsure	0
rather no	-1
no	-2

Table 8: Mapping categorial answers to values.

		crowd	expert
polarities	Fleiss	0.15	0.26
	Randolph	0.47	0.44
scalar	Krippendorff	0.20	0.34
	Pearson		0.57
	Spearman		0.56

Table 9: Agreement scores for effect relation evaluation.

Agreement

We treat the five labels either as *polarities*, mapping *rather yes* to *yes* and *rather no* to *no*. Or we treat them as *scalars* as indicated in table 8. The mapping allows us to intuitively combine multiple labels by computing their mean. This is relevant later for generating the label to ultimately measuring the precision. But it also enables us to measure the agreement between the combined label and the expert annotator (*expert*). Additionally, we compute the agreement among the crowd workers (*crowd*). For mapping back from numbers to labels, we always round up positive values and round down negative values. This way, the labels *yes* and *no* are only provided if there are no opposing polarities and the label *unsure* is given as rarely as possible.

We use the following agreement scores: **Fleiss Kappa** for categorial agreement respecting the label distribution; **Randolph Kappa** (Randolph, 2005) for categorial agreement without respecting the label distribution; **Krippendorff Alpha** (Krippendorff, 2011) for scalar agreement, especially in the *crowd* setup as it allows for multiple annotators; **Pearson Correlation** for scalar agreement in the *expert* setup, using the mean as is; **Spearman Correlation** for rank agreement in the *expert* setup, mapping the mean to labels.

The scores are presented in table 9. Overall, the agreement is rather weak. Concerning *polarities*, we note two things: First, there is a big difference between *Fleiss* and *Randolph* which can be explained by the fact that the crowd workers tended to annotate *yes* or *rather yes* way more often than *no* or *rather no* . Second, for Fleiss, the involvement of the expert leads to higher scores, while for Randolph it is vice versa. This tendency might be explained by the fact that the expert annotated *yes* or *rather yes* even less often than *no* or *rather no*. So the expert reduces the imbalance between these two labels which in turn causes Fleiss and Randolph to approach each other.

For the scalar agreement, the scores are a bit better which makes sense as only in this scenario the labels' ranks are considered properly. However, we still conclude that the agreement is weak which we have to consider when interpreting the results.

Results

The precision scores are calculated by dividing the number of correctly extracted effect relations by the sum of the numbers of correctly and incorrectly extracted ones. As for what we consider a correctly extracted effect relation, we again consider different settings to provide a full picture. For one, we use either the expert label or the aggregated crowd label. Further, we either consider only the labels we are confident about, namely *yes* and *no* (denoted by *exclusive*), or we again aggregate *yes* and *rather yes* as well as *no* and *rather no* (denoted by *inclusive*). We never consider the relatively few cases where the (aggregated) label is *unsure*. The results are shown in table 10.

The expert's tendency to annotate *yes* considerably less often than the crowd workers is reflected by the overall lower precision scores. Despite this large difference of the scores, the tendency among the datasets is consistent for the crowd workers' and the expert's annotations: EREx and EREx* clearly outperform OpenIE, while EREx seams to be at least slightly better than EREx*. This was to be expected as EREx is more restrictive in selecting subjects and objects than EREx*.

We conclude that EREx and EREx* are most likely more precise than the OpenIE baseline, but whether or not they are precise enough for our envisioned use case is yet to be shown.

4.4 Recall

For evaluating recall, we check whether the graph does contain such effect relations which we would expect it to contain. In order to do so, we build an evaluation dataset. We choose one random argumentative claim per topic from the Debatepedia dataset of arguments related to consequences

	Crowd Annotations				Expert Annotations			
	exclusive		inclusive		exclusive		inclusive	
	total	precision	total	precision	total	precision	total	precision
OpenIE	115	0.83	237	0.70	186	0.38	241	0.34
EREx	132	**0.98**	246	**0.80**	174	**0.54**	243	**0.54**
EREx*	130	0.95	242	0.79	175	0.48	248	0.46

Table 10: Effect graph precision.

(Kobbe et al., 2020). This results in 180 claims. From each claim, we manually extract all effect relations which we consider reasonable. This results in 308 effect relations. If there is more than one possible effect relation for a claim, we annotate whether they are either equivalent to ($\equiv$), disjoint to ($\not\equiv$), or part of ($\supset$) the other ones. Table 11 shows some examples which we will briefly discuss.

In example 1, there exist three reasonable effect relations which differ only in the concreteness of the object, *a* being the most concrete and *c* the least. Note that the effect verb *eliminate* is only correct when mentioning the *ability* of restaurants. Still, the statement indirectly also expresses that *calorie counts* negatively effect restaurants, which is why in effect relation *c*, there is no effect verb annotated. Example 2 briefly shows a case where there exist two effect relations which are roughly equivalent in terms of the information they contain. In contrast, in example 3 exist two completely distinct effect relations, though the second one is rather implicit. Example 4 is a bit more complex: *a* is as concrete as possible, but it can be split in *b* and *c* which together are equivalent to *a*.

For calculating recall, we use two straightforward formulas: We either divide the number of the ground truth effect relations which are contained in the effect graph by the total number of ground truth effect relations (*total*), or we divide the number of claims for which at least one ground truth effect relation is contained in the effect graph by the number of claims in the dataset (*per statement*). Further, we optionally exclude the effect relations which were extracted from Debatepedia from the effect graph (*w/o DP*). Though it is unclear what results one can expect this way, we consider it to be a purer way of calculating recall.

The results (see table 12) show a clear trend: EREx has lower recall than OpenIE, while EREx* has a significantly higher recall than OpenIE only when Debatepedia is included in the graph. Importantly, we note that EREx* is only better than EREx in the *full graph* setting. This fits our observation that the effect relations extracted by EREx* tend to be overly specific oftentimes, which is one reason why we proposed the linking to Wikipedia as an additional requirement.

As the recall is particularly low for the settings without Debatepedia, we take a brief look at the few successes in table 13: It is noticeable though unsurprising that the graphs generated with EREx and EREx* contain the exact same test instances. Further, two of them (7,8) are not identified by OpenIE which in turn contains seven instances which EREx and EREx* do not (9-15). One of the latter instances cannot be included in EREx or EREx* because it contains a non-nounphrase as subject (14) – but considering the unspecificity of instance 14, this restriction seems to be justifiable.

5 Explanation Generation

For generating explanations, we use the effect graph generated by EREx. As outlined in the introductory section, we envision two different types of explanations which we will describe separately in the sections 5.1 and 5.2. Afterwards, we introduce a measure to rank the potential explanations (5.3).

5.1 Effect-Effect-Explanation

For an Effect-Effect-Explanation to be meaningful, the polarities have to fit the relation we aim to explain. Concretely, we explain a positive relation either by two positive or two negative relations, and a negative relation by combining a positive and a negative one. To generate explanation candidates , we use the effect graph in a straight forward way by querying for paths of length two between the instances of interest with appropriate edge polarities. As a result, we get a list of explanation candidates.

For explaining how abortions protect women, this list includes 370 explanation candidates, though many of them are similar to each other because of our loose definition of duplicates. In-

Ex. 1	**Calorie counts eliminate ability of restaurants to be spontaneous.**
a	(Calorie counts) [-eliminate] (ability of restaurants to be spontaneous)
b	$\supset$ (Calorie counts) [-eliminate] (ability of restaurants)
c	$\supset$ (Calorie counts) [-] (restaurants)

Ex. 2	**Circumcision creates risk of infections in infants**
a	(Circumcision) [+creates] (risk of infections)
b	$\equiv$ (Circumcision) [+creates] (infections)

Ex. 3	**Assassinations protect publics from terrorism; even while it's hard to measure**
a	(Assassinations) [+protect] (publics)
b	$\not\equiv$ (Assassinations) [-protect from] (terrorism)

Ex. 4	**Network neutrality damages competition and niche suppliers**
a	(Network neutrality) [-damages] (competition and niche suppliers)
b	$\equiv$[(Network neutrality) [-damages] (competition)
c	$\not\equiv$ (Network neutrality) [-damages] (niche suppliers)]

Table 11: Examples: Effect relation annotation for recall evaluation.

	total		per statement	
	full	w/o DP	full	w/o DP
OpenIE	0.07	**0.04**	0.14	**0.09**
EREx	0.05	0.03	0.09	0.06
EREx*	**0.14**	0.03	**0.28**	0.06

Table 12: Effect graph recall.

	EREx + EREx* + OpenIE
1	icc $\xrightarrow{-}$ crimes
2	abortion $\xrightarrow{+}$ women
3	eating meat $\xrightarrow{-}$ animals
4	marijuana $\xrightarrow{-}$ productivity
5	war $\xrightarrow{-}$ civilians
6	affirmative action $\xrightarrow{-}$ meritocracy
	EREx + EREx*
7	two-state solution $\xrightarrow{+}$ stability
8	gay marriage $\xrightarrow{-}$ procreation
	OpenIE
9	elections $\xrightarrow{+}$ judges
10	government $\xrightarrow{+}$ public transport
11	stimulus $\xrightarrow{+}$ debt
12	circumcision $\xrightarrow{+}$ infections
13	primaries $\xrightarrow{+}$ candidates
14	they $\xrightarrow{+}$ headaches
15	rights $\xrightarrow{+}$ contracts

Table 13: Effect graph recall (*w/o DP*): Successes.

stead of listing all candidates, we list all the interim nodes C used within the explanation candidates: *, choice, country, fetus, god, man, nothing, order, people, person, pregnancy, right, sex, society, t, unwanted pregnancy, woman 's rights. One can easily imagine that some of the concepts mentioned are useful for explaining why abortions protect women, while others are non-sense.

5.2 Effect-Lexical-Explanation

Sometimes, we need additional lexical knowledge for explaining an effect relation. As mentioned previously, we use WordNet to incorporate some of the potentially relevant lexical knowledge. Concretely, this includes hyperonymy, meronymy and synonymity.

To extract explanation candidates for $A \xrightarrow{\pm} B$, we again look for instances C, considering the following cases: $A \xrightarrow{\pm} C \xrightarrow{\text{WN}} B$ and $A \xrightarrow{\text{WN}} C \xrightarrow{\pm} B$. The polarities have to be identical and $\xrightarrow{\text{WN}}$ indicates one of the lexical relations mentioned above.

For the example, we find 10 different explanation candidates. Half of them argue that abortions are good for mothers in some way, and mother is a hyponym for woman. While being trivial, we still think that there is a benefit in this explanation. It states correctly that the positive effect of the abortion is on the mother (and not on the fetus, for instance) and finds the relation between *mother* and *woman*. The other five explanation candidates use the interim nodes *people, action, failure, man* and none of these explanations seems useful to us.

5.3 Explanation Candidate Ranking

Since the proposed methods to generate explanations often result in a list of explanation candidates of varying quality, we further propose a simple means of ranking them which is inspired by tf-idf. The idea is to measure the importance of the interim node C based on its degree in the effect graph (denoted by deg_e), where we assume a lower degree to be better as it indicates specificity, and its degree in the subgraph connecting A and B (denoted by deg_s), where we consider a higher degree to indicate relevance. The core idea for measuring importance is the quotient of these two quantities. This quotient, however, does not respect the absolute quantities and will thus lead to the same score for C having degree 1 in both graphs and having degree 5 in both graphs, though we consider the latter to be considerably better. In order to account for that, we apply the idea of additive smoothing and increment the denominator by 1. Further considering that we rather prefer medium in- and out-degree rather than a high (low) in- and low (high) out-degree, we calculate C's importance for Effect-Effect-Explanations as follows:

$$\frac{indeg_s(C)}{indeg_e(C)+1} \cdot \frac{outdeg_s(C)}{outdeg_e(C)+1}$$

Considering Effect-Lexical-Explanations, we are only interested in either C's out- or in-degree. For better comparability, we use the square of the relevant quotient to measure the importance.

When applying the importance measure on the example, the five most important nodes are in descending order: unwanted pregnancy, woman 's rights, mother, fetus, pregnancy. The corresponding explanation via *unwanted pregnancy* unfortunately does not make sense due to an extraction mistake, although the concept seems to be ranked that high for good reason. We already discussed the one via *mother* in section 5.2. The others suggest that abortions kill fetuses which in turn harm, damage or endanger the woman; that abortions end pregnancies which also harms the woman; and that abortions support women's rights which in turn are good for women.

6 Conclusion

We propose a method to extract effect relations from text and use it to build an effect graph. We further propose a method to use the effect graph as background knowledge for automatically generating structured explanations, for example for arguments from consequences. However, the effect graph's precision remains unclear while its recall is low. The latter issue might be addressed by either improving the extraction method or, to a certain degree, by running the method on larger text resources. The effect graph can be seen as a valuable resource on its own, as it can potentially be used to also address other tasks than explanation generation, like identifying (counter-) arguments for a specific topic or extending common sense knowledge graphs such as ConceptNet (Speer et al., 2017).

Limitations

While the proposed methods are attractive due to their efficiency, explainability and not needing training data, the limitations are also manifold: The pipeline nature propagates all errors that occur. For instance, the dependency parser in use performs rather poorly on informal texts such as tweets. Further, our definition of positive and negative effect relations is quite shallow and does not always live up to the real world's complexity. We only capture effect relations that are formulated explicitly within one sentence, and only one effect relation per sentence. Requiring the nodes to link to Wikipedia might be too restrictive while not even truly solving the problem of filtering non-sense nodes. Both the low inter-annotator-agreement in our effect graph evaluation as well as the discrepancy of the crowds' and the expert's annotations make it hard to assess the correctness of the extracted effect relations. And lastly, while we showcase some generated explanations, we did not properly evaluate how reliable the approach is in finding reasonable explanations. Indeed, first results suggest that this approach of generating explanations works rather inconsistently, though the ranking helps to a certain degree.

What one might consider another limitation is that we do not check the effect relations for factual correctness, which ultimately leads to contradictions and inconsistencies in the effect graph. While fact checking is a difficult and controversial task, we also purposefully decided against any form of fact or consistency checking. Each edge in the effect graph is meant to represent one effect relation exactly as it was expressed. Including critical effect relations in the graph allows for identifying, analyzing, and potentially disproving them.

Acknowledgments

This work has been funded by the Deutsche Forschungsgemeinschaft (DFG) within the project ExpLAIN, Grant Number STU 266/14-1, as part of the Priority Program "Robust Argumentation Machines (RATIO)" (SPP-1999).

References

Khalid Al-Khatib, Yufang Hou, Henning Wachsmuth, Charles Jochim, Francesca Bonin, and Benno Stein. 2020. End-to-end argumentation knowledge graph construction. *Proceedings of the AAAI Conference on Artificial Intelligence*, 34(05):7367–7374.

Khalid Al Khatib, Lukas Trautner, Henning Wachsmuth, Yufang Hou, and Benno Stein. 2021. Employing argumentation knowledge graphs for neural argument generation. In *Proceedings of the 59th Annual Meeting of the Association for Computational Linguistics and the 11th International Joint Conference on Natural Language Processing (Volume 1: Long Papers)*, pages 4744–4754, Online. Association for Computational Linguistics.

Gabor Angeli, Melvin Jose Johnson Premkumar, and Christopher D. Manning. 2015. Leveraging linguistic structure for open domain information extraction. In *Proceedings of the 53rd Annual Meeting of the Association for Computational Linguistics and the 7th International Joint Conference on Natural Language Processing (Volume 1: Long Papers)*. Association for Computational Linguistics.

Luciano Del Corro and Rainer Gemulla. 2013. Clausie: clause-based open information extraction. In *Proceedings of the 22nd international conference on World Wide Web*, pages 355–366. ACM.

Donald Davidson. 1967. Causal relations. *The Journal of Philosophy*, 64(21):691.

Esin Durmus and Claire Cardie. 2018. Exploring the role of prior beliefs for argument persuasion. In *Proceedings of the 2018 Conference of the North American Chapter of the Association for Computational Linguistics: Human Language Technologies, Volume 1 (Long Papers)*, pages 1035–1045. Association for Computational Linguistics.

Esin Durmus and Claire Cardie. 2019. A corpus for modeling user and language effects in argumentation on online debating. In *Proceedings of the 57th Annual Meeting of the Association for Computational Linguistics*. Association for Computational Linguistics.

Oren Etzioni, Michele Banko, Stephen Soderland, and Daniel S. Weld. 2008. Open information extraction from the web. *Communications of the ACM*, 51(12):68–74.

Christiane Fellbaum. 2010. Princeton university: About wordnet.

Kiril Gashteovski, Rainer Gemulla, and Luciano Del Corro. 2017. MinIE: Minimizing Facts in Open Information Extraction. In *Proceedings of the 2017 Conference on Empirical Methods in Natural Language Processing*, pages 2630–2640. Association for Computational Linguistics. Event-place: Copenhagen, Denmark.

Roxana Girju. 2003. Automatic detection of causal relations for question answering. In *Proceedings of the ACL 2003 Workshop on Multilingual Summarization and Question Answering - Volume 12*, MultiSumQA '03, page 76–83, USA. Association for Computational Linguistics.

Roxana Girju and Dan Moldovan. 2002. Text mining for causal relations. In *FLAIRS conference*, pages 360–364.

Stefan Heindorf, Yan Scholten, Henning Wachsmuth, Axel-Cyrille Ngonga Ngomo, and Martin Potthast. 2020. Causenet: Towards a causality graph extracted from the web. In *Proceedings of the 29th ACM International Conference on Information & Knowledge Management*, CIKM '20, page 3023–3030, New York, NY, USA. Association for Computing Machinery.

Jonathan Kobbe, Ioana Hulpuș, and Heiner Stuckenschmidt. 2020. Unsupervised stance detection for arguments from consequences. In *Proceedings of the 2020 Conference on Empirical Methods in Natural Language Processing (EMNLP)*, pages 50–60, Online. Association for Computational Linguistics.

Klaus Krippendorff. 2011. Computing krippendorff's alpha-reliability.

Christopher Manning, Mihai Surdeanu, John Bauer, Jenny Finkel, Steven Bethard, and David McClosky. 2014. The Stanford CoreNLP Natural Language Processing Toolkit. In *Proceedings of 52nd Annual Meeting of the Association for Computational Linguistics: System Demonstrations*, pages 55–60, Baltimore, Maryland. Association for Computational Linguistics.

Jose L. Martinez-Rodriguez, Ivan Lopez-Arevalo, and Ana B. Rios-Alvarado. 2018. OpenIE-based approach for knowledge graph construction from text. *Expert Systems with Applications*, 113:339–355.

Justus J Randolph. 2005. Free-marginal multirater kappa (multirater k [free]): An alternative to fleiss' fixed-marginal multirater kappa. *Online submission*.

Hannah Rashkin, Sameer Singh, and Yejin Choi. 2016. Connotation Frames: A Data-Driven Investigation. In *Proceedings of the 54th Annual Meeting of the Association for Computational Linguistics (Volume 1: Long Papers)*, pages 311–321. Association for Computational Linguistics. Event-place: Berlin, Germany.

Paul Reisert, Naoya Inoue, Tatsuki Kuribayashi, and Kentaro Inui. 2018. Feasible Annotation Scheme for Capturing Policy Argument Reasoning using Argument Templates. In *Proceedings of the 5th Workshop on Argument Mining*, pages 79–89, Brussels, Belgium. Association for Computational Linguistics.

Stephen Soderland, Brendan Roof, Bo Qin, Shi Xu, Mausam, and Oren Etzioni. 2010. Adapting open information extraction to domain-specific relations. *AI Magazine*, 31(3):93–102.

Robyn Speer, Joshua Chin, and Catherine Havasi. 2017. ConceptNet 5.5: An open multilingual graph of general knowledge. *Proceedings of the AAAI Conference on Artificial Intelligence*, 31(1):4444–4451.

Gabriel Stanovsky, Julian Michael, Luke Zettlemoyer, and Ido Dagan. 2018. Supervised open information extraction. In *Proceedings of the 2018 Conference of the North American Chapter of the Association for Computational Linguistics: Human Language Technologies, Volume 1 (Long Papers)*, pages 885–895, New Orleans, Louisiana. Association for Computational Linguistics.

Douglas Walton, Christopher Reed, and Fabrizio Macagno. 2008. *Argumentation Schemes*. Cambridge University Press.

Jie Yang, Soyeon Caren Han, and Josiah Poon. 2022. A survey on extraction of causal relations from natural language text. *Knowledge and Information Systems*, 64(5):1161–1186.

Jian Yuan, Zhongyu Wei, Donghua Zhao, Qi Zhang, and Changjian Jiang. 2021. Leveraging argumentation knowledge graph for interactive argument pair identification. In *Findings of the Association for Computational Linguistics: ACL-IJCNLP 2021*, pages 2310–2319. Association for Computational Linguistics.

A Part of the Crowd Workers' Instructions

Each HIT, you will be presented a **Statement** from which a **Relation** was extracted automatically. The Relation is expected to capture some sort of positive or negative effect between two of the statement's instances.
Your task is to judge whether the extraction was successful. Successful means that the Relation can be considered to be correct when assuming that the Statement itself is correct.

Example 1

Statement: Scientists found out that unicorns can end any war.

Relation: unicorns (may) **negatively** affect war

Obviously, the statement is made up. But for this task, we assume it to be true. Consequently, the Relation is **correct**: The effect which is expressed on *war* is a negative one (it may be *ended* by unicorns).

Other words that trigger negative effects are for instance *decrease, damage, forbid, ban, reduce, ...*
Positive effects are triggered by words such as *increase, help, permit, cause, create, ...*

Example 2

Statement: Scientists found out that unicorns can end any war.

Relation: scientists (may) **negatively** affect war

This time, the Relation is **not correct**: It is not the *scientists* who have a negative effect on *war*, but the *unicorns*.

Your turn!

Statement: Throughout history, nuclear weapons have killed many innocents.

Relation: history (may) **negatively** affect innocents

Assuming the Statement is correct, is the Relation also correct?

- ○ No
- ○ Rather no
- ○ I am unsure
- ○ Rather yes
- ○ Yes

OPT-*R*: Exploring the Role of Explanations in Finetuning and Prompting for Reasoning Skills of Large Language Models

Badr AlKhamissi Siddharth Verma Ping Yu Zhijing Jin
Asli Celikyilmaz Mona Diab
Meta AI

Abstract

In this paper, we conduct a thorough investigation into the reasoning capabilities of Large Language Models (LLMs), focusing specifically on the Open Pretrained Transformers (OPT) models as a representative of such models. Our study entails finetuning three different sizes of OPT on a carefully curated reasoning corpus, resulting in two sets of finetuned models: OPT-*R*, finetuned without explanations, and OPT-*RE*, finetuned with explanations. We then evaluate all models on 57 out-of-domain tasks drawn from the SUPER-NATURALINSTRUCTIONS benchmark, covering 26 distinct reasoning skills, utilizing three prompting techniques. Through a comprehensive grid of 27 configurations and 6,156 test evaluations, we investigate the dimensions of finetuning, prompting, and scale to understand the role of explanations on different reasoning skills. Our findings reveal that having explanations in the fewshot exemplar has no significant impact on the model's performance when the model is finetuned, while positively affecting the non-finetuned counterpart. Moreover, we observe a slight yet consistent increase in classification accuracy as we incorporate explanations during prompting and finetuning, respectively. Finally, we offer insights on which skills benefit the most from incorporating explanations during finetuning and prompting, such as *Numerical* (+20.4%) and *Analogical* (+13.9%) reasoning, as well as skills that exhibit negligible or negative effects.

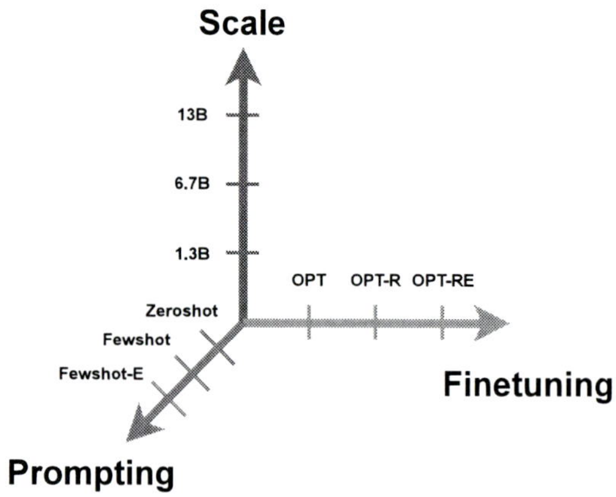

Figure 1: **Three-Dimensional Grid of Fine-Tuning, Prompting, and Scale.** Each dimension is represented as an axis, with three levels for each of finetuning, prompting, and scale plotted on each axis. The resulting grid consists of 27 different combinations evaluated on various reasoning tasks. It should be noted that there is a hidden dimension, the scoring function, comprising four components. This results in a comprehensive total of 6,156 evaluations.

1 Introduction

Recently, there has been a surge in the release of Large Language Models (LLMs) by both industrial and academic institutions. These models vary from open-source releases such as OPT (Zhang et al., 2022) and LLAMA (Touvron et al., 2023) to closed-source ones like GPT-3 (Brown et al., 2020) and PALM (Chowdhery et al., 2022). In addition, researchers have developed models that are finetuned on top of these foundational models to better follow instructions, such as OPT-IML (Iyer et al., 2022) and Alpaca (Taori et al., 2023). Despite the remarkable progress in LLMs' performance in Natural Language Processing (NLP) tasks, reasoning remains a challenging area. For example, prior work have shown that LLMs struggle with commonsense reasoning (West et al., 2022) and arithmetic reasoning (Hendrycks et al., 2021) to name a few.

Recent efforts have attempted to improve the reasoning performance of LLMs by decomposing answers into step-by-step reasoning chains using in-context learning (Wei et al., 2022b; Kojima et al., 2022) or during finetuning (Chung et al., 2022; Wei et al., 2021a). While these approaches have shown some improvement on benchmarks such as GSM8K (Cobbe et al., 2021), it is not clear how those explanations affect finetuning, prompting, or

Proceedings of the 1st Workshop on Natural Language Reasoning and Structured Explanations (@ACL 2023), pages 128–138
June 13, 2023

```
{Task Definition}

Provide your answer followed by a brief reasoning.

{In-Context Examples}

Input: {input}

Options: {options}

Output: The answer is {answer} because {explanation}
```

Figure 2: Template used during both training and inference. The model is tasked with predicting the answer followed by the explanation.

their combination. Concurrent work has investigated the generalization capability of such models to reasoning skills beyond those encountered during finetuning (Yu et al., 2022), but a comprehensive evaluation of the role of explanation during finetuning and prompting with respect to reasoning skills is still lacking.

In this paper, we aim to address this gap. We investigate OPT (Zhang et al., 2022) as a representative of such models and utilize it as our base model. Through finetuning OPT on a collection of carefully curated open-source reasoning datasets that come with explanations for each instance, we evaluate its performance on 57 tasks drawn from the SUPER-NATURALINSTRUCTIONS benchmark (Wang et al., 2022), covering 26 different reasoning skills. Our experiments are structured around three key dimensions: finetuning, prompting, and scale, each of which is comprised of three distinct components (See Figure 1). **Finetuning**: (1) a (vanilla) unfinetuned OPT model; (2) A finetuned OPT model without explanations (OPT-*R*); and, (3) A finetuned OPT model with explanations (OPT-*RE*). **Prompting**: (1) zero-shot prompting; (2) Fewshot prompting without explanations; and, (3) Fewshot prompting with explanations. Finally, **Scale**: (1) 1.3B; (2) 6.7B; and, (3) 13B. Accordingly, we create grid of 27 different components, providing a detailed analysis measuring the impact of explanations during finetuning and inference across different model scales.

Our findings reveals that finetuning on reasoning datasets leads to statistically significant improvements in seven reasoning skills, including *Numerical*, *Analogical* and *Reasoning on Objects*, with *Physical*, *Counting* and *Textual Entailment* showing a significant effect only for the OPT-*RE* model, across both fewshot prompting conditions and model sizes, as compared to the vanilla OPT model (see Table 2). However, we also find that this approach significantly hinders the performance of three other reasoning skills (see Table 3). We also investigate the impact of incorporating explanations during fewshot prompting and find that it does not have a significant impact on the performance of the finetuned models, as measured by the variance in the difference between both prompting methods across reasoning skills for each model. However, we notice that it has a more noticeable effect on the performance of the vanilla OPT model, as shown in Table 5. Additionally, we observe a consistent increase in the average performance across all tasks from Fewshot to Fewshot-E, as well as from OPT to OPT-*R* to OPT-*RE* models, indicating that explanations do have a small effect on performance during both finetuning and prompting. Finally, Table 4 presents a summary of the results, indicating which reasoning skills demonstrate improvement due to the incorporation of explanations during either finetuning or prompting, which skills show a negative effect, and which skills have negligible effects regarding explanations.

2 OPT-*R*: Finetuning on Reasoning Skills

2.1 Reasoning Datasets with Explanations

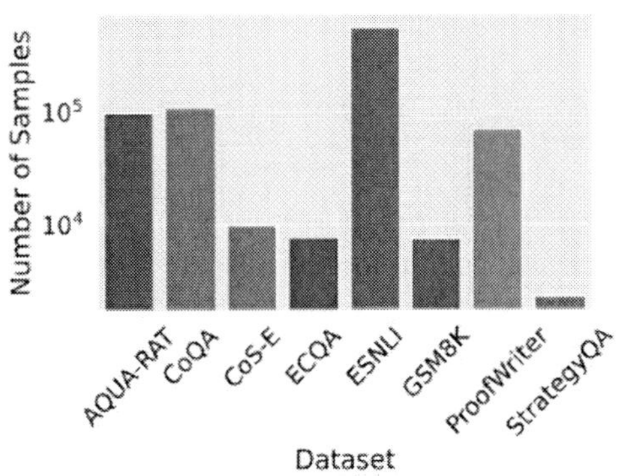

Figure 3: Number of samples in each dataset of the training corpus. Y-axis in log scale.

The finetuning corpus utilized to refine OPT is composed of various reasoning datasets, each of which includes a corresponding explanation or rationale for the answer. These rationales may consist of a sequence of smaller steps (i.e. chain-of-thought) or a free-form text that elucidates the reasoning behind the answer. As shown in Figure 2, we employ a uniform template for all tasks during the training process. The input to the model begins with a task definition, followed by an instruction to provide an answer followed by a brief reasoning. Next, we extract two random in-context examples uniformly from the training set that remain constant throughout training for each instance. The input for the current training instance is then presented in a format specific to each task. The options for the answer are then included in the input, but not in the in-context examples (see Appendix A for further details on task-specific definitions and options). The options are pre-shuffled for each training instance. The model is finally provided with the answer prefix, "`Output: The answer is`", and is tasked to predict the answer, followed by an explanation if OPT-*RE* is being finetuned. Similarly, the in-context examples only comprise an explanation when training OPT-*RE*.

Below is a brief description of each dataset used during finetuning. See Figure 3 for the relative size of each dataset.

AQUA-RAT The Algebra Question Answering with Rationales dataset (Ling et al., 2017) rendering the task of solving algebraic word problems more feasible by dividing the problem into a series of smaller steps. They create a 100k-sample dataset that contains questions, answers and rationales in natural language and human-readable mathematical expressions that can be used to derive the final answer.

CoQA The Conversational Question Answering dataset Reddy et al. (2019). It consists of 127k questions and answers, compiled from 8k conversations about passages from seven different domains. Given a passage that contains a conversation, the model is tasked with answering a question by highlighting the corresponding evidence from the passage.

CoS-E The Common Sense Explanations dataset Rajani et al. (2019) to induce language models with commonsense reasoning. In this dataset, the model is given a question and a set of choices and is tasked with selecting one of the provided choices along with providing an explanation in natural language as to why that choice is correct.

ECQA The Explanations for Commonsense Question Answering dataset Aggarwal et al. (2021). It is similar to CoS-E since it requires the model to choose one of the provided options to answer the given question, and also provide an explanation.

ESNLI The Stanford Natural Language Inference dataset with Explanations Camburu et al. (2018) to train models to provide interpretable and robust explanations for their decisions. The authors extend the SNLI dataset (Bowman et al., 2015) with human-annotated explanations. Similar to any NLI task, the model is given a premise and hypothesis and the task is to determine whether the hypothesis sentence entails, contradicts, or is neutral with respect to the given premise.

GSM8K The Grade School Math dataset Cobbe et al. (2021) to train models to better perform multi-step mathematical reasoning. It consists of 8.5k linguistically diverse grade school math word problems. Therefore, the task for the model is to answer the question by performing a series of arithmetic operations to obtain a final answer, while explaining it's reasoning steps.

ProofWriter The ProofWriter dataset Tafjord et al. (2021) to generate both the implications of a theory from the RuleTaker dataset (Clark et al., 2020) and the natural language proofs that support them. Specifically, given a sequence of facts and rules, the model is tasked with answering a question using "Yes", "No", or "Unknown" and provide the reasoning path by referring to the provided facts and rules. We consider the open-world assumption subset of RuleTaker with questions that requires reasoning up to a depth of 5.

StrategyQA The Strategy Question Answering dataset Geva et al. (2021) to improve multi-hop reasoning for questions where the required reasoning steps are implicit in the question. Therefore, the task of the model is to answer the question using "Yes" or "No" then provide a strategy that explains the answer by decomposing it into a number of steps.

2.2 Finetuning Procedures

OPT The Open Pretrained Transformers (OPT) models are a suite of decoder-only pre-trained transformers ranging from 125M to 175B parameters released by Zhang et al. (2022). In this work, we use three OPT models with sizes of 1.3B, 6.7B and 13B. The details of each model architecture, pre-training corpus and training configuration (e.g. weight initialization, optimizer, tokenizer, hyperparameters, etc.) can be found in Zhang et al. (2022).

Reasoning Skill	Task IDs
Abductive Reasoning	task854
Analogical Reasoning	task1287, task1288
Argument Reasoning	task514
Causal Reasoning	task1393
Commonsense Reasoning	task279, task156, task295
Commonsense Reasoning → Numerical Commonsense ...	task1403
Commonsense Reasoning → Physical Reasoning	task084
Commonsense Reasoning → Social Situations	task580, task937, task1606
Commonsense Reasoning → Spatial Reasoning	task082, task083
Deductive Reasoning	task221, task1568, task220
Ethics	task667, task724, task723
Grammatical Reasoning	task1712, task052, task1559
Logical Reasoning	task717, task211, task268
Logical Reasoning → Reasoning with Symbols	task923, task935
Mathematics → Counting	task523, task155
Multihop Reasoning	task1297, task056
Numerical Reasoning	task621, task1333
Reasoning on Objects	task1583, task1584
Reasoning on Social Interactions	task609, task881, task875
Reasoning on Strings	task1189
Relational Reasoning	task1380, task472, task1505
Scientific Reasoning	task1431, task228, task714
Temporal Reasoning	task018, task1549, task383
Textual Entailment	task738, task890, task463
Textual Entailment → Analogical Reasoning	task1347
Textual Entailment → Deductive Reasoning	task1612, task534, task1366

Table 1: Evaluation tasks from SUP-NATINST (Wang et al., 2022) used for each reasoning skill.

Implementation Details To finetune the selected models, we utilized the metaseq[1] implementation since it enables higher training efficiency compared to other codebases (Zhang et al., 2022). Each model is finetuned twice for 10 epochs, once with explanations and once without (i.e. OPT-*RE* vs OPT-*R*, respectively). Models are evaluated at the end of each epoch on a chosen set of SUPER-NATURALINSTRUCTIONS validation tasks, and the checkpoint with the best performance is selected for evaluation on the testing tasks. The loss is calculated only on the tokens the model is tasked to predict during inference, and not the full input, what is referred to as label-loss in (Iyer et al., 2022). The samples across all datasets are shuffled during training. Further, the model is provided with two in-context examples during finetuning in addition to the task definition to match inference time following (Wang et al., 2022).

[1]https://github.com/facebookresearch/metaseq

3 Evaluating the Models

3.1 SUPER-NATURALINSTRUCTIONS Tasks

In this study, we focus on a subset of the SUPER-NATURALINSTRUCTIONS benchmark version 2.6[2] (SUP-NATINST for short) proposed by Wang et al. (2022), which comprises 1,616 varied NLP tasks and includes meta-labels for each task, such as task type, domain and more importantly for this work: the underlying reasoning skills. Specifically, we select a subset of tasks that satisfy two key criteria: (i) the task focuses on a single reasoning skill, enabling us to evaluate a specific atomic skill, and (ii) the task can be tested using classification mode, as detailed in Section 3.2. Note that there is no data contamination between finetuning data and the evaluation benchmark.

[2]We downloaded the data from https://github.com/allenai/natural-instructions/tree/v2.6.

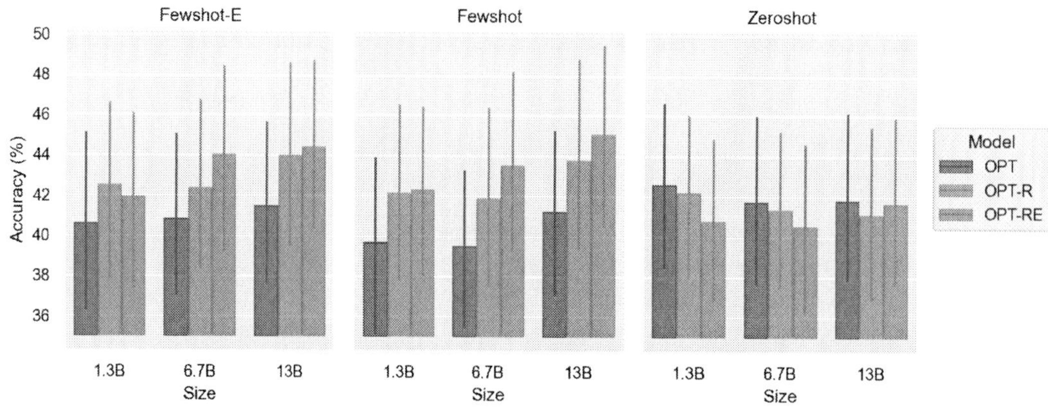

Figure 4: Results achieved across all tasks as a function of the three primary dimensions analyzed in this study: Finetuning, Prompting and Scale.

Benchmark Splits Following the task selection process, we apply a random sampling technique to ensure diversity within the testing set. Specifically, we select a maximum of three tasks from each reasoning skill, and allocate any remaining tasks to the validation set. Notably, this approach enables us to obtain a representative sample of the selected reasoning skills for testing, while also ensuring that our model's performance is not influenced by a particular subset of tasks. Table 1 shows the complete list of tasks used for evaluating our finetuned models for each reasoning skill.

3.2 Evaluation Setup

Earlier, we mentioned that we selected 57 tasks spanning 26 reasoning skills from SUP-NATINST to evaluate our finetuned models. To meet our criteria, as detailed in Section 3.1, each task had to fulfill two conditions. The second condition required that the task can be considered a classification task. That means there is a discrete set of candidates (one of which is correct) and thereby treating it as a classification problem where the highest-scoring candidate is considered the answer. To ensure this, we utilized a straightforward heuristic: we only sampled tasks that had no more than 10 possible candidate answers.

Classification Method To determine the correct answer, we conduct a forward pass for each potential candidate answer and utilize a scoring function to measure the likelihood that the candidate tokens follows the input, similar to Brown et al. (2020). This process is repeated four times using distinct scoring functions, as detailed in the subsequent paragraph. The highest accuracy score from the four scoring functions is considered as result of the task.

Scoring Functions This is considered the fourth dimension of this work since we evaluate each task using four different scoring functions and take the maximum accuracy as the result. The four scoring functions used are as follows: (1) **mean**, which involves computing the average of the log probabilities of candidate tokens, also referred to as token score. (2) **unconditional-norm**, which computes the difference between the sum of token scores of the candidate when unconditioned by any previous tokens and the sum of candidate token scores when conditioned by previous input. (3) **suffix**, which computes the sum of the conditioned candidate's token scores alone. Finally, (4) **sum**, which involves calculating the sum of all the token scores passed to the model. The reason we employed different functions is that we observed significant gains in performance when using one scoring function over the other for specific tasks. Therefore, in order to ensure fairness across all tasks, we selected the highest accuracy over all scoring functions for each task.

4 Results & Findings

In this section, we present the results and findings of our experiments. First, we illustrate in Figure 4 the outcome of our evaluation on the effectiveness of finetuned models as compared to the vanilla OPT model, across three different scales when using both fewshot prompting with and without explanations. Furthermore, we observe a monotonic increase in the performance of each model as we increase the scale under those two prompting condition, which indicates a positive correlation between the model's capacity and its overall performance. However, we note that this trend does not apply to the zeroshot prompting method, since we are testing out-of-distribution tasks and that the finetuned models were trained with fewshot exemplars in their context. This leads us to focus only on the fewshot prompting methods, with and without explanations, for the remaining of our evaluations. Specifically, we investigate the impact of finetuning the OPT models on reasoning datasets, as compared to the vanilla OPT model, and explore the effect of explanations during finetuning and prompting, both in terms of the reasoning skill.

4.1 Model Performance for Reasoning Skills

The results reported in this and the following section are the classification accuracy of each reasoning skill across different conditions, such as model sizes and fewshot prompting methods. Table 2 shows the reasoning skills where either OPT-*RE* or OPT-*R* are significantly better than the vanilla OPT model, as measured by Welch's t-test, where $p < 0.05$. Conversely, Table 3 show the reasoning skills where the vanilla OPT model performs significantly better than either of its finetuned counterparts.

Skill	OPT	OPT-*R*	OPT-*RE*
Numerical	44.8	**65.2***	64.7*
Analogical	49.0	**62.9***	60.8*
Counting	19.8	13.1	**31.3***
Physical	38.2	37.8	**49.1***
Entailment	42.6	47.2	**51.6***
Social Int	34.1	**43.0***	40.1
Objects	54.3	**62.6***	59.9*

Table 2: Performance as a function of the reasoning skills where OPT-*RE* or OPT-*R* performs significantly better than the OPT model as measured by Welch's t-test ($p < 0.05$) denoted by the * symbol. The performance is measured across Fewshot and Fewshot-E prompting, the three different scales and tasks under the corresponding reasoning skill. Best result indicated in **bold**.

The results reveal that the finetuned variants of the OPT model demonstrate a significant improvement on seven distinct reasoning skills, with particular emphasis on the *Numerical* and *Analogical* reasoning tasks. Specifically, for the *Mathematical*

Skill	OPT	OPT-*R*	OPT-*RE*
Argument	**57.9**	46.1^-	48.7^-
TE - Deductive	**36.0**	29.0^-	29.4^-
Commonsense	**33.4**	29.7	28.8^-

Table 3: Performance as a function of the reasoning skill where OPT performs significantly better than either OPT-*R* or OPT-*RE* as measured by Welch's t-test ($p < 0.05$) denoted by the $^-$ symbol. The performance is measured across Fewshot and Fewshot-E prompting, the three different scales and tasks under the corresponding reasoning skill. TE is Textual Entailment.

Counting skill, the OPT-*RE* variant outperforms both the OPT-*R* and OPT models, underscoring the criticality of incorporating explanations during the finetuning process for mathematical datasets. Likewise, the *Physical Reasoning* tasks exhibit a similar trend. On the other hand, we can see that for the *Argument*, *Deductive Textual Entailment* and *Commonsense* skills the non-finetuned version outperforms considerably.

4.2 Fine-Grained Skill Analysis

Table 4 shows the classification accuracy results obtained from the three models, in relation to the reasoning skill and few-shot prompting method used. The best accuracy value for each reasoning skill is indicated in **bold**, and the cells are shaded with colors ranging from green to white to indicate their position in the accuracy spectrum of each reasoning skill. The skills with similar performance across different models are assigned a lighter shade of green, indicating that their color spectrum ends earlier than that of other skills where the difference in performance between models is more significant. The table is divided into four blocks to distinguish effects of finetuning and prompting methods on reasoning skills: the first block showcases skills where the finetuned (OPT-*RE* and OPT-*R*) models outperform the vanilla OPT model, the second block highlights skills where OPT-*RE* has better accuracy than other models therefore illustrating the importance of finetuning on explanations on those skills. The third block displays skills where OPT outperforms other models showing that finetuning actually hurts performance in this case, and the fourth block identifies skills where the choice of model or prompting method has little impact on the overall performance.

Skill	OPT Fewshot	OPT Fewshot-E	OPT-*R* Fewshot	OPT-*R* Fewshot-E	OPT-*RE* Fewshot	OPT-*RE* Fewshot-E
Numerical	39.9	49.7	65.1	**65.3**	64.7	64.8
Analogical	51.9	46.2	**63.3**	62.5	60.7	60.9
Objects	53.5	55.1	61.4	**63.8**	60.0	59.7
Social Interactions	33.6	34.7	**43.8**	42.3	40.2	40.0
Textual Entailment	43.3	42.0	47.1	47.3	**51.9**	51.2
Grammatical	54.4	55.1	61.2	60.0	62.0	**63.1**
Multihop	36.6	31.7	38.9	**39.9**	39.5	37.0
Symbols	44.2	47.2	51.7	51.8	51.9	**52.4**
Spatial	44.1	47.1	49.8	**51.8**	49.6	49.2
Social Situations	46.3	46.6	53.2	53.2	51.9	52.3
Counting	19.6	20.0	13.5	12.7	29.8	**32.9**
Physical	35.8	40.6	36.9	38.8	48.1	**50.0**
Logical	31.7	33.4	33.7	34.1	36.9	**38.4**
Temporal	**50.7**	49.7	43.4	46.5	48.5	38.5
Argument	55.8	**60.1**	46.3	45.9	48.6	48.8
TE - Deductive	33.7	**38.3**	27.9	30.1	29.0	29.9
Relational	47.4	**51.1**	47.6	47.9	44.8	44.6
Commonsense	**35.0**	31.8	29.8	29.5	28.5	29.2
TE - Analogical	16.3	18.7	18.6	**20.7**	18.7	18.1
Abductive	33.9	36.1	**36.9**	34.4	34.2	35.3
Ethics	26.8	25.8	26.5	25.9	26.2	**27.6**
Deductive	39.4	40.4	39.4	40.4	40.0	**41.1**
Causal	50.2	**50.6**	49.1	48.9	50.1	50.5
Scientific	23.4	23.3	24.3	24.5	**25.0**	24.5
Numerical Commonsense	**59.5**	59.2	59.0	59.0	59.2	59.4
Strings	60.7	60.7	61.1	**61.2**	60.7	60.7

Table 4: Classification accuracy results achieved by different models as a function of the reasoning skill and few-shot prompting method employed. The best accuracy obtained for each reasoning skill is highlighted in bold. The cells are shaded with colors ranging from green to white to indicate their position in the accuracy spectrum. Reasoning skills with smaller variance in achieved results are assigned a lighter shade of green to convey the extent of similarity between models. The first block highlights skills where the finetuned models perform notably better than the vanilla OPT. The second block emphasizes the skills where OPT-*RE* outperforms other models. In contrast, the third block showcases the skills where OPT outperforms the other models. Lastly, the fourth block identifies skills where the choice of model or prompting method has little impact on the overall performance.

Explanations' Effect One of the central questions that we sought to investigate in this study is the extent to which explanations play a role in improving the reasoning capabilities of OPT models during finetuning and prompting. The results presented in Table 5 suggest that the presence or absence of explanations in the fewshot examples employed for prompting does not *significantly* impact the performance of the model when the model is finetuned on reasoning datasets. Concretely, in Table 5, we present the variance of the absolute accuracy difference for each model across reasoning skills by excluding the *Temporal* skill, which was identified as an outlier. Specifically, we compute the difference between the two corresponding columns for each model in Table 4. These values provide insights into the impact of including explanations during prompting on the performance of the models. Our findings reveal that the difference is negligible for OPT-*R* and OPT-*RE* models, suggesting that the choice of prompting method does not significantly affect the model's accuracy. However, for the vanilla OPT model, the difference is more substantial, emphasizing the importance of employing explanations during fewshot prompting. However, the mean performance of each model across the distinct fewshot prompting methods demonstrates a slight yet consistent increase in classification accuracy, from Fewshot to Fewshot-E (incorporating explanations), as well as from OPT to OPT-*R* to OPT-*RE* models showing that explanations do have a small effect on performance during both finetuning and prompting.

Model	Std(|F-FE|)	Avg(F)	Avg(FE)
OPT	2.31	40.68	41.82
OPT-*R*	0.84	43.44	43.68
OPT-*RE*	0.78	44.49	44.86

Table 5: The first column shows the variance of the absolute difference in accuracy for each model across different reasoning skills, when using Fewshot (F) and Fewshot-E (FE) prompting methods. The second and third columns show the average performance of each model across each prompting method. Results are obtained after dropping the outlier *Temporal* skill.

5 Related Work

Reasoning LLMs LLMs have made significant advancements in the field of NLP and related areas (Brown et al., 2020; Chowdhery et al., 2022; Chung et al., 2022), especially with the advent of the pre-train, prompt, and predict paradigm (Liu et al., 2021). This paradigm has enabled these models to solve a multitude of tasks through incontext fewshot or zeroshot learning using instructions (Wei et al., 2021b; Iyer et al., 2022). However, their reasoning abilities have been a subject of debate in recent literature (Huang and Chang, 2022; AlKhamissi et al., 2022). Several studies suggest that increasing the size of an LM trained through the same next-token prediction method can lead to the emergence of complex behaviors (Wei et al., 2022a), including reasoning. For instance, some research has demonstrated that sufficiently large LMs can use chain-of-thought prompting (Wei et al., 2022b) to simulate human-like reasoning. Other studies have shown that the addition of a simple prompt, such as "Let's think step-by-step" (Kojima et al., 2022) can elicit reasoning abilities in LLMs by generating explicit reasoning steps before decoding the final answer. However, some researchers contend that emulating the human reasoning thought process is distinct from claiming that the model can truly reason (Wei et al., 2022b).

Finetuned LLMs Concurrent studies have finetuned LLMs to follow instructions to improve their generalization ability to unseen tasks through zero and fewshot learning (Iyer et al., 2022; Chung et al., 2022). However, our approach differs in that we only finetune on a selected number of open-source datasets that provide explanations for each instance. This enables us to focus on the importance of explanations during finetuning in the context of reasoning skills. While concurrent works, such as (Iyer et al., 2022; Wang et al., 2022), have experimented with different prompting methods during finetuning and inference, our study focuses primarily on evaluating the reasoning ability of the finetuned models across a set of reasoning skills. Other concurrent studies have explored the impact of finetuning on a set of held-out reasoning tasks (Yu et al., 2022), but their evaluation approach, which involves generating answers, may be influenced by various factors such as decoding strategy, decoding parameters, and prompt templates. In contrast, we adopt a rank classification approach similar to (Brown et al., 2020), which better captures the reasoning performance of the model being evaluated, in addition to covering a larger number of reasoning skills and tasks.

6 Conclusion

In this study, we investigated the impact of incorporating explanations during finetuning and prompting on three different sizes of the OPT model. Through a systematic and comprehensive evaluation process that considered three key dimensions, we found that while explanations did provide a small improvement in performance, the effect was not significant when incorporated in the in-context demonstrations during inference for the finetuned models. Additionally, our results showed that both finetuned models exhibited significant improvements in reasoning skills such as *Numerical*, *Analogical* and *Reasoning on Objects*. Moreover, we demonstrated that skills such as *Physical*, *Counting*, and *Textual Entailment* benefited from incorporating explanations during the finetuning process. Overall, our findings provide insights into the impact of incorporating explanations on the reasoning capabilities of LLMs and offer guidance on which reasoning skills would benefit most from the inclusion and exclusion of explanations during finetuning and prompting.

Limitations

While our study provides valuable insights into the impact of finetuning on reasoning performance and the role of explanations during finetuning and prompting with respect to various reasoning skills, there are several limitations to our work. Firstly, we only consider a single LLM, OPT, as our base model. Our results may not generalize to other LLMs with different architectures or pretraining objectives. Secondly, we only use a limited set of reasoning datasets for finetuning due to the limited availability of open-source datasets with explanations. However, it is possible that our findings may not hold for models finetuned on larger closed datasets as usually seen in real-world scenarios. Thirdly, our experiments only cover a limited range of model sizes due to limitations in computational budget, therefore it is possible that our findings may not hold for much larger models. Finally, we only consider finetuning using fewshot prompting conditions in our experiments, and it is possible that our findings may not hold for models finetuned without in-context exemplars. Overall, while our study provides valuable insights into the impact of finetuning and explanations on reasoning performance, further research is needed to investigate these factors across a broader range of models, datasets, and finetuning strategies.

Ethics Statement

This work is based on analyzing and evaluating the performance of LLMs on reasoning tasks using existing public datasets. No personally identifiable information or sensitive data was collected or used in this research. We acknowledge the potential risks of developing LLMs, including their potential impact on spreading misinformation, generating unwanted content and the exacerbation of existing biases in datasets. Our work aims to contribute to improving the transparency and understanding of how LLMs can be optimized for specific reasoning skills. We hope our findings will inspire further research on developing ethical and responsible approaches for developing and deploying LLMs.

References

Shourya Aggarwal, Divyanshu Mandowara, Vishwajeet Agrawal, Dinesh Khandelwal, Parag Singla, and Dinesh Garg. 2021. Explanations for CommonsenseQA: New Dataset and Models. In *Proceedings of the 59th Annual Meeting of the Association for Computational Linguistics and the 11th International Joint Conference on Natural Language Processing (Volume 1: Long Papers)*, pages 3050–3065, Online. Association for Computational Linguistics.

Badr AlKhamissi, Millicent Li, Asli Celikyilmaz, Mona T. Diab, and Marjan Ghazvininejad. 2022. A review on language models as knowledge bases. *ArXiv*, abs/2204.06031.

Samuel R. Bowman, Gabor Angeli, Christopher Potts, and Christopher D. Manning. 2015. A large annotated corpus for learning natural language inference. In *Proceedings of the 2015 Conference on Empirical Methods in Natural Language Processing (EMNLP)*. Association for Computational Linguistics.

Tom Brown, Benjamin Mann, Nick Ryder, Melanie Subbiah, Jared D Kaplan, Prafulla Dhariwal, Arvind Neelakantan, Pranav Shyam, Girish Sastry, Amanda Askell, et al. 2020. Language models are few-shot learners. *Advances in neural information processing systems*, 33:1877–1901.

Oana-Maria Camburu, Tim Rocktäschel, Thomas Lukasiewicz, and Phil Blunsom. 2018. e-snli: Natural language inference with natural language explanations. In S. Bengio, H. Wallach, H. Larochelle, K. Grauman, N. Cesa-Bianchi, and R. Garnett, editors, *Advances in Neural Information Processing Systems 31*, pages 9539–9549. Curran Associates, Inc.

Aakanksha Chowdhery, Sharan Narang, Jacob Devlin, Maarten Bosma, Gaurav Mishra, Adam Roberts, Paul Barham, Hyung Won Chung, Charles Sutton, Sebastian Gehrmann, et al. 2022. Palm: Scaling language modeling with pathways. *arXiv preprint arXiv:2204.02311*.

Hyung Won Chung, Le Hou, Shayne Longpre, Barret Zoph, Yi Tay, William Fedus, Eric Li, Xuezhi Wang, Mostafa Dehghani, Siddhartha Brahma, et al. 2022. Scaling instruction-finetuned language models. *arXiv preprint arXiv:2210.11416*.

Peter Clark, Oyvind Tafjord, and Kyle Richardson. 2020. Transformers as soft reasoners over language. In *IJCAI*.

Karl Cobbe, Vineet Kosaraju, Mohammad Bavarian, Jacob Hilton, Reiichiro Nakano, Christopher Hesse, and John Schulman. 2021. Training verifiers to solve math word problems. *ArXiv*, abs/2110.14168.

Mor Geva, Daniel Khashabi, Elad Segal, Tushar Khot, Dan Roth, and Jonathan Berant. 2021. Did aristotle use a laptop? a question answering benchmark with implicit reasoning strategies. *Transactions of the Association for Computational Linguistics*, 9:346–361.

Dan Hendrycks, Collin Burns, Saurav Kadavath, Akul Arora, Steven Basart, Eric Tang, Dawn Song, and Jacob Steinhardt. 2021. Measuring mathematical problem solving with the math dataset. *NeurIPS*.

Jie Huang and Kevin Chen-Chuan Chang. 2022. Towards reasoning in large language models: A survey. *ArXiv*, abs/2212.10403.

Srinivasan Iyer, Xi Victoria Lin, Ramakanth Pasunuru, Todor Mihaylov, Dániel Simig, Ping Yu, Kurt Shuster, Tianlu Wang, Qing Liu, Punit Singh Koura, et al. 2022. Opt-iml: Scaling language model instruction meta learning through the lens of generalization. *arXiv preprint arXiv:2212.12017*.

Takeshi Kojima, Shixiang Shane Gu, Machel Reid, Yutaka Matsuo, and Yusuke Iwasawa. 2022. Large language models are zero-shot reasoners. *arXiv preprint arXiv:2205.11916*.

Wang Ling, Dani Yogatama, Chris Dyer, and Phil Blunsom. 2017. Program induction by rationale generation: Learning to solve and explain algebraic word problems. In *Proceedings of the 55th Annual Meeting of the Association for Computational Linguistics (Volume 1: Long Papers)*, pages 158–167, Vancouver, Canada. Association for Computational Linguistics.

Pengfei Liu, Weizhe Yuan, Jinlan Fu, Zhengbao Jiang, Hiroaki Hayashi, and Graham Neubig. 2021. Pretrain, prompt, and predict: A systematic survey of prompting methods in natural language processing. *ACM Computing Surveys*, 55:1 – 35.

Nazneen Rajani, Bryan McCann, Caiming Xiong, and Richard Socher. 2019. Explain yourself! leveraging language models for commonsense reasoning. In *ACL*.

Siva Reddy, Danqi Chen, and Christopher D. Manning. 2019. CoQA: A conversational question answering challenge. *Transactions of the Association for Computational Linguistics*, 7:249–266.

Oyvind Tafjord, Bhavana Dalvi, and Peter Clark. 2021. ProofWriter: Generating implications, proofs, and abductive statements over natural language. In *Findings of the Association for Computational Linguistics: ACL-IJCNLP 2021*, pages 3621–3634, Online. Association for Computational Linguistics.

Rohan Taori, Ishaan Gulrajani, Tianyi Zhang, Yann Dubois, Xuechen Li, Carlos Guestrin, Percy Liang, and Tatsunori B. Hashimoto. 2023. Stanford alpaca: An instruction-following llama model. `https://github.com/tatsu-lab/stanford_alpaca`.

Hugo Touvron, Thibaut Lavril, Gautier Izacard, Xavier Martinet, Marie-Anne Lachaux, Timothée Lacroix, Baptiste Rozière, Naman Goyal, Eric Hambro, Faisal Azhar, Aur'elien Rodriguez, Armand Joulin, Edouard Grave, and Guillaume Lample. 2023. Llama: Open and efficient foundation language models. *ArXiv*, abs/2302.13971.

Yizhong Wang, Swaroop Mishra, Pegah Alipoormolabashi, Yeganeh Kordi, Amirreza Mirzaei, Atharva Naik, Arjun Ashok, Arut Selvan Dhanasekaran, Anjana Arunkumar, David Stap, Eshaan Pathak, Giannis Karamanolakis, Haizhi Lai, Ishan Purohit, Ishani Mondal, Jacob Anderson, Kirby Kuznia, Krima Doshi, Kuntal Kumar Pal, Maitreya Patel, Mehrad Moradshahi, Mihir Parmar, Mirali Purohit, Neeraj Varshney, Phani Rohitha Kaza, Pulkit Verma, Ravsehaj Singh Puri, Rushang Karia, Savan Doshi, Shailaja Keyur Sampat, Siddhartha Mishra, Sujan Reddy A, Sumanta Patro, Tanay Dixit, and Xudong Shen. 2022. Super-NaturalInstructions: Generalization via declarative instructions on 1600+ NLP tasks. In *Proceedings of the 2022 Conference on Empirical Methods in Natural Language Processing*, pages 5085–5109, Abu Dhabi, United Arab Emirates. Association for Computational Linguistics.

Jason Wei, Maarten Bosma, Vincent Y Zhao, Kelvin Guu, Adams Wei Yu, Brian Lester, Nan Du, Andrew M Dai, and Quoc V Le. 2021a. Finetuned language models are zero-shot learners. *arXiv preprint arXiv:2109.01652*.

Jason Wei, Maarten Bosma, Vincent Y Zhao, Kelvin Guu, Adams Wei Yu, Brian Lester, Nan Du, Andrew M Dai, and Quoc V Le. 2021b. Finetuned language models are zero-shot learners. *arXiv preprint arXiv:2109.01652*.

Jason Wei, Yi Tay, Rishi Bommasani, Colin Raffel, Barret Zoph, Sebastian Borgeaud, Dani Yogatama, Maarten Bosma, Denny Zhou, Donald Metzler, Ed Huai hsin Chi, Tatsunori Hashimoto, Oriol Vinyals, Percy Liang, Jeff Dean, and William Fedus. 2022a. Emergent abilities of large language models. *ArXiv*, abs/2206.07682.

Jason Wei, Xuezhi Wang, Dale Schuurmans, Maarten Bosma, Ed Chi, Quoc Le, and Denny Zhou. 2022b. Chain of thought prompting elicits reasoning in large language models. *arXiv preprint arXiv:2201.11903*.

Peter West, Chandra Bhagavatula, Jack Hessel, Jena D. Hwang, Liwei Jiang, Ronan Le Bras, Ximing Lu, Sean Welleck, and Yejin Choi. 2022. Symbolic knowledge distillation: from general language models to commonsense models.

Ping Yu, Tianlu Wang, O. Yu. Golovneva, Badr AlKhamissi, Siddharth Verma, Zhijing Jin, Gargi Ghosh, Mona Diab, and Asli Celikyilmaz. 2022. Alert: Adapting language models to reasoning tasks. *ArXiv*, abs/2212.08286.

Susan Zhang, Stephen Roller, Naman Goyal, Mikel Artetxe, Moya Chen, Shuohui Chen, Christopher Dewan, Mona Diab, Xian Li, Xi Victoria Lin, et al. 2022. Opt: Open pre-trained transformer language models. *arXiv preprint arXiv:2205.01068*.

Dataset	Task Definition	Options
AQuA	You are given an algebraic word question. Questions in this task often requires executing a series of arithmetic operations to obtain a final answer. You are also given 5 answer options (associated with 'A', 'B, 'C', 'D', 'E'). Do not generate anything else apart from one of the following characters: "A", "B", "C", "D", "E" and the corresponding explanation.	-A -B -C -D -E
CoQA	You are given a passage that contains a conversation and a question. The task is to answer the question and provide an explanation that highlights the corresponding evidence in the passage.	Free-form text
CoS-E	You are given a passage that contains a sentence and a question. The task is to answer the question by selecting one of the provided choices.	Select one of the provided choices
ECQA	You are given a question that requires commonsense reasoning. The task is to answer the question by selecting one of the provided choices.	Select one of the provided choices
ESNLI	You will be presented with a premise and a hypothesis sentence. The task is to determine whether the hypothesis sentence entails (implies), contradicts (opposes), or is neutral with respect to the given premise sentence. Please answer with "Contradiction", "Neutral",or "Entailment".	-Contradiction -Neutral -Entailment
GSM8K	You will be presented with a passage that contains a grade school math word problem. The task is to answer the question by performing a series of arithmetic operations to obtain a final answer.	Number
ProofWriter	You are given a sequence of facts and rules followed by a question. The task is to answer the question using "Yes", "No" or "Unknown".	-Yes -No -Unknown
StrategyQA	You are given a sentence and a question. The required reasoning steps are implicit in the question. The task is to answer the question using "Yes" or "No" then provide a strategy that explains the answer by decomposing it into a number of steps.	-Yes -No

Table 6: Task definition and options used for each of the finetuning reasoning datasets.

A Finetuning Task Definition and Options

Table 6 shows the task definition and options provided as input to the template shown in Figure 2 during finetuning the OPT models on the reasoning datasets.

Deductive Additivity for Planning of Natural Language Proofs

Zayne Sprague **Kaj Bostrom** **Swarat Chaudhuri** **Greg Durrett**
Department of Computer Science
The University of Texas at Austin
{zaynesprague@, kaj@cs, swarat@cs, gdurrett@cs}.utexas.edu

Abstract

Current natural language systems designed for multi-step claim validation typically operate in two phases: retrieve a set of relevant premise statements using heuristics (planning), then generate novel conclusions from those statements using a large language model (deduction). The planning step often requires expensive Transformer operations and does not scale to arbitrary numbers of premise statements. In this paper, we investigate whether an efficient planning heuristic is possible via embedding spaces compatible with deductive reasoning. Specifically, we evaluate whether embedding spaces exhibit a property we call *deductive additivity*: the sum of premise statement embeddings should be close to embeddings of conclusions based on those premises. We explore multiple sources of off-the-shelf dense embeddings in addition to fine-tuned embeddings from GPT3 and sparse embeddings from BM25. We study embedding models both intrinsically, evaluating whether the property of deductive additivity holds, and extrinsically, using them to assist planning in natural language proof generation. Lastly, we create a dataset, Single-Step Reasoning Contrast (SSRC), to further probe performance on various reasoning types. Our findings suggest that while standard embedding methods frequently embed conclusions near the sums of their premises, they fall short of being effective heuristics and lack the ability to model certain categories of reasoning.

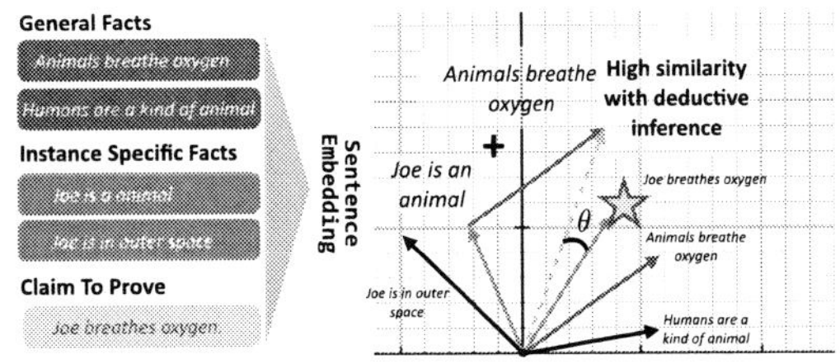

Figure 1: A visualization of an embedding space that has the Deductive Additivity property. When two facts (blue and red) are added together, their resulting vector (yellow) should have high similarity with the embedding of a statement that logically follows via deduction (green).

1 Introduction

One way to justify the truth of a statement is to give an explanation building logically towards that statement based on deduction from shared premises. The ways facts can be combined through reasoning are numerous, including many different modes of deduction like syllogism or modus tollens. This process can be automated with natural language processing, using systems to generate natural language proofs that use evidence to derive a claim through a structured argument. Large language models (LLMs) like GPT4 (OpenAI, 2023) have exhibited impressive performance in reasoning tasks. However, these models can still make unsound inferences (Ye and Durrett, 2022; Zhang et al., 2023; Xue et al., 2023).

One reason for these errors is that models may fail to plan reasoning effectively. LLMs do not have explicit planning capabilities: they generate conclusions in a way that conflates lexical choice and decisions of what content to generate, and no alternatives are materialized in typical greedy or sampling-based LLM inference. A recent line of work (Bostrom et al., 2021, 2022; Sprague et al., 2022; Creswell et al., 2023) explores how to decouple these stages. However, what is still missing is a scalable method for doing planning in these kinds of natural language reasoning settings: past work involves early-fusion invocation of pretrained LMs (Xiong et al., 2021) and does not scale to thousands of premises.

This work explores the feasibility of planning the reasoning process directly in a vector space, where combining statements and retrieving similar statements can be efficiently implemented as

Proceedings of the 1st Workshop on Natural Language Reasoning and Structured Explanations (@ACL 2023), pages 139–156
June 13, 2023

addition and cosine similarity, respectively. We introduce *deductive additivity (DA)*, a property of an embedding space necessary to enable this planning. A visualization of an embedding space with the deductive additivity property is shown in Figure 1. Each piece of evidence is embedded into a fixed-size vector, and the combined embeddings of two facts should be close to embeddings of statements that are entailed from those two facts via deduction. This property can help us plan when we are trying to derive a goal statement based on premise statements. New facts that bring us closer to that goal should be explored in the deductive reasoning process, so this vector space provides a natural heuristic: we want to find fact embeddings that, when summed, achieve the highest dot product with the encoding of our goal. Crucially, the vector-based nature of this heuristic facilitates rapid retrieval through efficient search algorithms.

Our experiments test both off-the-shelf embeddings (e.g., SimCSE (Gao et al., 2021)) as well as embeddings that are explicitly tuned for deductive additivity. First, we conduct intrinsic evaluations to see whether embeddings of standard encoders exhibit deductive additivity. We then test how well the method performs as a search heuristic on the natural language proof generation datasets EntailmentBank (Dalvi et al., 2021) and Everyday Norms: Why Not (Sprague et al., 2022, ENWN). Finally, we create the Single-Step Reasoning Contrast (SSRC) dataset to benchmark each method on how well they model different reasoning categories, like syllogism or modus tollens, and how robust they are to common errors in reasoning, like negation.

Our main contributions are threefold: (1) We propose a novel method for planning reasoning steps over a collection of facts purely based on vector arithmetic. (2) We show that several embedding methods have promise for deductive additivity but do not fully meet the properties required for planning in natural language deduction scenarios even when explicitly fine-tuned for it. (3) We present a new dataset meant to help diagnose and identify areas where deduction planning methods are underperforming across a range of different reasoning categories.

2 Problem Description and Motivation

Here we introduce the problem of proof generation, the system we use to generate proofs and deductive additivity.

2.1 Problem Setup

We explore the process of proving a goal statement (or claim) g by generating an entailment tree T, given a set of general-purpose facts $X = x_1, \dots x_n$ and a collection of instance-specific facts $F = f_1, \dots f_m$. Instance-specific facts typically pertain to the context or background of a particular scenario, while general-purpose facts can be applied more broadly. An example can be seen in Figure 1, where F consists of two statements, "*Joe is an animal*" and "*Joe is in outer space*", and all other facts belong to X. T is a binary-branching tree with its leaves being members of X and F while its non-leaf nodes (which we also call *intermediates*) are new statements generated via deductive reasoning. The root of T must logically entail g. We use the entailment models from past work (Bostrom et al., 2022; Sprague et al., 2022), which are based on WaNLI (Liu et al., 2022) to make this judgment.

The EntailmentBank dataset (Dalvi et al., 2021) formalizes three variants of this problem setting. The first setting, denoted as Task 1 (T1), provides only the general-purpose facts relevant to the construction of the gold entailment tree, making it the easiest setting as it eliminates the need to sift through irrelevant facts. Task 2 (T2) includes both the relevant facts and lexically similar distractor facts. Task 3 (T3) (Dalvi et al., 2021) includes all facts from a large corpus like Wikipedia as the general-purpose fact set X. In all these settings, the task involves iteratively building the entailment tree through deductions until the original goal g is entailed. Our experiments will focus on the T2 setting. [1]

2.2 Proof Generation

We follow past work on these tasks (Bostrom et al., 2022; Sprague et al., 2022) where the intermediate nodes of the entailment tree are generated from a pre-trained language model. Details on the model are in Appendix D. Specifically, given two premise statements p_a and p_b, we assume access to a model $P(d_{ab} \mid p_a, p_b)$ that places a distribution over valid

[1]While the T3 setting offers a large-scale stress test for retrieval-based approaches like ours, we found in practice that a first-stage retrieval (i.e., converting T3 to T2) with BM25 worked well for all datasets considered in this work. Nevertheless, models that scale to large X sets will be useful for future systems tackling more sophisticated problems like automatic fact-checking.

deductions d given the two premises. If the two premises do not combine to yield any meaningful new conclusions, the behavior of this system is not well-defined.

To produce an entailment tree T, we follow the proof generation algorithm from Bostrom et al. (2022); we outline it here and detail all modules of the search algorithm in Appendix D. We begin with our collection of premises $P = \{X \bigcup F\}$. In EntailmentBank and ENWN, the set P is given per dataset example. From P, a heuristic M ranks pairs of premises as to how useful their deduction will be in proving the claim g (also given per example). We denote a single ranked premise pair as a step in the search, and we term the current collection of steps at any moment in the search as the search fringe.

A deductive step model, S, pops the highest-ranked step (according to M) from the fringe and generates a set of deductions.[2] These deductions are validated and added back to the pool of premises P, where the heuristic will rank all potential pairs of the new set of deductions with all other previous premises to create new steps in the search fringe. This process is repeated until the $maxSteps$ limit is reached or the fringe has been exhausted.

Our work focuses on investigating if the heuristics used during the search can leverage embedding spaces that exhibit deductive additivity.

2.3 Deductive Additivity

Recall that d_{ab} represents a valid conclusion from a pair of premises p_a and p_b. Our heuristics are based on an embedding function $E : \Sigma^* \rightarrow \mathbb{R}^n$, embedding a sentence into n-dimensional space. We represent the sum of the embedded premises as the deductive trajectory embedding $\mathbf{e}^{'}_{a+b} = E(p_a) + E(p_b)$, where $\mathbf{e}^{'}$ signifies embeddings produced through arithmetic operations rather than the encoder E. An encoder E generates an embedding space exhibiting the property of deductive additivity if the deductive trajectory embedding has a higher cosine similarity with their embedded conclusion than any other statement, x, not entailed by the premises via deduction, denoted as $p_a, p_b \nrightarrow x$. That is, we want

$$\cos(\mathbf{e}^{'}_{a+b}, E(d_{ab})) > \cos(\mathbf{e}^{'}_{a+b}, E(x)) \quad (1)$$

[2]To thoroughly explore the space of all plausible deductions, we sample k generations each time ($k = 5$ in all our experiments).

When the condition in Equation 1 holds, the embedding space is capable of representing logical relationships strictly in their vectors and can be expressed through simple arithmetic operations such as addition.

2.4 Tuning for Deductive Additivity

Any sentence embedding method can be evaluated for whether or not it exhibits deductive additivity. However, we additionally describe a method for fine-tuning an embedding model to have this property.

We use EntailmentBank to obtain a collection of premise deduction triplets $D = \{p_a, p_b, d_{ab}\}$. Subsequently, we use a loss function to push the encoded representations of the premises closer to that of the deduction (Chen et al., 2020a; Gao et al., 2021).

$$l_{ab} = -\log \frac{\exp(\mathbf{e}^{'}_{a+b} \cdot E(d_{ab})/\tau)}{\sum_{i=1}^{N} \exp(\mathbf{e}^{'}_{a+b} \cdot E(d_i)/\tau)} \quad (2)$$

where N represents the batch size. Most deductions d_i will not entail the deduction d_{ab}, so they serve as suitable negatives from the perspective of Equation 1.

For training, we employ temperature scaling in the contrastive loss in Equation 2. Previous work has found that contrastive learning benefits from having large batch sizes, more in-batch negatives, and hard negatives (He et al., 2020; Karpukhin et al., 2020; Chen et al., 2020b; Radford et al., 2021; Xiong et al., 2021). To take advantage of hard in-batch negatives, we leverage the tree structures in our training data (EntailmentBank). Specifically, each batch in our training loop contains all the intermediate labeled steps for an entailment tree in EntailmentBank, covering multiple trees. We discover that triplets from the same tree serve as suitable proxies for hard negatives in our contrastive learning process, allowing us to bypass the need for hard negative mining. Our batches include 100 trees, as many as we could fit onto our GPU, which equates to 200-300 triplets in a batch. We found that increasing the batch size led to better performance. We implement our method with the PyTorch Metric learning library (Musgrave et al., 2020).

Following each epoch of training, we assess the encoder's performance by our second intrinsic evaluation, Ranking Gold Steps. We use the

EntailmentBank T2 development set for checking when to stop training the encoder.

2.5 Caching

Certain heuristics used in proof generation algorithms, such as the one we construct using deductive additivity, can cache the encodings of the initial evidence pool X. This offers significant time savings in completing the first step of a search procedure (where a non-cached method would need to set up and rank the pairs for the initial set). However, any subsequent deductions will need to be encoded since they cannot be precomputed and cached. We also found the time savings to be relatively limited in the $T1$ and $T2$ settings since n is relatively small, so we do not expand on this capability further.

3 Heuristics and Datasets

To measure the performance of using deductive additivity as a proof generation heuristic, we explore five heuristics and three datasets.

3.1 Baseline Heuristics

We consider two baseline heuristics for ranking and retrieving relevant statements: BM25, a sparse retrieval method, and the original heuristic from previous work, SCSearch, which employs an early-fusion premise ranker model.

BM25 BM25 (Robertson et al., 1995) matches items in an index with a query via sparse vector representations, capturing lexical overlap but not deeper semantic similarity. In the proof generation search procedure, we index all concatenations of strings in each step (two premises, generated deductions, or one of both), then retrieve the best step based on the goal.

SCSearch Past work (Bostrom et al., 2022) has used heuristics with a substantially different structure. These heuristics use language models like DeBERTa to score premise pairs conditioned on a claim. Specifically, these models are of the form $\mathbf{w}^\top E(p_1, p_2, g)$; they encode p_1, p_2, and g jointly with an encoder model. A linear layer $\mathbf{w}$ is then used to predict a logit value used for ranking. These models are trained as binary classifiers on EntailmentBank by selecting positive examples of premise pairs that eventually lead to g and negative examples of unrelated premise pairs. This allows the language model to determine if the immediate deduction would be beneficial towards deducing the claim that it is conditioning on. It also allows the language model to see the claim and premise pairs in context and model interactions between them. Because these methods use Transformers to score the premise pair and can model nonlinear interactions between the premises, these models are strictly more expressive than vector-based heuristics.

3.2 Embedding-based Heuristics

To test if embeddings with deductive additivity can be useful in proof generation, we employ three different heuristics that all use deductive additivity but with different encoders to compare different embedding spaces. A deductive additivity heuristic will, for each step, encode any new deductions from the previous step and then sum all the pairs to create deductive representations $\mathbf{e}_d^{'}$ for hypothetical deduced pairs. We then compute the cosine similarity of each $\mathbf{e}_d^{'}$ with $\mathbf{e}_g$ (the goal embedding), which is used as a score to select the next step $S_i = \underset{d}{\text{argmax}} \cos(\mathbf{e}_d^{'}, \mathbf{e}_g)$.

We consider the deductive additivity heuristic under three different encoders: SimCSE and GPT3 are used to test off-the-self sentence encoders for deductive additivity, and finally, we fine-tune GPT3 explicitly for deductive additivity.

SimCSE SimCSE (Gao et al., 2021) is an encoder that produces sentence embeddings optimized using a contrastive objective.[3] We test to see if this encoder produces an embedding space where deductive additivity holds.

GPT3 We use OpenAI's embedding endpoint to create sentence embeddings using the Ada model (Brown et al., 2020). We test to see if this encoder produces an embedding space where deductive additivity holds as well.

GPT3-tuned We combine OpenAI's embedding endpoint with three additional dense layers using the GLU activation function with residual connections between each layer. We then fine-tune these three layers using the EntailmentBank T1 dataset as described in Section 2.4.

[3]Note that this contrastive objective is different from ours. Training for SimCSE was performed on natural language inference (NLI) examples from MNLI and SNLI datasets. From the perspective of data assumptions, we place it in the "fine-tuned" category; although it hasn't been trained on EntailmentBank data explicitly, it uses related entailment data.

3.3 Datasets

EntailmentBank (EB) This dataset comprises annotated entailment trees for textbook-based science facts (Dalvi et al., 2021). We used this dataset for training the majority of our models in a T1 setting. We evaluate the models on the test slice of entailment trees for the T2 task setting.

Each example in EB contains a set of premises, P, and a claim g that we are trying to prove given P. To prove g, the system has to produce a series of deductions by combining two premises from the set P, then combining intermediate deductions and the premises in P until the claim is proven. Whether it is proven is determined via an entailment model scoring g above a certain threshold from some generated conclusion following previous work (Sprague et al., 2022; Bostrom et al., 2022) and detailed further in Appendix D. Planning heuristics must determine which premise-premise or premise-deduction pairs are most likely to help in proving the claim, as the set of pairwise premises and intermediate deductions can be large.

In the T2 setting, the number of premises n is fairly small; $n < 30$ for most examples. There are usually only 3 to 5 deductions involved to produce the annotated entailment tree. We allow for a total of 10 steps ($maxStep$), and for each step, we allow for five generations to be sampled (k).

Everyday Norms: Why Not (ENWN) ENWN (Sprague et al., 2022) contains annotated entailment trees for common everday scenarios. Structurally, ENWN resembles EntailmentBank but with a different domain of reasoning and a larger number of required deductive steps on average (4.71 to 4.26). ENWN aims to combine common social rules deductively to determine whether a person should perform a particular action (usually something they should not do). ENWN currently does not have a T2 or T3 setting.

3.4 Single-Step Reasoning Contrast Dataset

Both EntailmentBank and ENWN test a subset of logical inference types but do not necessarily have broad coverage. For example, EntailmentBank has very few examples involving negation, despite this being a very important phenomenon to model in practice. We want to test whether our embedding methods can handle a wider range of cases.

We construct a new dataset that examines common forms of logical reasoning[4] via synthesized examples. We consider fourteen categories: Analogy, Categorical Syllogism, Causal reasoning, Classification, Comparison, Composition, Division, Modus Ponens, Modus Tollens, Definition, Temporal Logic, Propositional Logic, Quantificational Logic, and Spatial Relationship. For each category, we use GPT-3.5 to generate ten examples of deductions given two premises using the corresponding reasoning category.

For every example deduction, we prompt GPT 3.5 further to perturb the premises in four ways creating additional examples of incorrect deductions. For each perturbation, we create three examples where one or both premises have been *negated*, three examples where one or both premises are a *false premise*, fifteen examples where one or both premises are an *irrelevant fact*, and three examples where one or both premises have an *incorrect quantifier* (usually meaning that "some", "all", or "none" has been prepended to the premise). Examples from the dataset from different reasoning categories and perturbation types are shown in Section B of the Appendix in Table 5. Prompts to create examples and perturb the examples can be found in Appendix E.

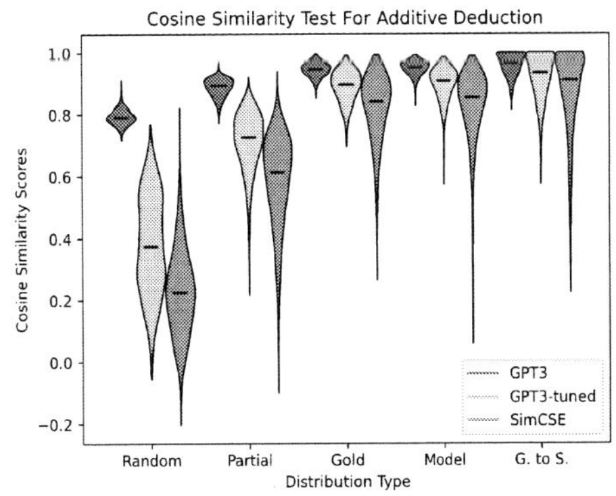

Figure 2: Distribution of cosine similarities for examples in EntailmentBank T2 and ENWN. All three encoders show little overlap between Random and Gold, showing that these embeddings support Deductive Additivity and the condition in Equation 1. However, the overlap with Partial is substantially higher.

[4]We initially employed ChatGPT for annotating examples in EntailmentBank and ENWN. However, it did not yield consistent labels, signaling an opportunity for further exploration in future research. Instead, we adopted a different approach, generating a selection of widely-used labels that we subsequently employed as the reasoning categories within the SSRC dataset.

4 Experiments

4.1 Intrinsic Evaluation

We perform two intrinsic evaluations to test if encoders exhibit the deductive additivity property: do they rank gold premise pairs in the proof generation task above incorrect pairs?

Comparing Deduction Embedding Representations In our first intrinsic evaluation, we measure the cosine similarity distributions of premise pairs and a deduction in three settings to test for deductive additivity. The first setting uses a deduction d_{ab} and measures the cosine similarity of its embedding $E(d_{ab})$ with a random premise pair $P_r = \{p_x, p_y\}$ where p_x and p_y are drawn randomly from the set of premises, $U(P)$. The next setting looks at partially random premise pairs, $P_p = \{p_a, p_y\}$ where p_a is one of the gold premises $P_g = \{p_a, p_b\}$ that yield the deduction d_{ab}. Finally, we measure the distribution of scores for the gold premise pair P_g and the following deduction from those premises d_{ab}. These three settings correspond to **Random**, **Partial**, and **Gold**, respectively, in Figure 2.

Additionally, we also compared the gold premise pair $P_g = \{p_a, p_b\}$ with model-generated deductions $S_d(p_a, p_b) = d'_{ab}$ and measured their cosine similarity $cos(e'_{a+b}, E(d'_{ab}))$. Finally, we measured the cosine similarity scores of the annotated deductions and the generated deductions $\cos(E(d_{ab}), E(d'_{ab}))$; this is a sort of sanity check to see if the deductive additivity property holds for proof generation. This experiment checks whether the step model introduces significant deviation in embedding similarity compared to using the gold steps. These settings correspond to **Model** and **G. to S.** respectively in Figure 2, all settings have their averages reported in Table 4 in Section A of the Appendix as well.

Embedding Representations Results Figure 2 shows a slight overlap between the cosine similarity score distributions of random and gold pairs, aligning with expectations and showing that Equation 1 roughly holds for all three encoders. However, the partial pairs have much more overlap with the distribution of gold pairs for each encoder. Concerningly, the partial pairs are much more numerous because these pair one of the ground truth statements with an irrelevant statement, forming a pair we do not want the heuristic to surface. We will see the performance ramifications of this in the end-to-end evaluation. On a positive note, we also see high agreement between the gold premise pair and the generated deduction, indicating that deductions generated by the step model are similar to the annotated deductions.

Heuristic	EB T2 Deductive	EB T2 Goal	ENWN Deductive
BM25	0.47	0.21	0.50
SCSearch	**0.78**	**0.39**	**0.82**
SimCSE (DA)	0.46	0.20	0.59
GPT3-tuned (DA)	0.54	0.23	0.54
GPT3 (DA)	0.54	0.24	0.56

Table 1: Comparison against different heuristics on the MRR of selecting gold premises conditioned on their immediate deduction and the goal of the tree. GPT3 outperforms BM25, indicating that there are more complex reasoning steps required than just lexical overlap. However, SCSearch still outperforms all methods by as much as 0.24.

Ranking Gold Steps The second intrinsic evaluation measures the rankings of premise pairs, P_{pairs}, conditioned on a deduction embedding, $E(d_{ab})$, where one pair is the gold premise pair $P_g = \{p_a, p_b\}$ which yield the deduction. All other pairs are either random $P_r = \{p_x, p_y\}$, where p_x and p_y are sampled uniformly from the set of premises $U(P)$, or are partially random $P_p = \{p_a, p_y\}$. The full list of premise pairs is the union of all these sets $P_{\text{pairs}} = P_g \cup P_p \cup P_r$. We calculate scores for each pair according to how each heuristic scores premise pairs, $\text{scores} = \{\text{heuristic}(P_s, d_{ab}) \mid P_s \in P_{\text{pairs}}\}$. For the heuristics using deductive additivity (DA), the scores are cosine similarities, $\text{scores} = \{\cos(e'_{n+m}, E(d_{ab})) \mid \{p_n, p_m\} \in P_{\text{pairs}}\}$. Finally, we sort scores and find the rank of the gold premise pair.

We calculate the mean reciprocal rank (MRR) using the ranks of the gold premise pairs across all examples in the EntailmentBank T2 and Everyday Norms: Why Not datasets. We also repeat this process for EntailmentBank T2 where we make the target of the search the claim g instead of the immediate deduction d_{ab}. Because the claim g is often a product of multiple deductions in the premise set P, we expect the MRR scores to be lower than the scores on the immediate deductions d_{ab}. ENWN does not have a T2 setting, so we do not show the claim-conditioned scores because every premise would be related to the claim g,

	EB		ENWN	
	Solved	**Steps**	**Solved**	**Steps**
BM25	43%	2.2	48%	5.1
SCSearch	**61%**	3.4	**86%**	9.8
SimCSE (DA)	44%	2.8	46%	2.7
GPT3-tuned (DA)	49%	2.1	46%	2.5
GPT3 (DA)	49%	2.2	41%	2.2

Table 2: Generated proofs per heuristic on the two datasets. BM25 has high performance on both of these datasets, indicating that textual overlap is enough to plan reasoning steps for nearly 50% of the examples. SimCSE (DA) and GPT3 (DA) underperform BM25 on ENWN; this could mean that these methods are not as sensitive to lexical overlap as BM25 is. SCSearch still outperforms every baseline by as much as 38%, showing that a lot of reasoning is unaccounted for in the other methods.

making nearly all pairs valid. These are shown in Table 1. A number closer to 1.0 indicates that the gold premise pair was consistently ranked higher than partial and random premise pairs.

Gold Steps MRR Results Table 1 shows the BM25 MRR scores as being quite competitive with the methods using deductive additivity, SimCSE, GPT3, and GPT3-tuned, all of which are within 0.1 of each other. BM25s high performance indicates that the datasets EB T2 and ENWN have many examples where the lexical overlap is enough to determine the gold premise pair P_g. GPT3 does outperform the BM25 baseline, however, and in nearly every case, the SimCSE heuristic does as well (except for ENWN). GPT3-tuned does slightly worse in both EB T2 and ENWN, showing that fine-tuning the embeddings to produce the deductive additivity property is not trivial. The degradation in performance is surprising given that the model was fine-tuned on a task very similar to the intrinsic evaluation being reported in Table 1. SCSearch still outperforms all leading methods. There is a significant drop across all methods between ranking premise pairs with the immediate deduction and the goal. Although this was expected, the drop is quite significant and is worth exploring further in future work on how it could be mitigated.

4.2 Extrinsic Evaluation: Generating Proofs

Next, we explore how well heuristics employing deductive additivity can perform on proof generation datasets detailed in Section 3.3.

Results We report the percentage of proofs that entailed the goal, g, as well as the average number of steps to prove the claim across all planning heuristics in Table 2. GPT3 (DA), GPT3-tuned (DA), and SimCSE (DA) are all able to produce slightly more proofs than BM25 on the EB T2 dataset but fail to outperform BM25 on ENWN. Because BM25 is a limited heuristic that only employs lexical overlap, this result shows that nearly 50% of examples in these datasets can have proofs generated using simple heuristics that use no deeper semantic representations. However, deeper reasoning does help, as shown by the fact that SCSearch is able to generate far more proofs than the other methods across both datasets by as much as 36%. This finding is also supported by the MRR results of the second intrinsic evaluation, shown in Table 1. Disappointingly, deductive additivity does not seem to be able to capture the same sort of benefits in the heuristic it provides.

4.3 Single-Step Reasoning Contrast Dataset

To best understand where the vector-based methods are lacking in performance and pinpoint where improvements can be made, we test each method across a variety of types of reasoning and common failure cases in the Single-Step Reasoning Contrast (SSRC) dataset. In this experiment, we perform the same evaluation as our second intrinsic evaluation, Ranking Gold Steps. Here we use examples from the SSRC dataset, which have been curated and labeled to allow for a report of an MRR on different types of deductions and error cases.

Encoder	**Overall MRR**
SCSearch	0.83
SimCSE (DA)	0.80
GPT3-Tuned (DA)	0.83
GPT3 (DA)	**0.85**
BM25	0.50

Table 3: Overall scores of each heuristic on the SSRC dataset. GPT3 (AD) outperforms SCSearch slightly on this benchmark, slightly contradicting the results of the previous experiments.

Results Table 3 shows the averaged MRR scores across all methods. GPT3 (DA) outperforms SCSearch slightly overall, but to better understand the performance, we plot the average MRR across the fourteen reasoning categories and perturbation types for each method compared to SCSearch in

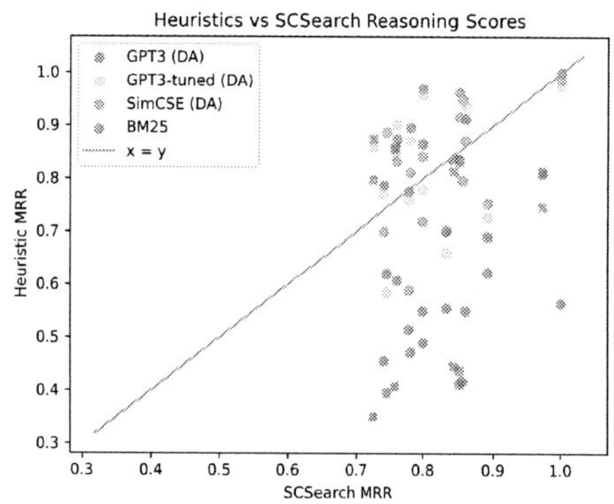

Figure 3: Comparison plot of the heuristic methods versus the SCSearch heuristic. If a point is above the green line, then that method outperformed SCSearch. Circles indicate reasoning categories, and X-marks indicate perturbation types. BM25 underperforms all other methods, showing that the dataset is not sensitive to lexical overlap.

Figure 3. GPT3 (DA) can outperform both BM25 and SimCSE (DA) consistently across nearly every reasoning category and all perturbation types. Furthermore, we see that GPT3 (DA) is capable of beating or matching SCSearch on half of the reasoning categories and perturbation types, contradicting previous results indicating that these datasets might be skewed in areas where SCSearch excels at.

GPT3-Tuned (DA) performs worse in 9 categories than GPT3 (DA) and better in only 3. This could be from the skewed reasoning categories in EntailmentBank, but it could also be that enforcing the condition in Equation 1 directly is counterproductive. Averaged scores for each reasoning category and perturbation type can be found in Appendix C, in Tables 6 and 7 respectively.

5 Discussion

Vector-based methods are not sufficient to capture all information for planning deductions. We've found that vector-based methods can represent complex reasoning but fall short in planning reasoning steps when compared to early-fusion premise rankers like SCSearch. Our results suggest a more complex and structured approaches may be necessary for step-by-step systems.

Skewed datasets provide optimistic benchmarks for weaker models. Our results focused on the T2 setting because we discovered that a BM25 + SCSearch pipeline did quite well and scaled to large numbers of premises. However, we believe this is an optimistic result and may not scale to production settings where claims may require more complex deductions that are less sensitive to lexical overlap. Developing datasets with more complex reasoning and benchmarking in real production settings is a focus for future work.

Training for Deductive Additivity can harm performance. We found that training deductive additivity directly improves categories of reasoning prevalent in the training dataset while harming other categories. Both larger and more diverse datasets may be a solution for this problem, but GPT3 embeddings already show deductive additivity without explicitly training for it. Developing different training objectives that result in embeddings with deductive additivity is another focus for future work.

6 Related work

Our work follows from models and methods done in the Question Answering domain where models are required to generate an answer or select evidence that leads to the answer through "multi-hop" reasoning (Chen et al., 2019; Min et al., 2019; Nishida et al., 2019). Although these end-to-end methods can be used in proof generation, understanding the underlying reasoning of the decisions being made is impactful for understanding the affordances of the model (Hase and Bansal, 2020; Bansal et al., 2021).

Step-by-step methods have been looked at for proof generation, detangling planning and reasoning into separate subsystems that work together as a whole when proving a claim (Dalvi et al., 2021; Ribeiro et al., 2022; Bostrom et al., 2022; Yang et al., 2022; Hong et al., 2022; Creswell et al., 2023; Yang and Deng, 2023). There has also been work on using similar modular systems in answering questions with a knowledge base and different types of embeddings (Bordes et al., 2013; Ren et al., 2020; Tran et al., 2022). Our work extends from this literature, focusing on exploring alternative heuristics for natural language deduction planning entirely in embedding space by tapping into the property of deductive additivity.

We also follow work being done in retrieval, which focuses on finding evidence from a large corpus that would help answer a query. State-of-the-art retrieval methods involve encoding the corpus into vector indexes that can be used to calculate the cosine similarity of an encoded query (Xiong et al., 2021; Karpukhin et al., 2020; Khattab and Zaharia, 2020). Sparse encoders, like BM25, have also been used to help reduce the search space for relevant passages (Valentino et al., 2022). However, none of the methods tap into the deductive additivity property in their embedding spaces and instead encode the query to find relevant passages and then re-encode the query with the appended passages to find additional relevant passages. We consider this to be similar to early-fusion premise rankers in the proof generation task.

Another line of relevant work deals with understanding reasoning errors from language models, like the detection of logical fallacies in text (Jin et al., 2022). We further this line of work with the SSRC dataset, building a contrast set (Gardner et al., 2020) for reasoning targeting certain types of deductions and common reasoning errors.

7 Conclusion

In this work, we have explored the property of deductive additivity in sentence embedding spaces. Results show that off-the-shelf sentence encoders exhibit the property somewhat; however, when used as heuristics in natural language proof generation, they are only slightly more successful than BM25. Furthermore, we see that fine-tuning for deductive additivity does not lead to better reasoning capabilities of the embedding space, and we posit that a large contributor to this could be skewed datasets. We introduced the Single-Step Reasoning Contrast dataset, which shows that these same skewed datasets provide over-optimistic results for inferior methods harming our ability to benchmark systems for their use in production settings. Lastly, we've shown that early-fusion premise rankers like SCSearch still outperform vector-based approaches. However, their ability to scale to more diverse reasoning datasets that are less sensitive to lexical overlap is still an open question for future work.

Acknowledgments

This work was partially supported by NSF CAREER Award IIS-2145280, the NSF AI Institute for Foundations of Machine Learning (IFML), a gift from Salesforce, Inc., a gift from Adobe, and a grant from Open Philanthropy. Thanks to the anonymous reviewers for their helpful comments.

References

Gagan Bansal, Tongshuang Wu, Joyce Zhou, Raymond Fok, Besmira Nushi, Ece Kamar, Marco Tulio Ribeiro, and Daniel Weld. 2021. Does the Whole Exceed Its Parts? The Effect of AI Explanations on Complementary Team Performance. In *Proceedings of the 2021 CHI Conference on Human Factors in Computing Systems*, New York, NY, USA. Association for Computing Machinery.

Antoine Bordes, Nicolas Usunier, Alberto Garcia-Duran, Jason Weston, and Oksana Yakhnenko. 2013. Translating embeddings for modeling multi-relational data. In *Advances in Neural Information Processing Systems*, volume 26. Curran Associates, Inc.

Kaj Bostrom, Zayne Sprague, Swarat Chaudhuri, and Greg Durrett. 2022. Natural language deduction through search over statement compositions. In *Findings of the Association for Computational Linguistics: EMNLP 2022*, pages 4871–4883, Abu Dhabi, United Arab Emirates. Association for Computational Linguistics.

Kaj Bostrom, Xinyu Zhao, Swarat Chaudhuri, and Greg Durrett. 2021. Flexible generation of natural language deductions. In *Proceedings of the 2021 Conference on Empirical Methods in Natural Language Processing*, pages 6266–6278, Online and Punta Cana, Dominican Republic. Association for Computational Linguistics.

Tom Brown, Benjamin Mann, Nick Ryder, Melanie Subbiah, Jared D Kaplan, Prafulla Dhariwal, Arvind Neelakantan, Pranav Shyam, Girish Sastry, Amanda Askell, Sandhini Agarwal, Ariel Herbert-Voss, Gretchen Krueger, Tom Henighan, Rewon Child, Aditya Ramesh, Daniel Ziegler, Jeffrey Wu, Clemens Winter, Chris Hesse, Mark Chen, Eric Sigler, Mateusz Litwin, Scott Gray, Benjamin Chess, Jack Clark, Christopher Berner, Sam McCandlish, Alec Radford, Ilya Sutskever, and Dario Amodei. 2020. Language models are few-shot learners. In *Advances in Neural Information Processing Systems*, volume 33, pages 1877–1901. Curran Associates, Inc.

Jifan Chen, Shih-ting Lin, and Greg Durrett. 2019. Multi-hop question answering via reasoning chains. *arXiv*, abs/1910.02610.

Ting Chen, Simon Kornblith, Mohammad Norouzi, and Geoffrey Hinton. 2020a. A simple framework for contrastive learning of visual representations. In *Proceedings of the 37th International Conference on Machine Learning*, volume 119 of *Proceedings of Machine Learning Research*, pages 1597–1607. PMLR.

Xinlei Chen, Haoqi Fan, Ross B. Girshick, and Kaiming He. 2020b. Improved baselines with momentum contrastive learning. *CoRR*, abs/2003.04297.

Antonia Creswell, Murray Shanahan, and Irina Higgins. 2023. Selection-inference: Exploiting large language models for interpretable logical reasoning. In *The Eleventh International Conference on Learning Representations*.

Bhavana Dalvi, Peter Jansen, Oyvind Tafjord, Zhengnan Xie, Hannah Smith, Leighanna Pipatanangkura, and Peter Clark. 2021. Explaining answers with entailment trees. In *Proceedings of the 2021 Conference on Empirical Methods in Natural Language Processing*, pages 7358–7370, Online and Punta Cana, Dominican Republic. Association for Computational Linguistics.

Tianyu Gao, Xingcheng Yao, and Danqi Chen. 2021. SimCSE: Simple contrastive learning of sentence embeddings. In *Proceedings of the 2021 Conference on Empirical Methods in Natural Language Processing*, pages 6894–6910, Online and Punta Cana, Dominican Republic. Association for Computational Linguistics.

Matt Gardner, Yoav Artzi, Victoria Basmov, Jonathan Berant, Ben Bogin, Sihao Chen, Pradeep Dasigi, Dheeru Dua, Yanai Elazar, Ananth Gottumukkala, Nitish Gupta, Hannaneh Hajishirzi, Gabriel Ilharco, Daniel Khashabi, Kevin Lin, Jiangming Liu, Nelson F. Liu, Phoebe Mulcaire, Qiang Ning, Sameer Singh, Noah A. Smith, Sanjay Subramanian, Reut Tsarfaty, Eric Wallace, Ally Zhang, and Ben Zhou. 2020. Evaluating models' local decision boundaries via contrast sets. In *Findings of the Association for Computational Linguistics: EMNLP 2020*, pages 1307–1323, Online. Association for Computational Linguistics.

Peter Hase and Mohit Bansal. 2020. Evaluating explainable AI: Which algorithmic explanations help users predict model behavior? In *Proceedings of the 58th Annual Meeting of the Association for Computational Linguistics*, pages 5540–5552, Online. Association for Computational Linguistics.

Kaiming He, Haoqi Fan, Yuxin Wu, Saining Xie, and Ross Girshick. 2020. Momentum contrast for unsupervised visual representation learning. In *Proceedings of the IEEE/CVF conference on computer vision and pattern recognition*, pages 9729–9738.

Ruixin Hong, Hongming Zhang, Xintong Yu, and Changshui Zhang. 2022. METGEN: A module-based entailment tree generation framework for answer explanation. In *Findings of the Association for Computational Linguistics: NAACL 2022*, pages 1887–1905, Seattle, United States. Association for Computational Linguistics.

Zhijing Jin, Abhinav Lalwani, Tejas Vaidhya, Xiaoyu Shen, Yiwen Ding, Zhiheng Lyu, Mrinmaya Sachan, Rada Mihalcea, and Bernhard Schoelkopf. 2022. Logical fallacy detection. In *Findings of the Association for Computational Linguistics: EMNLP 2022*, pages 7180–7198, Abu Dhabi, United Arab Emirates. Association for Computational Linguistics.

Vladimir Karpukhin, Barlas Oguz, Sewon Min, Patrick Lewis, Ledell Wu, Sergey Edunov, Danqi Chen, and Wen-tau Yih. 2020. Dense passage retrieval for open-domain question answering. In *Proceedings of the 2020 Conference on Empirical Methods in Natural Language Processing (EMNLP)*, pages 6769–6781, Online. Association for Computational Linguistics.

Omar Khattab and Matei Zaharia. 2020. Colbert: Efficient and effective passage search via contextualized late interaction over bert. In *Proceedings of the 43rd International ACM SIGIR Conference on Research and Development in Information Retrieval*, SIGIR '20, page 39–48, New York, NY, USA. Association for Computing Machinery.

Alisa Liu, Swabha Swayamdipta, Noah A. Smith, and Yejin Choi. 2022. WANLI: Worker and AI collaboration for natural language inference dataset creation. In *Findings of the Association for Computational Linguistics: EMNLP 2022*, pages 6826–6847, Abu Dhabi, United Arab Emirates. Association for Computational Linguistics.

Sewon Min, Victor Zhong, Luke Zettlemoyer, and Hannaneh Hajishirzi. 2019. Multi-hop reading comprehension through question decomposition and rescoring. In *Proceedings of the 57th Annual Meeting of the Association for Computational Linguistics*, pages 6097–6109, Florence, Italy. Association for Computational Linguistics.

Kevin Musgrave, Serge J. Belongie, and Ser-Nam Lim. 2020. PyTorch Metric Learning. *ArXiv*, abs/2008.09164.

Kosuke Nishida, Kyosuke Nishida, Masaaki Nagata, Atsushi Otsuka, Itsumi Saito, Hisako Asano, and Junji Tomita. 2019. Answering while summarizing: Multi-task learning for multi-hop QA with evidence extraction. In *Proceedings of the 57th Annual Meeting of the Association for Computational Linguistics*, pages 2335–2345, Florence, Italy. Association for Computational Linguistics.

OpenAI. 2023. GPT-4 Technical Report.

Alec Radford, Jong Wook Kim, Chris Hallacy, Aditya Ramesh, Gabriel Goh, Sandhini Agarwal, Girish Sastry, Amanda Askell, Pamela Mishkin, Jack Clark, et al. 2021. Learning transferable visual models from natural language supervision. In *International conference on machine learning*, pages 8748–8763. PMLR.

Hongyu Ren, Weihua Hu, and Jure Leskovec. 2020. Query2box: Reasoning over knowledge graphs in vector space using box embeddings. In *International Conference on Learning Representations*.

Danilo Neves Ribeiro, Shen Wang, Xiaofei Ma, Henghui Zhu, Rui Dong, Xinchi Chen, Zhu Peng, Zhiheng Huang, Andrew Arnold, and Dan Roth. 2022. Entailment tree explanations via iterative retrieval-generation reasoner. In *Proceedings of the 2022 Conference of the North American Chapter of the Association for Computational Linguistics: Human Language Technologies*, Online and Seattle, USA. Association for Computational Linguistics.

Stephen Robertson, S. Walker, S. Jones, M. M. Hancock-Beaulieu, and M. Gatford. 1995. Okapi at TREC-3. In *Overview of the Third Text REtrieval Conference (TREC-3)*, pages 109–126. Gaithersburg, MD: NIST.

Zayne Sprague, Kaj Bostrom, Swarat Chaudhuri, and Greg Durrett. 2022. Natural language deduction with incomplete information. In *Proceedings of the 2022 Conference on Empirical Methods in Natural Language Processing*, pages 8230–8258, Abu Dhabi, United Arab Emirates. Association for Computational Linguistics.

Khiem Vinh Tran, Hao Phu Phan, Khang Nguyen Duc Quach, Ngan Luu-Thuy Nguyen, Jun Jo, and Thanh Tam Nguyen. 2022. A comparative study of question answering over knowledge bases. In *International Conference on Advanced Data Mining and Applications*, pages 259–274. Springer.

Marco Valentino, Mokanarangan Thayaparan, Deborah Ferreira, and André Freitas. 2022. Hybrid autoregressive inference for scalable multi-hop explanation regeneration. In *Proceedings of the AAAI Conference on Artificial Intelligence*, volume 36, pages 11403–11411.

Wenhan Xiong, Xiang Li, Srini Iyer, Jingfei Du, Patrick Lewis, William Yang Wang, Yashar Mehdad, Scott Yih, Sebastian Riedel, Douwe Kiela, and Barlas Oguz. 2021. Answering complex open-domain questions with multi-hop dense retrieval. In *International Conference on Learning Representations*.

Tianci Xue, Ziqi Wang, Zhenhailong Wang, Chi Han, Pengfei Yu, and Heng Ji. 2023. RCOT: Detecting and Rectifying Factual Inconsistency in Reasoning by Reversing Chain-of-Thought. *ArXiv*, abs/2305.11499.

Kaiyu Yang and Jia Deng. 2023. Learning symbolic rules for reasoning in quasi-natural language. *Transactions on Machine Learning Research (TMLR)*.

Kaiyu Yang, Jia Deng, and Danqi Chen. 2022. Generating natural language proofs with verifier-guided search. In *Proceedings of the 2022 Conference on Empirical Methods in Natural Language Processing*, pages 89–105, Abu Dhabi, United Arab Emirates. Association for Computational Linguistics.

Xi Ye and Greg Durrett. 2022. The Unreliability of Explanations in Few-shot Prompting for Textual Reasoning. In *Advances in Neural Information Processing Systems*.

Muru Zhang, Ofir Press, William Merrill, Alisa Liu, and Noah A Smith. 2023. How language model hallucinations can snowball. *arXiv preprint arXiv:2305.13534*.

A Embedding Reconstruction Results

Table 4 shows the averaged cosine similarity of the random, partially random, and gold pairs, as well as the cosine similarities for the gold pairs with the step model generations. This provides complementary information to Figure 2.

B SSRC Dataset Examples

Table 5 shows four examples from the SSRC dataset that have been sampled from different reasoning categories and show different perturbation types for the premises.

C SSRC Dataset Results

We report the raw scores for both the reasoning categories and perturbation types in Tables 6 and 7 respectively.

D Proof Generation Modules

We outline in more detail the proof generation search algorithm we use in our experiments following work from Sprague et al. (2022) and Bostrom et al. (2022).

Algorithm 1 The main search function with a heuristic using the deductive additivity property. Given a set of premises and a goal claim, generate intermediate deductions until the claim is proven true or a termination criterion is met. E is a sentence encoder.

Input A list X of string premises $\mathbf{p}_i$ that will be used to search over to prove a string claim $\mathbf{g}$
Output A list of steps taken by the algorithm with their generations
Procedure SEARCH($X = \{\mathbf{p}_1, \dots \mathbf{p}_n\}$, $\mathbf{g}$):
$f \leftarrow \{E(\mathbf{p}_i) + E(\mathbf{p}_j) \mid \mathbf{p}_i, \mathbf{p}_j \in X, i \neq j\}$
$\hat{g} \leftarrow E(\mathbf{g})$
$gens \leftarrow \{\}$
$maxSteps \in \mathbb{N}$
$i \leftarrow 1$
while $|f| > 0 \wedge i \leq maxSteps$ **do**
  $step \leftarrow \underset{x_i \in f}{\text{argmax}}\, M(x_i, \hat{g})$
  $f \leftarrow f \setminus \{step\}$
  sample $\mathbf{y}_i$ from $p_S(\mathbf{y} \mid step)$
  if $\mathbf{y}_i \notin gens$ **then**
    $gens \leftarrow gens \bigcup \{\mathbf{y}_i\}$
    yield $(step, \mathbf{y}_i)$
    if entails$(\mathbf{y}_i, \mathbf{g})$ **then return**
    $f \leftarrow f \cup \{E(\mathbf{y}_i) + E(\mathbf{x}_j) \mid \mathbf{x}_j \in X\}$
    $f \leftarrow f \cup \{E(\mathbf{y}_i) + E(\mathbf{y}_j) \mid \mathbf{y}_j \in gens, 1 \leq j < i\}$
    $i \leftarrow i + 1$

D.1 Deductive Step Model

The deductive step model is trained using the EntailmentBank dataset following Bostrom et al. (2022). We transform the annotated entailment trees into individual steps $T_i = (x_1, x_2 \rightarrow c)$ and fine-tune a pre-trained language model to generate the deduction given a set of premises. We do not use data from (Bostrom et al., 2021).

D.2 Reasoning Validation

To ensure that the search space generates well-reasoned deductions, we implement a set of validators that examine both the types of steps being taken and the generations produced by the step models following Sprague et al. (2022). Firstly, we employ a Consanguinity Threshold step to ensure that the search procedure does not permit steps to consist of the same premise or premises that result in immediate deductions. For instance, if p_a and p_b create the deduction d_{ab}, we disallow a new step to be (p_a, d_{ab}). This approach effectively promotes diversity in the types of steps being taken. We also enforce that no generation from a step model is an exact duplicate of one of the inputs.

Furthermore, to avoid identifying high-ranking pairs of premises that result in illogical deductions due to hallucination, we devise a new validation method to ensure consistency. The Deduction Agreement validator compares the embedding of the added premises $e_{d'}$ with the embedding of the generated deduction e_d. If the cosine similarity falls below a threshold t_{da}, the step is filtered out. A running average of all $\cos(e_{d'}, e_d)$ scores for previous deductions is maintained. If a branch in the entailment tree generates too many deductions that have low cosine similarity with their summed premises, it will be filtered out.

D.3 Entailment Scores

We employ a DeBERTa model, fine-tuned on the MNLI and WaNLI tasks, to assess the entailment of each generated natural language deduction. If a deduction achieves a score above a predefined threshold, t_g, it is considered to have recovered the goal g. Once a deduction has successfully recovered the goal, we can trace back the steps used to create that specific deduction, resulting in a minimal proof tree that contains only the essential steps required to prove the goal.

	EB				ENWN			
Heuristic	**Rand**	**Partial**	**Gold**	**Model**	**Rand**	**Partial**	**Gold**	**Model**
SimCSE	0.25	0.62	0.85	0.85	0.14	0.48	0.72	0.76
GPT3-tuned	0.31	0.70	0.90	0.90	0.56	0.74	0.86	0.87
GPT3	0.79	0.88	0.93	0.94	0.79	0.89	0.95	0.95

Table 4: We look at the average cosine similarity score of different summed premise pairs with their textual deduction embedding. We see large gaps between a Random set of premises and the Partial/Gold set; however, Partial and Gold are less separated. The Model columns show that there is no loss in representing deductions if the deduction is the gold annotation or from the deduction step model.

Category and Perturbation	**Premises**	**Conclusion**	**Perturbed Premises**
Categorical Syllogism, Negation	All cats are animals. Whiskers is a cat.	Whiskers is an Animal.	Some cats are not animals. Whiskers is not a cat.
Causal Reasoning, Irrelevant Fact	High levels of stress cause anxiety. Linda has been under a lot of stress lately.	Linda may develop anxiety.	Anxiety disorders can also manifest as physical symptoms. ...
Comparative Reasoning, Incorrect Quantifier	John is stronger than Mary. Mary is stronger than Sue.	John is stronger than Sue.	Some women are stronger than Sue.
Temporal Reasoning, False Premise	The store is open for 12 hours. The store opens at 9 AM.	The store closes at 9 PM.	The store is open for 10 hours.

Table 5: Examples taken from the Single-Step Reasoning Contrast (SSRC) dataset. The Category and Perturbation column shows which reasoning category is used in the deduction as well as what type of perturbation is applied to the premise. The perturbed premise is then used to create invalid premise pairs (where one premise could be a gold premise, but the other is perturbed) such that when the two are combined, their deduction does not lead to the conclusion. There are ten examples per reasoning category, and each example has multiple perturbed premises for each of the four perturbation types.

	SCSearch	**SimCSE (DA)**	**GPT3-tuned (DA)**	**BM25**	**GPT3 (DA)**
Analogy	0.86	0.80	**0.95**	0.42	**0.95**
Categorical syllogism	0.80	0.72	0.78	0.55	**0.87**
Causal Reasoning	**0.78**	0.59	0.76	0.52	**0.78**
Classification	0.86	0.87	**0.94**	0.55	0.91
Comparative Reasoning	0.85	0.92	**0.96**	0.44	**0.96**
Composition	0.75	**0.89**	0.59	0.40	0.62
Definition	0.80	0.84	0.96	0.49	**0.97**
Divisions	**0.85**	0.83	0.83	0.41	0.84
Modus Ponens	**1.0**	0.99	0.98	0.56	**1.0**
Modus Tollens	**0.83**	0.70	0.66	0.56	0.7
Propositional Logic	**0.89**	0.75	0.73	0.62	0.69
Quantification Logic	0.76	0.83	**0.90**	0.61	0.87
Spatial Reasoning	0.78	0.81	0.87	0.47	**0.90**
Temporal Reasoning	0.74	0.70	0.77	0.46	**0.79**

Table 6: Results of each heuristic on SSRC are broken down by the reasoning category and averaged over the individual perturbation types of each category. We separate SCSearch and SimCSE (DA) from the BM25 and GPT3 (DA) heuristics as the BM25 and GPT3 (DA) have not been trained on any natural language inference data (with the possibility that GPT3 may have seen some incidental examples of inferences in its pretraining), making them close to zero-shot on this task. SCSearch and SimCSE (DA) have both been fine-tuned on reasoning datasets (EntailmentBank and NLI, respectively).

	SCSearch	SimCSE (DA)	GPT3-tuned (DA)	BM25	GPT3 (DA)
False Premise	**0.84**	0.81	0.81	0.45	0.81
Irrelevant Fact	**0.97**	0.75	0.82	0.81	0.87
Incorrect Quantification	0.76	**0.86**	0.84	0.41	**0.86**
Negated	0.73	0.80	0.86	0.35	**0.87**

Table 7: Results of each heuristic on SSRC are broken down by the perturbation type and averaged over the individual reasoning categories. We again separate SCSearch and SimCSE (DA) from the BM25 and GPT3 (DA) heuristics.

E SSRC Prompting

We use ChatGPT to prompt GPT3.5 and create the SSRC dataset. We followed the same template for all reasoning categories and then used a simple Python script to parse out the examples generated. Below is an example of how we prompted ChatGPT for the reasoning category Classification. All prompts are given to ChatGPT one after another.

F Examples of GPT ranking SSRC premise pairs

Here we show three examples from the SSRC dataset and place the premise pairs in order of how GPT3 ranked them. The **Category** indicates which reasoning category the example belongs to, **Perturbation** indicates which perturbation type the example is exhibiting, **Target** is the claim g, **Gold Premises** are the correct premises that yield the claim from a deduction, **Rank** is the Rank GPT3 gave the gold premises (1 being the best). We also include all premise pairs and their ranks below the **Rank** of the gold premises, and we mark the pair **(G)** for the gold premise pair.

Creating the ten examples

Create ten deductions that use classification in the example. A definition of classification in deductions and an example is below:

Definition:

Classification involves grouping things based on shared properties or characteristics and drawing conclusions based on these groupings.

Example:

P1: A dog is a type of animal.

P2: A cat is a type of animal.

C: Dogs and cats are both animals.

Each example should have 2 premises and 1 conclusion. They must all use classification to perform the deduction.

Figure 4: Prompt given to ChatGPT that creates the original ten deductions for the specific reasoning category. The premises given in this step are referred to as the "gold premises".

Negating the ten examples

For each of the ten generate negations of each premise and conclusion. If a premise begins with "All... are x" you should both negate the sentence and remove the word "All" at the beginning.

Just write the negations and put it in the format:

P1: Negated premise one

P2: Negated premise two

C: Negated conclusion

Figure 5: Once the ten reasoning examples have been generated, we then ask ChatGPT to negate the ten examples' gold premises.

Creating false premises

For each of the ten generate two false premises total, one for each premise. The false premise should make the original deduction invalid. Do NOT generate a false conclusion. Do NOT repeat the valid premises or conclusions. Only generate the False premises.

Put them in this format:

False P1: False premise for premise one

False P2: False premise for premise two

Figure 6: After the negated premises are generated, we ask ChatGPT to create false premises for the ten reasoning examples. False premises are not negated premises. Instead, they should employ some common sense from the model to make a statement false. An example from the SSRC dataset is "a granny smith is a type of fish." which is a false statement.

Generating irrelevant facts: Prompt 1
For each of the ten generate two facts that seem related to the deduction but are in fact irrelevant. They should not contribute to the deduction at all, but they should be close enough to trick someone. ONLY GENERATE THE NEW FACTS.

Put them in this format:

Irrelevant Fact 1: Irrelevant fact for premise one
Irrelevant Fact 2: Irrelevant fact for premise two

Generating irrelevant facts: Prompt 2
Do this again. For each of the ten generate two facts that seem related to the deduction but are in fact irrelevant. They should not contribute to the deduction at all, but they should be close enough to trick someone. ONLY GENERATE THE NEW FACTS.

Put them in this format:

Irrelevant Fact 1: Irrelevant fact for premise one
Irrelevant Fact 2: Irrelevant fact for premise two

Generating irrelevant facts: Prompt 3
Generate one more set of facts. For each of the ten generate two facts that seem related to the deduction but are in fact irrelevant. They should not contribute to the deduction at all, but they should be close enough to trick someone. ONLY GENERATE THE NEW FACTS.

Put them in this format:

Irrelevant Fact 1: Irrelevant fact for premise one
Irrelevant Fact 2: Irrelevant fact for premise two

Figure 7: After the false premises are generated, we ask ChatGPT to create irrelevant facts that are true but not helpful in deducing the original conclusion. We prompt ChatGPT three times for a set of six irrelevant facts per example.

Generating examples with incorrect quantifiers
Now generate premises from the original set of 10 examples that have incorrect quantifiers that would make the conclusion invalid. Use things like "All, some, none, etc.". Do not write the conclusion.

Put them in the format:
Incorrect P1: Incorrect quantifiers for p1
Incorrect P2: Incorrect quantifiers for p2

Figure 8: Finally, we prompt ChatGPT to adjust the quantifier on the original gold premises.

Category: spatial reasoning
Perturbation Type: NEGATED
Target: The pharmacy is on the same side of the street as the bank.
Gold Premises: The post office is on the same side of the street as the bank. The pharmacy is next to the post office.
Rank: 1

Rank (G) 1: the pharmacy is next to the post office. the post office is on the same side of the street as the bank.

Rank 2: the pharmacy is not next to the post office. the post office is on the same side of the street as the bank.

Rank 3: the pharmacy is next to the post office. the post office is not on the same side of the street as the bank.

Rank 4: the pharmacy is not next to the post office. the post office is not on the same side of the street as the bank.

Figure 9: An example of GPT3 embeddings using deductive additivity correctly ranking a spatial reasoning example with negation from the SSRC dataset.

Category: definition
Perturbation Type: FALSE PREMISE
Target: A Granny Smith is a type of fruit.
Gold Premises: An apple is a type of fruit. A Granny Smith is a type of apple.
Rank: 1

Rank (G) 1: an apple is a type of fruit. a granny smith is a type of apple.

Rank 2: an apple is a type of fruit. a granny smith is a type of fish.

Rank 3: a granny smith is a type of apple. an apple is a type of vegetable.

Rank 4: a granny smith is a type of fish. an apple is a type of vegetable.

Figure 10: An example of GPT3 embeddings using deductive additivity correctly ranking a definition example with false premises from the SSRC dataset.

Category: propositional logic
Perturbation Type: IRRELEVANT FACT
Target: The store is closed.
Gold Premises: If it is Sunday, the store is closed. It is Sunday.
Rank: 10
Rank 1: i need to buy groceries. if it is sunday, the store is closed.
Rank 2: i forgot to bring my reusable bag. if it is sunday, the store is closed.
Rank 3: if it is sunday, the store is closed. i prefer to shop on saturdays.
Rank 4: the store is near my house. it is sunday.
Rank 5: it is sunday. the store has a sale.
Rank 6: i need to buy groceries. the store has a sale.
Rank 7: i prefer to shop on saturdays. the store has a sale.
Rank 8: i forgot to bring my reusable bag. the store has a sale.
Rank 9: the store is near my house. i prefer to shop on saturdays.
Rank (G) 10: if it is sunday, the store is closed. it is sunday.
Rank 11: the store is near my house. i need to buy groceries.
Rank 12: i have a coupon for the store. it is sunday.
Rank 13: the store is near my house. i forgot to bring my reusable bag.
Rank 14: i have a coupon for the store. i prefer to shop on saturdays.
Rank 15: i have a coupon for the store. i need to buy groceries.
Rank 16: i have a coupon for the store. i forgot to bring my reusable bag.

Figure 11: An example of GPT3 failing to rank a propositional logic example of the SSRC dataset correctly amongst irrelevant facts.

Synthetic Dataset for Evaluating Complex Compositional Knowledge for Natural Language Inference

Sushma Anand Akoju, Robert Vacareanu, Haris Riaz, Mihai Surdeanu, Eduardo Blanco
University of Arizona
{sushmaakoju, rvacareanu, hriaz, msurdeanu, eduardoblanco}@arizona.edu

Abstract

We introduce a synthetic dataset called Sentences Involving *Complex* Compositional Knowledge (SICCK) and a novel analysis that investigates the performance of Natural Language Inference (NLI) models to understand compositionality in logic. We produce 1,304 sentence pairs by modifying 15 examples from the SICK dataset (Marelli et al., 2014). To this end, we modify the original texts using a set of phrases – modifiers that correspond to universal quantifiers, existential quantifiers, negation, and other concept modifiers in Natural Logic (NL) (MacCartney, 2009). We use these phrases to modify the subject, verb, and object parts of the premise and hypothesis. Lastly, we annotate these modified texts with the corresponding entailment labels following NL rules. We conduct a preliminary verification of how well the change in the structural and semantic composition is captured by neural NLI models, in both zero-shot and fine-tuned scenarios. We found that the performance of NLI models under the zero-shot setting is poor, especially for modified sentences with negation and existential quantifiers. After fine-tuning this dataset, we observe that models continue to perform poorly over negation, existential and universal modifiers.

1 Introduction

Natural language inference (NLI) has made tremendous progress in recent years, both in terms of datasets, e.g., SNLI (Bowman et al., 2015b), MultiNLI (Williams et al., 2018), Adversarial NLI (Nie et al., 2019), NLI_XY (Rozanova et al., 2021), MonaLog (Hu et al., 2019), and methods (Yang et al., 2020; Lan et al., 2020; Wang et al., 2021b,a; Devlin et al., 2019). However, many of these directions lack explainability, a critical drawback that limits their applicability to critical domains such as medical, legal, or financial. In contrast, Natural Logic (NL) (MacCartney, 2009) provides the necessary explainability through explicit *compositionality* that is driven by several relations that serve as building blocks (Forward Entailment (FE), Reverse Entailment (RE), Negation, Cover, Alternation, Equivalence, and Independence) as well as rules to combine them, which model changes in monotonicity.

In this work, we analyze how well transformer networks trained for NLI understand the atomic reasoning blocks defined in NL, and how well they can compose them to detect changes in monotonicity (Richardson et al., 2020; Joshi et al., 2020). To this end, we create a dataset containing 1304 sentences by modifying 15 premise/hypothesis pairs from the SICK dataset (Marelli et al., 2014). The dataset is generated by modifying the premise and hypothesis sentences selected, as follows:

- We append a series of modifiers to subject/verb/objects in the hypothesis/premise pairs. These modifiers include universal quantifiers (e.g., *every*, *always*), existential quantifiers (e.g., *some*, *at least*), negation, and adverbs/adjectives (e.g., *happy*, *sad*). Table 2 lists the complete set of modifiers used.

- We store the adjusted entailment label for each modifier pair to understand the shift in meaning from word-level changes within sentential contexts. More formally, we used the seven entailment relations as defined in (MacCartney, 2009). These labels were generated manually for each example by following monotonicity calculus and natural logic. For example, consider the premise: *an old man is sitting in a field* and the hypothesis: *a man is sitting in a field*, with the original SICK label: Forward Entailment. After adding the universal quantifier *every* to the aforementioned SICK example, the modified premise: *an old man is sitting in a field* and the original hypothesis: ***every** man is sitting in a field* are annotated

Proceedings of the 1st Workshop on Natural Language Reasoning and Structured Explanations (@ACL 2023), pages 157–168
June 13, 2023

with the adjusted label: Reverse Entailment.

Using this dataset, we analyzed the capacity of three different NLI methods to correctly capture the change in entailment given the modified texts. In particular, the contributions of this work are as follows:

1. We propose a mechanism to generate synthetic data for NLI that enforces compositionality in reasoning. Following this mechanism, we produce 1,304 examples from 15 SICK (Marelli et al., 2014) premise, hypothesis sentence pairs by modifying the sentences for subject, verb, and object respectively with a series of modifiers. The resulting dataset is freely available at `https://github.com/clulab/releases/tree/sushma/acl2023-nlrse-sicck`.

2. We define specific annotation guidelines based on monotonicity calculus and natural logic (MacCartney, 2009) for annotating the modified premise and hypothesis sentences in the dataset above. The resulting labels are included in the dataset.

3. We conducted an analysis to understand how well these structural and compositional changes are captured by neural NLI models, in both zero-shot and fine-tuned scenarios. Our analysis indicates that NLI models perform poorly over negation and several types of quantifiers. Fine-tuned NLI models do not show significant improvement in learning about compositional changes when compared to their zero-shot equivalent models over our dataset. This suggests that compositionality in reasoning remains a challenge for neural models of language.

2 Related Work

Natural Logic (NL) is a formal reasoning approach that makes use of syntactic structure and semantic properties of lexical items to understand compositionally (MacCartney, 2009).

Logical reasoning is a known challenge for neural NLI models (Ravichander et al., 2019). In particular, NLI models struggle to understand quantifiers, which is highlighted by the fact that these models do not generalize well over quantifier-driven inference tasks (Haruta et al., 2020). The monotonicity calculus over quantifiers with token-level polarity has been explored using the CCG parser over the SICK dataset to generate a synthetic dataset that considers compositional data augmentation (Marelli et al., 2014) and monotonicity calculus (Hu et al., 2019). Other recent research focused on language structures to highlight the importance of compositionality, i.e., the premise and hypothesis differ only in the order of the words, or the presence of antonyms, synonyms, or negation (Dasgupta et al., 2018). Having such data augmentation can help move closer to the compositional encoding of the language (Dasgupta et al., 2018). Our work extends this direction: our dataset captures both phrasal changes (e.g., synonyms, hypernyms), which we inherit from the SICK dataset (Marelli et al., 2014), as well as multiple types of modifiers that are critical for NLI such as universal, existential, negation, and adjectives/adverbs.

The FraCas test suite (Cooper et al., 1996) contains 346 examples that explore aspects of natural logic applied to NLI (MacCartney, 2009). The HELP dataset (Yanaka et al., 2019b) modifies phrases in premise/hypothesis sentences based on monotonicity reasoning from combinatorial categorical grammar (Steedman and Baldridge, 2011) and semantic tagging (Abzianidze and Bos, 2017). As mentioned above, our work is complementary to such datasets, as we cover other types of text modifications. The MED dataset (Yanaka et al., 2019a) is another manually-labeled dataset where hypotheses were also modified by the human labelers given the monotonicity information for the premises. Similarly, we manually labeled NLI information, but our work focuses mainly on compositional information in a sentential context.

Enhancing the dataset with data augmentation is another recent method to test the generalizability of NLI models (Jha et al., 2020). Lexical entailment acquired from the distributional behavior of word pairs (Geffet and Dagan, 2005) led to the subsequent work of (Bowman et al., 2015a), who produced a 3-way classification task for NLI dataset that serves as a benchmark for evaluating natural language understanding. Using Natural Logic as a means to learn and reason about the semantic and lexical relations is a common method used to improve the reasoning capabilities of the NLI models (Bowman et al., 2015c).

The NLI_XY dataset (Rozanova et al., 2021) conducts structural investigation over the transformer-based NLI models. In particular, the authors investigate how monotonicity (upwards or downwards) changes when the premises and hypotheses are modified through the insertion of hypernym/hyponym phrases. This work is complementary to ours: while they focus on monotonicity in lexicalization (e.g., changing from a hypernym to a hyponym), we focus on changes in monotonicity due to explicit modifiers applied on top of such lexical modifications.

The MonaLog system (Hu et al., 2019) introduces a simple yet explainable NLI method that relies on a simplified Natural Logic implementation. The proposed method operates by implementing monotonicity calculus over CCG syntactic trees using "a small inventory of monotonicity facts about quantifiers, lexical items and token-level polarity." Despite its simplicity, the authors report excellent performance on the SICK dataset. More closely related to our work, they use MonaLog to generate additional training data for NLI from the generated proofs.

3 Dataset

We introduce a synthetic dataset to facilitate the analysis of compositionality in logic. The dataset contains 1,304 sentences that were created by modifying 15 examples from the SICK dataset (Marelli et al., 2014) with a variety of modifiers. To this end, we used a set of phrases that correspond to universal quantifiers, existential quantifiers, negation, and other concept modifiers in Natural Logic (NL) (MacCartney, 2009). These modifiers were applied to syntactic constructs in both premise and hypothesis and the entailment labels are adjusted, as detailed below.

3.1 Overview

At a high level, our dataset creation followed the following steps:

1. We start with 15 seed pairs of premise and hypothesis sentences from SICK. Table 1 shows the seed sentence pairs.

2. We syntactically analyze these sentences to understand their subject-verb-object (SVO) structures. Each of the SVO elements is then modified using a subset of the applicable modifiers listed in Table 2. This process is detailed in Section 3.2.

3. Lastly, we re-annotate the entailment labels for the modified sentences, using the seven entailment relations defined in (MacCartney, 2009): Forward Entailment (FE), Reverse Entailment (RE), Negation (Neg) (or Contradiction), Alternation, Cover, Independence (Neutral) and Equivalence (Equiv). This step is detailed in Section 3.3. The labels are described in Table 3.

3.2 Sentence Modification Strategy

For each premise and hypothesis sentence pair, we modified individual subject, verb, and object phrases with the following approach:

1. To modify *subjects*, we used the Berkeley Neural Parser to extract the left-most noun phrases (NPs). We then append the applicable modifiers from Table 2. In particular, we used universal quantifiers, existential quantifiers, negations, and adjectives.

2. To modify *verbs*, we used the Berkeley Neural parser to extract the rightmost verb phrases (VPs) from the parse tree and appended the applicable modifiers. Verbs were modified using universal quantifiers (*always*, *never*), negations (*not*, *never*), and adverbs (*abnormally,elegantly*).

3. To detect *objects*, we used the syntactic dependency parser of (Vacareanu et al., 2020) to identify noun phrases attached to the main verb. Similarly to the subject modifications, these objects were modified using universal quantifiers, existential quantifiers, negations, and adjectives.

After modifying each of the premises and hypotheses sentences, we generate multiple new data points as follows: $f(P_i, H_i, m, SVO) = P_i^{'}, H_i^{'}$ where $m \in M$: all modifiers; SVO : subject/verb/object phrases for either one of the parts of the sentence; and P_i, H_i are premise and hypothesis from sentence pairs $S_i \in S$ where S is the set of 15 examples from SICK. Lastly, f is the function that modifies a given premise and hypothesis that follows one of the modification strategies described above. We generate the following pairs of combinations of the premise, and hypothesis sentences: $(P_i^{'}, H_i), (P_i, H_i^{'}), (P_i^{'}, H_i^{'})$. We repeat this process to modify each of the relevant sentence phrases, as well as a couple of combinations:

Premise	Hypothesis	SICK label
an **old man** is sitting in a field	a **man** is sitting in a field	Entailment
A boy is standing in the **cold water**	A boy is standing in the **water**	Entailment
Two children are **hanging on a large branch**	Two children are **climbing a tree**	Entailment
A **boy** is hitting a baseball	A **child** is hitting a baseball	Entailment
Two dogs are playing by a **tree**	Two dogs are playing by a **plant**	Entailment
A player is **throwing the ball**	**Two teams are competing in a football match**	Neutral
A man is **sitting** in a field	A man is **running** in a field	Neutral
Two dogs are **playing** by a tree	Two dogs are **sleeping** by a tree	Neutral
A girl with a black bag is on a crowded train	**A cramped black train is on the bag of a girl**	Neutral
A blond girl is **riding the waves**	A blond girl is **looking at the waves**	Neutral
The **turtle** is following the **fish**	The **fish** is following the **turtle**	Contradiction
A man is jumping into an **empty** pool	A man is jumping into a **full** pool	Contradiction
A deer **is jumping** over a fence	A deer **isn't jumping** over the fence	Contradiction
A child is **hitting** a baseball	A child is **missing** a baseball	Contradiction
A classroom is **full of students**	A classroom is **empty**	Contradiction

Table 1: 15 premise/hypothesis sentence pairs from the SICK dataset (Marelli et al., 2014) and corresponding NLI labels that form the seed of our dataset. The bold text highlights the lexically-driven compositional change in the premise and hypothesis sentences.

Modifier Type	Modifiers
Universal quantifiers	*every, always, never, every one of*
Existential quantifiers	*some, at least, exactly one, all but one*
Negation	*not every, no, not*
Adjectives	*green, happy, sad, good, bad, an abnormal,* and *an elegant*
Adverbs	*abnormally, elegantly*

Table 2: List of modifiers used to modify subject, verb, and object elements of sentences. They are applied to each of the premise and hypothesis sentences in Table 1.

subject, verb, object, subject + object, and verb + object.

3.3 Entailment Annotation Strategy

To annotate our dataset,[1] we created a set of annotation guidelines that follow Natural Logic and monotonicity calculus (MacCartney, 2009).

In general, to produce entailment relations we used a set theoretic approach to understand how the set of concepts that holds true in the premise overlaps with the set described in the hypothesis. To implement this set theoretic approach consistently, we defined the quantitative interpretation for several more ambiguous modifiers such as *all but one, all, not every* as follows:

1. For the modifier *all*, we consider the size of the set of elements X to be greater than 0: $|X| > 0$. For example, in the case of the phrase *all children*, we consider the size of the set of children to be greater than 0.

2. For the *all but one* modifier, we consider the size of *all* as N and the size of *all but one* to be $N - 1$. Note that the size of *all but one* could thus theoretically be 0, when $N = 1$.

3. For *not every* we consider the size of the corresponding set X to be 0 or larger: $|X| \geq 0$ where X is any set defined over the sentence. *not every man* would make X as a set of all men but there exists zero or one or more men that would not be included in this set.

4. When we cannot determine the size of the intersection of the two sets of premise and hypothesis, we resolved the annotation to be a Neutral label among all 7 entailment relations.

5. When comparing quantifiers between modified premise, and hypothesis sentence pairs, we denote the sizes of sets mathematically for $P \cup H$, $P \cap H$, and the Universal set. For example, consider the premise: ***every** turtle is following the fish* and the hypothesis: ***every** fish is following the turtle*. The set over the premise is P : $\forall X \in$ all turtles following one fish, and the set over hypothesis is H : $\forall X \in$

[1]The annotation guidelines we followed are detailed on this website https://github.com/clulab/releases/tree/sushma/acl2023-nlrse-sicck/annotations-guidelines/NLI_annotation_task_guidelines.pdf

Entailment Relation	Set Theoretic Notation	Examples using WordNet Hierarchy
Equivalence	$X \equiv Y$	*couch* $\equiv$ *sofa*
Forward Entailment (FE)	$X \subset Y$	Hyponym: *crow* $\subset$ bird.
Reverse Entailment (RE)	$X \supseteq Y$	Hypernym: *Asian* $\supseteq$ *Thai.*
Negation (Neg)	$X \cap Y = \phi \wedge X \cup Y = \mathbb{U}$	Antonym: *able* $\neg$ *unable*
Alternation	$X \cap Y = \phi \wedge X \cup Y \neq \mathbb{U}$	Typically caused concepts with a shared hypernym: *cat* $\|$ *dog*. The corresponding hierarchy is : *carnivore* $\rightarrow$ *feline*, *canine*; *feline* $\rightarrow$ *cat*; and *canine* $\rightarrow$ *dog*.
Cover	$X \cap Y \neq \phi \wedge X \cup Y = \mathbb{U}$	*animal* $\smile$ *non-ape*
Independence	all other cases	*hungry* $\|$ *hippo*

Table 3: Entailment relations as defined in (MacCartney, 2009) with explanations using the WordNet hierarchy (Miller, 1995).

Premise	Hypothesis	SVO	Modifier Type	Label
an old man is sitting in a field	a man is sitting in a field	None	None	FE
every old man is sitting in a field	a man is sitting in a field	Subject	Universal	FE
an old man is sitting in a field	**every** man is sitting in a field	Subject	Universal	RE
an old man is **elegantly** sitting in a field	a man is **elegantly** sitting in a field	Verb	Adverb	FE
an old man is sitting in **every** field	a man is sitting in a field	Object	Universal	FE
an old man is sitting in a field	a man is sitting in **every** field	Object	Universal	Neutral

Table 4: Premise, hypothesis examples where one or both of the premise and hypothesis were modified. The text in bold indicates the change from the original text. The *SVO* column indicates the part of the sentence that was modified: subject, verb, or object (SVO). The Modifier type indicates which type of modifier was used to modify the parts of sentences. The label is the Entailment relation annotated by the annotators over modified data.

all fishes following the turtle. Thus, $P \cap H = \phi$. In this case, the label is Negation (see Table 3). Table 4 includes more examples with the corresponding entailment labels.

A total of 1,304 modified premise and hypothesis sentence pairs along with original sentence pairs were included in the final SICCK dataset. The data was annotated by 5 annotators which were distributed between two sub-groups of annotators, based on the complexity of the labels. In the first two rounds of annotations, we re-grouped to develop concrete guidelines for annotations, without defining too strict rules by leaving room for more natural "if-this-then-that" deductions. There were disagreements between annotations which were resolved by verifying the sizes of sets mathematically over $X \cup Y$, $X \cap Y$ to follow the entailment relations defined as in (MacCartney, 2009). While in the initial round the inter-annotator agreement was low ($k < 0.4$), the annotations were revised until each group of annotators converged.

Tables 5, 6, and 7 provide summary statistics about the SICCK dataset.

Modifier type	# of sentence pairs
With universal quantifiers	217
With existential quantifiers	303
With negation	167
With adjectives/adverbs	602

Table 5: Sentence counts in SICCK based on types of modifiers.

SVO modified	# of sentence pairs
Subject	560
Verb	220
Object	509

Table 6: Sentence counts in SICCK based on which syntactic structures are modified.

4 Evaluation

We conducted an evaluation of how NLI methods capture the explicit compositionality in our dataset using two configurations: a zero-shot setting, in which we used NLI systems trained externally, and a fine-tuned setting, in which the same models were fine-tuned using our dataset.

Entailment relations	# of sentence pairs
Forward Entailment	223
Reverse Entailment	27
Alternation	121
Negation	54
Negation|Alternation	260
Neutral	393
Equivalence	7
Cover	1
Cover|FE	1

Table 7: Label counts in SICCK. Note that Negation|Alternation indicates ambiguous labels where the two annotators did not converge.

4.1 Zero-shot Analysis of NLI Models

For this analysis, we evaluate three pretrained neural entailment models on our dataset. However, all these systems emit just the three "traditional" entailment labels (Forward Entailment, Contradiction, and Neutral) whereas our dataset contains the seven labels from NL. To align these label spaces, we performed the following transformations:

1. In case a system produces a Neutral label, we run the prediction in the opposite direction, i.e., from hypothesis to premise. If the top label in the reversed direction is Forward Entailment (FE), we label the pair as Reverse Entailment. Otherwise, we keep the Neutral label. This heuristic allows these systems to produce four labels instead of three.
2. We convert our seven labels to four labels through the following heuristics: (a) Equivalence was removed since we had only one sentence pair labeled as Equivalence in our dataset; (b) Alternation is merged with Negation; (c) Cover and Independence become Neutral; and (d) the 7 examples that were annotated as Cover|FE were removed.

We conducted zero shot evaluation using three NLI models: the cross-encoder model of Reimers and Gurevych (2019) (`nli-deberta-v3-base` in our tables), the adversarial NLI model of Nie et al. (2020) (`ynie/roberta-large-. . .`), and ELMo-based Decomposable Attention model (Parikh et al., 2016) (`pair-classification-. . .`). We draw the following observations from this experiment:

- Table 8 indicates that the ELMO-based NLI model performs considerably worse than the other two transformer-based models. This is a testament to how far our field has progressed in just a few years. However, no model approaches 70 F1 points, which indicates that none of these models truly understand the task well.
- The NLI models do better over adjectives and adverbs, but they struggle to understand statements modified with universal and existential quantifiers, and negation. Tables 8–14 indicates that the transformer-based NLI models perform at over 70 F1 points on adjectives/adverbs, at over 65 F1 for universal quantifiers, at approximately 60 F1 for existential quantifiers, and at only 30–35 F1 for negation. This is a surprising finding considering how much attention negation has received in the NLP literature (Pang et al., 2002) (Hossain et al., 2022) (Hossain et al., 2020).
- Lastly, Tables 15–17 indicate that NLI models process objects best, followed by subjects, and, lastly, verbs. This is not surprising considering the increased semantic ambiguity of verbs.

4.2 Analysis of Fine-tuned NLI models

To understand if NLI methods are capable of learning this compositional information, we fine-tuned the two NLI models that performed better over the SICCK dataset. To maximize the data available, we implemented a 5-fold cross-validation evaluation over the entire SICCK dataset and experimented with multiple hyperparameters. In particular, we used 4 or 8 epochs, and batch sizes of 8, 16, or 32 data points.

The results of these experiments are summarized in Table 9. We draw the following observation from this experiment:

- The difference in F1 scores between the fine-tuned systems and the corresponding zero-shot setting ranges from -0.05 to 0.06. This indicates that these systems do not acquire substantial new knowledge despite the fact that they've been exposed to approximately 1,300 sentences with compositional information. This suggests that understanding compositionality is harder than expected.
- Similar to the zero-shot setting, NLI models did better over adjectives, and adverbs and

NLI system	F1	Precision	Recall	Accuracy
nli-deberta-v3-base	**0.5254**	**0.5601**	**0.5860**	**0.6579**
ynie/roberta-large-snli-mnli-fever-anli-R1-R2-R3-nli	0.5200	0.5156	0.5533	0.6334
pair-classification-decomposable-attention-elmo	0.0829	0.0497	0.2500	0.1986

Table 8: Overall scores for the three pretrained NLI modes under zero-shot setting, based on compressed 4-entailment relations: Forward Entailment, Reverse Entailment, Contradiction, and Neutral.

NLI model with epochs, batch size	F1	Precision	Recall	Accuracy
nli-deberta-v3-base-4-8	0.5392	0.5310	0.5546	0.5686
roberta-large-snli-mnli-fever-anli-R1-R2-R3-nli-4-8	0.4257	0.4708	0.4456	0.4460
nli-deberta-v3-base-4-16	0.5153	0.5072	0.5404	0.5556
roberta-large-snli-mnli-fever-anli-R1-R2-R3-nli-4-16	0.5177	0.5472	0.5239	0.5203
nli-deberta-v3-base-4-32	0.4871	0.4756	0.5109	0.5280
roberta-large-snli-mnli-fever-anli-R1-R2-R3-nli-4-32	0.4829	0.4941	0.4884	0.4904
nli-deberta-v3-base-8-8	**0.5876**	**0.5799**	**0.6024**	**0.6045**
roberta-large-snli-mnli-fever-anli-R1-R2-R3-nli-8-8	0.4433	0.4596	0.4385	0.4559
nli-deberta-v3-base-8-16	0.5464	0.5378	0.5636	0.5801
roberta-large-snli-mnli-fever-anli-R1-R2-R3-nli-8-16	0.4724	0.4723	0.4772	0.4828
nli-deberta-v3-base-8-32	0.5489	0.5408	0.5713	0.5785
roberta-large-snli-mnli-fever-anli-R1-R2-R3-nli-8-32	0.4281	0.4558	0.4319	0.4345

Table 9: Overall scores for two *fine-tuned* NLI models on SICCK dataset based on the compressed 4-entailment relations: Forward Entailment, Reverse Entailment, Contradiction, and Neutral. We report the results for 4 and 8 epochs and batch sizes of 8, 16, and 32 data points.

relatively better over universal quantifiers in comparison to that of the negation and existential quantifiers. We also observed that models seem to be confused when the annotated label was Neutral but the modifier types were negations.

- NLI models perform somewhat better over subject and object-modified examples than on examples with modified verbs. This indicates that the semantic ambiguity of verbs is likely to impact NLI models.

5 Error Analysis

We analyze the incorrect predictions of the NLI models over SICCK dataset in this section. We observed that NLI models performed better over adjectives and adverbs, and relatively well over universal quantifiers in comparison to sentences modified with negation and existential quantifiers under both fine-tuned as well as zero-shot settings. We also observed that models seem to be confused when the adjusted label was Neutral and the modifier types were negations.

SVO	# count	Neutral
subject	86	65
verb	41	35
object	40	22

Table 10: For all our SICCK dataset's 167 examples with negation modifiers, this table includes counts of all the modified subject, verb, and object parts of sentences respectively for each of the 4-Entailment adjusted labels from SICCK annotations. The last column indicates how many of these data points have the Neutral label.

5.1 Neutral Labels with Negation Modifiers

Negation understanding in natural language has been a challenging problem (Pang et al., 2002; Hossain et al., 2022). (Hossain et al., 2022) discussed that Negation is underrepresented in natural language corpora. Further, (Hossain et al., 2020) show that even though the transformers were fine-tuned with modified premises with negation (i.e., verb modifiers with negation), the transformers struggle with inference over negated sentence pairs.

In our SICCK dataset, there are 167 examples with negation modifiers. Table 10 shows some statistics relevant to this. Of these 167 examples with Negation modifiers, there are 122 Neutral examples. We observed that the NLI models correctly predicted ground truth for approximately 37% of these examples. For all the incorrectly predicted labels for negation-modified examples with Neutral labels, the models seemed to be confused for various compositional cases, i.e. subject or verb or object-modified examples almost equivalently. Modifiers such as *no*, *not every*, *not* with Neutral and Contradiction labels seem to contribute to the confusion. SICCK examples also include the format of alternating modifiers between premises, hypothesis, or both i.e. $(P_i^{'}, H_i), (P_i, H_i^{'}), (P_i^{'}, H_i^{'})$ Section 3 which further seems to confuse the NLI models. This is surprising since we have 593 Neutral examples in our SICCK dataset, albeit with fewer negation examples. As emphasized by the analysis from (Hossain et al., 2022) and (Hossain et al., 2020), detecting negation in natural language continues to be an unresolved problem.

5.2 Verb-modified Examples

For verb modifiers, we used modifiers *abnormally, elegantly, always, never.* Our SICCK dataset has a total of 220 verb-modified examples of which, we have 89 universal modifiers, 90 adverbs/adjectives, and 41 negation. Among the 31 verb-modified examples with negation with Neutral label, NLI models incorrectly alternate between Contradiction and FE for 99% of the examples. Of the 49 examples with universal modifiers over verbs with Neutral labels, approximately 69.4% were incorrectly predicted. This further emphasizes that negation (especially when occurring in Neutral examples) remains a challenge.

6 Conclusion

This paper introduced a new, synthetic dataset that facilitates analyses of how NLI models capture compositionality. The dataset contains 1,304 sentence pairs that were created by modifying 15 examples from the SICK dataset (Marelli et al., 2014) with a variety of modifiers that correspond to universal quantifiers, existential quantifiers, negation, and other concept modifiers in Natural Logic (NL) (MacCartney, 2009). We used these phrases to modify the subject, verb, and object parts of the premise and hypothesis. Lastly, we annotated these modified texts with the corresponding entailment labels following NL rules.

We conducted a preliminary analysis of how well the change in the structural and semantic composition is captured and detected by neural NLI models, in both zero-shot and fine-tuned scenarios. We found that the performance of NLI models is poor in both settings, especially for modified sentences with negation and existential quantifiers, and when verbs are modified.

Limitations

While this work explores the impact of the typical compositional modifiers on entailment relations, we did not consider other fine-grained information that further captures upward or downward monotonicity from the monotonicity calculus of the premise/hypothesis sentence pairs. Further, the dataset that we generated is relatively small, at approximately 1,300 sentences. We also did not evaluate the dataset over T5, BART, GPT-x, and other state-of-the-art LLMs, which may provide more insights. We also did not conduct any evaluation for explanations and interpretation of the evaluated NLI models, which could be future work. Lastly, we did not include a comparison with existing datasets that were created specifically for negation modifiers and universal & existential quantifiers. We see all these issues as exciting avenues for future work.

References

Lasha Abzianidze and Johan Bos. 2017. Towards universal semantic tagging. *arXiv preprint arXiv:1709.10381*.

Samuel R. Bowman, Gabor Angeli, Christopher Potts, and Christopher D. Manning. 2015a. A large annotated corpus for learning natural language inference. In *Proceedings of the 2015 Conference on Empirical Methods in Natural Language Processing*, pages 632–642, Lisbon, Portugal. Association for Computational Linguistics.

Samuel R Bowman, Gabor Angeli, Christopher Potts, and Christopher D Manning. 2015b. The snli corpus.

Samuel R. Bowman, Christopher Potts, and Christopher D. Manning. 2015c. Recursive neural networks can learn logical semantics.

Robin Cooper, R Crouch, Jan van Eijck, Chris Fox, Josef van Genabith, Jan Jaspars, Hans Kamp, David Milward, Manfred Pinkal, Massimo Poesio, et al. 1996. Using the framework. the fracas consortium. Technical report, Technical report, FraCaS deliverable D-16.

Ishita Dasgupta, Demi Guo, Andreas Stuhlmüller, Samuel J Gershman, and Noah D Goodman. 2018.

Evaluating compositionality in sentence embeddings. *arXiv preprint arXiv:1802.04302*.

Jacob Devlin, Ming-Wei Chang, Kenton Lee, and Kristina Toutanova. 2019. BERT: Pre-training of deep bidirectional transformers for language understanding. In *Proceedings of the 2019 Conference of the North American Chapter of the Association for Computational Linguistics: Human Language Technologies, Volume 1 (Long and Short Papers)*, pages 4171–4186, Minneapolis, Minnesota. Association for Computational Linguistics.

Maayan Geffet and Ido Dagan. 2005. The distributional inclusion hypotheses and lexical entailment. In *Proceedings of the 43rd Annual Meeting of the Association for Computational Linguistics (ACL'05)*, pages 107–114.

Izumi Haruta, Koji Mineshima, and Daisuke Bekki. 2020. Logical inferences with comparatives and generalized quantifiers.

Md Mosharaf Hossain, Dhivya Chinnappa, and Eduardo Blanco. 2022. An analysis of negation in natural language understanding corpora. In *Proceedings of the 60th Annual Meeting of the Association for Computational Linguistics (Volume 2: Short Papers)*, pages 716–723, Dublin, Ireland. Association for Computational Linguistics.

Md Mosharaf Hossain, Venelin Kovatchev, Pranoy Dutta, Tiffany Kao, Elizabeth Wei, and Eduardo Blanco. 2020. An analysis of natural language inference benchmarks through the lens of negation. In *Proceedings of the 2020 Conference on Empirical Methods in Natural Language Processing (EMNLP)*, pages 9106–9118, Online. Association for Computational Linguistics.

Hai Hu, Qi Chen, Kyle Richardson, Atreyee Mukherjee, Lawrence S Moss, and Sandra Kuebler. 2019. Monalog: a lightweight system for natural language inference based on monotonicity. *arXiv preprint arXiv:1910.08772*.

Rohan Jha, Charles Lovering, and Ellie Pavlick. 2020. Does data augmentation improve generalization in nlp? *arXiv preprint arXiv:2004.15012*.

Pratik Joshi, Somak Aditya, Aalok Sathe, and Monojit Choudhury. 2020. Taxinli: Taking a ride up the nlu hill. *arXiv preprint arXiv:2009.14505*.

Zhenzhong Lan, Mingda Chen, Sebastian Goodman, Kevin Gimpel, Piyush Sharma, and Radu Soricut. 2020. Albert: A lite bert for self-supervised learning of language representations.

Bill MacCartney. 2009. *Natural language inference*. Stanford University.

Marco Marelli, Stefano Menini, Marco Baroni, Luisa Bentivogli, Raffaella Bernardi, and Roberto Zamparelli. 2014. A SICK cure for the evaluation of compositional distributional semantic models. In *Proceedings of the Ninth International Conference on Language Resources and Evaluation (LREC'14)*, pages 216–223, Reykjavık, Iceland. European Language Resources Association (ELRA).

George A Miller. 1995. Wordnet: a lexical database for english. *Communications of the ACM*, 38(11):39–41.

Yixin Nie, Adina Williams, Emily Dinan, Mohit Bansal, Jason Weston, and Douwe Kiela. 2019. Adversarial nli: A new benchmark for natural language understanding. *arXiv preprint arXiv:1910.14599*.

Yixin Nie, Adina Williams, Emily Dinan, Mohit Bansal, Jason Weston, and Douwe Kiela. 2020. Adversarial NLI: A new benchmark for natural language understanding. In *Proceedings of the 58th Annual Meeting of the Association for Computational Linguistics*. Association for Computational Linguistics.

Bo Pang, Lillian Lee, and Shivakumar Vaithyanathan. 2002. Thumbs up? sentiment classification using machine learning techniques. In *Proceedings of the 2002 Conference on Empirical Methods in Natural Language Processing (EMNLP 2002)*, pages 79–86. Association for Computational Linguistics.

Ankur P. Parikh, Oscar T"ackstr"om, Dipanjan Das, and Jakob Uszkoreit. 2016. A decomposable attention model for natural language inference. *ArXiv*, abs/1606.01933.

Abhilasha Ravichander, Aakanksha Naik, Carolyn Rose, and Eduard Hovy. 2019. Equate: A benchmark evaluation framework for quantitative reasoning in natural language inference.

Nils Reimers and Iryna Gurevych. 2019. Sentence-bert: Sentence embeddings using siamese bert-networks.

Kyle Richardson, Hai Hu, Lawrence Moss, and Ashish Sabharwal. 2020. Probing natural language inference models through semantic fragments. *Proceedings of the AAAI Conference on Artificial Intelligence*, 34(05):8713–8721.

Julia Rozanova, Deborah Ferreira, Marco Valentino, Mokanrarangan Thayaparan, and Andre Freitas. 2021. Decomposing natural logic inferences in neural nli. *arXiv preprint arXiv:2112.08289*.

Mark Steedman and Jason Baldridge. 2011. Combinatory categorial grammar. *Non-Transformational Syntax: Formal and Explicit Models of Grammar. Wiley-Blackwell*, pages 181–224.

Robert Vacareanu, George Caique Gouveia Barbosa, Marco A. Valenzuela-Escárcega, and Mihai Surdeanu. 2020. Parsing as tagging. In *Proceedings of the Twelfth Language Resources and Evaluation Conference*, pages 5225–5231, Marseille, France. European Language Resources Association.

Boxin Wang, Shuohang Wang, Yu Cheng, Zhe Gan, Ruoxi Jia, Bo Li, and Jingjing Liu. 2021a. Info{bert}: Improving robustness of language models from an information theoretic perspective. In *International Conference on Learning Representations.*

Sinong Wang, Han Fang, Madian Khabsa, Hanzi Mao, and Hao Ma. 2021b. Entailment as few-shot learner. *arXiv preprint arXiv:2104.14690.*

Adina Williams, Nikita Nangia, and Samuel Bowman. 2018. A broad-coverage challenge corpus for sentence understanding through inference. In *Proceedings of the 2018 Conference of the North American Chapter of the Association for Computational Linguistics: Human Language Technologies, Volume 1 (Long Papers)*, pages 1112–1122. Association for Computational Linguistics.

Hitomi Yanaka, Koji Mineshima, Daisuke Bekki, Kentaro Inui, Satoshi Sekine, Lasha Abzianidze, and Johan Bos. 2019a. Can neural networks understand monotonicity reasoning? In *Proceedings of the 2019 ACL Workshop BlackboxNLP: Analyzing and Interpreting Neural Networks for NLP*, pages 31–40.

Hitomi Yanaka, Koji Mineshima, Daisuke Bekki, Kentaro Inui, Satoshi Sekine, Lasha Abzianidze, and Johan Bos. 2019b. Help: A dataset for identifying shortcomings of neural models in monotonicity reasoning. *arXiv preprint arXiv:1904.12166.*

Zhilin Yang, Zihang Dai, Yiming Yang, Jaime Carbonell, Ruslan Salakhutdinov, and Quoc V. Le. 2020. Xlnet: Generalized autoregressive pretraining for language understanding.

A Appendix

We provide the modifier-based evaluation results for zero-shot setting over NLI models and finetuned NLI models.

NLI system	F1	Precision	Recall	Accuracy
nli-deberta-v3-base	0.5333	0.5474	**0.5877**	0.6636
ynie/roberta-large-snli-mnli-fever-anli-R1-R2-R3-nli	**0.5597**	**0.5636**	0.5854	**0.6774**
pair-classification-decomposable-attention-elmo	0.0694	0.0403	0.2500	0.1613

Table 11: **Universal quantifiers**: scores based on compressed 4-entailment relations for zero-shot NLI evaluation.

NLI system	F1	Precision	Recall	Accuracy
nli-deberta-v3-base	**0.5101**	**0.5453**	**0.5608**	**0.6106**
ynie/roberta-large-snli-mnli-fever-anli-R1-R2-R3-nli	0.4932	0.4888	0.5348	0.5941
pair-classification-decomposable-attention-elmo	0.1044	0.0660	0.2500	0.2640

Table 12: **Existential quantifiers**: scores based on compressed 4-entailment relations for zero-shot NLI evaluation.

NLI system	F1	Precision	Recall	Accuracy
nli-deberta-v3-base	0.2678	**0.3556**	0.4637	**0.3054**
ynie/roberta-large-snli-mnli-fever-anli-R1-R2-R3-nli	**0.2996**	0.3470	**0.4690**	0.3533
pair-classification-decomposable-attention-elmo	0.0412	0.0225	0.2500	0.0898

Table 13: **Negation**: scores based on compressed 4-entailment relations for zero-shot NLI evaluation.

NLI system	F1	Precision	Recall	Accuracy
nli-deberta-v3-base	**0.5768**	**0.6088**	**0.6154**	**0.7741**
ynie/roberta-large-snli-mnli-fever-anli-R1-R2-R3-nli	0.5543	0.5618	0.5523	0.7126
pair-classification-decomposable-attention-elmo	0.1139	0.0687	0.3333	0.2060

Table 14: **Adjectives/Adverbs**: scores based on compressed 4-entailment relations for zero-shot NLI evaluation.

NLI system	F1	Precision	Recall	Accuracy
nli-deberta-v3-base	**0.5070**	**0.5469**	**0.5732**	**0.6429**
ynie/roberta-large-snli_mnli_fever_anli_R1_R2_R3-nli	0.4862	0.4812	0.5168	0.6054
pair-classification-decomposable-attention-elmo	0.0796	0.0473	0.2500	0.1893

Table 15: **Modified subject**: scores based on compressed 4-entailment relations for zero-shot NLI evaluation.

NLI system	F1	Precision	Recall	Accuracy
nli-deberta-v3-base	**0.4724**	**0.5141**	**0.5875**	**0.5727**
ynie/roberta-large-snli_mnli_fever_anli_R1_R2_R3-nli	0.4932	0.5082	0.5764	0.5955
pair-classification-decomposable-attention-elmo	0.0669	0.0386	0.2500	0.1545

Table 16: **Modified verb**: scores based on compressed 4-entailment relations for zero-shot NLI evaluation.

NLI system	F1	Precision	Recall	Accuracy
nli-deberta-v3-base	**0.5683**	**0.6166**	**0.6030**	**0.7073**
ynie/roberta-large-snli_mnli_fever_anli_R1_R2_R3-nli	0.5687	0.5638	0.5908	0.6778
pair-classification-decomposable-attention-elmo	0.0915	0.0560	0.2500	0.2240

Table 17: **Modified object**: scores based on compressed 4-entailment relations for zero-shot NLI evaluation.

NLI system	F1	Precision	Recall	Accuracy
nli-deberta-v3-base	**0.5393**	**0.5319**	**0.5542**	**0.5622**
ynie/roberta-large-snli-mnli-fever-anli-R1-R2-R3-nli	0.3960	0.4241	0.4046	0.3917

Table 18: **Universal quantifiers**: fine-tuned NLI models' evaluation scores based on 4-entailment relations. We report results for 8 epochs and a batch size of 32 data points.

NLI system	F1	Precision	Recall	Accuracy
nli-deberta-v3-base	**0.5470**	**0.5373**	**0.5729**	**0.5611**
ynie/roberta-large-snli-mnli-fever-anli-R1-R2-R3-nli	0.4649	0.5101	0.4633	0.4653

Table 19: **Existential quantifiers**: fine-tuned NLI models' evaluation scores based on 4-entailment relations. We report results for 8 epochs and a batch size of 32 data points.

NLI system	F1	Precision	Recall	Accuracy
nli-deberta-v3-base	0.3476	0.3634	0.4064	0.3952
ynie/roberta-large-snli-mnli-fever-anli-R1-R2-R3-nli	**0.3979**	**0.4420**	**0.4536**	**0.4671**

Table 20: **Negation**: fine-tuned NLI models' evaluation scores based on 4-entailment relations. We report results for 8 epochs and a batch size of 32 data points.

NLI system	F1	Precision	Recall	Accuracy
nli-deberta-v3-base	**0.5862**	**0.5803**	**0.5998**	**0.6412**
ynie/roberta-large-snli-mnli-fever-anli-R1-R2-R3-nli	0.4191	0.4350	0.4201	0.4252

Table 21: **Adjectives/Adverbs**: fine-tuned NLI models' evaluation scores based on 4-entailment relations. We report results for 8 epochs and a batch size of 32 data points.

NLI system	F1	Precision	Recall	Accuracy
nli-deberta-v3-base	**0.5920**	**0.5848**	**0.6154**	**0.6107**
ynie/roberta-large-snli-mnli-fever-anli-R1-R2-R3-nli	0.4681	0.4872	0.4778	0.4768

Table 22: **Modified subject**: fine-tuned NLI models' evaluation scores based on 4-entailment relations. We report results for 8 epochs and a batch size of 32 data points.

NLI system	F1	Precision	Recall	Accuracy
nli-deberta-v3-base	**0.5203**	**0.5114**	**0.5454**	**0.5545**
ynie/roberta-large-snli-mnli-fever-anli-R1-R2-R3-nli	0.3750	0.4102	0.3864	0.3955

Table 23: **Modified verb**: fine-tuned NLI models' evaluation scores based on 4-entailment relations. We report results for 8 epochs and a batch size of 32 data points.

NLI system	F1	Precision	Recall	Accuracy
nli-deberta-v3-base	**0.5501**	**0.4945**	**0.5342**	**0.5058**
ynie/roberta-large-snli-mnli-fever-anli-R1-R2-R3-nli	0.4047	0.4410	0.4011	0.4053

Table 24: **Modified object**: fine-tuned NLI models' evaluation scores based on 4-entailment relations. We report results for 8 epochs and a batch size of 32 data points.

Author Index

Association for Computational Linguistics
209 N. Eighth Street
Stroudsburg, Pennsylvania 18360

ISBN 978-1-7138-8179-7

9 781713 881797

CURRAN ASSOCIATES INC.
proceedings.com